THE RESTORATION OF
BLYTHBURGH CHURCH
1881–1906

Concerning Blythburgh Church

One of the Finest Specimens of Gothic Architecture in the County falling to pieces for want of **£3,000.**

From the Sketch]   BLYTHBURGH CHURCH.   BUILT A.D. 1460. *[by Ernest Crofts, R.A.*

RESTORATION COMMITTEE.

Patroness: H R.H. THE PRINCESS LOUISE, DUCHESS OF ARGYLL

The Bishop of Norwich	Sir Caspar Purdon Clarke, G.S.I., F.S.A.
The Archdeacon of Suffolk	Sir Augustus Helder, M.P.
Rev. Canon Raven, R.D.	E. Crofts, Esq., R.A., F.S.A.
The Vicar of Blythburgh	Luke Fildes, R.A.
Lady Blois	C. F. Egerton, Esq.
Mrs. Seymour Lucas	J. Seymour Lucas, Esq., R.A., F.S.A.
Mrs. Egerton	Carmichael Thomas, Esq.
Mrs. Hamilton	Norman Graham, Esq.
Sir Ralph Blois, Bart., Lord of the Manor	

Hon. Secretary: Sir Ralph Blois, Bart.   Hon. Treasurer: C. F. Egerton, Esq.
Cockfield Hall, Yoxford, Suffolk.   Bulcamp, Wangford, Suffolk.

The first page of the 1905 appeal prospectus, illustrated by Ernest Crofts RA, a Blythburgh resident, and listing the eminent restoration committee. BCP, Blue Scrap Book

THE RESTORATION OF BLYTHBURGH CHURCH 1881–1906

THE DISPUTE BETWEEN THE SOCIETY FOR THE PROTECTION OF ANCIENT BUILDINGS AND THE BLYTHBURGH CHURCH RESTORATION COMMITTEE

Edited by
ALAN MACKLEY

General Editor
RICHARD HALSEY

The Boydell Press

Suffolk Records Society
VOLUME LX

A Suffolk Records Society publication

First published 2017

The Boydell Press, Woodbridge

ISBN 978-1-78327-167-2

Issued to subscribing members for the year 2016–17

The Boydell Press is an imprint of Boydell & Brewer Ltd
PO Box 9, Woodbridge, Suffolk IP12 3DF, UK
and of Boydell & Brewer Inc.
668 Mt Hope Avenue, Rochester, NY 14620–2731, USA
website: www.boydellandbrewer.com

The publisher has no responsibility for the continued existence or
accuracy of URLs for external or third-party internet websites referred to
in this book, and does not guarantee that any content on such websites is,
or will remain, accurate or appropriate

A catalogue record for this book is available
from the British Library

This publication is printed on acid-free paper

MIX
Paper from
responsible sources
FSC® C013056

CONTENTS

ILLUSTRATIONS

Map

PREFACE AND ACKNOWLEDGEMENTS

The origin of this volume lies in a letter from Norman Kelvin, professor of English, The City University of New York, written in 1992 to the then vicar of Blythburgh, the Revd Harry Edwards. Professor Kelvin, editor of *The Collected Letters of William Morris* (4 volumes, Princeton University Press, 1984–2014), referred to a visit made by Morris to Blythburgh church in 1895 and wished to identify the incumbent. I replied on the vicar's behalf, providing some information about the vicar of Blythburgh at that time, the Revd Thomas Oakes. Coincidentally I had just visited the British Architectural Library and in the journal *The Architect* had noticed serendipitously a letter from the secretary of the Society for the Protection of Ancient Buildings (SPAB) to another Blythburgh vicar in 1883. The society and the local building committee were clearly at loggerheads over the restoration of the church. Later, Professor Kelvin told me that the SPAB library was a potentially rich source on the subject of Blythburgh church restoration. I visited the library in 1995 and copied the nearly 250 documents in the Blythburgh boxes.

The first use of this material was at the behest of The Blythburgh Society when Owen Thompson wrote an article for the *Suffolk Review,* 'The Rev. Henry Sykes and the restoration of Blythburgh church: late Victorian church restoration', 31 (1998), pp. 2–15. Owen Thompson also used related documents held by Suffolk Record Office at Ipswich.

Achieving the marriage of the SPAB and Suffolk documents has been a slow process, with many diversions along the way. I wish to thank the council of the Suffolk Records Society for accepting my proposal and its general editor, Richard Halsey MBE, for his guidance on content and the shape required by the society. Thanks are due to the staffs of the SPAB library, the Norfolk and Suffolk Record Offices, and the library of the University of East Anglia. Institutions and individuals that have responded to my requests for help include the libraries of the City University London, Clare College Cambridge, the RIBA, Peterborough Cathedral, the Institution of Civil Engineers, Lambeth Palace and Ruskin College Oxford. I am also grateful to James Bettley, Alan Greening, David Lindley and Oliver Henderson Smith. There was a most unexpected and welcome communication from Rose Sanguinetti, granddaughter of the influential Blythburgh churchwarden Claude Egerton. She gave me information about the family that I could not have found elsewhere.

Living in Blythburgh has added to the pleasure of my research. The names of the places and people in this volume still resonate today. The churchwardens, Jenny Allen and Thomas Lond-Caulk, and the Revds Joan Lyon and Malcom Doney provided valuable support when I exposed a late draft of my introduction to public gaze. And I thank my wife Ursula for her tolerance when, having removed from our house an eighteenth-century family, the subject of an earlier publication, I repopulated it with a feuding nineteenth-century group that seemed to demand my attention even more.

I am grateful to the SPAB, the Suffolk Record Office, Ipswich, and the church-wardens and parochial church council of Holy Trinity, Blythburgh, for permission to publish their documents. The Suffolk Records Society acknowledges with thanks grants from the Blythburgh Society and the Remembering Blythburgh Project; also the Adnams Community Trust for a grant to cover the cost of the colour plates in this volume.

Alan Mackley
Blythburgh, May 2016

ABBREVIATIONS

Bt	Baronet, a member of the lowest hereditary order
BCP	Blythburgh Church Papers
Crockford	*Crockford's Clerical Directory*
CWA	Blythburgh churchwardens' accounts
FSA	Fellow of the Society of Antiquaries of London
IJ	*Ipswich Journal*
ODNB	*Oxford Dictionary of National Biography*
PSIAH	*Proceedings of the Suffolk Institute of Archaeology and History*
RCMB	Blythburgh church restoration committee minute book
RIBA	Royal Institute of British Architects
SPAB	Society for the Protection of Ancient Buildings
SROI	Suffolk Record Office, Ipswich branch
VMB	Blythburgh vestry minute book

Unless otherwise stated, the place of publication is London. For Suffolk places, the county name has not been included.

INTRODUCTION

> The Church's Restoration
> In eighteen-eighty-three
> Has left for contemplation
> Not what there used to be.
>
> John Betjeman, 'Hymn', *Mount Zion* (1932) in *Collected Poems* (1958)

Blythburgh is a small village in northeast Suffolk, with some 300 inhabitants, situated on the river Blyth, four miles inland from the sea at Southwold. It is renowned for its grand parish church, which from its prominent location overlooking the marshes has for centuries been a beacon for travellers on the road from London to Yarmouth. The church has a fifteenth-century nave and chancel, with a notable painted ceiling with carved angels, and an older tower. Visitors may wonder why a small community boasts such a large church. Probably few of them realise that in 1881, the year with which the story described in this volume begins, the church was in an extreme state of disrepair and became the focus of a rancorous twenty-five year long battle between those who wished to restore the building and those who supported preservation, fearing the destruction of the character of the church.[1]

On Thursday 8 December 1881 the London newspaper *The Morning Post* carried this news item:

> The parish church of Blythburgh, Norfolk, has been closed by order of the Bishop of Norwich on account of the dangerous condition of its fine hammer-beam roof. The church is one of the best examples of semi-Flemish 13th century architecture, but is altogether in a very dilapidated condition.

This short report is remarkable for the number of errors it contains. Blythburgh is in Suffolk, not Norfolk; its church does not have a hammer-beam roof; and, setting aside the now archaic term 'semi-Flemish', the church is not of the thirteenth century but of the fifteenth. However, two essential facts were correct: Blythburgh church was in a very dilapidated condition, and it had been closed.

The closure of Blythburgh church precipitated a bitter dispute between a succession of incumbents and restoration committees, on the one hand, and the Society for the Protection of Ancient Buildings (SPAB), on the other. Blythburgh's community wanted a secure, restored structure, with the sweeping away of accumulated unsightly repairs. The SPAB, in contrast, regarding Blythburgh as a fine example

---

[1] A summary of the background to the 'restoration versus conservation' issue is in John Delafons, *Politics and preservation: a policy history of the built heritage, 1882–1996* (1997), pp. 13–21, and in Chris Miele, 'Morris and conservation' in Chris Miele (ed.), *From William Morris: building conservation and the Arts and Crafts cult of authenticity, 1877–1939* (New Haven and London, 2005), pp. 31–65. There are references to the Blythburgh dispute in Anne Riches, 'Victorian church building in Suffolk' in H. Munro Cautley, *Suffolk churches and their treasures* (5th edn, Woodbridge, 1982), pp. 381–2, and in James Bettley and Nikolaus Pevsner, *The buildings of England: Suffolk: East* (New Haven and London, 2015), p. 128.

of an unrestored church, strongly opposed the loss of any historic fabric, including post-medieval repairs, and any replacement by modern copies. John Betjeman's line 'Not what there used to be' aptly describes the result feared by the SPAB. The stage was therefore set for a 'restoration versus conservation' conflict. It was fought not only through private correspondence and meetings between the parties, but also in the national and local press. This volume presents documents from both sides of the dispute.

The documents

I. SPAB files. Blythburgh Box I, 1881–95, Blythburgh Box II, 1901–6, and Additional Documents. This collection covers the whole period of the society's involvement with the work at Blythburgh. It includes not only the society's papers but also letters received and other material collected, including newspaper reports. These documents provide the single most extensive coverage of the subject.[2]

II. Blythburgh church restoration committee minute book. This records the proceedings of meetings held between October 1881 and May 1884. Inserted in the book are numerous press cuttings and newspaper reports of the progress of the appeal for subscriptions to the restoration fund.[3]

III. Blythburgh churchwardens' accounts from Easter 1879 to Easter 1911.[4]

IV. A collection of papers from F.C. Brooke of Ufford Place, Suffolk, for the period 1882–4, comprising correspondence with the Blythburgh incumbent, and newspaper reports and other documents saved by Brooke.[5]

V. Other relevant documents held by the Suffolk Record Office, Ipswich.[6]

VI. Blythburgh church papers. A miscellaneous collection of documents, scrapbooks and photographs, deposited in the Suffolk Record Office, Ipswich, May 2016. References are to a provisional list compiled by the editor, dated March 2016.

The documents from the collections have been integrated and presented thematically and chronologically in Correspondence, Architects' Reports and other sections, with appropriate source references.

---

[2] The documents are held in the SPAB library, 37 Spital Square, London, E1 6DY. They are here referred to as SPAB I and SPAB II.

[3] SROI FC 198 E 2 1. Hereafter RCMB.

[4] SROI FC 185 E 1 1. Hereafter CWA.

[5] SROI HD 80 4 2. Hereafter Brooke.

[6] SROI FC 185 E 3 2, Parts 1–3. Hereafter SROI 2, 1–3. Use has also been made of the Blythburgh vestry minute book (1884–1902), SROI FC 198 A1 1.

Plate 1. The church exterior before restoration. This illustration used for the 1882 appeal pro-spectus shows that the tracery of four of the south aisle windows had been lost, and that the south porch and chancel windows were bricked up. © SROI, HD80 4 2

Blythburgh church: the road to near ruin

There can be no doubt about the state of Blythburgh church in 1881. Early in that year Ernest Geldart, a 'priest-architect' known as an expert on church furnishing and decoration, visited the church.[7] His diary entry for 26 February records its condition a few months before the church was closed:

> A civil woman ... let me in to a splendid ruin – a church of almost cathedral size having 18 or 20 windows in its clerestory on either side a flat painted roof with angels at the intersection of the cross beams, wh. angels in some cases had fallen off altogether and in others had dropped their wings or let them droop feebly. Down the walls green streams show the inroads of the weather, and from one end to the other the place is tottering to its death. The rood screen has been sawn down sheer off at the panel tops, and the screen to the side chapels mutilated and then whitewashed. At the north of the sanctuary is an altar

---

[7] James Bettley, 'A month in the country: Revd Ernest Geldart at Kelsale, 1881', *PSIAH* 42 Part 4 (2012), pp. 490–503. Before entering the church Geldart (1848–1929) was a pupil of Alfred Waterhouse. In 1881, between appointments, he visited a friend and colleague at Kelsale.

Plate 2. The interior of the nave and chancel before restoration showing box pews, the absence of the central section of the screen, and the loss of the tracery from the east window. Probably 1870s. BCP, Blue Scrap Book

tomb of the latest Perpendicular to the memory of King (Neddy it sounded like), a Saxon king the sextoness told me, who certainly received honours late in the day.[8] The alms box is a curiosity and would look better if the vicar had not decorated it by painting forget me nots or some such flowers in the panels. The stalls (those wh. remain) are richly carved and the wonder is they have not been sold or burned for fire wood. The sanctuary decorations

---

[8] This is presumably a reference to the tomb of John Hopton, lord of the manor (d. 1478). See Colin Richmond, *John Hopton: a fifteenth-century Suffolk gentleman* (Cambridge, 1981).

consist of red, blue and gold paper banners and texts plastered into one enormous dossal and covering the whole east wall up to the great east window, wh. poor window has been robbed of all its tracery and filled in solid down to the spring of the arch. The lower part is filled with neat and inexpensive quarry glass of this pattern. Many of the other windows are filled in a more solid manner with brickwork pure and simple, wh. keeps out the rain at the same time as the sunshine.

This was a very sad state indeed for the parish church of one of the earliest Christian sites in East Anglia.

Early records

The first documentary source implying the existence of a church at Blythburgh is a twelfth-century history of Ely. It records that in AD 654 the Christian East Anglian king, Anna, and his son, Jurmin, were killed in battle (at Bulcamp) with the pagan Mercian king, Penda, and their bodies brought to Blythburgh.[9] It is probable that Blythburgh had an Anglo-Saxon minster, of the reign of King Ælfwald (d. 749).[10]

By the eleventh century Blythburgh was a prosperous town with a market. The Domesday Book records that the church was one of the richest in Suffolk (a rich county) and had two dependent churches or chapels.[11] It is highly likely that the rich church had descended from the pre-Conquest minster. The dependent churches were possibly those serving Blythburgh and Walberswick.

Blythburgh was part of the royal estate, and early in the twelfth century its church was granted by Henry I to the Augustinian canons of St Osyth Priory, Essex, founding the priory of the Blessed Virgin Mary. It is possible that canons were established at Blythburgh during Henry's reign (he died in 1135); they were certainly there by 1147. The canons would have occupied the wealthy mother church; the parish

---

[9] Janet Fairweather (trans.), *Liber Eliensis: a history of the Isle of Ely* (Woodbridge, 2005), p. 22. A separate tradition names Bulcamp, a hamlet of Blythburgh parish, as the site of the battle. Anna was a nephew of King Raedwald, identified as the most probable occupant of the Sutton Hoo ship burial. Rosalind C. Love (ed.), *Goscelin of Saint-Bertin: the hagiography of the female saints of Ely* (Oxford, 2004), pp. lxxxvii, 90–1, refers to the cult of Anna, still venerated at Blythburgh in the twelfth century, and to Jurmin, whose relics were translated to the new Norman church at Bury St Edmunds in the mid eleventh century. See also Norman Scarfe, *Suffolk in the Middle Ages* (Woodbridge, 1986), p. 44.

[10] John Blair, *The church in Anglo-Saxon society* (Oxford, 2005), p. 203. A leaf from an eighth-century writing tablet was found on the Blythburgh priory site before 1902. It has been suggested that it is the remains of a diptych of the kind used during the mass of the early medieval church. The discovery of styli is further evidence of a literate presence at Blythburgh (Leslie Webster and Janet Backhouse (eds), *The making of England: Anglo-Saxon art and culture AD 600–900* (1991), p. 81). The discovery of Ipswich ware on the priory site and elsewhere in Blythburgh suggests occupation during the seventh century (Suffolk County Council Archaeological Service, Sites and Monuments Records BLB001, 004 and 016). Two inhumation burials of the middle to late Anglo-Saxon period (radiocarbon dated to AD 670–780 and AD 890–1020) were found in 2008 during excavations on the site of the priory church. They had been disturbed by the construction of the nave, probably in the eleventh or twelfth century (*Blythburgh priory, Blythburgh, Suffolk: archaeological evaluation and assessment of results*, Wessex Archaeology, Ref. 68742, 2009).

[11] Ann Williams and G.H. Martin (eds), *Domesday Book: a complete translation* (1992), p. 1186.

church, Holy Trinity, was one of its two dependents.[12] From the twelfth century to the dissolution of the priory in 1537 the prior was rector of Blythburgh.[13]

Rebuilding the church

The parish church was rebuilt in the fifteenth century. It has a large, simple, rectangular plan enclosing the nave and chancel with aisles running the length of the church. There is no chancel arch, and the clerestory and open roof run in an unbroken line for the length of the building. This plan originated in the second half of the fourteenth century in urban areas roughly centred on Norwich. Blythburgh is one of a Suffolk coastal group begun in the first half of the fifteenth century; four in south-west Suffolk followed later in the century. It is a plan generally achievable only when the whole church is rebuilt, with the possible exception of the tower, as at Blythburgh.[14]

Its form before rebuilding is not known, with only the tower, dating from the first half of the fourteenth century, surviving from the earlier church.[15] That the church should be rebuilt at this time, with the priory in decline and doubt about the extent of Blythburgh's recovery from the impact of the Black Death, demands an explanation.[16]

A study of taxes levied in 1428 and 1449 shows that depopulation and reduced levels of wealth were widespread throughout Suffolk. The Blything hundred was granted an average tax relief of 19.2 per cent. Blythburgh and Walberswick received a 14.83 per cent reduction in 1449 (compared with a 1334 assessment), but the relief was entirely for Blythburgh.[17]

In the agrarian depression of the early fifteenth century the rental value of the demesne fell by over 30 per cent. Arable was abandoned in the 1450s, and income from the mill fell by 29 per cent between the 1420s and 1460s, not recovering before

---

[12] The possibility that the canons occupied the rich mother church and that the parish church was one of the dependent churches was first considered by Norman Scarfe in 'Blythburgh, Holy Trinity Church', *PSIAH* 34 Part 2 (1978), p. 155.

[13] Christopher Harper-Bill (ed.), *Blythburgh priory cartulary*, I (Suffolk Charters 2, Woodbridge, 1980), pp. 1–5. Blythburgh priory was never large, although by the end of the thirteenth century the original royal endowment had been augmented by the acquisition of other parish churches and grants of generally small properties in some forty parishes, mostly in Suffolk. The number of canons may have reached double figures, but by 1407 the institution was in decline and there were only seven including the prior. The priory's income fell from about £86 per annum in 1291 to some £50 in the 1530s. Nevertheless the priory church had been extended and in the thirteenth century was an impressively large cruciform structure.

[14] Birkin Haward, *Suffolk medieval church arcades* (Ipswich, 1993), pp. 35–6. There are eleven such churches in Suffolk. Neighbouring examples are at Covehithe, Southwold and Walberswick.

[15] An earlier date for the tower depends on the restored west window being an accurate copy of the original work, which stylistically would then be of *c*. 1350 (Eric Gee, unpublished typescript of a visit made in August 1964, now in the National Monuments Record). Gee speculates that the nave and north aisle were built first, followed by the south aisle, when a clerestory was put over both arcades *c*. 1420. The chancel followed after 1442, with the choir aisles built at the same time. The work was complete by *c*. 1470. The church fabric incorporates fragments of an earlier church of *c*. 1070.

[16] As rector, the prior would have been responsible for the church chancel. The Blythburgh 'community', which could well have meant just the Hopton family, would have been responsible for the nave and tower.

[17] David Dymond and Roger Virgoe, 'The reduced population and wealth of early fifteenth-century Suffolk', *PSIAH* 36 (1986), pp. 73–99.

the early sixteenth century. In the 1460s the income from Blythburgh fair reached its lowest level.[18]

However, in these apparently unpropitious times, Blythburgh's lord of the manor, John Hopton (succ. 1430, d. 1478), did not have to rely only upon his Suffolk income. He lived in Blythburgh, but his Yorkshire property was worth as much as, if not more than, all his Suffolk properties put together. He had, at the lowest estimate, a clear income of £300 per year, of which Blythburgh contributed perhaps £40. The other Suffolk estates delivered maybe £150, plus something from sheep farming. From Yorkshire it is unlikely that he received less than £100 and it could have been as high as £300 per annum. Blythburgh therefore provided a relatively small proportion of Hopton's total income. John Hopton has been described as more than merely well-off: he was just less than very rich.[19]

We do not know how much money Hopton contributed to the cost of the new church. Certainly, he founded a chantry in 1451 in the north chancel chapel, where the Blythburgh priest was to celebrate mass daily for the good estate of John, his benefactors and the soul of his late wife, Margaret.[20] And, in expressing his wishes for his interment, he referred to the church 'by him lately edified and built'.[21] He was buried in a swagger tomb, at his request between the chancel and the north chapel.[22]

The reason for the rebuilding of Blythburgh church in a splendid manner should not be sought in either the size of the community or its wealth. The explanation lies in the obsession in the Middle Ages with death. This is thus described by Eamon Duffy:

> The extensive and often sumptuous rebuilding of so many of the churches of East Anglia in the fifteenth century was an expression not simply of … bourgeois prosperity … but the concern of [the] rich to use their wealth as post-mortem fire insurance. The flinty splendour of Blythburgh … was certainly a testimony of the desire of the … Hoptons … for a perma-nent reminder to their neighbours of their family wealth and status. But first and foremost, their benefactions were prompted by a concern to erect before God a permanent witness to their piety and charity, which would plead for them at the Judgement Seat of Christ.[23]

The Hoptons were not the only benefactors of the new church. Building was sup-ported by other donations, both large and small. Some expenditure was deliberately conspicuous: the names of John Masin and his wife Katherine, for example, were inscribed on the seven-sacrament font and the now lost central boss of the vaulted roof of the south porch.[24] Heraldic shields in windows and along the length of the

---

[18] Mark Bailey, *Medieval Suffolk: an economic and social history, 1200–1500* (Woodbridge, 2007), pp. 207, 211 and 233.

[19] Richmond, *John Hopton*, pp. 32 and 95.

[20] John Hopton married twice, first to the widow Margaret Saville (she died by December 1451) and then to the twice widowed Thomasin Barrington (d. 1498). Richmond, *John Hopton*, pp. 100–1.

[21] Judith Middleton-Stewart, *Inward purity and outward splendour: death and remembrance in the dean-ery of Dunwich, Suffolk, 1370–1547* (Woodbridge, 2001), p. 272.

[22] Richmond, *John Hopton*, p. 156, n. 224. This is the most prestigious site in the church and, because it affects the rector's chancel, would need his permission.

[23] Eamon Duffy, *The stripping of the altars* (New Haven and London, 1992), pp. 301–2. Suffolk exam-ples of the purchase of remission from the torments of purgatory are described in David Dymond and Clive Paine, *Five centuries of an English parish church: 'the state of Melford church'*, Suffolk (Cambridge, 2012), and in Peter Bloore and Edward Martin (eds), *Wingfield College and its patrons: piety and prestige in medieval Suffolk* (Woodbridge, 2015).

[24] Alfred Suckling, *The history and antiquities of the hundreds of Blything and part of Lothingland, in the county of Suffolk* (1847*)*, p. 152, says 'Masin', quoting the inscription on the porch boss, although

roof did celebrate the Hoptons, but these emphasised family descents and alliances rather than benefactors.[25] (The Anglo-Saxon past was kept alive with the depiction of kings and bishops of Dunwich in the windows.)[26] The long list of testators also includes the name of Alice Stapleton, whose benefactions of 1494 included money for a canopy over the high altar. Having previously been arraigned for keeping a brothel, she was perhaps more in need than most for advocacy at the seat of final judgement.[27]

The sixteenth and seventeenth centuries: radical change

Less than a century after the completion of the new parish church came the dramatic changes of the sixteenth century, with the dissolution of the priory, the Reformation and the separation of the English church from Rome. The priory's property passed into lay hands,[28] Blythburgh church was left with meagre endowments and a perpetual curate served the parish with a small income. Little is known of the direct religious impact upon Blythburgh, but there was no preacher in the whole of the Suffolk coastal zone in 1567.[29] More is known about the havoc wreaked by a violent thunderstorm that swept across east Suffolk on 4 August 1577, damaging both Blythburgh and Bungay churches.[30] A man and a boy died in Blythburgh church, presumably struck by lightning. Suckling wrote 'The parish registers mention, that the spire-part of the steeple was thrown down, and the standing remains greatly rent and torn by the tempest'.[31]

Blythburgh church suffered further during the seventeenth century, when on 9 April

---

Enid Radcliffe and Nikolaus Pevsner, *The buildings of England: Suffolk* (Harmondsworth, 1974), p. 103, identifies the donors as 'Mason'. This is repeated in Bettley and Pevsner (2015).

[25] Anon., Heraldry of Suffolk churches, *Suffolk Heraldry Society* 10 (1980). Many of the series of 25 bosses and shields on the roof are now indecipherable. Some are thought to be merely heraldic ornamentation and not authentic coats of arms. See also Middleton-Stewart, *Inward purity*, pp. 248–50.

[26] Much of this glass was lost to seventeenth-century iconoclasm, but a considerable debt is owed to Hamlet Watling (see n. 143 below) and other antiquaries for recording the glazing programme before the further losses of the nineteenth century. Middleton-Stewart, *Inward purity*, p. 241.

[27] Middleton-Stewart, *Inward purity*, p. 49, n. 2 and p. 51.

[28] The suppression of Blythburgh priory was authorised by the Pope in 1528 to provide for the endowment of Cardinal College, Ipswich. The death of Wolsey reprieved Blythburgh until its dissolution in February 1537. The priory's property passed to Walter Wadelond of Needham Market. He became the lay owner of the tithes – the impropriator. In 1548 the reversion was granted to Sir Arthur Hopton of Blythburgh (Harper-Bill, p. 4). Hopton's Blythburgh, Walberswick and Westleton estate was sold in 1592 to Alderman Robert Brooke (d. 1601), a successful London grocer, and soon after he added Cockfield Hall, Yoxford (Peter Warner, *Bloody marsh: a seventeenth-century village in crisis* (Macclesfield, 2000). The village of the title is Walberswick.

[29] Diarmaid MacCulloch, *Suffolk and the Tudors: politics and religion in an English county, 1500–1600* (Oxford, 1987), pp. 189–90.

[30] Abraham Fleming, *A strange and terrible wonder* (1577). This pamphlet is the source of an enduring myth that the devil, in the guise of a black dog, leapt from the rood screen, coursed down the nave terrorising the congregation, and left by the north door, on which he left its claw marks. The earliest printed references to this story date from the 1950s, including a report of a visit to Blythburgh by the Plebs League, a group of Marxist students from Ruskin College, Oxford. *The Plebs*, vols 44–7 (1952), p. 116. Although Fleming wrote that the creature 'flew with wonderful force to no little fear of the assembly, out of the Church in a vicious and hellish likeness', his only reference to marks left on church fabric relate to Bungay, not Blythburgh. The marks on the Blythburgh door are burns from candle or taper flames.

[31] Suckling, *History and antiquities*, p. 158.

1644 Puritan iconoclasts, implementing a parliamentary ordinance of August 1643 and led by William Dowsing, arrived in Blythburgh. The Puritan lord of the manor, Sir Robert Brooke of Cockfield Hall, Yoxford, no doubt agreed with the ensuing destruction,.[32] This included the smashing of stained glass and other 'superstitious' imagery, the ripping up of monumental brass inscriptions, the destruction of altar rails and the pulling down of crucifixes and crosses. Dowsing's journal records that crosses on the outside of the church went, as did more than 200 'pictures' – i.e. stained glass – in the nave and chancel. Some of these were ordered destroyed within eight days. Twenty cherubim – the angels in the roof – were targeted, but their height seems to have put them beyond the reach of the iconoclasts. Brasses were removed from monuments, and the decorative panels in the font chiselled flat. The scars of this work are still visible in Blythburgh church.[33] The archdeacon's parochial visitation book of 1663 recorded that there had been no communion celebrated for twelve years. [34]

By the latter half of the seventeenth century the size and wealth of the Blythburgh community were much reduced. The hearth tax returns of 1674 show that Blythburgh, including the hamlets of Bulcamp and Hinton, had fewer hearths than other thoroughfare communities on the London–Yarmouth major road.[35] To compound matters, in 1676 Blythburgh suffered a disastrous fire.[36] Gardner wrote that some inhabitants were unable and others chose not to rebuild their properties. Blythburgh was reduced to poverty. The number of dwellings was no more than 21 and the population 124. It was still a poor community in 1881, when the church closed. Although the Blyth navigation, opened in 1761, had stimulated investment and building in Halesworth and Southwold, it had left no mark on Blythburgh – substantial buildings of the eighteenth and nineteenth centuries found in other thoroughfare communities on the trunk road, in Saxmundham, Yoxford, Wangford and Wrentham for example, are absent from Blythburgh. No prominent citizen or merchant chose to build in the village. There are no such buildings on the line of the turnpike cut through Blythburgh in 1785. The patron and vicar of the church both lived elsewhere.[37] Although Blythburgh's pop-

---

[32] Sir Robert Brooke (1573–1646) inherited his father's Suffolk estate in 1601. As MP for Dunwich from 1624, he was a member of the parliamentarian Suffolk county committee during the civil war. Andrew Thrush and John P. Ferris (eds), *The history of parliament: the House of Commons, 1604–1629* (Cambridge, 2010).

[33] Trevor Cooper (ed.), *The journal of William Dowsing: iconoclasm in East Anglia during the English Civil War* (Woodbridge, 2001), pp. 299–300. The account of Dowsing's work at Walberswick on 8 April 1644 is the only one to mention him by name or the presence of soldiers. The rings in the pillars of Blythburgh church to which by tradition troopers' horses are supposed to have been tethered are of recent date. The myth that muskets were fired at the angels in the roof also has no foundation. Lead shot found in the angels' wings are of a type not known in the sixteenth century. An entry in the churchwardens' accounts for 1761 of payments for the shooting of jackdaws in the church provides a more likely explanation. Norman Scarfe, 'Blythburgh', pp. 155–6. See Appendix A 17 for references to cracks in the tower walls in the report of William Weir.

[34] Suckling, *History and antiquities*, p. 158.

[35] S.H.A. Hervey (ed.), *Suffolk in 1674: being the hearth tax returns, 1674* (Woodbridge, 1905). Blythburgh had 175 hearths, whereas Saxmundham (247), Yoxford (272) and Wrentham (187) were larger. The nearby market towns of Halesworth (500), Beccles (929) and Bungay (589), and the port of Southwold (399), had far outstripped Blythburgh. Of these communities, only Beccles and Bungay had been ranked above Blythburgh on the basis of tax assessments in 1327. Frank Grace, 'A historical survey of Suffolk towns', *Suffolk Review* 5 (1982), pp. 105–13.

[36] Thomas Gardner, *An historical account of Dunwich, Blithburgh and Southwold* (1754), p. 121. The statistics presumably do not include the outlying hamlets of Bulcamp and Hinton.

[37] The vicarage for the combined living of Walberswick with Blythburgh was at Walberswick. The living's gross/net income in 1875 was £140/135. This had fallen to £131/124 in 1898. *Crockford 1875,*

Plate 3. The north aisle chapel (the Hopton chapel dedicated to St Anne) before the removal of stalls to the chancel. Probably 1870s. © SPAB

ulation rose steadily through the nineteenth century, peaking in the census of 1851, it was a community of poorly paid farmworkers and small shopkeepers. A handful of farmers were tenants of landed estates. Blythburgh church mouldered away. If the residents worshipped at all, they were more likely to be found in the Primitive Methodist chapel in Dunwich Road than in the established church.[38]

p. 883 and 1898, p. 1198. The Brooke estate passed to the Blois family by marriage in the late seventeenth century. This family, descended from Robert Blois (d. 1559), an Ipswich mercer and chandler, established their gentry status through the purchase of a farmhouse, called Sigers, in Grundisburgh, afterwards calling it Grundisburgh Hall. John, heir to Sir Robert Brooke (d. 1646) died in 1652. The last Brooke in the male line was then his brother, Sir Robert (c. 1637–69). Sir William Blois (1626–75) married first, in 1647, Brooke's sister and co-heir Martha (d. 1657), and then, in 1660, Jane, John Brooke's widow. Sir William Blois's son Sir Charles, 1st Bt (1657–1738), finally inherited Cockfield Hall on the death of his aunt Mary Brooke in 1693.

38 T.C.B. Timmins (ed.), *Suffolk returns from the census of religious worship, 1851* (Suffolk Records Society 39, 1997), pp. 143–4. The population was 607, excluding 511 in the Union workhouse at Bulcamp. The average attendance at Holy Trinity Church was 35 plus 21 scholars in the morning and 60 plus 20 scholars in the afternoon. There was an average of 10 communicants. The average morning attendance at the Primitive Methodist chapel was 170. Nonconformism was evident in Blythburgh early in the nineteenth century with the granting of a license for what is now Chantry Cottage in Priory Road to be used as a meeting house (private communication). The Primitive Methodist chapel was opened in 1837 and rebuilt in 1860. C.F. Stell, *Nonconformist chapels and meeting-houses in eastern England* (Swindon, 2002), p. 280.

The condition of Blythburgh church before closure

The journals of visitors to the church in the nineteenth century describe its decay in great detail. For example, in 1808:

> The church is kept in a very bad state; many of its fine windows are closed with red bricks; the carvings on the roof, consisting of angels bearing shields, on which are painted the arms of divers benefactors to the church, are in such a condition that they are continually falling. An altar tomb in the chancel (one of those engraved in Gardiner's 'History of Dunwich') now serves as a base for two or three clumsy square columns of bricks; so that the deceased, whatever he might have been in his lifetime, is now unquestionably a firm supporter of the church. D. Davis.[39]

Also in 1808:

> It seems [*on the dissolution of Blythburgh priory*] no provision was made for a clergyman; he receives so scanty an allowance that, in a parish containing 363 persons according to the return in 1801, 438 by the return in 1811, divine service is performed but once a fortnight, by a curate who resides at a distance of six miles! Has the bishop no power in such a case? If he has not, it is to be hoped that Parliament, under the very laudable care which they are exerting for the benefit of the Church, will find some mode of making a provision for such cases. G. and B.[40]

Later, in 1832, Sir Stephen Glynne, visiting Blythburgh, described a very spacious and beautiful church in a sad state of mutilation and decay.[41] And in 1874 J.J. Raven was even more dismayed:

> Re the (now) choir stalls: 'The woodwork which is now in the chancel has been recently removed from the Hopton chantry at the end of the north aisle [*and*] the screen which, with its coats of whitewash, well typifies the insolvent condition of the benefice ... The condition of Blythburgh is a sore scandal. Here is one of the finest Churches in Suffolk, in a place of historic note, and surrounded by fair estates, shorn of its architectural ornaments and reduced to the lowest point of squalor; the nave filled with rickety pews of the meanest deal; the windows, many of them blocked up with red brick and plaster; the flooring loose and broken; and the whole plentifully smeared with whitewash, which dose was being administered at the time of one of my visits by workmen with caps on their heads and pipes in their mouths'.[42]

---

[39] Sylvanus Urban, *The gentleman's magazine and historical chronicle for the year 1808*, 78 Part 2, p. 776. The reference is to John Hopton's tomb.

[40] Sylvanus Urban in George Laurence Gomme (ed.), *Topographical history of Staffordshire and Suffolk* (1899), p. 201.

[41] Sir Stephen Glynne, 9th Bt (1807–74), of Hawarden Castle, Flintshire, brother-in-law of the statesman, William Gladstone, was an assiduous visitor of churches from 1825 to 1874. Flintshire Record Office, Church Notes of Sir Stephen Glynne, GB 0208 SG, Notes on Suffolk Churches, Blythburgh, pp. 39–41. The church attracted many visitors. Between 8 September 1896 and 25 September 1900, over 3,000 people signed the visitors' book. Visitor numbers were highest between July and September. BCP, Books 2, Visitors' Book.

[42] J.J. Raven, 'Blythburgh', *PSIAH* 4 (1874), pp. 236 and 241. Sir W.R. Gowers in 'The flint-work inscription on Blythburgh church', *PSIAH* 11 (1901), states that shrubs were flourishing in the north aisle about 1878. He was anxious that the inscription under the east window was preserved. This was restored over a hundred years later, paid for by Mrs Audrey Malan of The Green, Blythburgh, in memory of her husband, Edward. The dedication service was held on 16 May 1982. BCP, 1–49.

Plate 4. The interior of the south aisle before restoration, showing box pews and whitewashed screen. Probably 1870s. © SPAB

And so it was in 1881, finally, that the bishop ordered the church closed.

Restoration: phase one, 1881–4

The Blythburgh vicar in 1881 was the Revd Henry Sykes,[43] who had come to the parish in 1879. Determined to save the church, Sykes announced in a notice dated

---

[43] The Blythburgh incumbent was a perpetual curate, paid by the diocese. Before the dissolution of Blythburgh priory the parish was served by the Augustinian canons. Thereafter the curate was nom-inated by the impropriator of the tithes and licensed by the bishop. Only the bishop could remove him. Sykes, ordained in 1877, was vicar of Walberswick with Blythburgh, 1879–85. He came from

4 October 1881 a meeting for parishioners to discuss the restoration of the church.[44] He encouraged them to attend with the words:

> As the Church belongs to the whole parish, it is hoped all will feel a deep interest in preserving 'Our holy and our beautiful house in which our fathers praised' from further decay, and in handing down to future generations this noble monument of the piety of former times. Let no one say 'I am too poor.' Read 2 COR. VIII. 1 to 12v. Remember what the Saviour said of the Widow's mite, and of another, 'She hath done what she could.' Read also PROV. III. 9 and 10v. Come to the meeting and encourage your Vicar and Churchwardens in this great undertaking.

Sykes had already written to the *Ipswich Journal*, on 3 October, covering a letter signed by A.G. Adamson, drawing attention to the state of the church and the need to raise money for its restoration..[45] Sykes noted that two collections had already been made in the church, a bank account opened and contributions to a restoration fund solicited.

Parishioners gathered in Blythburgh's National School on 8 October 1881. The meeting agreed that an effort should be made at once towards raising funds for the restoration of the church. A committee was formed, headed by Sykes and comprising the two churchwardens, local farmers, the landlord of the White Hart and their wives.[46] Meeting for the first time three days later, the committee decided to print 100 small collecting cards and agreed that Sykes should write to the architect George E. Street to ascertain his fee for inspecting the church and reporting on its condition.[47] Sykes had already been advised that 'He [*Street*] knows better how to touch old [*buildings*] without disenchanting them of their own special character than, perhaps, any living architect'.[48] Sykes was authorised to engage Street provided that his fee did not exceed ten guineas plus travelling expenses.[49] Street visited the church on 3 November, and the committee was told at its meeting on 10 November that a report was expected within a few weeks with estimates of the cost of each stage of any proposed work. Street's involvement with Blythburgh was brief – he died on 18

Freethorpe, Norfolk. He returned to Norfolk as vicar of Potter Heigham. An Act of Parliament of 1868 permitted perpetual curates to describe themselves as vicar, and the term became the popular title for the various grades of parochial clergy, replacing 'parson'. It is used generally in this volume.

[44] Appendix C 3.

[45] Correspondence 1. In speculating about the role a large church like Blythburgh could play, Adamson used the phrase 'a sort of pro-cathedral in the district'. Is this the origin of the often-used description of Blythburgh church, 'the cathedral of the marshes'?

[46] The first appointments to the committee were the churchwardens Robinson Briggs and Charles Youngs; farmers Arthur Cooper, Thomas Tuthill and Thomas Rawlinson; George Mills, landlord of the White Hart; and Mrs Cooper, Briggs, Youngs, Sykes and Tuthill. Blythburgh schoolmistress Miss Mary Sainty and coal merchant and Sunday school teacher Charles A. Bicker were added to the committee on 10 October 1881. Lady Eliza Blois and Miss Clara Cooper joined on 21 January 1882; and on 21 August, the Revd G.I. Davies, rural dean, and Samuel Wilton Rix, a Beccles solicitor. The youth of Blythburgh was represented by Mary Sainty and Arthur and Clara Cooper, all in their early twenties. RCMB 1.

[47] George Edmund Street (1824–81), architect and major shaper of 'High Victorian' style.

[48] Correspondence 56. In a letter to F.C. Brooke, 27 February 1883, Sykes quotes advice he had been given by the Revd Sidney Pelham, vicar of St Peter Mancroft, Norwich, in a letter of 30 September 1881.

[49] The churchwardens paid Arthur Street's ten guineas fee. CWA 1881/82.

December – but his son, Arthur E. Street, completed his proposals without delay and sent them to Sykes on 31 December.[50]

Street proposed an extensive programme of work on the church, including re-leading the chancel roof, renewing bays at the west end of the nave roof and repairing the north and south aisle roofs. Blocked windows in the clerestory, chancel and nave aisles would be reopened and the tracery restored. The east and west windows would be restored. The nave columns and arches were found to be in good condition, but stonework would be cleaned and the nave replastered. The monumental stones in the floor would be relaid and the church paved with glazed and encaustic tiles, although Street noted that money could be saved by using simpler tiles. Other work proposed included the renewal of six angels in the roof, the restoration of the screen, the removal of the brick piers from the Hopton tomb and the repair of the wall above it. Externally, work was needed on the south porch, the parapet of the south aisle, the plinths and walls of the church, and the tower. The total cost of the work proposed by Street was £4,865.[51] Within this sum the estimated cost of work on the chancel was £745. The raising of this formidable sum was clearly beyond the means of the parish alone: at Easter 1881 the balance held by the churchwardens was a mere £44 9s. 5d.[52]

London supporters of the church responded to the notice in the *Morning Post*. Arthur C. Pain, who knew Blythburgh well, wrote to the paper proposing the formation of a committee to raise the 'necessary funds to render the edifice safe and fit for public worship'.[53] S. Sutherland Safford wrote to *Building News* in May 1882 that a London committee had been formed and asked for subscriptions or promises of assistance.[54]

At a meeting held on 21 January 1882, with the knowledge that some £5,000 was needed to restore the church, the restoration committee agreed to hold a bazaar in Blythburgh in the coming summer. Other fundraising events were arranged; for example, Miss Sainty organised an entertainment in the school on 10 February, which raised £3, and a concert at Yoxford contributed £18 10s. 0d.[55]

By now Street's report had been discussed and forwarded to the bishop of Norwich. Sykes met the bishop on 23 January to discuss the report and estimate of costs. The bishop suggested that the works be divided into three classes: those that were urgent, those that might be postponed and those that might be considered questionable. The architect should be asked to estimate the cost of each class of work to provide guidance on the sums that would have to be raised. No help could be expected from the ecclesiastical commissioners, because they had no property in the parish.[56]

---

[50] Arthur Edmund Street (d. 1938). He oversaw the completion of many of his father's works.

[51] Proposal and estimates for the restoration of Blythburgh church, 31 December 1881, Appendix A 1. The condition of the church may be judged from the extract of specification, Appendix A 4.

[52] The church owned little property. The annual rental income from 'Penny Pightle' and 'Thistley Meadow' was less than £30. See CWA 1881/82, for example.

[53] Correspondence 3. Arthur C. Pain, MICE (1844–1937), was the engineer who supervised the construction of the Southwold Railway, which opened in 1879 and ran through Blythburgh.

[54] Correspondence 12. Samuel Sutherland Safford (b. 1853) of Parkshot, Richmond, Surrey, was founder and secretary of a short-lived London committee (1882–3) of which the composition is not known. His Suffolk connections included his grandfather John Sutherland, surgeon and mayor of Southwold, after whom Sutherland House in the High Street is named.

[55] At the 14 April meeting it was agreed to put an advertisement in the *Ipswich Journal* and the *East Anglian Daily Times* and to print circulars announcing that the fundraising bazaar would be held in August 1882 and saying where contributions could be made. RCMB 10.

[56] The commissioners would meet a benefaction for the improvement of the living but not for the

At the committee meeting on 31 March 1882 it was unanimously agreed that the restoration of the church and chancel should proceed as one work, with the funds invested in the names of the vicar and churchwardens. Street should be instructed to prepare plans and specifications for a new roof for the south aisle, alongside both the nave and the chancel, the repair of the south aisle parapet, and those windows considered to be in a dangerous condition. The aim of this work was to keep out wind and water, and deal with those parts of the structure in a dangerous condition. Untouched at this stage would be the roofs of the nave and north aisle, both in a bad state, the bricked-up windows and the seating and flooring of the church. However, the committee was told at its next meeting, on 14 April, that the archdeacon had stated that because the correct procedure for approval of the work had not been followed, the committee did not have the authority to carry out the work, and resolutions passed at the previous meeting could not be executed on the terms proposed. Only the vestry could take such decisions.[57] The committee adopted Street's plans and asked him to prepare specifications to submit to a vestry meeting for approval. The vestry meeting was duly called and the plans and specifications passed without dissent. They were then sent to the bishop for his sanction and approval. He signed them on 7 July 1882.

A notable absentee at this stage was the patron, Sir John Blois.[58] Lady Blois's name had been added to the committee in January 1882, and she attended meetings from 31 July. It became apparent that the Blois family, responsible for the chancel, would not accept the committee's original position that the church should be considered as a whole and one fund invested. At the meeting on 3 July the committee considered a proposal from Lady Blois that funds be divided – subject to the approval of the archdeacon and the bishop – two-thirds to the church and one-third to the chancel.[59]

The involvement of the Blois family was crucial for fundraising. For example, Lady Blois arranged an amateur concert given in July 1882 at 38, Queen's Gate, the home of Mrs Smith-Bosanquet. Arrangements were made by Viscountess Midleton, Lady Blois, Lady Colthurst and Mrs Frederick Gaussen. Mr D'Oyly Carte gave

---

restoration of buildings. The bishop endorsed the appointment of Arthur Street as architect, in conjunction with Arthur William Blomfield (1829–99), architect.

[57] The vestry, a meeting of all parish ratepayers, churchgoers or not, and so-called because parishioners had originally met in the church vestry, was from the sixteenth to the twentieth century the local body responsible for the administration of Anglican parish churches. It had the authority to propose repairs and alterations to the church. Vestry meetings had to be convened with proper notice – on the church and school doors for two Sundays. See Appendix C 1 for the Norwich diocese's regulations respecting faculties. Some of the vestry functions were transferred to other bodies in the nineteenth century by, for example, the creation of civil parish councils in 1894. Vestries were eventually replaced by parochial church councils, set up in 1921.

[58] Sir John Ralph Blois, 8th Bt (1830–88), was a second son, his older brother Charles Samuel (1828–49) having died unmarried. Sir John had lived in Australia and was said to have been more at home in open spaces than in London, with no aptitude for politics. He was not an ideal church patron: 'His agnostic attitude towards religion caused anxiety to his earnestly pious lady: but after he had brought *The Times* to church, for comfortable reading during the sermon, she ceased to urge his attendance'. He had twelve children and 'became too penurious, even in respect of petty disbursements which were necessary to maintain a creditable appearance for his house and family. But the benefit was reaped later: people said that the improvements by which his son transformed Cockfield Hall were paid for entirely out of Sir John's savings'. Robert T.L. Parr, *Yoxford yesterday,* SROI, S. Yoxford 9.

[59] In pre-Reformation England the responsibility for the maintenance of the chancel rested with the rector, in the case of Blythburgh the prior until the dissolution of the priory in 1537. The responsibility then passed with the priory property, ultimately to the Blois family, as lay impropriators or lay rectors, enjoying the tithes from the parish.

permission for the performance of a selection of solos and choruses from 'Patience', enjoyed by 'a fashionable audience'. The concert raised £54.[60]

The Blythburgh bazaar was held over two days (9–10 August 1882) under the patronage of eminent local ladies: the countess of Stradbroke, Lady Constance Barne, Lady Huntingfield, Lady Blois, Lady Knightley, the Hon. Mrs Morton North, the Hon. Mrs Henry Brodrick, the Hon. Misses Thellusson, Mrs Blois, Mrs Frederick Gaussen, Mrs Sykes and Mrs Cooper. The first thought was to hold the event in the priory grounds, but this was found to be impracticable, so George Mills, landlord of the White Hart and member of the restoration committee, offered the meadow behind the inn. On the day of the bazaar, there was a large central marquee and tents pitched around the grounds, decorated with flags and banners. The result exceeded all expectations. Net receipts were £211 14s. 2d.

In long and detailed accounts the county newspapers reviewed the background to the dereliction of the church and the urgent need for action. They stressed the lead taken by Lady Blois in the campaign to restore the church:

> Lady Blois and a number of other ladies resident in the neighbourhood, with the ready assistance and co-operation of Sir John Blois, the patron of the living, have taken the subject up in a way that undoubtedly signifies a successful result … Lady Blois carried out the onerous duties of superintending the fancy fair generally admirably and proficiently.[61]

Mrs Cooper 'proved herself quite equal' to the task of planning out the ground. There were stalls in 'every conceivable form and fashion', with Lady Blois and family members prominent in manning them. Refreshments were under the direction of Mrs Blois.

On the first day there was an exhibition of mechanical toys; on the second, a magician came from Norwich. The band of F Company (Halesworth) Volunteers was in attendance, playing a choice selection of music during the day. The Southwold Railway was crowded. Concerts given in a room at the White Hart by ladies and gentlemen volunteering their services 'proved to be an excellent break in what might otherwise have been a somewhat monotonous time'! The event was, the *Norfolk Chronicle* reported, 'largely patronized by the elite of the neighbourhood'.[62]

These accounts of the bazaar incensed Sykes and precipitated public attacks by the vicar upon his patron. In the restoration committee minute book he annotated the report published in the *Halesworth Times*. Against the mention that Sir John and Lady Blois had been the principal movers in the matter, Sykes wrote 'A pure invention'. The newspaper stated that Lady Blois had secured all the subscriptions up to the date of the bazaar. Sykes wrote alongside, 'Lady Blois helped to raise this sum'.

Sykes did not stop there. He wrote to the *Ipswich Journal* on 16 August 1882 with an explicit attack on his patron. He claimed that statements in the paper's report of the bazaar 'may prove prejudicial to the great object we have set before us'. His main point was that those who had started the movement had been unfairly ignored.

---

[60] See reports in Appendix C 11–12.
[61] The fancy fair became a popular form of charity bazaar by the mid nineteenth century, selling a variety of fancy goods and ornaments from stalls manned by volunteers. The fairs were organised mostly by middle-class women, and securing a prominent female patron was important. See Susie Steinbach, *Women in England, 1760–1914: a social history* (2013).
[62] Appendix C 18.

Although Lady Blois had worked 'with a will', she was not an original member of the restoration committee and she had not been the means of collecting all the money collected so far. Sykes claimed that had the preservation of the church depended upon Lady Blois and the cooperation of Sir John, 'It is to be feared the church ... must have become a heap of ruins'. Sykes wrote, intriguingly, 'I might add much more but I forbear'.[63] The paper published a letter of the same date from 'Churchman' of East Suffolk. 'He' also referred to the report of the bazaar and pointedly criticised Sir John for having set an inadequate example, asserting that Sir John's contribution should have been £500, not the £100 with which he had headed the list of subscribers.[64] Was 'Churchman' in fact Sykes? Sykes added to 'Churchman's' barb about Sir John's appearance at the top of the subscription list by pointing out that the honour of leading the list really belonged to a Walberswick widow who had been the first to respond to the appeal: 'She hath given more than they all'.[65]

A printed fundraising leaflet was circulated in August 1882[66] that included a list of subscribers and showed that the sum collected thus far was £596 13s. 4¾d. Further subscriptions were solicited, and collecting cards could be had on application to the vicar. This appeal was reinforced by inclusions in Suffolk and Norfolk newspapers of further regular reports of the progress of the appeal.

The restoration committee agreed that the whole sum collected up to that date, including the bazaar proceeds, should go to a general fund, to be divided two-thirds to the church and one-third to the chancel as Lady Blois had proposed. The bazaar funds had been invested by her in Beccles, and Sykes had invested restoration fund contributions separately in Southwold. This separation was maintained throughout the project, but the parties agreed to release money under their control in the agreed proportions.

Tenders from five building contractors were received on 7 September 1882.[67] The costs were broken down into five groups, separating the chancel from the nave, the

---

[63] Correspondence 32. See n. 59 above. Parr's acerbic account of the history of the Blois family shows that their ability to support Blythburgh church would have been compromised even before the nineteenth century. Sir John Blois, 5th Bt (1740–1810), sold the Grundisburgh estate in 1772 to settle debts. The rest of his estate was held by trustees from 1772 and reconveyed to him in 1779. Cockfield Hall was leased for 21 years (1772–93) to Chaloner Arcedeckne. Sir John was reputed to have lost much of his money to 'a Mr Fitzgerald, a well-known Irishman ... This was the notorious bully George Robert Fitzgerald – Fighting Fitzgerald was his nickname – he was hanged in 1786'. R.T.L. Parr, *Yoxford yesterday*. See also Rachel Lawrence, *Southwold river: Georgian life in the Blyth Valley* (Exeter, 1990), pp. 44–51.
   This was not the first time Sir John had been accused of inaction. In 1865 he was blamed for the neglect of Blythburgh priory ruins. The architect R.M. Phipson (1827–84), responding to a report that part of the ruin had collapsed, wrote that the expenditure of a few pounds by the patron would have preserved it for some generations. Phipson's view on restoration accorded well with that of the SPAB, formed a few years later: 'It is perhaps better they [*the ruins*] should fall altogether than suffer such an infliction; but a few brick piers and struts judiciously and obviously placed ... in no way destroys the interest of the ruins'. *The Times*, 24 June 1865. In 1871 Phipson was appointed surveyor for the Norwich diocese. Baty (1987) lists no fewer than fifteen churches on which he worked. Sir John's priorities were revealed when he supported a proposal to build a Blyth Valley railway with the words: 'Some men when they had acquired wealth spent their money in building Churches and hospitals, and at any rate the opening of their [*Southwold*] harbour would do them as much good as Churches and hospitals'. *The Ipswich Journal*, 23 December 1865.

[64] Correspondence 31.
[65] Correspondence 32.
[66] Appendix B 1, 1.
[67] Appendix A 7.

latter estimate separating aisle and tower windows, the clerestory, and the south aisle roof and parapet. The lowest tender, for £1,049 10s., was submitted by R.J. Allen, a Southwold builder. The chancel cost was expected to be £363, just over one-third of the total.

At the committee meeting held in the White Hart on 21 September 1882, almost one year after the church had been closed, Sir John attended for the first time. He set the committee in a more business-like direction. It was agreed to form a building committee, which was to meet monthly. The architect was to be asked how the restoration work could be adjusted to meet the sum of £730 currently available.[68] Advice from Street and the Southwold builder Allen was available to the committee at its next meeting on 12 October. The sum in hand had increased to £808, but the committee deferred a decision to proceed with the contracts. However, Sir John was unwilling to release any money from accounts under his control, because a dispute had arisen as to what part of the building actually constituted the chancel, for which he was legally responsible.[69] The committee, aware how difficult it would be to raise the sum originally estimated as needed for the restoration of the church, agreed to save money by restricting advertising to the *Norfolk Chronicle* and the *Ipswich Journal*.

The chancel question was still open at the building committee's meeting on 1 January 1883. However, Sir John Blois agreed to sign the contracts as set forth in the specifications but upon protest that he should not in consequence be held responsible for the north and south chapels in the future, unless it could be proved that he was legally liable. Arrangements for the first stage of restoration were now well advanced, although Blythburgh did not yet have the funds to cover the full cost of the work. Nevertheless, the building committee wished the work to go ahead, so it accepted Allen's proposal and asked him to prepare to start work in the early spring of 1883, or as soon as the weather permitted. Allen was to be asked not to press for payment for the whole amount of the contract until the required sum had been collected. At the meeting of 5 February it was reported that contracts drawn up by the architect had been signed by the contractor, but Sir John asked for the requirement not to press for full payment until funds were available to be written into the contract.

Sykes wrote a letter to the *Ipswich Journal* published on 13 January 1883[70] seeking support from the county at large and reporting that as soon as the weather permitted 'the contractor will commence the actual work of restoration'. Work started in the spring of 1883. Sykes, having already attacked his patron in the public press, now found himself in dispute with the Society for the Protection of Ancient Buildings.

---

[68] The building committee was Sykes, Blois, Briggs, Youngs, Rix, Davies and Cooper. Three were to form a quorum. RCMB 22.

[69] See n. 59 above. The area of the chancel, including the north and south aisles (chapel and vestry) to the east of the screen, is one-third of the total area of church (excluding the tower and south porch). If the aisles are excluded, the chancel area is 14 per cent of the total. The documents do not reveal what conclusion was reached about the extent of Sir John's responsibility.

[70] Correspondence 40.

The Society for the Protection of Ancient Buildings and Blythburgh church

The prospect that Blythburgh church would be restored had come to the attention of the SPAB when it was alerted by a supporter to the report in the *Morning Post* of 8 December 1881 about the closure of the church.

The SPAB, popularly known as 'Anti-Scrape', from its opposition to the destructive scraping of plaster from church walls to reveal the underlying fabric, had been founded in March 1877 by William Morris, its first honorary secretary and treasurer. The formation of the society was a response to the threat that the drastic restoration of medieval buildings would result in their destruction.[71] The case for the preservation of ancient buildings had already been argued in the eighteenth century by the Society of Antiquaries of London. It had opposed, for example, the radical restoration of Salisbury and Durham cathedrals by James Wyatt, 'fam'd for knocking down our ancient buildings', between 1780 and 1800.[72]

The SPAB condemned the restoration programmes of ecclesiological reformers who were inspired by John Ruskin's writing on architecture and the Gothic revival movement spurred by A.W.N. Pugin.[73] Notwithstanding his credit with ecclesiologists, Ruskin expressed concern about the 'deceit' of restoration. Morris deplored the reckless stripping from buildings of some of their most interesting features stopping at some arbitrary point in the past for the imaginative recreation of what the earlier builders should or might have done. The unsightliness of a structural aid did not matter: 'better a crutch than a lost limb'. Morris argued that, in the past, church buildings had been added to in the styles prevailing at the time. The effect, whatever its faults, was genuine. This contrasted with the attempts of architects to restore a building 'to the best time of its history'. Being unable to distinguish between what was admirable and contemptible within each period, the result was sheer fakery. Our descendants will, argued the society's manifesto, 'find them useless for study and chilling to enthusiasm'.[74]

The infant society agreed to approach bishops and clergy and others in charge of ancient buildings to seek their cooperation. The society set out to identify all unrestored buildings in an attempt to forestall their alteration. Morris knew Blythburgh from a visit he had made in 1868.[75] The SPAB regarded the church as an unrestored

---

[71] William Morris (1834–96), socialist, campaigner, writer and designer (Fiona MacCarthy, *William Morris* (1994), pp. 375–8).

[72] Nikolaus Boulting, 'The law's delays: conservationist legislation in the British Isles' in Jane Fawcett (ed.), *The future of the past: attitudes to conservation, 1147–1974* (1976), pp. 14–16. Charles Dellheim, *The face of the past: the preservation of the medieval inheritance in Victorian England* (Cambridge, 1982).

[73] Founded in Cambridge in 1839 as the Camden Society and renamed in 1845, the Ecclesiological Society was inspired by the Gothic revival and reform movements within the Anglican Church. Through the study of churches and their furnishings, the society determined 'scientifically' that the ideal form for a church was the Decorated form of English Gothic of the late thirteenth to mid fourteenth century. The society strongly influenced the wave of Victorian church restorations. All later additions were stripped away and buildings returned to their original, or assumed original state; in some cases, buildings were effectively rebuilt (Delafons, *Politics and preservation*, p. 14). James F. White, *The Cambridge movement: the ecclesiologists and the Gothic revival* (Cambridge, 1962).

[74] 'Manifesto of the Society for the Protection of Ancient Buildings' in Chris Miele (ed.), *William Morris on architecture* (Sheffield, 1996), pp. 52–5.

[75] MacCarthy, p. 217. The trenchant language used by the SPAB is illustrated by its description of the restoration of Ely cathedral as 'lamentable bedizenment and falsification which has degraded the great

building of considerable importance,[76] and the choice of G.E. Street as Blythburgh's architect alarmed it, because the immediate spur to the foundation of the SPAB had been a visit Morris made in 1876 to Burford church, Oxfordshire. It was being restored by Street in a way that infuriated Morris. Morris later stated that Street 'would restore every building in England if he could, and to our minds with the necessary result of ruining them'.[77]

The Blythburgh situation was considered by the society's restoration committee, and on its behalf the architect Philip Webb visited the church in January 1882.[78] Webb's report demonstrates the SPAB's uncompromising opposition to restoration, opening with the recommendation that '[O]n no account should the repairs be let on contract for the whole'.[79] This reflected the society's distrust of letting fixed-price contracts to a general contractor, fearful that such a contractor would skimp work to maximise profit, and that the standard of workmanship could not be assured. It was better to employ an experienced clerk of the works to let portions of the work to different tradesmen working under his supervision. The chosen contracting process for Blythburgh and the use of a single contractor was therefore the reverse of what the SPAB desired. Webb's recommendation for dealing with decayed window tracery reveals the way in which the SPAB rigorously applied its policy on preserving existing fabric and avoiding restoration: 'Where any window mullions and tracery are too much decayed or too unstable to be remedied by slight though carefully done repairs, it would be well to brick them up (there being an excess of light in the church)'.[80] In contrast to the reports of visitors over many decades who had deplored the church's dilapidated state, Webb concluded that the church was generally in a satisfactory condition and its appearance 'most dignified and uninjured by the restorer'. Webb saw not dilapidation and makeshift repairs, but a building that revealed a history worth preserving. He stressed that priority should be given first to the foundations and then to the repair of all the roofs.

Sykes wrote to the SPAB at the end of January 1882 noting that the visit had been made. He had received Arthur Street's report and estimates of cost for work on the church. The papers were with the bishop and would be put before the Blythburgh committee on their return. If a report from the SPAB reached him in time, it could also be put before the committee.[81]

Then followed a frustrating period for the SPAB as it sought to see Street's proposals. The architect wrote on 2 March that he would be happy to let the SPAB see

---

minster' (*Restoration in East Anglia. No. 1*, SPAB 1879). This publication, which was circulated to members, listed some unrestored churches, but not Blythburgh.

[76] Baty in his study of church building and restoration in the Norwich diocese in the nineteenth century concludes that the greatest activity correlates with the period of agricultural prosperity from the early 1850s to the early 1870s. On pp. 85–122 he considers restoration in the period 1837–1901 but refers to the SPAB only briefly, describing its influence in the diocese as marginal, p. 121.

[77] Morris had been a pupil of Street's from 1856. MacCarthy, *William Morris*, pp. 102–8, 376 and 378. Baty lists five churches in Norfolk on which Street worked between 1854 and 1870.

[78] Philip Speakman Webb (1831–1915). He met Morris in 1856 while an assistant with G.E. Street, then Oxford diocesan architect. He designed Red House, Bexleyheath, for Morris (1859–70).

[79] Appendix A 2.

[80] This was Webb's draft opinion. It became 'The church is light enough as it is' in later documents.

[81] Correspondence 7. When Sykes wrote to the SPAB he had already met the bishop and a way forward agreed. It is noteworthy that there is not a single reference to the SPAB in the restoration committee minute book. See n. 90 below.

them but 'at present nothing is being done'.[82] In April, S. Sutherland Safford wrote to the SPAB and learned that it had not yet received any information about restoration plans.[83] The London committee of which Safford was secretary had more success than the SPAB in gaining access to Street's plans, because by 27 May they were in Safford's hands and he offered to show them to the SPAB.[84] However, the SPAB initially preferred to repeat its direct request to Street for sight of the plans. The architect's response was that he would let the SPAB know 'when the plans come from Blythburgh. It will probably not be for a couple of months'.[85] Then the SPAB sought to see the plans in Safford's hands, only to receive the frustrating news that he had returned them to Sykes, although he had taken some tracings, and the SPAB could see those.[86] Thus it was not until July 1882 that the SPAB saw any plans. They did include the full specification, borrowed again by S. Sutherland Safford from Sykes and lent to the SPAB; however, the bishop had already approved the restoration of Blythburgh church on the basis of Street's proposals.[87]

J. Henry Middleton and George Wardle visited Blythburgh in August 1882 and reported to the SPAB's restoration committee.[88] In the light of their report (and Philip Webb's visit in January 1882), the SPAB wrote to Sykes on 27 September.[89] Their advice reflected fundamental SPAB beliefs in the preservation of original fabric if at all possible, and contractual and management practice to achieve this. The SPAB advised that on no account should the work be let under one contract. A responsible clerk of the works should be appointed and the repairs contracted in small portions to men working under constant supervision. If parts of the structure had to be replaced by new work, this new work should not reproduce or imitate the old work. The roof paintings 'cannot be restored'. Only essential repairs should be done to the windows. Windows should not be unblocked, and the wooden mullions and transoms should remain. In the case of clerestory windows where the tracery was beyond repair the openings should be bricked up and whitewashed. Philip Webb's report was echoed in the comment that 'there is more than a sufficiency of light in the church'. The society hoped that '<u>nothing</u> that belongs to the original aspect of this church will be destroyed'. The SPAB considered the church generally to be in a substantial condition and stressed that 'there is no reason why money subscribed for its repair should be used for any of the purposes usually included in a scheme of 'restoration'.

Sykes acknowledged receipt of the report and wrote that it would be laid before the Blythburgh committee on the following Monday. He wrote on 2 October that the report had been brought before the committee, but that discussion had been deferred to allow committee members to study the report. However, there is no reference to

---

[82] Correspondence 9.
[83] Correspondence 10–11.
[84] Correspondence 13.
[85] Correspondence 16.
[86] Correspondence 17–18.
[87] Strictly speaking, approval from Blythburgh, as the client, was needed before plans could be sent to the SPAB.
[88] Appendix A 6. Professor John Henry Middleton (1846–96), architect and archaeologist, member of SPAB committee and honorary secretary 1882–95. George Wardle (d. 1910), bookkeeper and draughtsman to Messrs Morris, Marshall, Faulkner & Co. (Morris & Co. 1874) and business manager, 1870–90. Founder member of the SPAB.
[89] Correspondence 35.

the SPAB report in a minute listing the business transacted at that meeting, nor is the SPAB mentioned in any subsequent minute.[90]

Six weeks later the SPAB was still waiting for a response from Blythburgh. There was clearly confusion about the relative status of the local Blythburgh committee and the London-based one. The SPAB wrote to A.G. Hill, a member of the latter, believing him to be a member of the Blythburgh committee and able to inform the society about the position. Hill knew nothing: he thought he was a member of the committee, presumably the London one, which he had joined to avert, if possible, 'restoration', but had never received notice of any meetings.[91]

The SPAB then became aware of the letter from Sykes published in the *Ipswich Journal* of 13 January 1883, in which Sykes had sought support from the county at large and stated that as soon as the weather permitted 'the contractor will commence the actual work of restoration'.[92] The SPAB wrote to Sykes pointing out that it had had no response to its report on the church and asking whether the proposed works were those recommended by the society.[93] Sykes responded on 22 January, nearly four months after receiving the SPAB report, and three weeks after the committee had formally accepted Allen's tender for the first stage of the work.[94] The SPAB report, Sykes wrote, had been carefully perused by every member of the building committee,[95] but its proposals were unacceptable, because it would result in the church being further disfigured by unsightly makeshifts and every window would have to be bricked up and the church rendered useless as a place of worship. But if the society could raise the money for its scheme, the building committee might put the work in the society's hands and devote itself to raising funds to build a chapel of ease.[96]

After months of discussion with Sykes, and intensely frustrated at its apparent inability to influence events at Blythburgh, the SPAB concluded that it had to resort to the newspapers to present its views. On 14 February 1883 the SPAB wrote lengthy letters to the *Ipswich Journal* and *Suffolk Chronicle* presenting the 'restoration' versus 'preservation' arguments.[97] The SPAB did not mince words, expressing candidly its disapproval of the committee's restoration plans. 'Cathedral glass' was described as 'the most offensive and vulgar of all glazing materials'.[98] The SPAB protested that 'With this and such like vulgarities the beautiful architecture of Blythburgh church would be replaced' and asked subscribers to say whether their contributions should be spent in the preservation of the church or in 'the delusive and mischievous pretence of restoration'.

---

90 Correspondence 36–7. RCMB 23 and 26. The minute for 4 December 1882, when only Sykes, Rix and Youngs were present, records that Rix presented his opinion on restoration and that this was rebutted by the chairman, Sykes. Rix was a preservationist who in 1891 argued against the restoration by Sir Arthur Blomfield of the church tower in Beccles, maintaining that the most interesting monument in the town would be destroyed and replaced by a model. *Beccles Paper*, 31 March 1891.
91 Correspondence 39.
92 Correspondence 40.
93 Correspondence 42.
94 RCMB 27.
95 See n. 81 above.
96 Correspondence 43.
97 Correspondence 44–5 and 53.
98 Cathedral glass is a rolled glass first produced commercially around the 1830s. It can be textured but lacks the richness and versatility of hand-blown glass. It is much cheaper. Sarah Brown, *Stained glass: an illustrated history* (1995), pp. 134–5.

Sykes responded with a speed he had failed to show in dealing with the SPAB's report. The day after the SPAB's letter appeared in the *Ipswich Journal*, he wrote to the newspaper that there was 'another side to the picture'. In a letter published a week later, on 3 March, he wrote at greater length to justify Blythburgh's position, explaining that the SPAB's proposals had come too late to be of service to the restoration committee[99] and that the architect's brief was to do the minimum required to ensure the safety of the building and make it again usable for worship. He emphasised that the architect understood that old work should be preserved wherever possible and new work inserted only if absolutely necessary. Describing the SPAB as 'an irresponsible body of men', he argued that it was unreasonable to expect the work of eleven months to be set aside in deference to last-minute suggestions and asserted that it 'were impossible to paint the hideous picture' the church would present if treated in the manner suggested by the SPAB. Addressing subscribers directly, as the SPAB had done in its letter, he said that a meeting of subscribers might be called before any further restoration was decided upon and commended subscribers for the sincerity of their affection for the church, in contrast to the SPAB's 'empty-handed sympathy'.

The SPAB had already written to Sir John Blois and the prominent neighbouring estate owner, the earl of Stradbroke,[100] on 2 March 1883, asking them to use their influence to stop the work until the London committee for the restoration of Blythburgh church had had time to consider the SPAB report.[101] The society hoped that the church would 'be saved the present destruction with which it is threatened'. At the same time the SPAB wrote again to the Suffolk newspapers, referring to the 'haste to destroy the beautiful old building' and the London committee's apparent ignorance of the SPAB's report. The society noted that Sykes had long delayed responding to the report, and questioned, justifiably it seems, whether any member of the building committee had actually seen it.[102]

The SPAB met Sir John at a date after 9 March.[103] An undated draft note states that Sir John sympathised with the society and agreed with its views as far as he had seen them. However, he could not see how the society could object to the replacement of a rotten wooden window by new stone tracery. With the exception of the proposed use of 'cathedral glass', he did not know what the society could object to. He criticised Sykes, describing him as 'No one. He is hopeless. He is only a commercial traveller. The bishop appointed him by mistake'.[104] Sir John reported that only £1,000 had been collected, and he thought that correspondence in the local papers, initiated by Sykes, could only harm the campaign for subscriptions.

---

[99] Correspondence 58. The SPAB's advice was dated 27 September 1882, more than three months before the decision to proceed with the work. Tenders for the restoration had been received earlier in September, but the decision to do the work was not taken until January 1883.

[100] John Edward Cornwallis Rous (1794–1886), 2nd Earl of Stradbroke, of Henham Hall. He owned land in Blythburgh. Henham adjoined the parish to the north.

[101] Correspondence 60 and 63.

[102] Correspondence 61–2.

[103] This could have been well into April, in the light of an exchange of letters with Lady Blois about her husband's health. Correspondence 63, 67–9.

[104] Correspondence 70. Sir John's criticism was disingenuous. His neglect to exercise his right to nominate a vicar is indicated by an announcement of the appointment of Sykes that included the words 'in the gift of the said Lord Bishop (by reason of lapse)', whereas the appointment of his successor the Revd Henry James in 1885 was described as 'on the nomination of Sir John Ralph Blois, Bart'. *Bury and Norwich Post and Suffolk Herald*, 22 July 1879 and 27 October 1885.

The correspondence noted by Sir John was not restricted to the local papers; Sykes and the SPAB also argued in the columns of *The Athenaeum*. Here, the SPAB made the first move, with a letter from George Wardle published on 17 February setting out the society's position.[105] Sykes countered on 27 February,[106] asking readers to judge whether the Blythburgh proposals for 'restoration' or its critics' proposals for 'modest repair' were more in accordance with the dictates of common sense. The journal *The Architect* also published letters from both sides, provided by the SPAB, setting out the positions of the advocates and opponents of restoration.[107]

Sykes's views of the SPAB can be seen in a letter to F.C. Brooke of Ufford Place dated 27 February 1883.[108] Summarising the state of affairs at Blythburgh and explaining the choice of G.E. Street as architect, he wrote: 'I will say privately to you that I would not have promised a subscription myself to carry out the recommendations of their committee, nor would I have dared to appeal to the country for such an object as they have in view', adding that 'For 50 years this Church has been a scandal. Why did not the 'Ancient Buildings Society' interfere to prevent a total wreck till they saw others in the field determined on action?'[109]

The public dispute continued through March and April 1883. The SPAB's attempt to involve the London committee failed: Safford wrote to Wardle on 21 March that the committee had been dissolved, noting that a local committee was in full working order and had opened a general list of subscriptions. No money had been received by the London committee.[110]

The SPAB's report on Blythburgh church was published in the Suffolk newspapers. An editorial comment in the *Suffolk Chronicle* revealed doubt about the SPAB's position. The desire to preserve all old work and reject reproduction or imitation in any new work made the writer 'fear to attempt to face the actual appearance of a building treated after this method'.[111]

The SPAB file is silent after 7 April 1883. On that date the SPAB made its final appeal to subscribers, through the county press, asking whether they had 'fully considered their duty towards the building which is now practically at their mercy'.[112] In his report to the annual meeting of the SPAB on 6 June 1883 William Morris referred to its 'ill-success at Blythburgh'. Instead of a 'moderate and carefully-considered plan for the repair of the building', the local committee had 'preferred the one which offered all the attractions of modern "cathedral glass", shiny encaustic tiles, new carving, and the ordinary paraphernalia supplied by the fashionable ecclesiastical tailors, though the estimate for this was a minimum of £5,000, against the £2,000 for which the really necessary works might have been done'.[113]

---

[105] Correspondence 51.

[106] Correspondence 64.

[107] Correspondence n. 35.

[108] Correspondence 56. Francis Capper Brooke (1810–86). He was related to the Blois family by descent through his mother from Sir Charles Blois, 1st Bt. Brooke's donation of £5 to the restoration fund was acknowledged by Sykes in a letter of 19 February. Brooke visited Blythburgh in March 1883 and met Sykes. Brooke seems to have been specially favoured. A copy of Street's estimate is in the Brooke collection, lent to him by Sykes and never returned.

[109] The condition of the church may well have been a scandal for fifty years, but the SPAB was founded in 1877, only four years before the church was closed.

[110] Correspondence 72.

[111] Correspondence 73.

[112] Correspondence 76.

[113] 'Report of the committee' in *SPAB Report, 1883*, pp. 7–30.

Meanwhile, in May 1883, Sykes wrote in the *Ipswich Journal* of the progress of the restoration: 'truckloads of new mullions and tracery for the windows are on the spot'. The cost of this work would be £1,049, but the amount promised was only £958. The work, which had started on the church before sufficient money had been collected to completely cover the cost, was expected to be finished by the end of September. Sykes made an urgent appeal for funds.[114]

In October 1883 the vicar proposed a plan for reseating the church. It was agreed to remove old square pews (which resembled sheep pens, according to the *Ipswich Journal*) and rearrange existing benches and stalls. An example of the work generally being constrained by lack of money is the decision to repair the floor with brick only 'where absolutely required.'[115] The encaustic tiles abhorred by the SPAB were never used.

In January 1884 the committee looked forward to a second phase of restoration. It was agreed to ask the architect to prepare plans and estimates for the roofs of the nave and north aisle. These were produced and sanctioned by the committee on 24 March and forwarded to the bishop for approval.[116] However, by the end of March 1884 the total sum collected was only £1,065, just enough to meet the contractor's bill for the first phase of restoration, with nothing in hand for additional work.

The Blythburgh work was still being questioned in the press. A correspondent to the *East Anglian Daily Times*, writing from St James' Street, London, on 2 January 1884 and identifying himself as only as 'A', said that on a visit to Blythburgh church two days earlier,[117] he had been impressed by what the local committee had achieved on a limited budget, but that details of the work savoured of mutilation rather than restoration. He thought that his letter might draw out explanations for the examples he quoted. Sykes responded at length on 9 January 1884. He wrote, he said, with indignation and pity. He seems to have known the letter writer, referring to his residence near the church and the probability that the letter was inspired 'from a house a hundred miles nearer Blythburgh than London'. Sykes concluded with 'unfeigned pleasure' to assure readers that those who had undertaken the restoration of the church would not relax their efforts until their architect's proposals had been carried out.[118]

The meeting of the building committee held on 7 April 1884 was the last before the reopening of the church. Sir John Blois expressed his satisfaction at the manner in which the business had been conducted hitherto; care had been taken in keeping the accounts, and expenses were not excessive in proportion to the funds collected. Sir John then announced that he and Lady Blois would retire from the committee on the completion of the present contract. Three heavy vertical lines were drawn in the minute book against this statement. A comment from Sykes perhaps?[119]

---

[114] Correspondence 77.
[115] RCMB 38.
[116] RCMB 43.
[117] Correspondence 78.
[118] Correspondence 80.
[119] RCMB 44.

The reopening of the church

Blythburgh church reopened on Easter Day, 13 April 1884. Sykes was assisted by vicars from neighbouring parishes at the three services. Sykes preached at the morning service, the Revd P.L. Cautley from Southwold preached the sermon in the afternoon and the Revd R. Gathorne from Wenhaston in the evening. A further three services were held on the following Wednesday. The Revd J.J. Raven, D.D., headmaster of Yarmouth Grammar School, preached in the morning and the bishop of Norwich, the Rt Revd John Thomas Pelham, in the afternoon. The Revd J.A. Clowes preached the evening service, standing in for Archdeacon Groome, who had been taken ill.[120] The press reports of the reopening, in contrast to its reports of the bazaar in 1882 that had so angered Sykes, credited Sykes for having led the restoration campaign and congratulated him for having nearly completed the first portion of the work.[121]

The church had been closed for nearly two and a half years. It was now partially restored. The contract with R.J. Allen had cost £1,064 10s. 0d. The south aisle had a new roof of English oak and the lead had been recast. The parapet on the south aisle had been secured. All the windows had been restored except two in the chancel, six in the clerestory on the north side of the chancel and one near the north door. These nine windows were still bricked up. Internally, old deal box pews had been removed and the oak benches restored to their original position. The stalls in the chancel had been moved further apart. The floor, where absolutely necessary, had been levelled and paved with light-coloured bricks. The leads on the roofs of the nave and north aisle had been repaired. Ancient coloured glass in the windows had been cleaned and replaced with new lead. Six new coloured emblems had been placed in the south windows.[122]

The building committee met again on 5 May 1884. It is the last meeting recorded in the minute book. After what was described as desultory conversation, it was decided not to apply for a building society grant, or to hold a fundraising bazaar. With the church reopened after a hard and, for some, bruising campaign, there was no enthusiasm for more of the same.[123] There was, however, much still to be done. Since the reopening, a beam had fallen from the north aisle roof, and other parts of the church required immediate attention. Sykes wrote to the *Ipswich Journal* on 26 November 1884 that a small sum was still outstanding on the first contract, and a further £1,000 was required to make good all the remaining roofs, unblock windows, and generally make the building weathertight.[124] Raising this money would be a difficult task.

Fundraising

From the list of subscribers included in the August 1882 appeal leaflet, and the regular publication of newspaper reports, it is possible to analyse the progress of

---

[120] See p. xxiii above for Canon Raven's comments on the condition of the church in 1874. See also Raven, 'Blythburgh'.
[121] Appendix C 21–3.
[122] The emblems were paid for by Ronald J. Cobbold of Dedham Lodge, Essex. Appendix B II 20 and 23.
[123] RCMB 46.
[124] Correspondence 81.

the appeal and identify the main sources of funds.[125] Between October 1881 and November 1884 £1,201 17s. 7¼d. was collected. The sources of this money are shown in Table 1.

Table 1
Sources of money collected, 1881–4

Source	Sum	£	s.	d.	% of total
Events		289	3	0	24.1
Gentry		208	12	0	17.4 (1)
Clergy(2)		200	3	6	16.7
Churchwardens[126]		64	2	0	5.3
Collected by individuals		60	11	5	5.0 (3)
Building society		25	0	0	2.1
Collection boxes		13	19	5	1.2 (4)
Interest		11	7	11	0.9
Church services		8	8	5	0.7
Other individuals		320	9	11¼	26.6
Total		1,201	17	7¼	100.0

Notes

(1) Probably understated, because only the names of the local gentry can be confidently identified. The landed families named as patrons for fundraising events are shown with the location of their seats in Figure 00.
(2) There were 65 clergymen in the list.
(3) Includes collections made by gentry families.
(4) In the church, rectory, and Blythburgh station.

Of the £596 received by early August 1882, excluding the proceeds of concerts and the donations of the Blois family and Sykes, some £354 was generated by appealing to the public in the nine months after the church was closed, or nearly £40 per month. In February 1883 a further appeal for funds from Sykes took the form of letters to newspapers and also individual letters to potential subscribers. However, the flow of donations was now slower, as the monthly additions to the fund (to the nearest pound) in Table 2 demonstrate.

---

[125] Appendix B I, 1 and 3, II, 2–24.
[126] The churchwardens' accounts show that as a body they paid the architect Arthur E. Street's £10 10s. 0d. fee in 1881/82, £36 6s. 7d. to the restoration fund in 1883/84 and a further £13 0s. 0d. in 1884/85. This last payment was approved by the vestry meeting on 17 April 1884. The churchwardens' accounts cannot be reconciled with the subscription list, which shows £42 donated before August 1882, £21 0s. 0d. in May 1884 and a further £1 2s. 0d. in November 1884. After the church reopened, the vestry meeting on 9 April 1885 approved the payment by the churchwardens of £15 to the restoration fund. CWA 1881/82, 1883/84, 1884/85, VMB minutes 17 April 1884 and 9 April 1885. Robinson Briggs, churchwarden, donated £15 0s. 0d. Appendix B I, 1.

Table 2
Monthly contributions to the appeal fund

Report dates	£
1882	
26 August	16
2 September	4
9 September	4
23 September	14
30 September	4
7 October	11
14 October	21
21 October	15
28 October	14
9 December	15
1883	
13 January	3
10 February	11 (1)
10 March	11
12 May	7
9 June	3
July	8
11 August	18
13 October	22 (2)
1884	
12 January	30
29 March	14 (3)
10 May	24 (4)
November	35

Notes
(1) Renewed appeal.
(2) Net of interest on deposits. Renewed appeal for £100 to clear debt on contract.
(3) Renewed appeal.
(4) Net of collections at services, and churchwardens' and building society grants.
    Renewed appeal after church reopened.

Only £35 was raised in the six months after the church reopened, of which £29 came from donations from past subscribers. From August 1882 to November 1884, £1,021 had been collected, of which the public appeal generated £304, or £11 per month. As time passed, Blythburgh found it increasingly difficult to raise money.

Although Sir John Blois headed the subscription list with his donation of £100, Sykes criticised him for his parsimony.[127] Sir John was responsible for the upkeep of the chancel, but the one-third of his donation that went to the chancel fund was his only direct contribution to the £363 cost. The balance, over ninety per cent, came from the restoration appeal. On the other hand, without the Blois family's donations and the income from the Blythburgh bazaar, the London concert, and subscribers encouraged by the family, the money available for restoring the church would have been very much less. And yet, even with the Blois family, less than a quarter of the architect's £5,000 estimate was collected. The London committee had failed to attract any subscriptions at all. Sir John's fear that Sykes's public dispute with the SPAB could harm the prospects of the appeal for funds was probably correct. The extent of restoration was constrained not directly by the SPAB's efforts, but by a shortage of money. Sykes won a victory for restoration, but it was a pyrrhic one.

Restoration: phase two, 1889–90

Blythburgh church had reopened in 1884 with the north aisle still unrestored and with no money immediately available to do the work. In 1889 a new vicar, the Revd Thomas Henry Royal Oakes, arrived in Blythburgh. Letters from the period of his incumbency reveal when further restoration work was done. They also reveal continuing tensions in Blythburgh.[128] Oakes was a combative individual, questioning the bishop, fighting the parish council, having a tetchy relationship with the patron, and upsetting Arthur Street so much that Street washed his hands of Blythburgh.

Oakes's first vestry meeting was in March 1889.[129] Tension between Oakes and his churchwardens and the parishioners grew quickly. A meeting held on 13 May 1890 was found to be illegal, and at the meeting on 14 August to elect churchwardens the question of legality was again raised. Oakes objected that a notice had been posted without his authority and a motion to elect a churchwarden could not be put to the meeting. When he asked if there was any other business, the meeting became disorderly in spite of his protests. The meeting, attended by an unprecedented number of parishioners, did not end until 20 minutes to one the following morning.[130]

Another distraction from building issues arose in 1893 with the raising at a vestry meeting of the question of Neale's Charity, established by Thomas Neale's will dated 1701.[131] The church found itself in dispute with the parish council, newly formed

---

[127] Sir John's rental income is not known, but his estate could not have been immune from the agricultural depression from the mid 1870s. By 1900 average Suffolk rents had fallen by 50 to 60 per cent, and many landed families struggled financially. Edward Bujak, *England's rural realms: landholding and the agricultural revolution* (2007), p. 52.

[128] T.H.R. Oakes (*c.* 1854–1945), vicar of Walberswick with Blythburgh, 1888–96. Born in India and educated at theological colleges in the USA and London. Curate at St Philip's, Girlington, Bradford, Yorkshire, before coming to Suffolk. He left to become vicar of St Matthew's, Netley, Hampshire, 1896–1921 (exchanging with the Revd Arthur Woodruff) and was, finally, rector of Thurgarton, Norfolk, until retirement in 1932.

[129] See n. 57 above.

[130] VMB minutes 13 May 1890 and 14 August 1890.

[131] At stake was the annual payment of £3 out of an estate in Bramfield, £2 10s. 0d. to be used for teaching five poor children of the parish to read and 10s. to buy bibles or other religious books for young persons. It had become customary at some date after the formation of the Blythburgh school board in 1878 for the churchwardens to pass £2 10s. 0d. (and on at least one occasion the full £3) to the board. The question was: should Neale's Charity be regarded as ecclesiastical or parochial? Should the church

Plate 5. The exterior of the church at the end of the nineteenth century, after the restoration of the south aisle windows, but before the repair of the south porch. BCP, Blue Scrap Book

by the Local Government Act of 1894. The parish council applied successfully to the Charity Commission to transfer control of the charity away from the church to themselves.

Further restoration work on the church (once again closed) was almost complete by June 1890. It was still in the hands of Arthur Street and Allen. Plans were being made for a reopening service.

Oakes reported to the bishop in July 1890 that the roof and wall of the north aisle had been restored at a cost of £500, but that only £300 was available. They were still £80 short in January 1891. Oakes pressed the bishop for the second instalment of £10 he had promised (the bishop had paid the first instalment towards a total of £20 in 1882). Oakes also questioned his position as vicar, quoting church law in that he had never been inducted.[132] The bishop replied that the second £10 was conditional upon £300 having been collected for the north aisle, 'connected with the church as distinct from the chancel'. He sought an assurance that these conditions had been met before

---

or the parish council control the funds? When the parish council applied to the Charity Commission to transfer control of the charity away from the church to themselves, Oakes objected, wanting the money for his Sunday school. He argued that payment to the school board ultimately helped the ratepayers and not children, hardly a charitable objective. The parish council could have countered that restricting the benefits to those attending the church's Sunday school (probably a minority of the children in Blythburgh at the time) was a constraint not within the spirit or law of Neale's bequest. In a letter dated 28 January 1896 (inserted in VMB) the Charity Commission found for the parish council, which then appointed trustees in place of the churchwardens. The churchwardens protested, but to no avail. A scheme of administration dated 13 July 1905 established the parish council's authority. The parish council continued to appoint trustees and distribute the funds until inflation wiped out the real value of the bequest. Neale's Charity did not survive into the twenty-first century, but Neale is remembered through his ledger stone in Blythburgh church and the books he left to Clare College library.

[132] Correspondence 90.

subscribing his £10. As far as Oakes's status was concerned, he was a perpetual curate and induction was not necessary. Oakes held the freehold of the glebe house and any lands, tithes or appurtenances belonging to the benefice, but the impropriator (i.e Blois, the patron) held the freehold of the church and churchyard.[133]

Oakes's relationships in Blythburgh were also sensitive. A phrase in a letter from Oakes to Patterson, in Street's office, is revealing: Oakes thought better of approving a course of action proposed by Patterson, because 'my patron and churchwardens are only too ready to resent any neglect of their authority'.[134]

A serious dispute arose between Oakes and Street about the ownership of drawings. Street had been paid £5 by the Revd Henry James, Oakes's predecessor, but Street argued that this was for the preparation of drawings not their ownership.[135] Oakes accused Street of bad faith and extravagance. In response to a letter from Oakes that has not survived, Street stated bluntly: 'It does not encourage me to do work for nothing, if the sole result is an abrupt "Stand and Deliver" without a semblance of thanks'.[136] An increasingly polarised debate (there were other matters at issue, including the contractor's shortcomings – work not being completed on time, losing opportunity for opening service and collection, and not saving old materials of value) led Street to suppose that Oakes was not aware of what was usually done and that in ten years of architectural practice he had never been asked to hand over drawings. Street found it especially odd that this first case should be one where he was actually out of pocket instead of making a profit. In July 1890, Street washed his hands of Blythburgh: 'I think we had better have no <more> fresh business transactions'.[137]

Friction between Oakes and his patron is evident from correspondence about arrangements for a fundraising bazaar planned for August 1890. Miss Alice Blois, on behalf of her mother, wrote to Mrs Oakes about the plans. She hoped that Mr Oakes would write to Lady Stradbroke and other potential patronesses. He was also asked to arrange the printing of circulars and help organise entertainment by finding a conjuror. Mrs Oakes was also expected to have a stall.[138] Mrs Oakes replied that she was concerned that too much was expected of her and her husband. She pointed out that they had worked very hard for a bazaar the previous year with discouraging results. The sale of work was ignored and it was evident that they had no influence with the ladies to whom it was suggested that they now write. Mrs Oakes thought it better for Lady Blois to write to them this time. It would also be more appropriate because, and here Oakes's voice can be heard, Sir Ralph and not her husband held the freehold of the church. The Oakeses would be away during August but would attend the bazaar. This was a clear statement of disengagement.[139] It is not known how much money was raised by the bazaar, but £80 of the restoration bill was still outstanding in January 1891.

---

[133] Correspondence 95.
[134] Correspondence 87.
[135] Henry Lionel James (b. *c*. 1858), vicar of Walberswick with Blythburgh, 1885–8. Came to Blythburgh from Laxey, Isle of Man, and left for St. Cuthbert's, Everton. He preached at the reopening of the church in 1884. Correspondence 86.
[136] Correspondence 86.
[137] Correspondence 94.
[138] Correspondence 96.
[139] Correspondence 97.

SPAB involvement from 1894

The SPAB file is silent on Blythburgh during the work on the north aisle. It became involved again in 1894 (after an interval of 10 years), when Oliver Baker wrote to the secretary, Thackeray Turner.[140] Baker referred to an unnamed friend who had described Blythburgh church as splendid and unique. The south porch was very dilapidated and in danger of collapse. Apart from that, and a leak in the roof, the church was perfect. Little work was needed to make the church sound. 'Micklethwaite would be sure to know'.[141] Turner wrote to Micklethwaite that the SPAB thought that the church had been thoroughly restored. Could he give them some more information? Micklethwaite replied that he had not visited the church, but that he believed that it had been much restored by Street (G.E.) and that his son had been working there since his father's death. The SPAB then received a letter from the artist Evacustes Phipson.[142] He referred to a restoration of Blythburgh church 'now in progress' and the careless treatment of painted glass windows. Such of the fragments that had not been stolen were lying about in confusion. The services of Hamlet Watling, the only person able to rearrange the glass, had been declined.[143] Unless the SPAB intervened, a large number of the most valuable and interesting windows would be 'utterly dispersed and destroyed'.

Thackeray Turner then wrote to Oakes,[144] saying that the society had received letters from two or three different quarters about the church's restoration and expressing concern about the painted glass windows. He also asked Oakes if he had a copy of the SPAB's 1882 report. Oakes replied that no work was in progress. He was trying to obtain funds but had met with little encouragement. He could only 'partially approve' of the work done some ten or twelve years before. If any more work was done, Street would be in charge of it.[145] The south porch was rapidly falling into ruin, but without funds nothing could be done. Oakes did have a copy of the SPAB's report.[146] The SPAB responded, setting out its philosophy regarding restoration and, on the subject of new tiles for the sacrarium (raised by Oakes), thought

---

[140] Oliver Baker (1856–1939), artist and antiquary. Member of the SPAB committee. Hugh Thackeray Turner (1853–1937), architect. Pupil of George Gilbert Scott but became revolted by 'Gothic Revival' design. Paid secretary of SPAB, 1883–1912. Ardent traveller and promoter of the society. His insistence that additions to old buildings should be 'frankly modern' remains a current idea. Correspondence 104.

[141] John Thomas Micklethwaite (1843–1906), architect and ecclesiologist. Not a member of the SPAB but frequently consulted by it. In Suffolk he restored the tower of Walberswick church, 1892–3, and the nave and aisles of Orford church, 1894–7; and he restored the screen at Ranworth, Norfolk.

[142] Correspondence 107. Evacustes (Edward) Arthur Phipson (1854–1931).

[143] Hamlet Watling (1818–1908), schoolmaster and antiquarian. He had a long interest in the church and wrote of his visits between 1837 and 1894. His coloured illustrations of the window glass are in SROI Sq.9, Suckling, Grangerized version, 6 vols. See Appendix C 2 for his published articles on the glass. See also Stephen J. Plunkett, 'Hamlet Watling: artist and schoolmaster', *PSIAH* 39 Part 1 (1997), pp. 48–75. Watling wrote of the glass in 1894 that 'the late restoration too has hastened its destruction'. Hamlet Watling, 'Blythburgh church. Also the painted glass in the church windows and other antiquities', (no date), p. 1. Bound manuscript in the possession of the editor.

[144] Correspondence 108

[145] A remarkable statement from Oakes given Street's disengagement in 1890. Correspondence 94 and 109. The SPAB replied: '[*The Society is*] fully alive to the fact that Mr Street does not agree with this Society, and this puts a difficulty in the Society's way'. Correspondence 110.

[146] Oakes attempted to discover the names of the SPAB's informants but was unsuccessful. He was told that the society never divulged names. 'Impossible it would be for the society to obtain information if it had not such a rule'. Correspondence 112. See Correspondence 35 for the SPAB report.

that a visit was needed before a just opinion could be formed. So Turner and William Morris visited the church on 17 July 1895. Oakes proposed that they come first to Walberswick, to inspect the church there; then, after lunch at the vicarage, he would drive them the three miles to Blythburgh. They rejected his proposal and went directly to Blythburgh, spending all their time there.[147]

Turner wrote to Oakes two days after the visit stating that the SPAB approved the advice that they had given to Oakes during the visit. The SPAB's rigid position on the alteration of buildings in the name of restoration was reflected in advice first stated in Philip Webb's report of 1882: the SPAB reprised Webb's comment, 'The church is so light already that nothing would be gained by opening out any of the blocked-up windows'. The most urgent work should be done first and this included attending to the south porch without delay.[148]

Oakes's last vestry meeting was in April 1896. In 1897 the Revd A.W. Woodruff was appointed the new vicar.[149] No major work was to be done to the church for another seven years. The churchwardens' accounts and the vestry minute book confirm the continuing poverty of Blythburgh church:[150] in April 1898 the restoration fund balance was £100 9s. 1d; a year later, it was £33 17s. 6d; in 1900, £52 8s. 7d. On 21 April vestry agreed that steps should be taken to repair the south porch as far as the restoration fund would permit. In 1901 the balance was £70 14s. 11d, when the vicar proposed tenders be invited for the scraping and replastering of the central aisle of the nave. The south porch was referred to, but no action taken. In 1902 the balance was £87 18s. 5d.[151]

Restoration: phase three, 1901–6

In October 1901 the Revd Arthur Woodruff wrote to *The Times* appealing for help: Blythburgh church was in peril, and could meet the same fate as part-ruined Covehithe and Walberswick, and threatened Dunwich. Part of its roof was in danger of collapse, as was the south porch (about which concern had been expressed seven years earlier).[152] The SPAB, reacting to the letter, wrote to Woodruff seeking more information.[153] Woodruff replied that an architect would visit soon and report upon the problems.[154] In March 1902 the SPAB saw copies of the architect's report. The society's committee was 'absolutely astonished and taken aback' by what it had read.[155] In its response to Woodruff, the society stated that it had not seen such drastic

---

[147] Correspondence 115–18.

[148] Correspondence 119.

[149] Arthur William Woodruff (c. 1858–1919), BA Oxon. 1880, MA 1884, ordained 1881. Vicar of Walberswick with Blythburgh, 1896–1902. Came to Blythburgh from Netley St. Matthew, Hampshire, and left Blythburgh to become licensed priest in Winchester diocese before appointment as rector of Ardley, Oxfordshire, in 1904.

[150] See CWA 3 and VMB. The first mention of the restoration fund in the VMB (the book starts in March 1884) is on 17 April 1884, when it was agreed to transfer £13 from the churchwardens' account to Sykes for the church restoration fund. On 9 April 1885 it was agreed to transfer £15.

[151] VMB 1901/02.

[152] Correspondence 120.

[153] The letter has not survived.

[154] Correspondence 121.

[155] Correspondence 124. The reports for Blythburgh and Walberswick churches have not been located. The architect was the little-known Charles Arthur Ford Whitcombe, of 5 Newman Street, London, W. BCP Blue Scrap Book, p. 17, 2.

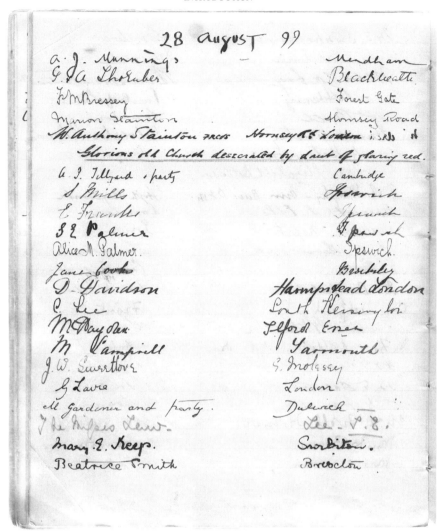

Plate 6. At the turn of the nineteenth century the church attracted many visitors, and each year over a thousand signed the visitors' book. They came from every continent and included the writers Henry Rider-Haggard and Clement Scott, known for his promotion of the north Norfolk coast as 'Poppyland'. His description of visitors to the Suffolk coast is apt: 'all middle-class people of the highest respectability'. This page records the visit of a young Alfred Munnings, artist, and one of ten vehement protests about the use of red paint on the chancel walls, that included such words as 'barbarous', 'disfigured', 'reckless' and 'tawdry'. BCP, Books 2. Visitors' Book, 1896–1900

and thoroughgoing restoration advocated for many a year. It was unthinkable that Blythburgh, 'of wide-world reputation', should be treated in such a way. The society hoped that 'restoration' would be abandoned and the building repaired in the simplest possible way. Woodruff replied that, being fully acquainted with the SPAB's position, he was not surprised by their response, but that nothing would be done while he was vicar. He was leaving and could not bind his successor, who would probably come into office in July or August.[156]

Aware of the risk to, at least, the south porch, the SPAB set out to identify the new incumbent so that action could be taken without delay. The society wrote again to Woodruff, and also to Sir Ralph Blois, and then, in September, to the churchwardens,[157] who it asked whether the porch could be supported temporarily, repeating its view that the porch could and should be repaired, not rebuilt. It hoped that it would be allowed to report upon the porch.

A significant new name appeared in September 1902: Claude Francis Egerton, churchwarden. Egerton was a professional civil engineer, practising in London.[158] Resident in Blythburgh, he was to play an important role over the next four years in an increasingly strained relationship between the SPAB and the Blythburgh church restoration committee. Before the new vicar was appointed, Egerton explained to the SPAB that Blythburgh was a poor parish, having only about £200 in hand or promised, but that the SPAB should arrange for the church to be reported upon. The society, though, preferred to wait for the new incumbent to be appointed before arranging an inspection.[159]

The new vicar was the Revd R.P. Wing.[160] The SPAB wrote to him in April 1903,[161] expressing its shock at the architect's proposals (forwarded by Wing's predecessor) and urging that they should not be carried out, hoping that the building would be treated in accordance with the society's principles. The society received no reply. Once again an SPAB supporter, the artist Joseph Southall, who was staying in Southwold, visited Blythburgh. He expressed concern at what he had seen:[162] rain

---

[156] Correspondence 125.

[157] Correspondence 126–8. Sir Ralph Barrett Macnaghten Blois, 9th Bt (1866–1950), of Cockfield Hall, Yoxford. Succeeded his father, Sir John, in 1888. He married Winifred Grace Hegan (d. 1963) in 1898. Secretary restoration committee appeal 1905. He inherited his father's local reputation for parsimony, and was ambitious socially rather than intellectually or politically, according to Parr.

[158] Claude Francis Arthur Egerton (1864–1957), MICE, a civil engineer who built railways in India, 1887–98, before becoming a partner in the London firm of Barry, Leslie and Partners. Ironically, on returning by rail from London one day with a cheap first-class ticket, he left the station at Halesworth instead of continuing his journey to Blythburgh by the Southwold railway. When a ticket collector noted that his ticket was not valid for journeys to Halesworth, Egerton refused to pay the difference in the fare, so the Great Eastern Railway took Egerton to court and won. *Southwold Railway Society Newsletter*, 33, August 2002, p. 16. A churchwarden and hon. treasurer restoration committee appeal 1905. He rented White House farmhouse, Bulcamp, from the earl of Stradbroke. Well connected as a member of the Leveson-Gower family, related to the earls of Sutherland. In 1900 he married Alexandra Elizabeth Ritchie, widow of Charles Bellairs, a supporter of Blythburgh church and previous tenant of White House (d. 1898), for whom he had been best man at his wedding. Thanks are due to the librarian of the Institution of Civil Engineers for providing details of Egerton's professional career.

[159] Correspondence 129–30.

[160] Richard Plowman Wing (1852–1936), BA Cantab., 1876, vicar of Walberswick with Blythburgh 1902–23. He came to Blythburgh from Huntingfield with Cookley and retired to Walberswick.

[161] Correspondence 131.

[162] Joseph Edward Southall (1861–1944), artist and pacifist. From a Quaker background, he trained as an architect. Active in the Arts and Crafts Movement. He often visited Southwold.

was coming through the roof, and timbers were beginning to give way. The 'care-taker' had told him that a thorough overhaul was in prospect with the possibility of repainting the roof. The south porch and tower were also in a bad way. Southall asked whether anything could be done to advise those responsible for the church.[163]

The SPAB briefed Southall on its understanding of the position at Blythburgh. It declared its astonishment at the architect's proposals, 'which might have been written 15 or 20 years ago', and described Egerton's response to its letter to the churchwardens as very unsatisfactory. The SPAB envisaged that if such destructive proposals for Blythburgh were adhered to, the society would have to appeal to the public through the press – a repeat of their experience in the 1880s. Southall was asked to assist the society by visiting Blythburgh again and talking to Wing.[164] Southall met Wing on 6 July 1903. He found that Wing was not very interested in the artistic or historical aspect of the church and because he had only recently come to the living, the restoration question was not altogether in his hands. Wing suggested that they should together meet the churchwarden Egerton. In a later letter Southall described the vicar as a mere nobody compared to Egerton. Egerton, 'who is a racing man, fond of dogs and horses', was found to have no particular views on restoration, but wanted to raise the necessary money and was disappointed that the SPAB could not help. Southall thought it fortunate that Blythburgh did not yet have funds for restoration, because Egerton had such 'an easy faith' in their architect.[165] There were, however, some encouraging signs for the SPAB: Egerton seemed to understand the SPAB's principles for repairing and preserving the fabric, although they appeared to be new to him, and he agreed that the roof should not be repainted. Egerton said he would be glad if it was not necessary to rebuild the porch. It was agreed that the church should be inspected on behalf of the SPAB.[166]

The architect Alfred H. Powell visited Blythburgh on 1 August 1903 and prepared a report for the SPAB.[167] Powell recommended that the south porch should be shored up at once. The work was to be done by an old millwright who lived in the village. Powell impressed upon the vicar and churchwarden that the work on the south porch could not be done satisfactorily unless it was supervised by someone recommended by the SPAB. This was agreed, and Powell promised to ask the society to find some-one as soon as possible. He thought that £150 of the £250 Blythburgh had collected so far would have to go on the porch.

The nave roof was also in a very poor state. Even from the ground it could be seen that some timbers were broken, wet through and probably rotten. The lead covering was in a bad condition throughout. There was an urgent need to erect scaffolding and closely inspect the roof. The condition of the church floor and the cracked tower also attracted Powell's attention. Powell's report was sent to Blythburgh with the SPAB's recommendations. The SPAB added that it was willing to write a letter supporting an appeal for funds, provided that the work would be properly done. The SPAB's requirements for the management of a project were set out in a letter dated 11 August

---

[163] Correspondence 132.
[164] Correspondence 133.
[165] Correspondence 134.
[166] Correspondence 135.
[167] Alfred H. Powell (1865–1960), 'Arts and Crafts' artist, designer and decorator of pottery. Supporter of SPAB. Appendix A 11.

1903:[168] an architect should be engaged who would stay at Blythburgh for the duration of the work; the architect would employ labour and buy materials as the work progressed, thus avoiding unnecessary profits passing into contactors' hands; and an architect such as Alfred Powell should be willing to do the work. The SPAB understood that Blythburgh was still collecting funds. The SPAB learned from Egerton that the porch had been shored up but it was not possible to start on the roof: there was only £200 in hand.[169]

The SPAB continued to press Blythburgh for an assurance that work would be done in accordance with its principles. Egerton, who clearly was handling matters rather than Wing, replied that they wished to do nothing to the church except what was necessary to prevent further decay. They would be quite willing for the work to be done under the personal supervision of someone recommended by the society.[170] The SPAB then provided Egerton with a letter to help in raising funds and told Powell that Blythburgh would engage him.[171]

Nearly a year passed and, having heard nothing from Blythburgh, the SPAB wrote to discover the latest position. Egerton replied that nothing other than shoring up the porch had been done. They were still raising money.[172] Uncertain about the adequacy of the support to the porch, the SPAB asked Powell to visit Blythburgh to look at the porch again. Powell visited Blythburgh with Randall Wells and met Wing.[173] The shoring for the porch seemed satisfactory. Wing had said that Blythburgh had collected £400, and Powell saw no reason why work on the porch should not start, certainly no later than spring 1905. Powell gave his recommendations on how the work should be done.[174]

In January 1905, Wing wrote to the SPAB asking it to communicate at once with Sir Ralph Blois, because he desired an interview about the church.[175] There appears to have been a meeting on 2 February and on the next day Blois wrote that he thought that the porch and nave roof should be repaired before further damage was done. He sought the society's view on which work should be done first.

In May 1905, Wing requested an estimate of the cost of repairing the porch. A further visit to Blythburgh, this time by the architect William Weir, was necessary before a cost estimate could be provided.[176] Weir visited Blythburgh in June 1905.

---

[168] Correspondence 146.

[169] Correspondence 150.

[170] Correspondence 152.

[171] Correspondence 153.

[172] Correspondence 155–6. Egerton refers to an approach made by Blythburgh resident John Seymour Lucas, RA, to Carmichael Thomas, editor of *The Graphic*, to arrange a series of pictures with an appeal. This weekly illustrated newspaper was founded by his father, William Luson Thomas (1830–1900), and published between 1869 and 1932. The paper published an appeal for Blythburgh in its issue of 22 July 1905, p. 98. The text drew from the restoration committee's appeal leaflet, including a sketch of the church by Ernest Crofts, RA. A reference to raising funds 'to preserve, not to restore, this magnificent building' is interesting and does not appear in the appeal leaflet. See Appendix B I, 5. Carmichael Thomas was a member of the church restoration committee.

[173] (Albert) Randall Wells (1877–1942), architect, joined the SPAB in 1901 and became an active campaigner against over-restoration of ancient buildings. As a 'wandering architect' he worked with Edward Shroeder Prior on Voewood, Holt, Norfolk (1905). Correspondence 159–61.

[174] Appendix A 12. Excluding the conditional £50 promised by an SPAB supporter, the restoration fund had increased by about £125, or little over £10 per month, in the previous year.

[175] Correspondence 166.

[176] William Weir (1865–1950), principal architect for the SPAB and a committee member from 1902. Had early positions with Philip Webb and J.T. Micklethwaite. Michael Drury, *Wandering architects*

He met Sir Ralph Blois and reported to the SPAB on the condition of the porch and his recommendations for repairing it.[177] The estimated cost was £200. The society was now dealing with Sir Ralph Blois rather than with Wing. Sir Ralph thanked the SPAB for Weir's report, which would be put before the Blythburgh committee on 8 July. Blois had also hoped that Weir would provide an estimate of the cost of repairs to the nave roof.[178]

The SPAB then learned of a serious setback to their hope that they would be involved with work on Blythburgh church. Responding to a request from the SPAB for the repair committee's decision, Blois wrote that Archdeacon Lawrence of Suffolk, giving no reason, had refused the SPAB to touch the church.[179] Matters were deadlocked.

In response, the SPAB embarked on a high-level lobbying exercise. It was obviously aware that another appeal for funds for Blythburgh had been launched. The patroness of the new restoration committee was HRH Princess Louise, Duchess of Argyll.[180] The committee included no fewer than three royal academicians: the Blythburgh residents John Seymour Lucas and Ernest Crofts, and Luke Fildes.[181] Sir Caspar Purdon Clarke, director of the South Kensington, later the Victoria and Albert Museum, was also among the committee members, as was Archdeacon Lawrence.[182] This was a very high-powered and potentially influential group.

The SPAB drafted a statement that reviewed the matter of Blythburgh church from 1901, when the vicar had appealed for funds, to 1905. It referred to the deadlock with Archdeacon Lawrence.[183] It sought comments from Prince Frederick Duleep

---

(Stamford, 2000), pp. 215–33. Wing requested a cost estimate in a letter dated 8 May 1905, but Weir did not visit Blythburgh until 24 June. Among the causes for the delay was the postponement of arrangements by Wing. Correspondence 172–7.

[177] Appendix A 13.

[178] Correspondence 170.

[179] Correspondence 195. The Ven. Charles D'Aguilar Lawrence (b. *c.* 1848), BA Oxon. 1872, MA 1874, archdeacon of Suffolk, 1901–16, rector of St Margaret's, Lowestoft, 1889–1901, and rural dean of Lotthingland from 1892.

[180] HRH the Princess Louise, Duchess of Argyll (1848–1939), daughter of Queen Victoria. She married the Marquess of Lorne, 1871. Artist and sculptor and active president for the infant National Trust. See Appendix B 1, 5 for the appeal leaflet. For her life see Lucinda Hawksley, *The mystery of Princess Louise, Queen Victoria's daughter* (2013). There is evidence that John Seymour Lucas, RA (see n. 183 below) could have been influential in recruiting the princess and the strong artistic representation on the committee. Lucas was a friend of the princess's equerry, William Probert (see n. 187 below). Lucas's son Sydney Seymour was the princess's architect for a proposal to create a new house on her estate in 1912–13 from the Wool Hall removed from Lavenham. James Bettley, 'The Wool Hall, Lavenham: an episode in the history of preservation', *Transactions of the Ancient Monuments Society* 57 (2013), pp. 26–55. The Wool Hall was saved through, among other protests, the intervention of the SPAB. William Weir and Philip Norman, active in the Blythburgh story, were among those involved. It may also be significant that the Blythburgh churchwarden Claude Egerton was related to the princess's mother-in-law, the duchess of Argyll, both being members of the Leveson-Gower family (personal communication from Rose Sanguinetti).

[181] John Seymour Lucas (1849–1923), RA, FSA, artist. Created picturesque house Priory Place, later The Priory, Priory Road, Blythburgh, from old cottages in the early twentieth century. Ernest Crofts (1847–1911), RA, artist. A neighbor of Lucas at The Green, Priory Road, Blythburgh, similarly created from old cottages at about the same time. Samuel Luke Fildes (1843–1927), RA, FSA, illustrator, and genre and portrait painter. Knighted, 1906.

[182] Sir Caspar Purdon Clarke (1846–1911), GSI, FSA, museum director and architect. Director of the South Kensington Museum (later renamed the Victoria and Albert Museum), 1896–1905. Director of the Metropolitan Museum, New York, 1905–11.

[183] Correspondence 199.

Singh[184] and also set out to influence Princess Louise, first through Philip Norman, and then through Captain Probert, the princess's equerry. The society sought to put the facts before her, feeling 'sure H.R.H. would not wish to help in bringing about a "restoration" of the building and might be willing to use her influence in favour of the repairs being carried out under the auspices of the Society'.[185] Norman replied that he had spoken to Probert and the SPAB's paper would be put before the princess, who was opening a fundraising event at Cockfield Hall, the Blois family seat.[186]

Meanwhile, Prince Frederick had established from Sir Ralph Blois that the archdeacon had 'climbed down' and had never meant to object to the SPAB's involvement. Sir Ralph had asked the prince to become a member of the Blythburgh committee and had explained to him that at its next meeting a resolution might be moved that the services of the SPAB should be engaged immediately to repair the porch under the supervision of someone like William Weir.[187]

At last it seemed to the SPAB that work on Blythburgh church would proceed in accordance with its principles and that it would be involved. Then a further bombshell fell. Sir Ralph wrote to Prince Frederick regretting that the Blythburgh committee had opposed his and his mother's wishes, with the result that 'a lot of money had been withdrawn'.[188] Duleep Singh's own contribution was returned, as conditions were not being complied with.[189] The roof would be repaired with the money in hand and 'under no circumstances is the society to be employed'. The porch would be left as it is. Sir Ralph and his family were annoyed at the Blythburgh committee's 'ill advised' action. Most of its members, Sir Ralph wrote, had been elected only because they were able to give professional help to raise money. The SPAB contacted Philip Norman again, hoping that Princess Louise could be informed of the state of affairs. Norman agreed to send extracts of the correspondence to Captain Probert with a request to lay the points of them before the princess. Norman, however, noted that 'The difficulty is that he is a Suffolk man and I have a sort of half suspicion that he may have taken the side of the committee; however if he has done so it would be though ignorance, as he is a gentleman and a fairminded man'.[190]

However, the Blythburgh committee had not yet definitely decided who should do the work. At its meeting on 9 July 1906, Sir Ralph was asked to get from the SPAB a report from William Weir on the repairs to the porch and nave roof with costs. The committee would then compare this with a report it had already received from the architect Philip Johnston.[191] Johnston had visited the church in December 1905,

---

[184] Prince Frederick Duleep Singh (1868–1926), of Old Buckenham Hall, Norfolk, landowner and antiquarian. He was the son of Duleep Singh (1838–93), former Maharaja of Lahore, deposed by the British and established at Elveden Hall.

[185] Philip Norman (1842–1931), FSA, artist, author and antiquary. Treasurer of the Society of Antiquaries, 1897–1913, and vice-president, 1913–17. Member of the SPAB committee. Correspondence 200. Captain (later Col.) William Geoffrey Carwardine Probert (1864–1938) of Bevills, Bures. Soldier, scholar and antiquarian. From 1903, equerry and subsequently comptroller to HRH Princess Louise, duchess of Argyll.

[186] Appendix B I, 5. An art exhibition and fancy fair on 5 August 1905.

[187] Correspondence 203.

[188] Correspondence 205.

[189] This was presumably the £50 conditional donation from 'a SPAB supporter'.

[190] Correspondence 212.

[191] Correspondence 215. Philip Mainwaring Johnston (1865–1936), FSA, FRIBA, architect, restored numerous churches and houses and designed war memorials. He was very active in Sussex and also worked on Prittlewell church and priory, and Southchurch Hall (Essex) after the First World War

returning in July 1906 to provide a costed proposal for restoration work. Sir Ralph gave a copy of Johnston's report to the SPAB. Weir, who made yet another visit to Blythburgh, commented on it. He was critical. Johnston's estimate of the cost for the work was £426 2s. 6d. Weir thought that the costs for the main roof, the tower and the south porch were all misleading. The proposed work on the vaulting of the porch 'would soon thrust the walls out again'. Weir produced his own detailed report on the church's condition, estimating the cost of the work to be £800.[192] Weir's report was sent to Sir Ralph, who replied that the Blythburgh committee would meet on 8 August and that Prince Frederick would attend. The SPAB's reservations about Johnston's estimate were also sent to Sir Ralph.[193]

At the crucial August 1906 meeting the Blythburgh committee decided to employ Philip Johnston as architect for the church, if he would work under the SPAB's supervision. Sir Ralph wrote that this was against both his and Prince Frederick's advice. Sir Ralph had offered to guarantee the money if the cost of the work recommended by the SPAB exceeded their £800 estimate.[194]

The SPAB responded to Sir Ralph on 5 October, proposing that as it was to be claimed that the work was carried out in accordance with the society's principles, it was essential that the society should inspect it from time to time. If the society's principles were departed from, then the society would persuade the architect to conform; and, if this was not possible, the Blythburgh committee would be informed.[195] The SPAB made this suggestion reluctantly. John Seymour Lucas, RA, responded on behalf of the Blythburgh committee, saying the society's representative could inspect the work now in progress.[196] So Weir again visited Blythburgh on behalf of the SPAB, meeting Philip Johnston at the church. His report to the SPAB was damning. It described the work in progress at Blythburgh as 'hopeless ... It appears a very great misfortune that the funds, which are not sufficient to undertake the necessary repairs, in order to make the fabric weatherproof, should be spent in useless restoration'.[197]

Having considered Weir's report, the SPAB committee concluded that it must disassociate the society from the work at Blythburgh, it being contrary to the society's principles. The SPAB wrote to Sir Ralph that it could take no other possible action and that it was a matter of deep regret that things had turned out as they had.[198] An exchange of letters between the SPAB and Prince Frederick Duleep Singh suggests that most of the Blythburgh committee were happy with what was being done.[199] The prince undertook to press the SPAB's position at the next Blythburgh meeting. He commented in respect of the restoration work and Philip Johnston, architect, that 'It is a grievous pity that it ever got into the hands of such a man'. That was the last word on Blythburgh in the SPAB file, ending a twenty-five year long battle to have work on Blythburgh church done in accordance with its principles.

(personal communication from James Bettley). It is not known how Johnston came to be involved with Blythburgh. Appendix A 15.

[192] Appendix A 17.
[193] Correspondence 224.
[194] Correspondence 227.
[195] Correspondence 229.
[196] Correspondence 230.
[197] Correspondence 235 and Appendix A 18.
[198] Correspondence 236.
[199] Correspondence 241.

The great achievement of the campaign, which had started in 1881, was that Blythburgh church was saved from ruin. In the process the east and west windows and the nave windows were all restored, giving the church the benefit of light that became one of its defining characteristics. The clerestory windows were also restored, but two blocked windows in the chancel have never been reopened. The screen, too, was restored, and its missing middle section replaced. The roofs of the north and south aisles were repaired. Box pews were removed and fifteenth-century benches revealed. Essential repairs were done to the nave roof. Externally, the south parapet was repaired. In all this work, in stone and timber, SPAB principles were ignored and medieval work copied.

But if the SPAB lost the battle, perhaps eventually it won the war. Blythburgh never had enough money to do all the work that was wanted or needed: the decorated nave roof and the angels were not touched, the original floor remained, and the south porch was repaired instead of being rebuilt. Thus the hands of the most enthusiastic restorers were stayed until attitudes changed.

Postscript

William Weir, the architect whose critical reports of the work done at Blythburgh in 1905 and 1906 had been a significant factor in the SPAB's decision to withdraw from any involvement, maintained an interest in the church, preparing further reports in 1926, 1933 and 1947.[200] The context was now quite different: he worked on behalf of the advisory committee of the diocese of St Edmundsbury and Ipswich, founded in 1914, of which Blythburgh was part. Advisory Committees (DACs) were established by the early 1920s to help the chancellor of each diocese assess applications for faculties (permission) to undertake work on churches. Although they were not decision-making bodies, the committees helped to ensure that changes to buildings and their furnishings were planned and executed in the most appropriate way, respecting the historic importance of a building, while maintaining it as a functioning place of worship.[201]

In 1934 Weir wrote of repairs to John Hopton's tomb. At last the disfiguring brick supports to the canopy were to be removed.[202] They had been noticed by a visitor in 1808, 126 years before. The report of a survey of the church in 1981 includes the words: 'It should be recorded with triumph that the major overhaul of the building undertaken by the parish in 1931 is now, after 50 years, complete. [*The church*] is safe for the conceivable future'; that is, one hundred years after the work to save Blythburgh church began. Restoration work at Blythburgh, always constrained by the availability of money, proceeded very slowly.[203]

---

[200] Appendix A 19–24.

[201] Richard Morrice, *Ecclesiastical exemption in England*, www.buildingconservation.com, accessed 24 March 2015.

[202] Appendix A 22.

[203] *Report on survey under the 1955 inspection of churches measure* by Caroe and Martin, 9 September 1981, p. 3. BCP 29/1.

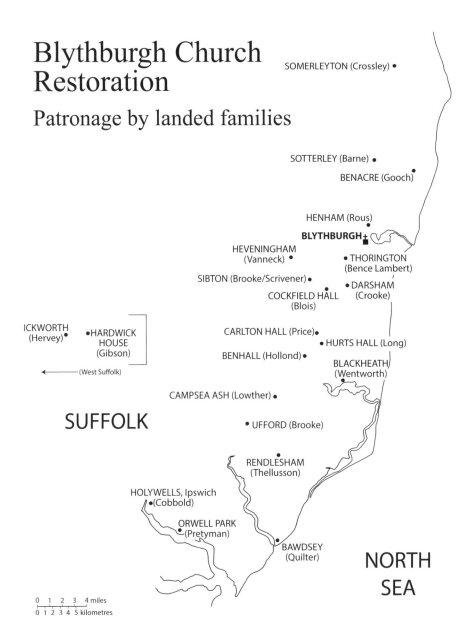

Blythburgh Church Restoration

Patronage by landed families

SOMERLEYTON (Crossley) •

SOTTERLEY (Barne) •

BENACRE (Gooch) •

HENHAM (Rous) •

BLYTHBURGH •

HEVENINGHAM (Vanneck) •

• THORINGTON (Bence Lambert)

SIBTON (Brooke/Scrivener) •

• DARSHAM (Crooke)

COCKFIELD HALL (Blois) •

ICKWORTH (Hervey) •

• HARDWICK HOUSE (Gibson)

CARLTON HALL (Price) •

• HURTS HALL (Long)

BENHALL (Hollond) •

BLACKHEATH (Wentworth)

(West Suffolk)

CAMPSEA ASH (Lowther) •

SUFFOLK

• UFFORD (Brooke)

RENDLESHAM (Thellusson)

HOLYWELLS, Ipswich (Cobbold) •

ORWELL PARK (Pretyman) •

BAWDSEY (Quilter) •

NORTH SEA

0 1 2 3 4 miles
0 1 2 3 4 5 kilometres

Map of Suffolk, showing the location of Blythburgh and the patronage by landed families of church appeals and fundraising events. Drawn by Mike Durrant.

EDITORIAL PRACTICE

The collections

Printed documents have been transcribed as such. In manuscripts original spelling has been retained. Underlinings have been shown as used by the authors. '&' has been changed to 'and' and '&c' to 'etc'. Punctuation has been modified where necessary for clarity, and capitalisation modernised and used sparingly. Abbreviations have been expanded when required for clarity. Editorial additions are shown in italics, within the text in square brackets. Money has been represented in the form £100 10s. 6d., and dates as 10 January 1885.

People have been identified in footnotes where necessary to assist understanding of the text. Generally, their details are in Appendix D, Notes on People. Further information has not been given for people mentioned only in subscription lists or as performing at or attending events.

Editorial symbols

\ /	for insertions
/ /	marginal entry or annotation
< >	for deletions which are legible in the original
[*sic*]	for all editorial insertions, italics within square brackets
[*illeg.*]	illegible words or sections
[*blank*]	empty spaces in the text
[*deleted*]	deleted and unreadable sections
[*damaged*]	for damaged and unreadable sections
[*?*]	for a reading which is not certain, preceding the word in question

GLOSSARY

Agnus Dei: the invocation of the 'Lamb of God'

aisle: the side of a church separated from the nave and chancel by an arcade or columns

alb: a white liturgical vestment, coming down to the ground and secured at the waist with a belt

altar pace: or footpace, the platform immediately before the altar at the top of the altar steps

Arca Domini: literally Lord's chest or coffer, in Blythburgh church the fifteenth-century 'Peter's Pence' box once used to collect taxes for Rome

arcade: a series of arches carried on columns

archdeacon: a senior member of the clergy with administrative functions within a diocese, delegated to him by the bishop

Arts and Crafts: a late nineteenth-century movement in Britain which sought to revive medieval craftsmanship

ashlar: cut stone shaped with even faces and edges to cover the face of a building

Augustinians: an order of canons inspired by the teaching of St Augustine of Hippo (354–430). In the twelfth century Henry I granted Blythburgh church to the canons of St Osyth Priory, Essex, founding Blythburgh priory

balk: beam

bay: a structural division in the architectural arrangement of a building

box pew: a pew of the eighteenth century, enclosed with high sides and commonly used by one family

buttress: a projection from a wall, bonded to it to create extra support and strength

came: lead used to hold glass in position in a stained-glass window

capital: the upper part or head of a column, set over the shaft

casement: an opening frame for a window

cathedral glass: manufactured glass promoted for glazing ecclesiastical buildings, first produced commercially around the 1830s

centre: a wooden frame used in arch or vault construction, removed when the mortar has set

chancel: the part at the east end of a church, set apart for the officiating clergy

chantry: a medieval endowment established to pay for the singing of masses for the soul of a particular deceased person. Also used to describe the chapel set aside for the performance of chantry duties by the priest

chapel: a part of a church (or a separate building) set aside for a religious purpose, with a separate dedication

chapel of ease: a church building within a parish, other than the parish church, for the convenience of parishioners who could not easily get to the church

chasuble: the outermost liturgical vestment worn by clergy in the Christian church for the celebration of the Eucharist

clerestory: a row of windows in the upper part of the nave and chancel, over the arcade and above the roofs of the aisles

column: an upright supporting a lintel, generally consisting of a base, shaft and capital

coping: the covering course, or capping, of a wall or parapet, to throw off water

cornice: an ornamental moulding around the top of a wall

cramp: a piece of metal bent to hold stones together

crosier: a hooked staff carried by a bishop as a symbol of his office

crypt: a vault beneath a building

curate: a cleric who assists a parish priest

deal: now any kind of softwood, but originally small thicknesses of timber

dean: a member of the clergy with administrative responsibilities within a diocese, typically for a group of parishes in a deanery

decorated: a style of English Gothic architecture from the late thirteenth to the second half of the fourteenth century characterised by window tracery, complex vaulting, and surface decoration

discharging arch: a relieving arch, built into a wall flush with the surface over a lintel to relieve it of the weight of the masonry above

dowel: a pin or peg of metal or wood to secure stones or other material together

dripstone: a projecting moulding over the head of a window, doorway, etc., to throw off rainwater

ecclesiology: from the 1830s used to define the science of the building and decoration of churches

encaustic tile: a decorative patterned floor or wall tile with inset colour glazed and fired

Eucharist: Holy Communion

faculty: permission granted by a diocese to undertake work on a church, its contents or churchyard

flag: stone used for paving

flashing: sheet metal let into joints of brick or stonework to lap over gutters to prevent the penetration of water at the junctions

flushwork: the decorative use of knapped flint in patterns with the split side set flush with the wall

Gothic: an architectural style prevalent in Europe from the latter part of the twelfth until the sixteenth century. Characterised by pointed arches, elaborate traceried windows and a vertical emphasis

Heptarchy: the collective name for the seven Anglo-Saxon kingdoms of the English early Middle Ages

iconoclasm: the attack of religious icons and other images for religious or political purposes, in particular post-Reformation destruction in English churches in the sixteenth and mid-seventeenth centuries

Jack o' the clock: a mechanical figure, dressed in armour, as in Blythburgh and Southwold churches, which strikes a bell to mark the hour or start of a service

jamb: the side of a window or door opening

lead: the metal most commonly used for roofing, flashing and decorative work. 'Leads' refers to roof coverings

lord of the manor: originally a feudal lord with certain rights over a unit of territory held as a tenant-in-chief of the crown. Gradually diminishing rights could pass, with the courtesy title, by inheritance or purchase of landed estates to the present time

louvre: an opening covered with horizontal, sloped boards, spaced to allow ventilation

mitre: the traditional ceremonial headgear worn by bishops

monial, mullion: the vertical pier that divides the lights of a window

nave: the central body of a church, reserved for the laity

nimbus: a halo or ring of light surrounding a saint in a work of art, traditionally surrounding a deity when on earth

parapet: a low wall, sometimes ornamented, at the edge of a wall, balcony or terrace

parish: an administrative part of a diocese, typically having its own church and priest. From the late-nineteenth century also the smallest unit of civil local government

parvis: a court or portico in front of a church, often the west porch itself, or a space over it. 'Parvise' is also a term used for a room over the church porch

patron: the individual or body with the right to select a new incumbent of a parish for presentation to the bishop when a vacancy occurs

Perpendicular: a late Gothic style of architecture which flourished in England from the fourteenth to the sixteenth century, characterised by straight verticals and horizontals, flat arches and roofs, and controlled rhythmic panelling with extensive use of glass

perpetual curate: an incumbent supported by a cash stipend, in the absence of an ancient rectory or vicarage, as at Blythburgh, where the responsibility for the parish had rested with the priory of St Osyth before dissolution

pew: a fixed wooden bench with a back in a church

pillar: generally a free-standing supporting construction

piscina: a stone bowl with a drain in the south wall of a church, used by the priest to wash his hands or receive the water used to rinse the chalice

plinth: the base course of a wall of a building, suggesting the platform on which the building sits

poppyhead: the carved termination of a pew-end, in the shape of a fleur-de-lys, foliage or figures

Portland cement: a light grey cement originally made from limestone from Portland, Dorset

Premonstratensians: an order of white canons founded by St Norbert at Prémontré, France, in 1120

press: a device for copying documents invented in the eighteenth century, using special copying inks and papers

Purbeck marble: dark stone from Purbeck, Dorset, capable of taking a high polish

purlin: the horizontal structural timber of a roof, resting upon the principal rafters

quarries: square or diamond-shaped pieces of window glass. Also floor tiles

quatrefoil: a decorative form in the shape of a flower with four leaves, much used in bands in Perpendicular architecture

rafter: an inclined timber forming the sides of a roof

rector: the parish priest historically entitled to the tithes

Reformation: the sixteenth-century movement against abuses in the Roman Catholic Church which led to the creation of Reformed and Protestant churches, including the Church of England

ridge: the upper angle of a roof

ridge roll: a wooden roll to take a lead ridge cover, and also the lead covering itself

rood: a cross or crucifix, often set up on a beam across the chancel arch, in the case of Blythburgh above the screen separating nave and chancel

sacrarium, sanctuary: the area around the altar of the church enclosed by the altar rail

saddle bars: iron bars set in stone to which leaded window lights are tied

scaffolding: a temporary erection of poles and planks to support platforms from which building work can be done

scarf: a form of bevelled joint for joining two pieces of timber so that they appear to be one continuous piece

screen: in a medieval church a partition between the nave with its aisles from the chancel, choir and chapels

sedilia: seats recessed in the south wall of a church, near the altar, used by the officiating clergy

sepulchre: a tomb

shore: a prop to support part of a building

sill: or cill, the piece of stone or timber forming the horizontal bottom of a door or window opening, designed usually to throw water off

soffit: the lower exposed part of a beam.

spandrel: the space between an arched doorway, or the top of a window, and the rectangle formed by the outer mouldings

spire: the pointed termination of a tower, of stone, or wood covered with stone, slates, tiles, wood shingles or lead

stall: a seat in the chancel of a church

stanchion bar: the upright iron bars between the mullions of Gothic windows

steeple: the combination of tower and spire of a church

stoup: a vessel placed near the entrance to a church, often in a niche, for holding holy water

string course: a horizontal band of mouldings on a building

tarpaulin: a large flexible sheet of water-resistant or waterproof material

tau: a Christian cross symbol named after the Greek letter it resembles

tie beam: the horizontal beam supporting a roof, jointed into wallplates to tie the walls together

tippet: a ceremonial scarf-like narrow piece of material worn over the shoulders

tithe: one tenth of produce or earnings formerly taken as a tax to support the clergy or the church

tracery: the pattern of intersecting mullions and transoms in a window

transom: the horizontal bars in windows, separating the lights

tunicle: a vestment worn over the alb by a priest at the celebration of Mass

vaulting: an arched structure over a space in a building

vestry: the meeting of parishioners to conduct parochial business. Also the room in a church (in Blythburgh church at the east end of the south aisle) where the vestments are kept

vicar: the priest officiating in a parish as deputy to a rector or a body or lay individual enjoying the benefit of the tithes. Commonly now the priest in charge of a parish

wall-piece: a wall-plate or a board set vertically against a wall

wall-plate: timber laid horizontally on a wall to which joists, rafters and roof trusses are fixed

THE DOCUMENTS

CORRESPONDENCE[1]

1. Newspaper cutting. Restoration of Blythburgh church. The Revd H. Sykes to the *Ipswich Journal*, 3 October 1881[2]

BLYTHBURGH CHURCH
To the Editor,
SIR, – Will you kindly find room in your next issue for the following letters, and oblige.
Yours faithfully,
    H. SYKES.

To the Editor of the Ipswich Journal.
SIR, – I should like to be allowed to call the attention of the Church people of the diocese to the state of Blythburgh Church. (1.) To show that, architecturally at any rate (setting aside for a moment other reasons), it is worth preserving, I extract the following words of that eminent antiquarian, John Henry Parker, from the 'Ecclesiastical and Architectural Topography of Suffolk': 'Blythburgh is a fine and large church. There is an elegant parapet of open work to the south aisle; on the angles of the porch are figures of an angel and an eagle, in the place of pinacles. The roof retains the old painting throughout. Some very fine old desks and seats remain in the North-east chapel, also some curious poppies. The original perpendicular poor's box remains, also a perpendicular lectern. The font is very fine, the tower arch very lofty.'[3] So much for my first point, that the church is well worth preserving. (2.) That there is crying need that something should at once be done. In 1855 the same great authority quoted above was obliged to add to his account – 'The whole church is in a miserable condition.' Things have not, I fear, mended since then. I visited the church myself last October. Rain came on while I was inside, and immediately came through the roof. Indeed, I have been told that the congregation assembled for service have sometimes had to shelter themselves under umbrellas. I need say no more to prove my second point, that something ought to be done, and at once. (3.) Some may ask, is it worth while to spend money on a church which is so far from

---

[1] Details about people can be found in Appendix D. Further information has been included in this section where thought necessary to explain the text. Unless otherwise referenced, documents 1–119 are from SPAB Box, Blythburgh Church, Suffolk, file I.

[2] SROI FC198, E2 1, Church Restoration. The Blythburgh church restoration committee minute book. Hereafter RCMB.

[3] J.H. Parker, *The Ecclesiastical and Architectural Topography of England: Part VII Suffolk* (Oxford and London, 1855).

modern centres of life at Blythburgh, and so much larger than the actual population of the place requires? To this I answer, surely a building so fine from an architectural point of view ought to be thought worth saving; surely the fact that it is a church solemnly dedicated to the service and worship of God ought to make us ashamed to let it go to ruin; and lastly, now that there is a railway to Blythburgh, might not the fine church of which I write be of some practical use in the diocese? We hear much now-a-days of the large size of the diocese of Norwich; many parts of it are therefore far removed from the Cathedral. Might not a large church like Blythburgh be of real service as a sort of pro-cathedral in the district in which it stands? The Bishop might, perhaps, use it for meeting his clergy, choral festivals, and other large gatherings of Church folk might be held in it. I would commend these three points to the notice of your readers:- (1.) That Blythburgh church is worth preserving. (2.) That it must be saved now if at all. (3.) That there are real reasons, religious, artistic, and practical, why it is a duty to preserve it. I do not wish to be thought to cast a slur on the various clergy who have held the living of late years, nor on the churchwardens and other inhabitants of the parish. The work needed to be done is much, and would be a costly one to be undertaken by a single parish, but if spread over the Churchpeople of the diocese it would be easy.

Trusting that my calling attention to the case will not be in vain,

I am, Sir, yours faithfully,

A.G. ADAMSON.

I am much obliged to Mr. Adamson for drawing attention to the state of the above church, and have pleasure in being able to state that very shortly the public will be made acquainted with the report of an eminent architect on what ought to be done, and the probable cost of the undertaking. In the meantime I wish to inform Mr. Adamson, and all who take an interest in the restoration of this noble edifice, that two collections have been made in church for that object. A banking account has been opened, a subscription list has been handsomely headed by a widow lady of this parish, and the following notice hangs over the 'original perpendicular poor's box':-

'BLYTHBURGH CHURCH RESTORATION FUND.

'Contributions may be deposited in this Box, and subscriptions will be thankfully received and acknowledged by the vicar and churchwardens – The Rev. H. Sykes, Walberswick vicarage, Wangford; Robinson Briggs, Esq., Bulcamp; Charles Youngs, Esq., Hinton; and at the banks at Southwold.'

The roof and windows are in a dangerous state, and something must be done speedily. Action has been taken, and it is to be hoped that the appeal for help, shortly to be made, will meet with a ready response from the public generally.

I am, Sir, yours faithfully,

H. SYKES.

Walberswick Vicarage, October 3rd, 1881.

2. Newspaper cutting. Support for church. S. Sutherland Safford to *The Morning Post*, **9 December 1881**[4]

BLYTHBURGH CHURCH.
TO THE EDITOR OF THE MORNING POST.

SIR, – I take the following from this week's ecclesiastical news in your paper –'The parish church of Blythburgh has been closed by order of the Bishop of Norwich, on account of the dangerous condition of its fine hammer-beam roof. The church is one of the best examples of semi-Flemish 13th century architecture, but is altogether in a very dilapidated condition.'[5] This fine old church is in the eastern part of the county of Suffolk, near Southwold. In Gardner's History, 1754, in speaking of the church he says: – 'It is 127 feet in length and 54 feet in width, the windows thereof are very numerous, and were once extremely beautiful, as may now partly be seen by what remains of the painted glass. They were adorned with a great many coats of arms, of which only seven remain entire. The roof is an exceeding good one, is painted and gilded, and upon it in almost innumerable places are the characters I.H.S. The church is decorated with many figures and devices. King Anna was buried here A.D. 654. In the church are the arms of the Swillington, Hopton, Brooke, and Blois families.'[6] In another local work by Wake, 1839, p. 330, I find the following remarks:- 'It is impossible to see the work of ruin passing stealthily, and without such prevention as might be effected by timely repair, upon the grandeur and venerable portions of so noble a pile, and to remain untouched by the spectacle. Would that those who are more concerned in the blame of neglect and indifference than we could but feel, in turning from it, the regret which we feel.'[7] With these facts placed prominently before those who have a feeling for antiquity, surely no time will be lost in taking steps to preserve, by public subscription if necessary, a venerable and magnificent pile gradually but assuredly smouldering [*sic*] into sad decay, desolation, and ruin. – I am sir, your obedient servant,

S. SUTHERLAND SAFFORD.

Parkshot, Richmond, Dec. 9. [*1881 added by Sykes.*]

3. Newspaper cutting. Proposal to form fund-raising committee. Arthur C. Pain to *The Morning Post*, **15 December 1881, published 20 December**[8]

BLYTHBURGH CHURCH.
TO THE EDITOR OF THE MORNNG POST.

Sir, – Permit me to confirm all the statements of your correspondent, Mr Stafford [*sic*], in your paper of Monday.[9] I feel sure that it only requires organisation to band together a great many persons, who, loving the fine old church, would willingly give time and money to preserve it from ruin and decay. The parish itself is poor, and without help from the outer world can do nothing. I would suggest that a committee

---

4   RCMB.
5   Appendix C 4, 'Closure of Blythburgh church'.
6   Gardner, pp. 122–7.
7   R. Wake, *Southwold and its vicinity, ancient and modern* (Great Yarmouth, 1839).
8   Also RCMB.
9   See Correspondence 2.

should be at once formed to raise the necessary funds to render the edifice safe and fit for public worship. – Yours obediently,

ARTHUR C. PAIN.

Claremont-road, Surbiton, Dec. 15. [*1881 added by Sykes.*]

4. Blythburgh brought to the attention of the SPAB. S. Wayland Kershaw to Thomas Wise, SPAB, 20 December 1881

/Received 22/12/81 Blythburgh church/
<35a Russell Road Kensington. W>

Lambeth Palace.
20 December 1881

Blythburgh Church

Dear Sir,

I send you another extract <u>re</u> this church and shall be obliged if you will bring the matter before the restoration committee.

It appears to me a fortunate time for our society to suggest <u>before further</u> steps are taken; The church may be described in the 'Report of the Churches in East Anglia' published by our society.[10]

I think it would be well also to send our papers to Mr Pain who seems from his letter inclined to our views.

Very truly yours,

[*signed*]   S.W. Kershaw FSA

Thomas Wise Esq.

5. Newspaper cutting. Restoration of church. The Revd H. Sykes to *The Morning Post*, 22 December 1881[11]

BLYTHBURGH CHURCH.
TO THE EDITOR OF THE MORNING POST.

SIR, – I beg to reply to the letter on the above subject which appeared in your issue of the 12th inst. It is quite true, as your correspondent states, that this 'venerable and magnificent pile is assuredly mouldering into sad decay, desolation, and ruin.' The spectacle is painful in the extreme to any person who has a spark of love for what is grand and beautiful in architecture, but the question arises, what can be done to prevent the further decay and ultimate ruin of this noble building? I am thankful to say some steps have been taken already. A meeting of parishioners, convened by circular, was held in the school on October 7, when a committee was appointed to consider the matter. Mr. G. E. Street, R.A., Cavendish-square, was engaged by the committee to inspect and report. Mr. Street and his son made a thorough inspection of the building in the early part of November, and promised to draw out estimates for the various portions of the work to be undertaken. The architect's reports and estimates have been delayed by the illness and lamented death of Mr. Street, but as soon as these have been received they will be printed for circulation and extensively advertised in

---

[10] See Introduction, n. 75. Blythburgh was not mentioned in the report.

[11] RCMB. The greater part of this letter was reprinted in *The Builder* on 31 December 1881. 'Blythburgh Church. – The Rev. H. Sykes, in a letter to the *Morning Post*, says, in replying to a previous letter on the state of the church, "that it is quite true … and extensively advertised in the public papers"'.

the public papers. A subscription list has been opened and a considerable number of collecting cards issued. Subscriptions will be thankfully received and acknowledged by the vicar and churchwardens, or may for the present be paid into the following banks – Messrs, Gurneys, Birkbeck, Barclay, Orde, and Buxtons, at Halesworth and Southwold; Messrs. Lacon's, also of Halesworth and Southwold. I will only add that the parishioners will do all they can for the restoration of the church, but as there are no wealthy families in the parish, they cannot be expected to raise more than a tithe of the amount required. I ought also to state that as the population is only a little over 600, a smaller church would have been far more convenient and comfortable. They are very willing, however, to waive their own interests, and help to the utmost of their power in restoring their grand old church. It is hoped that their appeal to the country for help will be liberally responded to by all who take an interest in the preservation of this noble edifice. – I am, sir, your obedient servant,

    H. SYKES.

Walberswick Vicarage, Southwold, Dec. 22 [*1881 added by Sykes.*]

6. Restoration of church. Thomas Wise, SPAB, to S. Wayland Kershaw, 22 December 1881

22 December 1881

S. Wayland Kershaw, Esq.,
Lambeth Palace.

Dear Sir,

Blythburgh Church

I have to acknowledge the receipt of your letter of yesterday's date enclosing extract from paper relating to the restoration of this church which shall be brought before the committee today.

    I am, dear Sir

        Yours faithfully,

[*signed*]   Thomas Wise

          Secretary

7. SPAB visit to Blythburgh church. The Revd H. Sykes to J.H. Middleton, 31 January 1882

/Re Blythburgh Church, Suffolk/

Walberswick Vicarage,
Southwold.
31 January 1882

Dear Sir,

I am sorry your letter did not reach me till the 29th, but hope you found no difficulty in gaining entrance into Blythburgh church.

    You are probably aware that the late Geo. E. Street Esquire inspected the church a little before his death. His report was not completed when that event took place, but on the first of January I received the report from Mr Arthur Street together with estimates of the work in several portions. Without taking a copy of his recommendations I sent them off to the bishop of the diocese and have not yet had them returned, so that the committee have not yet fully decided upon what is to be done and if your report reaches me before the next meeting I may be able to lay them side by side for the committee's consideration. I am sure we shall be most grateful for any hints you may be able to offer and for such advice as may help us in this great but much needed work.

I will just add that <any> communications addressed to me at Blythburgh are frequently detained for several days and it will be well, in future, to direct them as at the head of this letter.

Believe me, dear Sir,
Yours faithfully,
[*signed*]   H. Sykes

J.H. Middleton, Esq.

8. Request to see plans. SPAB to A.E. Street, 27 February 1882

27 February 1882

Street Esq.
Dear Sir,

Re <u>Blythburgh Church</u>

The committee of this society believe that you are likely to be engaged in the restoration of this church and as they are very much interested in the preservation of such a remarkable building they will be much obliged if you will allow two of their members to wait upon you to [*see*] the plans and to receive any [*letter incomplete*]

9. Concerning plans for Blythburgh. A.E. Street to SPAB, 2 March 1882

/Received 3/3/82
Answered/

14 Cavendish Place,
Cavendish Square, W.
2 March 1882

Sir,
When the plans of Blythburgh church are prepared I shall be most happy to let you see them. At present nothing is being done.

Yours truly,
[*signed*]   A.E. Street

10. Request for information about restoration. S. Sutherland Safford to SPAB, 4 April 1882

/re, Blythburgh Church. Received 5/4/82. Answered 14/4/82/

Parkshot,
Richmond,
Surrey.
4 April 1882

Dear Sir,
I shall be much obliged if you can inform me what is known by your society of Blythburgh church, Suffolk, and the proposed restoration of it. Have you had a report on the subject and can I obtain any particulars from your society.

Yours faithfully,
[*signed*]   S. Sutherland Safford

11. Thomas Wise, SPAB, to S. Sutherland Safford, 14 April 1882

14 April 1882
S. Sutherland Safford, Esq.,
   Parkshot, Richmond,
      Surrey.

Dear Sir,

<u>Blythburgh Church</u>

I am sorry your letter has been so long unanswered but absence from town during Easter has prevented me from attending to it earlier.

The attention of the society was called to the proposed restoration of this church and Mr Street was asked to give some idea of what was to be done. The plans are not yet finished but Mr Street has kindly promised to show them, when completed, to a deputation from the Society.

When I am in possession of the information I shall be glad to communicate with you again.

Yours faithfully,
[*signed*]   Thomas Wise
                  Secretary

12. Newspaper cutting. Formation of London committee. S. Sutherland Safford to *Building News*, 18 May 1882, published 19 May[12]

BLYTHBURGH CHURCH, SUFFOLK

Sir, I shall be greatly obliged if you will kindly permit me to state that a Committee has been formed in London for the preservation of this magnificent ecclesiastical monument – now on the verge of ruin.

The Church of Blythburgh, in the eastern part of the county of Suffolk, is one of the finest specimens of semi-Flemish 13th century architecture in this country; and the Committee seek the assistance of those who would regret to think that such a fabric should become a ruin, and this will be inevitable in the course of a very short time, unless an immediate effort be made to avert such a catastrophe.

The Bishop of Norwich has ordered the Church to be closed, for it is no longer safe in its present state. The late Mr. Street, R.A., had, within a few weeks of his death, examined and reported upon the building. The sum required for even ordinary repair is far in excess of the amount which can be collected by the Local Committee. The General Committee, therefore, appeal to all who are interested in the preservation of our grand old churches and monuments for help in this great work, by donations or by acting upon the Committee.

In consequence of Mr Street's decease, the Committee have conferred with Mr A.W. Blomfield, M.A., the eminent architect, who is willing to take up the work either alone, or in conjunction with his partner, the son of the late Mr Street, as may

---

[12] Also in SROI HD 80 4 2, F.C. Brooke of Ufford Place. Hereafter 'Brooke'. Reprinted in the *East Anglian Daily Times*, 20 May 1882.

be arranged. Subscriptions, or promises of assistance, will be gladly acknowledged, and any information will be given by, Sir, your obedient servant,

S. SUTHERLAND SAFFORD

Hon. Sec. Blythburgh Church Preservation Fund.

4, Garden-Court, Temple, London, E.C.

18th May 1882.

13. Restoration plans. S. Sutherland Safford to SPAB, 27 May 1882[13]

/Blythburgh Church. Received 29/5/82. Answered 6/02/

Parkshot,

Richmond,
Surrey.
27 May 1882

Dear Sir,

I should be glad if you would kindly let me know when I could see you at your office to show you the plans prepared by Mr Arthur Street for the preservation of Blythburgh church, Suffolk.

Yours faithfully,

[*signed*]   S. Sutherland Safford

14. Thomas Wise, SPAB, to S. Sutherland Safford, [?]6 June 1882

/Enclosure/

[*?*]6 June 1882

To S. Sutherland Safford Esq.,

Parkshot,

Richmond.

Dear Sir,

Blythburgh Church

I have been awaiting the instructions of my committee before answering your letter of the 27th May relating to the proposed restoration of this church. Mr Street has now been asked to fulfil his promise to send his plans to the committee [*three words*] it does not seem worth while to put you to any trouble or any work just yet. Upon hearing from Mr Street, I shall be pleased to [*four words that cannot be read*].[14]

The annual meeting of this society is arranged for Friday next. I have the pleasure to enclose your two invitations herewith. If you are unable to use them please do not trouble to return them.

Yours faithfully,

[*signed*]   Thomas Wise
Secretary

---

13 Street was happy that the SPAB should see the plans (Correspondence 9), but the view of the Blythburgh client, from whom presumably Safford had received the plans, was not known at this stage. However, Correspondence 23 shows that Sykes was happy that the SPAB should see them.

14 Concerning that Mr Street has not yet sent a copy of the plans to the SPAB.

15. Request to see plans. Thomas Wise, SPAB, to A.E. Street, 6 June 1882[15]

6 June 1882
A. Street Esq.,
    14 Cavendish Place,
        Cavendish Square.

Dear Sir,

<u>Blythburgh Church</u>

The committee of this society beg to remind you of your promise to let them see the plans for the restoration of this church as soon as they were completed. From a letter they now notice in the papers it appears that the work is to be undertaken without delay. Will you be so good then as to name an early date when it would be convenient for you to show the plans to a deputation from the committee? If you will kindly let me have an answer by return of post it would be in time for the meeting on Thursday next so that no time would be lost.

Yours faithfully,
[*signed*]   Thomas Wise
            Secretary

16. Plans. A.E. Street to Thomas Wise, SPAB, 8 June 1882

/Blythburgh Church. Received 9/6/82. Answered/

14 Cavendish Place,
Cavendish Square, W.

8 June 1882

Dear Sir,

I was out when your letter came and away this morning otherwise I would have answered it. I will let you know when the plans come from Blythburgh. It will probably not be for a couple of months.

Believe me,
Yours faithfully,
[*signed*]   Arthur E. Street

Thomas Wise

17. Request for plans. Thomas Wise, SPAB, to S. Sutherland Safford, 1 July 1882

9 Buckingham St,
Adelphi.
1 July 1882

S. Sutherland Safford Esq.,

---

15 Although the SPAB had been offered sight of the plans by S. Sutherland Safford on 27 May (Correspondence 13), at that stage the society preferred a formal request to the architect. However, Correspondence 15 shows that they decided to accept Safford's offer when it became clear that Street had to wait for the return of plans from Blythburgh. Unfortunately, by then Safford no longer had the plans (Correspondence 18).

Parkshot,
    Richmond,
       Surrey.
Dear Sir,

re <u>Blythburgh Church</u>

Referring to your letter of the 27th May, the committee will be much obliged if you will be so good as to allow them to inspect Mr Street's plans of the work proposed to be done to this church. The next meeting of the committee takes place on Friday next at 5 o'clock and if you would be so kind as to allow the plans to be inspected then, I will send for them to The Temple at any time you name.

    Yours faithfully,
[*signed*]   Thomas Wise
         Secretary

18. Plans. S. Sutherland Safford to Thomas Wise, SPAB, 3 July 1882

/Blythburgh Church. Received 5/7/82. Answered/
Parkshot,
Richmond, Surrey.
3 July 1882

Dear Sir,
I returned Mr Street's plans to the Rev. H. Sykes (Walberswick Vicarage, Southwold) the vicar of <u>Blythburgh</u>, about ten days ago but should you not be able to get the plans in time for the meeting, I have by me here, some <u>rough tracings</u> I took of them which if they are of any use I shall be very pleased to lend \<you\> on receiving word from you.

    Yours faithfully,
[*signed*]   S. Sutherland Safford

Thomas Wise, Esq.

19. Plans. Thomas Wise, SPAB, to S. Sutherland Safford, 5 July 1882

9 Buckingham St,
Adelphi.
5 July 1882

S. Sutherland Safford, Esq.,
    Parkshot,
      Richmond,
         Surrey.
Dear Sir,

re <u>Blythburgh Church</u>

I have to thank you for your letter of yesterday's date kindly offering the loan of the tracings of the plans for the restoration of Blythburgh church. There is a meeting here on Friday next, and if you could let me have the drawings by then I need hardly say I shall be greatly obliged.

    Yours truly,
[*signed*]   Thomas Wise
         Secretary

20. Publication of SPAB report in newspapers. Draft unsigned letter to Thackeray Turner, SPAB, no date[16]

My dear Turner,

<Send the two> If Sir John Blois makes an appointment for Monday afternoon as you proposed please send me a telegram.

> Morris and Company,
> Merton Abbey Works,
> Surrey.

If he does not, please send the two copies of the report to the Suffolk Chronicle and Ipswich Journal begging them to publish. Say the committee will be obliged if the editor will give space for the report. [*damage*] which we think will be very interesting to some of their readers. If the report is too long for insertion all at once we suggest they should print one half this week and one the next.

Ask them to head it.

Copy of the report made by the Society for Protecting Ancient Buildings on the necessary repairs of Blythburgh church.

[*unsigned*]

21. Request for specifications. Thomas Wise, SPAB, to S. Sutherland Safford, 18 July 1882[17]

18 July 1882

S. Sutherland Safford Esq.,
> Parkshot,
> > Richmond, Surrey.

Dear Sir,

re <u>Blythburgh Church</u>

I am instructed to thank you for the abstract of specification and for the two plans of Blythburgh church.

The committee of the Society for the Protection of Ancient Buildings has carefully read through the abstract but does not find any description of the works to be done under tender no. 4 nor for those in the chancel comprised under the etcetera of tender no. 5.

This church is of so great value and every part of the scheme for restoring it is necessarily so important, the committee feels it could not do justice either to the church or to the intention of those who have undertaken to restore it without having the whole scheme under consideration.

To enable the committee therefore to arrive at a clear opinion it is desirable that [*the complete copy of the specification should be before it and if you will kindly allow*] this, I am authorized to pay for the cost of a written copy supposing the lithographed copies to be exhausted.

I need not add that the committee is most anxious to give this case not only a careful but their immediate attention and it hopes to resume the consideration of it with the help of the full specification at the next meeting.

---

[16] Probably mid-July 1882.

[17] This letter also exists in draft form, from which the words in italics are taken.

I am, dear Sir,
Yours obediently,
[*signed*]   Thomas Wise
         Secretary

PS. The next meeting of the committee is arranged for Friday next, at 5 o'clock.
TW

22. Legal opinion on SPAB letters. Vernon Lushington to George Wardle, dated 'Wednesday evening'

(No longer 21 New Street but) 36, Kensington Square,
Kensington, W.
Wednesday evening

Dear Mr Wardle,
I have just received and read your two letters. They are in my opinion quite unexceptionable from the legal point of view. They are also I think very well calculated to make the impression you desire.

I don't send the letter on to the Athenaeum,[18] partly because I don't know Mr McColl, and also because I notice that in pages 2 and 3, certain figures are omitted, which you might like to insert. As regards the Ipswich letter:

p.1. I would omit 'if made in good faith', because while offensive, it seems to me inappropriate or at least without apparent justification. The sentence I think should be recast, or omitted.

p.12. I would omit the forecast of failure. It sounds faint-hearted. Might you not say, 'They have appealed but apparently so far in vain to those responsible etc'.

p.13. Substitute 'or in carrying out the miserable delusion of restoration'.

I send both letters to you at Charlotte Street, according to your directions as I understand them.

I will do my best to come to the meeting on Friday, but I have to hold a court that day at Epsom.

Yours very truly,
[*signed*]   Vernon Lushington

George Wardle, Esq.

23. Specifications. The Revd H. Sykes to S. Sutherland Safford, 20 July 1882

Walberswick Vicarage,
Southwold.
20 July 1882

Dear Sir,
I am sending the specifications by rail and if you have got Mr Street's consent you can take them to the 'Society' at once, but if you have got a copy from Mr Street please to return these and oblige.

      Yours truly,

---

[18] *The Athenaeum* was a literary and scientific journal published from 1828 to 1923. It eventually became *The New Statesman.*

[*signed*]   H. Sykes

24. Specifications. S. Sutherland Safford to Thomas Wise, SPAB, 21 July 1882

Parkshot,
Richmond, Surrey.
21 July 1882

Dear Sir,

I am much obliged to you for your letter of the 18th instant. Since receiving it I have been endeavouring to obtain a copy of the specification in full of the Blythburgh church work, and I find that the one the vicar has is the only one in existence.

I enclose you the note I have received from Mr Sykes (the vicar)[19] and I hope to receive the specification today in time for the meeting.

Should it not arrive soon enough the only thing I can do is to ask you to kindly postpone the consideration of it till the next meeting if necessary.

Believe me

Yours faithfully,

[*signed*]   S. Sutherland Safford

Thomas Wise, Esq.

P.S. The specification accompanies this letter.[20]

25. Specifications. Thomas Wise, SPAB, to George Wardle, 27 July 1882

27 July 1882
G. Y. Wardle Esq.,
    9 Charlotte Street,
        Bedford Square.

Dear Sir
    Re Blythburgh Church
Will you kindly let me know if you want a fair copy made of the 'General Condition' as well as one of the 'Specification'.

Yours truly,

[*signed*]   Thomas Wise
              Secretary

26. Request for return of specifications. S. Sutherland Safford to Thomas Wise, SPAB, 31 July 1882

/Received 1/8/82. Answered Blythburgh Church/

Parkshot,
Richmond, Surrey.

---

[19] Correspondence 23.

[20] For an extract of the specifications see Appendix A 4, 'Extract of Specifications'.

31 July 1882

Dear Sir,

I have received the enclosed note[21] from the vicar of <u>Blythburgh</u> who lent me the specifications. When will you be able to let me have them?

    Yours faithfully,

[*signed*]   S. Sutherland Safford

Thomas Wise, Esq.

27. Specifications. Thomas Wise, SPAB, to George Wardle, 1 August 1882

1 August 82

Dear Mr Wardle,

<u>Blythburgh Church</u>

Herewith I send you fair copy specification of the work.

    The original I have returned to Mr Safford who was pressed for it by the vicar. I hope this was right?

    Yours faithfully,

[*signed*]   Thomas Wise

28. Specifications. Thomas Wise, SPAB, to S. Sutherland Safford, 1 August 1882

1 August 1882

To S. Sutherland Safford Esq.,
    Parkshot, Richmond,
      Surrey.

Dear Sir,

re <u>Blythburgh Church</u>

The specification of the work to be done to this church has been in the hands of two members of the committee of the society, to whom the task of reporting upon the proposed restoration was entrusted, until this morning – it is now returned to me and I have the pleasure to forward it to you by this post, as requested in your letter of yesterday's date.

    I have to thank you very much for your kindness in obtaining for the committee the plans and specification at so short a notice. I hope you are not wanting the tracings for a short time as they are still in the hands of the two members above referred to – if I do not hear from you that you require them I will [? *words*] but I don't anticipate that they will be long.

I am, dear Sir,

    Yours faithfully,

[*signed*]   Thomas Wise

---

[21] Not in the SPAB file.

29. Specifications. S. Sutherland Safford to Thomas Wise, SPAB, 3 August 1882

/Received 4/8/2/

Parkshot,
Richmond, Surrey.
31 July 1882

Dear Sir,

Blythburgh

Many thanks for the specification received safely. Pray keep the tracings as long as necessary as I do not want them just now at all.

Yours faithfully,

[*signed*]   S. Sutherland Safford

30. Comments on restoration proposals. Arthur G. Hill to George Wardle, 9 August 1882

20 Lascelles Terrace,
Eastbourne.
9 August 1882

Society for the Protection of Ancient Buildings

Dear Sir,

My friend Mr H.W. Brewer has written to me concerning the 'restoration' of Blythburgh church, Suffolk.

He informs me that you and Mr Morris are about to visit the church with the view of forming an opinion as to the necessity of carrying out the scheme of restoration that <the> has been suggested.

I am writing now to say that I know Blythburgh church tolerably well, and I took notes etc upon its architecture etc when there in 1880.

I venture to express an opinion (not as an architect, but as one who gives the greater portion of his time to the study of medieval architecture) that nothing else but structural reparation is required, the church being singularly complete in fittings etc.

I am one of the committee for the 'restoration' but have as yet attended no meetings (if any such have been held) and merely allowed my name to appear because I thought I might be able to do good in averting the proposed modernizing of one of the grandest Perpendicular churches in England.[22]

I trust that the SPAB will be able to protect this fine work.

The parapets are wonderfully fine, and the exterior is much enriched with flint panelling.[23]

The roofs are splendid open timber examples with original colouring, and there are noble screens (whitewashed) and benches.

The windows have fragments of old glass.

There is an old alms box and several other objects of this class.

I have heard that it is proposed to add new pinnacles, parapets, and even roofs: also greater portion of the window tracery.

---

[22] The London committee referred to in Correspondence 12.

[23] Flushwork, the decorative use of knapped flints in patterns with the split side set flush with the wall. John Blatchly and Peter Northeast, *Decoding Flushwork on Suffolk and Norfolk Churches* (Ipswich, 2005).

I feel sure that when you have seen the church you will come to the conclusion that such acts would be vulgar and <vandal> and entirely to be deprecated.

I fancy that 'shoring up' will be required in one or two places, but my impression is that <u>no</u> <u>new work</u> whatever is required, and this applies equally to the <u>fittings</u> which are very fine.

Having visited nearly every important church in Norfolk and many in Suffolk I can join with the SPAB in lamenting over the fearful restorations that have taken place in a county which is richer than any other part of England in fittings and Perpendicular work generally.

I trust that some way may be found whereby the work can be put in the hands of a thoroughly conservative and learned architect (such as Mr Bodley or G.G. Scott) for I believe that the late Mr Street prepared plans for the restoration and, with all deference to his original genius, I do not think that his scheme would do any good to Blythburgh.

The above is my address for the next fortnight or so.

With apologies for my suggestions.

Believe me,

    Faithfully yours,

[*signed*]   Arthur G. Hill BA, FSA.

G. Wardle, Esq.

31. Newspaper cutting. Criticism of patron. 'Churchman' to the *Ipswich Journal*, 16 August 1882, published 19 August[24]

BLYTHBURGH CHURCH RESTORATION

SIR, – The long and valuable article in your issue of Saturday last on Blythburgh Church will have been read by many beside myself with more than common interest.[25] There can be no doubt that a building possessing so many points of an architectural and historical character claims more than a local sympathy. These are times in which certain economists would persuade us that utility must be the altar upon which the ancient and the historical should be sacrificed. Some such persons, it is reported, have gone so far as to suggest that the grand old church of Blythburgh should be demolished, and its *débris* used for building barns and cottages. There is often a lack of wisdom in these narrow calculations of present utility. We are not, however, justified in excluding from our calculations utility, especially when dealing with public money, in the restoration or building of edifices for sacred or other purposes. It is proposed, therefore, I learn, at once to restore the South Aisle from East to West, and make it in every way fit for Divine worship. What may be the estimate for that part of the work I do not know, but most sincerely do I hope that the praiseworthy and arduous efforts of Lady Blois and others may be realised in seeing that part of the work soon completed, and the services and ordinances of the Church held therein.

But supposing that part of the work be accomplished, how are the funds to be raised to preserve the entire fabric of the grand old church as a provincial and national monument? On certain conditions I do not despair of such a result. It may

---

[24] Also in RCMB. If this letter was not written by Revd Sykes himself, it would seem to have been inspired by him.

[25] The *Ipswich Journal*, 12 August 1882. See Appendix C 17.

be the work of time, perhaps considerable time. But in dealing with a restoration like Blythburgh, it cannot be that the spiritual wants of the place will ever need a building of such large dimensions; the appeal must be made for help upon national grounds for the restoration of the beautiful fabric of this fine old church. Englishmen, as a rule, are not guilty of the vice of vandalism, either by omission or commission. They are ready to aid in the restoration of churches perhaps more than any other edifices, but there are certain conditions instinctively possessing the English character, when appealed to for aid in restoration or any good work. What are the grounds of the appeal? Who are the persons locally interested? What are their abilities to give? What are the sums contributed respectively by those who may be more immediately benefitted by the undertaking? These inquiries arise in the mind.

In round numbers I learn that the estimated cost of restoring the entire edifice is £5,000. The list of contributors is published and their respective contributions. Considering the circumstances of the locality, the people of Blythburgh have promised well. But if the grand old church is to be restored, and appeal is to be made to the county in particular and the nation at large, the patron must set a more noble example. Instead of the sum of £100 which now is the head of the list, there should be no less than £500, *i.e.*, £100 for every 1,000 of the estimated cost of the entire restoration. I am credibly informed that the patron of the living is the owner of a great part of the parish and the hamlet of Hinton and Walberswick; also that he has so far been a benefactor to Blythburgh as to have erected at his own cost the new school buildings. Now, if that gentleman would take the lead in the undertaking, and the other noble landowners support him, there would be more hope of the speedy rescue of Blythburgh Church 'from further decay and ultimate ruin.' Until some such example is set and its influence felt, the restoration is doubtful.

I am, Sir, yours faithfully,
[*signed*]   CHURCHMAN
East Suffolk, August 16th 1882.

32. Newspaper cutting. Criticism of patron. The Revd H. Sykes to the *Ipswich Journal*, 16 August 1882, published 19 August[26]

SIR, – Many thanks are due to you and to all who have assisted in the preparation of such an admirable report of the bazaar lately held at Blythburgh,[27] but as there are some statements which may prove prejudicial to the great object we have set before us, I think it my duty to reply at once.

In the first place, the church would never have become so 'thoroughly dilapidated' had there been any adequate effort made to prevent it by those who ought to have taken an interest in its preservation, and now, had it depended upon Lady Blois and the co-operation of Sir John, it is to be feared the church, beautiful as it is, must have become a heap of ruins. No, the movement has originated where reason and common sense say it ought, viz., with the Vicar and churchwardens, and were they not to carry it on the restoration of Blythburgh Church, like the Walberswick Bridge,[28] would come to nothing; but, with the quiet, plodding perseverance which has characterised

---

[26] Also in RCMB.
[27] The *Ipswich Journal*, 12 August 1882. See Appendix C 17.
[28] The reference to Walberswick Bridge is not understood. A bridge across the river Blyth was built to carry the Southwold railway that opened in 1879. Otherwise, there was a long-established ferry for

their proceedings hitherto, there is no fear but that the work will be brought to a successful issue. All honour to Lady Blois and her family for the way in which they have laboured to collect subscriptions, and especially in the matter of the bazaar, but the public will need to be assured that the restoration, as a whole, rests upon a surer basis. The Vicar and churchwardens claim no honour in this matter. They felt that an imperative duty rested upon them, and their only desire is to discharge their responsibilities and to do what can be done to prevent their church from falling into further decay.

Though Sir John's name occurs first, on account of the sum promised, the honour of leading the list belongs to another. Mrs. Cape, a widow, of Walberswick, was the first to respond to the Vicar's appeal, and her subscription of £5 5s. 0d. was given as a thank-offering for the religious instruction she received as a Sunday scholar within the walls of Blythburgh Church. This donation was the outcome of a grateful heart, and it may truly be said of her as of a widow before, 'She hath given more than they all.'

The next step was an invitation, by circulars distributed through the parish, inviting all 'to come to the meeting, and encourage their Vicar and Churchwardens in this great undertaking.'

This meeting, held October 7, 1881, was well attended. The Vicar promised his subscription, the scheme was approved, a bazaar suggested, and a Restoration Committee appointed. The late Mr Street was communicated with, and, in answer to some inquiries, he wrote:- 'I should be only too glad to have a hand,' etc., – a very different thing from saying that 'Mr Street expressed a wish to have a hand,' etc., which gives a wrong impression, and one which needs to be corrected.

Again, instead of Lady Blois having started the movement, as your report implies, her name was not added to the Committee till January 21th, 1882, and at the same meeting the proposed bazaar was determined upon. Lady Blois has since worked 'with a will,' both in collecting subscriptions, holding concerts, and taking the management of the bazaar; but it is wrong to state that she has been the means of collecting the £600 already promised. Besides Sir John's subscription, she has been the means of raising £265 of the £600. I might add much more, but I forbear.

The attempt to ignore those who have started the movement, and upon whom the responsibility rests of carrying it forward, is not only unfair, but I fear will have a prejudicial influence in many quarters.

The claim which the Committee have upon a sympathizing public for help in such an undertaking, is quite sufficient, apart from any personal obligations, to ensure the support that is needed.

I remain, yours respectfully,
[*signed*]   H. SYKES.
Walberswick Vicarage,
August 16th, 1882.

---

pedestrians between Southwold and Walberswick. See Dani Church and Ann Gander, *The Story of the Southwold-Walberswick Ferry* (Holton, 2009).

Plate I. An aerial view of Blythburgh church in the early 1970s. The church's location on a knoll above the river Blyth is clearly demonstrated. The ruins of Blythburgh priory are concealed by trees 150 m north-east of the church. BCP, 36/12/9

Plate II. Blythburgh church interior in the early nineteenth century. Watercolour by Isaac Johnson (1753–1835). The artist has moved the font to the south to improve the view. His representation that tracery survived in the east window may not be reliable. See Blatchly 2014, pp. 98–100. © Society of Antiquaries of London

Plate III. Representations of St Bartholomew and St Helen in Blythburgh church window glass. Watercolours by Hamlet Watling, 1840s. © SROI, Sq9

Plate IV. The church from the south-east. This image published in the mid nineteenth century shows the east window of the chancel bricked up, and the heads of four windows in the south aisle, and the porch windows blocked. Suckling, 1847. BCP, 16/1

Plate V. The north aisle looking west, not east as the image caption states. The stalls in the chapel have not yet been moved to the chancel. The head of the west window is blocked. Suckling, 1847. BCP, 16/1

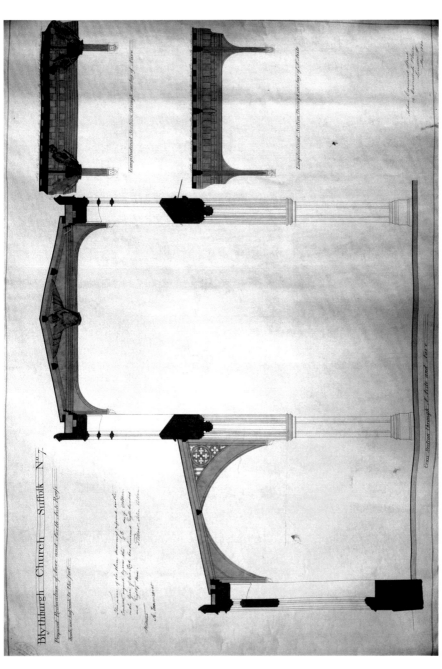

Plate VI. Proposed restoration of nave and north aisle roofs by Arthur Edmund Street, architect, March 1884. Signed by the contractor Robert Allen, 11 October 1889. © SROI, FC185/E3/3

Plate VII. Blythburgh church roof with angels. The roof escaped restoration in 1881–1906 and was conserved in the 1970s, including the removal of staining caused by treatment with insecticide. Photographed by Alan Mackley

Plate VIII. St Andrew's, Covehithe, and St Andrew's, Walberswick, two grand fifteenth-century churches nearby, comparable with Holy Trinity, Blythburgh, but reduced in size in the seventeenth century because they were too expensive for small communities to maintain. Photographed by Alan Mackley

33. Return of specifications. The Revd H. Sykes to S. Sutherland Safford, 27 August 1882

Walberswick.
27 August 1882

Dear Sir,

Please to send by return if possible the specifications as they may be required before I can get them. Mr Street is asking for tenders for south aisle roof (£600).

Yours faithfully,
(in haste)
[*signed*]   H. Sykes

S.S. Safford, Esq.

34. Request for SPAB report. The Revd H. Sykes to George Wardle, 7 September 1882

Walberswick Vicarage,
Southwold.
7 September 1882

Dear Mr Wardle,

I have just left Mr Debney[29] who has put into my hand a letter from you in which you give £2,000 as the probable cost of real repairs in Blythburgh church.

This sum is slightly in excess of the sum named by Mr Street for the same purposes. The roof and those windows which are considered to be in a dangerous condition are probably all that your society would have done and Mr Street's estimate for those portions and the securing of the parapet on the south aisle is £1,800. So far it is very satisfactory to know that our architect and yours quite agree, but how far their opinions may coincide with respect to other matters must be seen. My object in writing at present is to urge your society to let us have their report as soon as possible. This is very necessary inasmuch as the tenders for some portion of the work are to be sent in today to Mr Street and I expect our committee will have to meet shortly to decide upon them, and I should like to have your report to present before any decision is come to.

I am thankful to say the subscriptions are coming in very satisfactorily at present and encourage me very much.

Yours very truly,
[*signed*]   H. Sykes

George Wardle, Esq.

35. SPAB report. Thomas Wise, SPAB, to the Revd H. Sykes, 27 September 1882[30]

Re. Blythburgh Church

---

[29] Possibly of H.J. Debney and Sons, Family Grocers and General Drapers, of Southwold and Walberswick, with whom Oakes had an account. A link through Walberswick church may be assumed.

[30] An undated draft is in SPAB I, annotated 'To be returned to Thackeray Turner, Secretary, 9, Buckingham

The Society for the Protection of Ancient Buildings,
9 Buckingham Street,
Adelphi.
27 September 1882

To the Revd H. Sykes, Vicar,
Walberswick, Southwold.

Reverend Sir,

The Committee of this Society having considered the report of the two members who visited the church in August last, beg to offer their advice as follows:-

On no account should the repairs be let under one contract. A responsible clerk of works should be appointed with instructions for letting the work by portions to local or other men, who would work under his constant supervision, small portions only being done at one time. By this means a careful superintendence would be possible, the uncovered parts might be well secured from the weather and experience would be gained as the work proceeded from the easier parts to the more difficult. The scaffolding should be a good one but it need not be larger than the largest section undertaken at one time and would be moved on as the work proceeded. A comparatively small scaffold would thus serve for the whole and the church would not be seriously incommoded while the repairs were going on. It may be advisable in some parts of the work to proceed without contract. The clerk of the works would then obtain a schedule of prices for the material scaffolding etc. to be used.

In the first place the foundations of the church should be carefully examined all round, particularly at the north east end of chancel, where the only crack of importance in the solid masonry was noticed. There is evidently a vault or crypt under the north aisle of chancel at its east end. This should be opened and from the crypt the foundation of the cracked wall would probably be seen.

The next work of importance is the repair of <u>all</u> the roofs. This repair must be done with the conviction that to lift any of the roofs would be a dangerous expedient, only to be resorted to in case no other way is possible. This committee is of opinion that all the roofs may be well and solidly repaired without displacement of the timbers. The removal of an aisle roof would be sure to affect the stability of the clerestory. At present the north arcade and clerestory seem perfectly upright, but on the south there is a slight set outwards and that is a strong reason against subjecting this wall to the loss of the abutment and the steadying influence of the aisle roof. The repair of the roofs involves the careful recasting of the old lead. This should be done either in the churchyard or close by, and the plumber should have strict orders to cut out and save all the dates of repairs now existing and to solder them to the new roof after it is laid. The date of the present repair should be marked in a similar way. The lead should be stript, recast and replaced piece meal and *pari passu* with the rest of the roof, i.e. one bay at a time. The same scaffolds set up inside and out would so serve for the whole of the repair at that part. After the lead and boarding of the bay are lifted and a tarpaulin has been carefully fitted over, the woodwork should be examined piece by piece and the perished timbers replaced with new oak. Timbers must not be considered

St., Adelphi'. The final written version is in SROI, FC185 E3 2 Pt 3. It is also in RCMB, as published in the *Suffolk Chronicle*, and *the Ipswich Journal*, 24 March 1883. The SPAB proposals also reflect the report of Philip Webb. See Appendix A 2.

perished so long as there is a sufficient depth of heart wood unaffected. (If sap wood only is decayed, it is evident that removal is not needed). Any new oak that may be inserted must be perfectly plain without moulding or ornament, though the parts to which it joins be finely moulded. It is possible that a great length of the wall plates may need renewal. If the ornamental facia in those lengths of it to be replaced is lost or too much decayed, it must not be reproduced or imitated with new work. Many ornamental parts may be preserved, though partially decayed, so long as the roof be not disturbed, which would be hopelessly lost if the rough and wholesale fashion of removing the old roof for repair were adopted. Should any of the principals of the aisle roofs need strengthening, new oak must be laid on the top and bolted through. In repairing the nave roof, great care should be taken so as not to hurt any of the ancient painting; this is work that cannot be restored. Advantage should be taken of the scaffold to secure any loose pieces of carving and to replace any that have fallen down, the greatest delicacy and tenderness being used in so doing as before said – no attempt must be made to restore with new work any lost parts of the old. As regards the aisle roofs, it would be well, after strengthening unsafe timbers as aforesaid, to lay on the top of the outside face of the common rafters, oak rafters of small scantling, say 3″ x 4″ and 12 inches apart running lengthwise from east and west, and on these rafters new boarding for the lead having rolls 2 ft apart. This new boarding would be a little higher than the present aisle roofs, but there is sufficient space below the clerestory windows and the appearance of the church will not be affected externally. If this plan be adopted, the damaged walling under the clerestory windows must be carefully repaired and prepared for the lead curtains before hand.

In laying the new boarding it would be worth consideration if one drip between wall and gutter might not be got. This would shorten very advantageously the length of the sheets of lead. Memo: The lead should be recast to nothing less than 8 lbs to the foot. One of the most serious causes of mischief to the nave roof has been the want of a ridge roll. For want of this the water has been driven by the wind under the lap of the lead and the plumbers to stop the drift have most unwisely soldered the joint at the lap and have so lost the freedom for expansion and contraction which always goes on, and in consequence the lead has been cracked severely. A ridge roll ought certainly to be supplied and the other repairs executed as described above, but we may say that an intermediate drip between ridge and gutter would be even more advantageous to the nave than to the aisle roofs.

Portions of the lead spouting from the gutters of nave roof to the aisles need repair and perhaps renewal, but of this a careful clerk of works anxious to preserve the most possible of the old building would give instructions. The outlets of the spouts from the aisle roofs ought to be guarded and lead roses provided for the inlets.

The window frames <splaying> and glazing are the <west> next points that demand attention. As the building is evidently subject to very strong winds it would be unwise to remove the wooden transomes which have been placed across the mullions on the inside of some of the aisle windows; indeed, it would be right when any of the other windows show signs of needing such support to put exactly similar transomes across. It is on every ground desirable that the old windows should be disturbed as little as possible and as much of the old tracery be preserved as may by any means be kept together. For this reason we advise you not to remove the wooden mullions which have been inserted in several windows and where the stonework of others is dangerously decayed to repair it only where it is dangerous and not in a wholesale way. By so doing the removal of the old glass will also be avoided. This glass is all very beautiful and the painted glass is most precious. The removal of it from the stonework would be a certain cause of injury to the old tracery, even to the extent of making the entire renewal of it necessary, and the glass itself would suffer as seriously. The repair of the glass therefore, whether white or colored, should be done <u>without removing it</u>. The old lead cames of the painted glass are probably very brittle and the task of repair would be a ticklish one, but if entrusted to an ingenious workman who would aim at nothing beyond strengthening weak places, there is no doubt it could be done. Of course it would be a work of time, one man and his assistant only being employed. New <u>colored</u> glass must not be used to replace defects in the painted work. Powell's strong antique white glass should be used for filling all vacancies after all the bits of old glass, white or colored found in the church have been used up. 'Cathedral Glass' must on no account be used. Merely cracked quarries may be mended by what glaziers call a string. The clerestory windows should be mended on the same plan. In cases where the mullions and tracery of windows are too much decayed or too unsafe to be left with the simple repair we have suggested, it would be better to brick up the openings as has been done in the chancel, making the brickwork flush on the outside. There is more than a sufficiency of light in the church and there is nothing injurious to the effect, in blank panels of brickwork set in a moulded framing; inside, the brickwork would of course be whitewashed. If this course is adopted, the glass taken out will be available for mending the other windows and must be carefully saved for that purpose.

When the roofs and windows are repaired, the essential repairs are almost complete. The plastering of the walls of the church is on the whole in good state and should certainly not be disturbed except in those parts where from the soaking from the roof the plaster may have become rotten. It would be well to postpone the treatment of these cases until the water has had time to dry out and the proof of the unsoundness of the plaster is indisputable. Then, the rotten plaster should be taken off and renewed with <u>thin</u> tough common hair plaster, plainly and neatly trowelled, but not finished with a sandy surface in the modern fashion. This new plaster, when quite dry, should be whitened to match the rest of the church. The holes which have been made in the plastering by the careless use of nails for fixing decorations should be neatly filled up and touched with whitewash when dry, and the use of nails should be prohibited for that purpose henceforth.

The pavement of the church is too good in appearance to be interfered with in any wholesale way. Such parts as have sunk over graves or from settlements must be lifted, the ground levelled with concrete, and the paving relaid. When new tiles are needed, the buff paving bricks used already on the floor ought to be repeated. The memorial stones ought not to be displaced and those of them which have incised patterns and inscriptions ought to be protected from passing feet by matting.

The seats of the church will naturally be considered at a time when such extensive repairs are going on. It is the fashion to condemn all square pews without in every case giving due consideration to the circumstances; whatever may be the wish of the congregation as regards the 4 square deal pews on the north side of the nave, the original seating of the church ought not to be disturbed, even the remains of it. The original sills are easily seen, and all oak framing into these ought to be respected. At the back of the third pew west of the screen on the north side is a piece of an old screen, the end of it in line with the pier on which are the remains of a corbel or bracket. There are corresponding marks and remains on the south side. As the interest that is now growing in all matters of church architecture and archaeology generally is not likely to diminish but increase, all traces of the original disposition of parish churches and other ancient buildings will increase also and we shall be responsible to future times for whatever has been lost or sophisticated by our negligence or act, more than if the thought that such things were interesting had not been born; we ourselves, beginning to appreciate the importance of genuine history, ought to be more scrupulous about preserving it, than those who have no idea that the ways and deeds of former times, can have any value for us, and our scruples should equally protect things we think small as well as the great. For this reason the society hopes that nothing that belongs to the original aspect of this church will be destroyed and that the few mutilated remains of the old seating at the point now mentioned may be preserved. On the north side, plain new oak benches may be put in place of the deal pews, leaving the remains of the old screen untouched. Where there are deal floor boards these may be removed to enable you to get to the damp earth below, which should be dug out and the space filled with concrete, and the boarding made good with oak or elm boards. On the south side after the deal pews were removed, supposing this to be resolved by the parish, the remains of the oak seating should also be kept as they stand for occasional use. The bulk of the congregation will be accommodated, it is presumed, on the north side, as there the old seating is more perfect. As a means of making the congregation more comfortable, of keeping them together and so of helping the reader in such a large church, the committee suggests that a heavy cloth or carpet hanging should be hung on the north and west sides of these seats, say 8 feet high. This could be supported on oak posts with trussed bases, quite moveable and therefore without injury to the fabric. The slight sketch appended will shew what is meant by this.

The old oak choir stalls belonging to the chapel on the north side ought to be replaced – they were removed within the last 20 years and the man who took them away and put them together in the main chancel is we believe still active.[31] He ought to be employed in the replacing of them, but the superintendence of some one who knows what chancels were like in times past and what is the proper arrangement of a choir ought to be engaged to assist his memory. There is also a piece of the chancel screen now in the tower, which must have been removed at about the same time; it belongs to the south half of the screen. This also ought to be replaced, exactly as it before stood.

After the removal of the stall work now in the choir to its proper place, the space may be occupied with new choir seats of the simplest possible construction in solid oak set clear of the pillars. It would be well if the injurious and vulgar altar rail might be removed and a plain moveable rail of solid oak put in place of it. This should stand clear of the walls at each end, and the holes made in the walls by the present rail should be filled up as recommended for the holes caused by the nails used in fixing decorations. If the north, south and east walls of this end of the church could be hung with some heavy stuff of good but quiet color, a look of warmth and richness would be got at slight expense. The hangings should be supported, as those in the north aisle, upon posts standing clear of the walls and should cover the wall up to the sill of the east window.

Outside. The masonry generally is in good condition; on no account should the facings be repointed. Where any facings are loose they should, if shallow, be

---

[31] The stalls were to remain in the choir.

reset with good common mortar not stained with soot or tinted \in any way/ and, if deep, should be run <in any way> in behind with liquid cement and sand as will be described below. Repointing, beyond being injurious to the look of an old building, has the demerit of coming out bodily after a short exposure to frost and weather. The part of the masonry which needs most serious attention is the crested parapet on the south aisle. It will be easily understood that to take down and reset the stones of this parapet would be a most disastrous and costly work. The joints of the old stones have been secured with iron dowels and cramps, and to separate the stones would be to shatter them. Any parts quite loose should be lifted and reset, but the greater part must be dealt with differently. Proceed in this way: after cleaning out the joints without disturbing the stones or lichen, the outside faces should be stopped with stiff clay, and liquid Portland Cement, mixed with about one third to one half of fine sharp sand, should be poured into the beds and joints, and a piece of hoop iron or a wire should be used to work the cement fairly into the joints. This is a tedious work, but if carefully performed will be the saving of the old parapet; its success will depend on the patience and faithfulness of the mason and on the good quality and carefully adjusted proportions of the cement and sand. The cement should be of the slower setting kind, and the joints should be well wetted before the cement is run in. Every year in the thorough examination of the building this parapet ought to be specially looked to and weak parts treated as described. Only small portions of the other parapets would need lifting and resetting, the north pinnacle of chancel may be noted – but all the coping stones should be run with cement as above described. It will be of course understood that the clay is used in this process only as a dam or stop for the cement while in the liquid state, and that it must be removed when the cement is set.

From the above remarks it will be understood that the committee of the Society for \the/ <Protecting> \Protection of/ Ancient Buildings considers that after the foundations have been attended to, the repair of the roofs and the recasting and relaying of the lead should follow as being of next importance. These works involve considerable cost but they are vital in respect of the security of the building and should not be delayed. Otherwise, the church is generally in a substantial condition and there is no reason why money subscribed for its repair should be used for any of the purposes usually included in a scheme of 'Restoration'.

The committee of the Society for the Protection of Ancient Buildings will very gladly give any further advice or explanation that may be desired.

I am, Sir,

    Your obedient servant,

[*signed*]   Thomas Wise
          Secretary

36. Acknowledgement of SPAB report. The Revd H. Sykes to Thomas Wise, SPAB, 28 September 1882[32]

/Blythburgh Church. Received 2/10/82. Answered/

Walberswick Vicarage,
Southwold.
28 September 1882

---

[32] For the SPAB report see Appendix A 6.

Dear Sir,

I beg to acknowledge, with thanks 'Report on Blythburgh Church' from the 'Society for the Protection of Ancient Buildings' and will lay it before our committee at the meeting to be held on Monday next.

Yours respectfully,

[*signed*]   H. Sykes

Thomas Wise, Esq., <u>Secretary</u>

37. SPAB report and Blythburgh committee. The Revd H. Sykes to Thomas Wise, SPAB, 2 October 1882

/<u>Blythburgh Church 1208</u> Received 4 Oct/82/

Walberswick Vicarage,
Southwold.
October 2 1882

Dear Sir,

I brought your 'Report' before our committee today and they beg your society to accept their best thanks for the interest they take in our grand old church of Blythburgh. Discussion, however, is deferred to another meeting and in the meantime the report will go round to the members of our committee for their private perusal.

Yours faithfully,

[*signed*]   H. Sykes, vicar and chairman

[*Thomas*] Wise, Esq., Secretary to the 'Society for the Protection of Ancient Buildings'

38. Request for reaction to SPAB report. Thomas Wise, SPAB, to A.G. Hill, 14 November 1882

14 November 1882
A.G. Hill Esq.,
   47 Belsize Avenue.

Dear Sir,

Blythburgh Church

The committee of this society being informed that you are on the restoration committee of Blythburgh church apply to you as a member of this society for information as to how this society's report has been received.[33] Mr Sykes wrote some time ago to inform the committee that the report was under consideration but as nothing further has been heard from him I am desired to ask you how far their report was brought before your committee and how the whole matter of the restoration at present stands.

Trusting you will be able to furnish this information.

I am, dear Sir,

   Yours faithfully,

---

[33]   This letter confuses the Blythburgh restoration committee formed by Sykes with the London committee established by S. Sutherland Safford. See Correspondence 12.

[*signed*]   Thomas Wise
                    Secretary

39. SPAB report. Arthur G. Hill to Thomas Wise, SPAB, 15 November 1882

/ Blythburgh Church. Received 16/11/82. Answered /

47 Belsize Avenue,
Hampstead, N.W.
15 November 1882

Dear Sir,

I am sorry to say that I have received no information concerning the way in which the SPAB's report on Blythburgh church was received by the 'restoration committee' of that place.

Although I am a member of the committee – which I joined so as to have a hand, if possible, in averting the 'restoration' – I have never attended any meetings of the same, having never received any notice that such were to be held.

I have written to Mr Sykes, asking for information concerning the reception of the SPAB's report, but shall not receive an answer for a day or two, as I have lost his address, and have had to write through a friend.

When I do, I will communicate with you again.

Sincerely yours,
[*signed*]   Arthur G. Hill

Thomas Wise, Esq.
Society for Protection of Ancient Buildings

40. Newspaper cutting. Appeal for funds. The Revd H. Sykes to the *Ipswich Journal*, 10 January 1883, published 13 January

BLYTHBURGH CHURCH RESTORATION

SIR, – When so many appeals are being made for similar objects it is only right that reasons should be shewn for the proposal to restore another church.

First and foremost, we are driven out of our accustomed place of worship and are obliged to hold our services in the school-room, where the fixed desks and low seats, although ample for children, are most uncomfortable for adults. The arrangements for the administration of the Sacraments are far from satisfactory, and we long to return to the house of God in which provision has hitherto been found for the due order of Divine service.

Our second reason justifies us in making an appeal to the county at large. It is quite true that for less than one half of the sum required for the restoration of the old church we might have built a small one far more suitable for the needs of the present population, but we could not have looked for support outside the parish in an attempt to provide for our own comfort and convenience, and at the same time allowing one of the finest and noblest of our national churches to fall into ruins.

We consider we are responsible to the whole country for the preservation of such a rare specimen of the Perpendicular style of architecture. There is not to be found in all the kingdom a finer and more beautiful country parish church, and were we, without any adequate effort to prevent it, to allow this noble pile to become a heap of ruins, we should deserve the execrations of the hundreds of visitors who invariably find fault with the Vicar, the lay rector, or the lord of the manor for allowing the church to fall into such a state of dilapidation. Now that we are rising to a sense of our duties, and endeavouring to wipe out the 'scandal'* which attaches to us, we feel we have a claim upon the sympathies of all admirers of ancient buildings, and trust the many promises of support given, in order to urge us to make the attempt, will be fulfilled, and that others, being made acquainted with the circumstances of the case, will come forward and help us with their contributions, and we assure them that the funds entrusted to us shall be well and wisely spent.

As soon as the weather permits, the contractor will commence the actual work of restoration, and before next Christmas, so much will, we hope, be accomplished as to satisfy the subscribers that the Committee and their architect are well able to lay out economically the funds entrusted to them.

The Vicar could fill a large space in your valuable columns with the encouraging letters he is receiving from all parts of the diocese, and he hopes that all who take an interest in this truly great and necessary undertaking, will respond early to the appeal which is made in your advertising columns.

Let us all bear in mind (1) that we have no church fit for the worship of Almighty God; (2) that we desire to discharge our solemn responsibility to preserve this fine old building from imminent ruin; and (3) we cannot do this without external help.

Hoping to add from time to time additional particulars of our proceedings,

I remain, yours respectfully,

[*signed*]   H. SYKES

Walberwick Vicarage,

January 10th, 1883.

• See Dr. Raven's paper in the 'Proceedings of the Suffolk Archaeological Institute'.[34]

41. Request for work programme. George Wardle to Thomas Wise, SPAB, 14 January 1883

/Received 15/1/83. Answered Blythburgh Church/

Charlotte Street, Bedford Square.

14 January 1883

Dear Mr Wise,

I enclose a cutting from newspaper about Blythburgh. Will you write to Mr Sykes – vicar – in the name of the society and ask him to kindly inform us whether the works he proposes to begin so soon as the weather is fit are those recommended to him by the society or those which were described in Mr Street's specification.

Very truly yours,

[*signed*]   George Wardle

Keep note of the name of the newspaper; it is perhaps the one we ought to send communications to regarding church matters in eastern counties.

---

[34]   J.J. Raven, 'Blythburgh', *PSIAH* 4 (1874).

42. Request for response to SPAB proposals. Thomas Wise, SPAB, to the Revd H. Sykes, 17 January 1883

17 January 1883

The Revd H. Sykes,
    Walberswick Vicarage.

Dear Sir,

Re <u>Blythburgh Church</u>

The committee of this society notices from your letter in the papers that the works in connection with Blythburgh church are shortly to be commenced. [*?words*] they have not yet had any intimation of the amount of sympathy felt by the restoration committee with the suggestions of the society they will be exceedingly glad to know as far as possible the nature of the proposed work. Allow me, therefore, to ask, on behalf of the committee, if you will be so good as to let me know whether the works now proposed to be carried out are those recommended in the society's letter to you of the [*blank*].

    I am, dear Sir,
    Yours faithfully,
[*signed*]   Thomas Wise
                Secretary

43. Rejection of SPAB proposals. The Revd H. Sykes to Thomas Wise, SPAB, 22 January 1883[35]

/Blythburgh Church. Received 23/1/83. Answered/

Walberswick Vicarage,
Southwold.
22 January 1883

Dear Sir,

In answer to your inquiries respecting Blythburgh church I have to inform you that the portion of work to be first undertaken is from the plans and specifications of Mr Street, a copy of which, I believe, your society possesses. You will also find it specified at the head of the slip accompanying the enclosed circular.[36]

    Your society's report was carefully perused by every member of the building committee and all felt how deeply we were indebted to your society for the kindly interest taken in our church and its preservation so clearly indicated in the very elaborate and carefully drawn up report you have presented.[37]

    From a purely theoretical point of view your proposals are undoubtedly admirable but practically we regret to say, they are simply inadmissible. Take for example your proposed treatment of the windows. As the object of your society is the protection of

---

[35] This letter was reprinted in *The Architect*, 10 March 1883, together with Correspondence 53, under the heading: 'BLYTHBURGH CHURCH'. The following letters from the Secretary of the Society for the Protection of Ancient Buildings and from the Revd H. Sykes, the vicar, concerning Blythburgh Church, suggest the differences between the advocates and the opponents of restoration:- I *The Society's Theory'* and II *The Vicar's reply to the Society'*. In *The Architect*'s version the SPAB is incorrectly described as the Society for the Preservation of Ancient Buildings.

[36] Presumably the appeal leaflet dated 15 August 1882. See Appendix B I, 2.

[37] There are no references in the RCMB to the SPAB or the report.

ancient <u>work</u> your proposals are just what we might expect them to be, but you will not be surprised to find that they run counter to our ideas of restoration.

Again, we consider the church has been disfigured long enough by 'transomes' and 'bricked-up windows', and I am sure it would be most repugnant to the feelings of the parishioners and to the notions of the general public, to see the fine old church further disfigured with such unsightly make-shifts. Were your scheme carried out the ultimate result would be that every window must be walled up and the building rendered useless as a place of worship.

Our object in restoration is to preserve this noble edifice from the ruin which is imminent and to make it again fit and becoming for the worship of Almighty God – an object compared with which, purely scientific fancies must sink into insignificance.

I cannot think that many members of your society would like such a scheme as you propose to be applied to a place of worship they attend. Let them bring the matter home and ask themselves if they could bear to see their church, or chapel disfigured with unsightly 'transomes' and 'bricked-up windows' and adorned with 'posts' and 'curtains' such as you suggest.

From some expressions used in your report you evidently anticipate that your proposals will not coincide with our notions of restoration and you will quite understand that we should not feel justified in appealing to the country for funds to carry out such a scheme as you propose.

Could your society guarantee the money necessary for such a purpose then it might be a question whether it would not be wise on the part of our committee to place the business in your hands and apply themselves to raising funds for a chapel of ease.

Till some proposition of this kind be made to us we feel we must adhere to the course recommended by our architect and trust that a liberal response will be made to our appeal from every part of the country and to the list of subscriptions already published we shall be most happy to add a donation, however small, from the 'Society for the Protection of Ancient Buildings'.

With many thanks for the interest your society has taken in our proceedings.

I remain,

Yours most respectfully,

[*signed*]   H. Sykes

Thomas Wise, Esq.
Secretary etc.

44. Proposed letters to newspapers. Thomas E. Wardle to [?Thomas Wise], [?1] February 1883

The Society for the Protection of Ancient Buildings,
9, Buckingham Street, Adelphi, W.C.

Thursday Morning 9.45

Sir

I have called here at Mr Wardle's request to bring you the enclosed letter, which he requires you to make two copies from, one for the Suffolk Chronicle and the other for the Ipswich Journal, also to bring them over the first thing tonight and should they pass you will see that they are posted before six o'clock at the district post office.

[*signed*]   Thomas E. Wardle

/February 1883/

45. Statement of SPAB position. Draft letter SPAB to the editors of the *Ipswich Journal* and the *Suffolk Chronicle*, February 1883, unsigned[38]

(not to be sent to the Norfolk News)
    To the editors {Ipswich Journal
               {Suffolk Chronicle
    Both published at Ipswich on Saturdays

Blythburgh Church

Sir,

The committee for the restoration of Blythburgh church appeals 'to all lovers of the grand and beautiful in architecture, to help in raising funds for the preservation of this noble edifice from the ruin which is imminent.'

The Society for the Protection of Ancient Buildings was not slow to offer its assistance. A careful survey was made and a report sent to the building committee. This report described with great minuteness every source of present danger to the fabric, and the best means for <preventing> repairing and checking decay.

The recommendations of the report were all founded on a long experience in dealing with ancient buildings, and were in the strictest sense practical. The cost of the repairs <recommended by the society> as estimated by the society would amount to £2,000, or perhaps £3,000. These recommendations were in all senses too moderate for the committee, whose professed intention was but the 'preservation of the building from ruin'. At least £5,000 would be required under the plan that has been adopted, and as Mr Street said to the vicar, 'There is no limit to what may be spent on such a church,' if the kind of expense he proposed were indulged in. Mr Street's proposals were of the stereotyped sort, familiar to all who have known anything of restoration for the last 20 years. New windows, new roof, new plaster on the walls, the more or less complete renewal and entire modernizing of the church; for such treatment is modernization, call it by what other name you will. Take for example the windows: the mullions and greater part of the tracery will be taken out and new stone work substituted, the new being in sort a copy of the old, but still new in material and workmanship. How much loss of refinement and beauty this change alone will bring, only those who can distinguish modern work from ancient are competent to say. Between 15th century stone cutting and that of today the difference, <as are> as <between> works of art, is <in a sense> infinite, and with this difference, the preservation by <the> copying of traceries so refined as those of Blythburgh is an impossibility. We are aware that Mr Street did not agree with the society in this opinion, <but> that he thought stone cutting below the rank of carving, a mechanical art, and as well done now as ever. Unfortunately as respects modern stone cutting he had but too much reason for <his opinion> thinking it mechanical. As regards ancient work <the opinion is> he was obviously and strangely wrong. You have but to look at the windows of Blythburgh church to be convinced of this, if you can look with eyes sensitive to delicacies of curvature and accustomed to comparisons of size and shape. These windows <were never made by geometrical rules nor> have no geometrical

---

[38]   For the published letter see Correspondence 53.

exactness, nor any uniformity, <except in> though all are made from one or two designs.

The first appeal of the restoration committee is for £1,049 10s. 6d., to be <chiefly> partly spent in the destruction and renewal of the windows <whereas protection instead of a less ?happy> which, under a more protective treatment, <they> might remain <original and> with their glass and ironwork for the pleasure and instruction of those who really love what is beautiful in architecture for 200 years to come. How this might be done the report of the society carefully described, and the vicar acknowledges that 'its object being the protection of ancient work, the proposals of the society were just what might have been expected,' though 'they run counter to his ideas of restoration.' This is quite true. They are contrary to <u>all</u> ideas of restoration, they are conceived purely in the spirit of preservation, the purpose which the committee professes to have in view.

As a miserable consequence of the removal of the ancient stone-work of these windows, the old glass will also be sacrificed. This is of three kinds. There are in all the windows some remains of the original glazing, beautiful stained and painted glass, the leading of which is in a very tender condition, needing the greatest delicacy in <its> handling, but nevertheless capable of repair without disturbance. This old glass will be taken out, and what is not lost will be \cleaned/, re-leaded, <cleaned and put back in again as new and perh> and perhaps, rearranged. There <were> are here and there, but chiefly in the clearstory, remains of the old, quarry glazing, the glass being of very beautiful tint and quality; and there is the later glazing of poorer glass comparatively, but still of much better kind than church restorers are in the habit of using – infinitely better than the so-called cathedral glass prescribed in Street's specification. This 'cathedral glass,' it may be explained to the uninitiated, has no right to the name, other than what a prudent inventor had <it> in his power to give to his own production. It is the most offensive and vulgar of all known glazing materials. It is unlike ancient glass in all essentials of beauty, <and it is past belief for some reason it finds favour with those who see no difference between ancient and modern art> but it is nevertheless the chosen material with those who presume to 'restore' our ancient buildings. With this and such like vulgarities we are asked to replace the beautiful architecture of Blythburgh <church> , and to make <it> this noble church 'again fit for the worship of Almighty God.'

In the last 200 years this church, as finally left by the Reformation, has not been thought by bishop or clergy or congregation unfitted for its holy purpose, and it has not yet lost the sanctity of ancient origin, and of a beauty almost like that of nature. The new modernized church which will come out of this restoration will appeal only to a temporary fancy, and to undiscerning tastes.

The society would gladly save this noble building from a fate which has befallen so many of the most precious monuments of ancient art, but it has failed so often it almost despairs of being able to impress <on> those responsible for the preservation with the real nature of the duty that lies before them.

It remains for the subscribers to say /over/ whether the funds they contribute shall be spent in the <u>preservation</u> of the church, or in the delusive and mischievous pretence of <u>restoration</u>.

46. Letters to newspapers. Thomas Wise, SPAB, to George Wardle, 5 February 1883

5 February 1883

G.Y. Wardle Esq.,
  9 Charlotte Street,
    W.C.

Dear Sir,

re <u>Blythburgh Church</u>

I send you, as requested, the papers and letters on the above subject.
  Yours faithfully,
[*signed*]   Thomas Wise
        Secretary

P.S. I cannot place my hand on your abstract of Mr Street's report but I fancy I have a paper or two on the subject.

/Enclosure/

47. Abstract of A.E. Street's report. Thomas Wise, SPAB, to George Wardle, 6 February 1883

6 February 1883

G. Y. Wardle Esq.,
  9 Charlotte Street,
    W.C.

Dear Sir,

re <u>Blythburgh Church</u>

I send by this post the remaining papers on the above subject among which is, I think, your abstract of Mr Street's report.
  Yours faithfully,
[*signed*]   Thomas Wise
        Secretary
/Enclosure/

48. SPAB Report. Thomas Wise, SPAB, to editor of the *Suffolk Chronicle*, 14 February 1883

14 February 1883

The Editor,
  The Suffolk Chronicle.
    8 Princes Street,
      Ipswich.

Sir,

The committee of the above society would be greatly obliged if you could find room in your next issue to insert the enclosed letter on Blythburgh church.

I should be obliged if you would kindly send me a copy of the paper when published.

Yours obediently,

[*signed*]   Thomas Wise

    Secretary

/Enclosure/

49. SPAB Report. Thomas Wise, SPAB, to editor of the *Ipswich Journal*, 14 February 1883

14 February 1883

The Editor,

    The Ipswich Journal,

        Princes Street.

Sir,

The committee of the above society would be greatly obliged if you would kindly insert in your next issue the enclosed letter on Blythburgh church.

I should be greatly obliged if you would forward me a copy of the paper when published.

Yours obediently,

[*signed*]   Thomas Wise

    Secretary

/Enclosure/

50. Appeal for funds. The Revd H. Sykes to F.C. Brooke, 15 February 1883[39]

Walberswick Vicarage,

Southwold.

15 February 1883

Dear Sir,

May I ask you to give us a helping hand in this great undertaking?

The need is pressing that something be done to save our beautiful old church from further decay.

The parish is a poor one and we are utterly unable to raise the necessary funds. We are therefore appealing to a very wide circle for assistance in our great but necessary undertaking.

For 15 months our church has been closed as unfit for the Sunday services, and we are obliged to hold them in the school-room which is unsuited for the purpose, and very uncomfortable for the congregation.

The contracts for the first portion of the work are being signed (see slip) and when completed (Sep 30) we shall be able to return to our dear old church and the rest will be proceeded with as the funds come in.

To complete all that is needed to render the church secure and suited for Divine worship, we shall require a further sum of nearly £4,000 and towards this large sum we shall be most thankful to receive the smallest contributions.

On behalf of the committee, I beg to be, dear Sir,

---

[39] Brooke.

Yours very respectfully,
[*signed*]   H. Sykes

F.C. Brooke, Esq.,
   Ufford Place,
      Woodbridge.

51. Restoration of Blythburgh Church. George Wardle to *The Athenaeum*, 17 February 1883[40]

BLYTHBURGH CHURCH

VISITORS to Southwold, among whom are many artists, will hear with regret that the beautiful church of Blythburgh is about to be subjected to 'restoration.' The usual course is proposed. As a first step all the windows are to be renewed. The windows at Blythburgh are peculiarly beautiful and delicate examples of a time not always associated in popular estimation with delicacy and beauty. Perpendicular architecture is usually called stiff and mechanical.[41] Blythburgh church is a convincing proof that these faults do not unavoidably belong to the style. The plan of the church is extremely simple. The nearly flat roof extends without break from tower to east end, about 130 feet. The arcade is peculiarly fine in proportion and in the sweep of the arches. There is no chancel arch. The aisles are nearly the full length of the church. There are seven windows on each side, of which ten are of one pattern, and the rest but of slightly different design. There is no carving inside except for the seats and font; yet with this simple plan and the few elements of variety we have mentioned the church is full of architectural beauty. The moulding of the arches and capitals, the easy and beautifully modulated lines of the cusping of the windows, the perfect feeling for surface everywhere, give such a sense of finish as makes this spacious building one of the most refined and impressive of its type.

The degradation with which it is threatened will begin by the substitution of dull mechanical masonry for the beautiful and thoroughly artistic stonework of the windows. This degradation is certain, if the intention is to replace the old traceries and mullions by modern stone masonry is persisted in. The destruction of last century glass will accompany the destruction of the stone framing; and in lieu of it, that precious and strictly modern variety called cathedral glass will be substituted. Perhaps, as at Southwold Church, lately restored, the pinky-greeny-yellowy kind may be used. The ancient iron-work will go with the glass and the stone. Artists will appreciate the difference these changes will make in the character of the building.

As funds allow, other parts of the church will be dealt with in similar fashion; the walls will be new plastered, the floor laid with the inevitable encaustic tiles, and, in the usual way, a church which, sadly maimed, is still a most precious work of art, will become a vulgar parody of itself.

---

[40] RCMB. Part of this letter was reprinted in the *East Anglian Daily Times*, 21 February 1883: 'BLYTHBURGH CHURCH. G. W. writes in the Athenaeum: Visitors to … parody of itself.' Brooke. See Correspondence 56 and 58 for the Revd Henry Sykes's response.

[41] J. Mordaunt Crook in *The Dilemma of Style* (1987), p.151, summarises the antipathy of the ecclesiologists of the first half of the nineteenth century towards the Perpendicular style, quoting Ruskin's description of it as 'weak, dangerous [and] disagreeable'. By the 1870s, however, Perpendicular was described as the climax of Gothic art.

To those who do not know Blythburgh, we may say that the church was built for a large congregation, and that the decay of the town has left it but a very small one. Instead of a thousand people on Sunday there may be not more than twenty or thirty. It would have better befitted the circumstances of the place if a very modest repair of the building had been proposed. The committee asks for 5,000*l*.; probably half that sum would do all that is needed for useful repair. The Society for Protecting Ancient Buildings has made a careful survey, and provided the building committee with a full description of what is needed and how it ought to be done. If the instructions it gives were followed, the church might be put into a durable state of repair, all injurious defects made good, and, except for the absence of damp and decay, there would be no sign that any alteration had been made. The church would remain the same building in fact and appearance that we have received from our predecessors. Unfortunately, the advice which would have led to this desirable result has been rejected, and the more costly and destructive plan adopted.

G[*eorge*] W[*ardle*]

52. Acknowledgement of donation. The Revd H. Sykes to F.C. Brooke, 19 February 1883[42]

Walberswick Vicarage,
Southwold.
19 February 1883

Dear Sir,

Accept my best thanks for your kind and liberal donation.[43]

I may just \add/ with reference to the 'roof' and other portions of the building that the committee have steadily set before them the securing of the structure from the effects of wind and water – security first, comfort and convenience second.

In all things preserving all we can of the original material and inserting new only where absolutely necessary.

Yours very gratefully,
[*signed*]   H. Sykes

F.C. Brooke, Esq.,
Ufford Place,
Woodbridge.

53. Newspaper cutting. Statement of SPAB position. Thomas Wise, SPAB, to editor of the *Ipswich Journal*, published 20 February 1883[44] [45]

BLYTHBURGH CHURCH

SIR, – The Committee for the restoration of Blythburgh Church appeals to all lovers of the grand and beautiful in architecture, to help in raising funds for the preservation of this noble edifice from the ruin which is imminent.

The Society for the Protection of Ancient Buildings was not slow to offer its

---

[42] Brooke.
[43] Five pounds in the list published 10 March 1883.
[44] Also in RCMB and Brooke (the version printed in the *Ipswich Journal* on 24 February 1883).
[45] See n. 35 to Correspondence 43 concerning the reprinting of letters in *The Architect*.

assistance. A careful survey was made and a report sent to the building committee. This report described with great minuteness every source of present danger to the fabric, and the best means for repairing and checking decay. The recommendations of the report were all founded on a long experience in dealing with ancient buildings, and were in the strictest sense practical. The cost of the repairs as estimated by the Society would amount to £2,000, or perhaps £3,000. These recommendations were in all too moderate for the Committee, whose professed intention was but the preservation of the building from ruin. At least £5,000 would be required under the plan that has been adopted, and as Mr. Street said to the Vicar, 'There is no limit to what may be spent on such a church,' if the kind of expense he proposed were indulged in. Mr. Street's proposals were of the stereotyped sort, familiar to all who have known anything of restoration for the last 20 years. New windows, new roof, new plaster on the walls, the more or less complete renewal and entire modernizing of the church; for such treatment is modernization, call it by what other name you will. Take for example the windows: the mullions and greater part of the tracery will be taken out and new stone work substituted, the new being in sort a copy of the old, but still new in material and workmanship. How much loss of refinement and beauty this change alone will bring, only those who can distinguish modern work from ancient are competent to say. Between 15th century stone cutting and that of to-day the difference, as works of art, is infinite, and with this difference, the preservation in copying of traceries so refined as those of Blythburgh is an impossibility. We are aware that Mr. Street did not agree with the Society in this opinion, that he thought stone cutting below the rank of carving, a mechanical art, and as well done now as ever. Unfortunately as respects modern stone cutting he had but too much reason for thinking it mechanical. As regards ancient work he was obviously and strangely wrong. You have but to look at the windows of Blythburgh church to be convinced of this, if you can look with eyes sensitive to delicacies of curvature and accustomed to comparison of size and shape. These windows have no geometrical exactness, nor any uniformity, though all are made from one or two designs.

The first appeal of the Restoration Committee is for £1,049 10s. 6d., to be partly spent in the destruction and renewal of the windows which, under a more protective treatment, might remain with their glass and ironwork for the pleasure and instruction of those who really love what is beautiful in architecture for 200 years to come. How this might be done the report of the Society carefully described, and the Vicar acknowledges 'that its object being the preservation of ancient work, the proposals of the Society were just what might have been expected,' though 'they run counter to his ideas of restoration.' This is quite true. They are contrary to all ideas of restoration. They are conceived purely in the spirit of preservation, the purpose which the Committee professes to have in view.

As a miserable consequence of the removal of the ancient stone-work of these windows, the old glass will also be sacrificed. This is of three kinds. There are in all the windows some remains of the original glazing, beautiful stained and painted glass, the leading of which is in a very tender condition, needing the greatest delicacy in handling, but nevertheless capable of repair without disturbance. This old glass will be taken out, and what is not lost will be cleaned, re-leaded, and perhaps, re-arranged. There are here and there, but chiefly in the clerestory, remains of the old quarry glazing, the glass being of very beautiful tint and quality; and there is the later glazing of poorer glass comparatively, but still of much better kind than church restorers are in the habit of using – infinitely better than the so-called 'Cathedral glass' prescribed in Mr. Street's specification. This 'Cathedral glass,' it may be explained to the uninitiated, has no right to the name, other than what a prudent inventor had in his power to give to his own production. It is the most offensive and vulgar of all known glazing materials. It is unlike ancient glass in all essentials of beauty, but it is nevertheless the chosen material with those who presume to 'restore' our ancient buildings. With this and such like vulgarities we are asked to replace the beautiful architecture of Blythburgh, and to make this noble church 'again fit for the worship of Almighty God.'

In the last 200 years this church, as finally left by the Reformation, has not been thought by Bishop or clergy or congregation unfitted for its holy purpose, and it has not yet lost the sanctity of ancient origin, and of a beauty almost like that of nature. The new modernized church which will come out of this restoration will appeal only to a temporary fancy, and to undiscerning tastes.

The Society would gladly save this noble building from a fate which has befallen so many of the most precious monuments of ancient art, but it has failed so often it almost despairs of being able to impress those responsible for the preservation with the real nature of the duty that lies before them.

It remains for the subscribers to say whether the funds they contribute shall be spent in the preservation of the church, or in the delusion and mischievous pretence of restoration,

Yours faithfully,

THOMAS DIX [*sic*], Secretary.[46]

The Society for the Protection of Ancient Buildings,

9, Buckingham Street, Adelphi, W.C.

February, 1883.

/Ipswich Journal 20/2/83/

54. Newspaper cutting. Reaction to SPAB position statement. The Revd H. Sykes to the *Ipswich Journal*, 21 February 1883, published 24 February[47]

BLYTHBURGH CHURCH

SIR, – My attention has been drawn this evening to the letter of Mr. Wise* in yesterday's issue, but as I have lent the report furnished by the Society he represents, I will postpone any remarks upon the letter referred to till next week. If you will kindly insert the enclosed letter in your issue of Saturday it will be sufficient to shew your readers that there is another side to the picture.

For the present I beg to be

Yours truly,

[*signed*]   H. SYKES

Walberswick Vicarage,

February 21st, 1883.

*   This name was misprinted on Tuesday.

---

46   The *Ipswich Journal* typesetter misread 'Wise'.

47   Below this letter the *Ipswich Journal* printed the letter dated 22 January 1883 from Sykes to the SPAB. See Correspondence 43. Also in Brooke and RCMB.

55. Progress of restoration work. Extract of letter from the Revd H. Sykes to S. Sutherland Safford, 24 February 1883

Extract of letter from the Revd H. Sykes re. Blythburgh, dated 24 February 1883, to S.S. Safford.

I may just add here that the contractor has signed the contracts and is pushing forward the work of restoration.

He hopes in a few <days> weeks to have some of the windows completed. I called the other day at his works and found five men engaged on the stone work.

Mr Allen has erected a scaffold (moveable) inside the church to take dimensions of the wood work of the south aisle roof, and by the end of September we hope to see the first portion of the work completed.

56. Restoration plans and dispute with the SPAB. The Revd H. Sykes to F.C. Brooke, 27 February 1883[48]

Walberswick Vicarage,
Southwold.
27 February 1883

Dear Sir,

I am pleased to find you are so deeply interested in the restoration of Blythburgh church and shall be glad to give you every information I possess with reference to it.

If you could meet <you> me at the church at some time convenient to yourself I might be able to explain matters more fully than I am able to do in a letter. In the meantime you will be interested to know what is the exact position of affairs.

Contracts are signed by the contractor himself and will be signed by myself and churchwardens probably today. They would have been signed yesterday but I was not able to meet them for the purpose. Sir John has not signed I believe, for the chancel portion, though the contract has been altered to meet his own suggestions.

The first portion of the work will be for the purpose of keeping out the wind and water and includes the south aisle roof, the parapet on the south front and those windows which are not already bricked up. These are all in a dangerous condition and in consequence we have, with the bishop's permission, <we have> held our services in the school-room.

The next portion will be the north <N.> aisle roof and probably the nave roof. These are in a bad state. Though the nave roof in some parts of it is very good, yet there are other parts requiring attention.

When the roof is completed other portions of the building such <at> as the bricked up windows the flooring and seating of the church must be considered.

There may be a difference of opinion as to the desirability of <tiling> paving with encaustic tiles. The bishop's opinion is in favour of the common sort, which is an alternative suggested by the architect.

I may say here, that our sole reason for selecting the \late/ G.E. Street, Esq., was because we were assured 'He knows better how to touch old without disinchanting them of their own special character than, perhaps, any living architect.' This extract

---

48 Brooke.

is from a letter of the 30th September 1881 written in answer to several questions I addressed to the Revd Sidney Pelham, then vicar of Saint Peter Mancroft, Norwich.

I met the late George E. Street and his son in the church and told them our wishes were that every portion of the old work, both in stone and wood, should be scrupulously preserved and new inserted only where the old was entirely gone or was too much decayed to be retained. I enclose the report which was not quite complete at the father's death and I know from the clerks in Mr Street's office that the son is working from the plans laid down by Mr Street before his death.

Mr Street Junior has carried out the work from his father's plans at Saint Peter Mancroft to the entire satisfaction of the working committee under whose direction the restoration of that church has been completed.

I am writing a letter to the Ipswich Journal which will give you an idea what is my dispute with the 'Society for the Protection of Ancient Buildings' and I will say to you privately that I would not have promised a subscription myself to carry out the recommendations of their committee, nor would I have dared to appeal to the country for such an object as they have in view.

I would prefer taking the ease and quiet of my predecessors in the benefice <to> than to aggitate [*sic*] for a scheme which would make our grand old church a laughing stock to all, but the 'artists' <and visitors> 'who visit Southwold' and \which/ would render this house of God unseemly and uncomfortable as a place of worship.

For 50 years this church has been 'a scandal'. Why did not the 'Ancient Buildings Society' interfere to prevent a total wreck till they saw others in the field determined on action? I will mention 'the meeting' you suggest to our local committee and believe me dear Sir

Yours faithfully,
[*signed*]   H. Sykes

F.C. Brooke, Esq.

P.S. These pencil marks were made by the bishop at an interview I had with him January 23 1882.

You will kindly return the 'report' when you have perused it thoroughly and oblige.[49]

H. S

57. Proposal to seek support in Suffolk. George Wardle to Thackeray Turner, SPAB, 27 February 1883

9 Charlotte Street,
Bedford Square.
27 February 1883

Blythburgh Church

Dear Mr Turner,

Please sketch out a letter to be sent after approval by the committee to <Lady St> Lord Stradbroke, Henham Hall, Wangford, Suffolk and Sir John Blois ? ? Suffolk, asking each to use his influence to <stop the> obtain from the restoration committee

---

[49]   The 'pencil marks' refer to G.E. Street's report. See Appendix A 1. It was never returned to Sykes. Brooke died in 1886.

at Blythburgh a <further> fuller consideration of the proposals of the society. Enclose copies of the Athenaeum of last week but one[50], marking the paragraph and give as a reason for not proceeding hastily with the restorations that we <are su> know that the London committee for restoration are wholly ignorant of our proposals and only since the publication of our letters to the Suffolk papers have they learnt that we had made one and that they are anxious to consider it.

Say also we have heard that the works have been actually commenced and that one window is already taken out. Put all this into a polite and politic form and have ready to send if the committee approves.

Very truly yours,

[*signed*]   George Wardle

I will get Sir John Blois's address.

58. Newspaper cutting. Reaction to SPAB position statement. The Revd H. Sykes to the *Ipswich Journal*, 28 February 1883, published 3 March[51]

BLYTHBURGH CHURCH

SIR, – In pursuance of what I promised last week, I beg to give the other side of the picture which I think Mr. Wise has most unfairly represented.

In the first place, the proposals of the 'Society for the Protection of Ancient Buildings' came too late to be of any service to the Restoration Committee. In October, 1881, the late Geo. E. Street, Esq., was engaged by the Committee to inspect the building and report upon the minimum of what was required to be done to insure the safety of the building and render it again suitable and comfortable for Divine worship.

Mr. Street quite understood that we wished to preserve the old work and only to insert new where it was absolutely necessary to secure the above objects.

The opinion of one qualified to judge of Mr. Street's competence for such an undertaking, may be given in a brief extract of a letter addressed to the Vicar, and dated September 30th, 1881:- 'He (Mr. Street) knows better how to touch old buildings without disenchanting them of their own special character than, perhaps, any living architect.'[52]

When Mr. Street's report was presented, the Committee were gratified to find that for £5,000 all they desired could be effected.

It was most important that those parts of the building should be first treated which admitted wind and water, and at the Committee's request the architect prepared plans and specifications for the thorough repair of the South aisle roof, the parapet on the South side, and those windows which required immediate attention. These plans, etc., were adopted by the Committee, passed at a vestry meeting, received the sanction of the Archdeacon, were signed by the Bishop; tenders were invited and received from five builders. All this was done, occupying about eleven months' time before the proposals of the Society which Mr. Wise represents were received. Now, however reasonable their proposals might have been in themselves, they clearly came too late to be considered. It were most unreasonable to expect the Committee to set aside

---

[50] See Correspondence 51.
[51] Also in RCMB.
[52] See Correspondence 56.

their architect and to undo the work of eleven months in deference to the advice of an irresponsible body of men, who at the last moment thought fit to make suggestions. In the second place, not only were these men too late in the field, but the scheme they proposed ran in direct opposition to the object we had in view; and, whether that object was a good one, I will ask your readers to judge, and will give them an extract from the 'Proceedings of the Suffolk Archaeological Institute,' volume IV.[53]

At the close of an ably written paper upon Blythburgh Church, the writer concludes as follows:- 'At the present day, which has seen the restoration of so many houses of God in our land, the condition of Blythburgh Church is a sore scandal. Here is one of the finest churches in Suffolk, in a place of historic note, and surrounded by fair estates, shorn of its architectural ornaments, and reduced to the lowest point of squalor; the nave fitted with rickety pews of the meanest deal; the windows, many of them blocked up with red brick and plaster; the flooring loose and broken; and the whole plentifully smeared with whitewash.'

Now Mr. Wise knows well that the above description of the state of the church is but a faint echo of complaints made long ago, by such writers as Old Gardiner, Wake, and Suckling,[54] and yet this scientific society would perpetuate several parts of the 'scandal' referred to.

The windows, 'blocked up with red brick and mortar,' must not be disturbed, but as time passes on, other windows are treated in the same manner, and yet Mr. Wise tells your readers that if their proposals had been adopted, 'these windows,' many of which are already propped up with unsightly transomes, and others with wooden mullions inserted to sustain the tracery in some cases, and in others ugly brickwork, fitted in with glass of every hue and colour 'might remain with their glass and ironwork . . . for 200 years.' It is more likely, considering the decay which is fast going on, that in far less time than '200 years,' these windows now containing 'old and valuable painted glass,' would, by their scheme being carried out, be replaced throughout by the 'red bricks and mortar,' which go to make up the 'scandal' the Committee are seeking to wipe out. It were impossible to paint the hideous picture which 'this house of God' would present, if treated in the manner suggested by this preserving society.

The stone work of the windows is rapidly decaying and falling down, and yet it does not coincide with their artistic notions that any restoration of the original work should be attempted. They admit that many lengths of the wall plate must be renewed, and that new beams for the roof may be required, but here again they insist that no imitation of the old work must be thought of, but the new beams and plates must be of plain oak, even where they are to join the finely carved and moulded portions.

The flooring must only be repaired with buff coloured paving bricks, and no attempt must be made to imitate the ancient tiles. In short, distinction and not correspondence is the rule to be observed throughout the whole building.

I freely admit that their scheme is consistently carried out in accordance with their notions of artistic propriety. When, however, one reflects that no regard is paid to the seemly appearance of a place of worship, and but scant regard to the comfort and feelings of the congregation, I cannot but think but that there are to be found in the country many who think with us, that the great object which ought to be constantly

---

[53] Raven,'Blythburgh'.
[54] Gardner, *Dunwich*; Wake, *Southwold*; Suckling, *Blything*.

kept in view is to secure the safety of the building and see that the restoration, when completed, shall leave a church consistent in its several parts, and rendered suitable and becoming the worship of Almighty God, even though artistic fancies may in some cases be disregarded.

In conclusion, I will just say that before any other portion of the restoration scheme is decided upon, a meeting of the subscribers to the fund may be called and the opportunity given to those who have proved the sincerity of their affection for the dear old church by the substantial help which is worth a great deal of empty-handed sympathy.

Yours faithfully,

[*signed*]   H. SYKES

Walberswick Vicarage, February 28, 1883.

59. Visit to Blythburgh. The Revd H. Sykes to F.C. Brooke, 2 March 1883[55]

Walberswick Vicarage,
Southwold.
2 March 1883

Dear Sir,

I believe you may take a ticket from Woodbridge to Blythburgh; if not you can book to Halesworth, and then to Blythburgh by the Southwold Railway. The station is close by the church, which is handy for you.

The train you mention as arriving at Darsham \at 11.31/ would not be a convenient one for Blythburgh. I have given on the other side three trains which would serve you better, and when convenient if you will kindly say by which train I may expect you at Blythburgh I shall be pleased to meet you at the station.

I have not seen the letter of Mr Watling's you allude to, could you kindly supply a copy?[56]

I did not come to the parish until June [*18*]79 and was a perfect stranger to Suffolk till then.

Believe me,

Yours very truly,

H. Sykes

F.C. Brook[*e*], Esq.

These times are taken from the latest time table I possess, but I don't think there is any material change beyond a few minutes.

Leaves Woodbridge at

7.36   12.15   2.23

Returning from Blythburgh at

11.15   2.43   5.10

Allowing at Blythburgh about

2¾ hours   1¼ hours   1½ hours

---

55   Brooke.
56   The letter from Hamlet Watling is not in the collection.

60. Request for support. Thackeray Turner, SPAB, to the earl of Stradbroke, 2 March 1883[57]

2 March 1883

To the Earl of Stradbroke

<u>Re Blythburgh Church</u>

My Lord,

I trust you will forgive me for calling your attention to the restoration of the very interesting church of the Holy Trinity at Blythburgh.

The Society for the Protection of Ancient Buildings has done all it can to save this church from the proposed restoration, and I am now writing on the behalf of the society to ask if you will aid it by using your influence to stay the progress of the works which have, I regret to say, been actually begun; some of the windows having been already removed.

This society only desires that the works should not proceed, until the London committee for the restoration of Blythburgh church has had time to consider the society's report.

The London committee were never even informed that we had issued a report and it was only by its publication in the Suffolk papers that they knew of its existence. <u>We now learn that they are very anxious to consider our report</u>.

We trust that if only the present work can be stopped until the Blythburgh London committee have time to consider what we advise should be done, they will approve of our views, and this interesting church will be saved the present destruction with which it is threatened.

In case, my Lord, you should not have seen it, I take the liberty of sending a copy of the 'Athenaeum' with this containing an article on the subject.[58]

I have the honour to remain,

    Your Lordship's most obedient servant,

[*signed*]   Thackeray Turner
              Secretary

61. Draft letters for newspapers. George Wardle to Thackeray Turner, SPAB, undated

Dear Mr Turner

I send draft written for Ipswich Journal and Suffolk Chronicle. Be sure you write very plainly for the Journal. They have a very bad printing staff and will make awful blunders if everything is not very plain.

I think we had better not add that tag to the letter to <Boar> Office of Works. They will reply. [*?*Ask Mr Kershaw about these views] and formed our opinion upon them. Let the letter stand as I have written it.

    Very truly yours,

[*signed*]   G. W.

Send me all papers relating to Blythburgh once more.

---

57   An identical letter was sent to Sir John Blois, Bt.
58   See Correspondence 51.

62. Newspaper cutting. Statement of SPAB position. Thackeray Turner, SPAB, to the *Suffolk Chronicle*, 2 March 1883, published 6 March[59]

BLYTHBURGH CHURCH RESTORATION

To the Editor of the Suffolk Chronicle.

SIR, – The committee of the Society for the Protection of Ancient Buildings has just heard that the restoration at Blythburgh is begun, one of the windows being already taken out. This haste to destroy the beautiful old building is of a piece with the information brought to the Society within these few days, that the London Committee of the Blythburgh Restoration Fund has not seen the report made by this Society, nor was the committee aware that such a report had been made.

When the report was sent to the Vicar, he wrote in grateful terms acknowledging the trouble the Society had taken, and giving the committee to understand that he would postpone any remarks on the report itself until the Building Committee had seen and considered it. Whether any member of that committee has seen it Mr. Sykes knows, but not until many weeks after the receipt of the report, and in reply to our urgent inquiry, did the Society receive the letter Mr. Sykes published last week. The tone of that letter will best show the spirit in which the restoration is being carried on. It may be a good joke to ask the Society to contribute to a work which it has plainly said will be the destruction of a most beautiful and remarkable building, but the earnestness of the Society's efforts to save it ought have secured it from the insult.

This letter will, I fear, be too late for insertion this week. I would, therefore, to prevent confusion, ask your readers to note the date. The letter of Mr. Sykes, which will probably appear on March 3rd, will receive due consideration from the Society.

I am, Sir, etc.,

[*signed*]   THACKERAY TURNER,
           Secretary.

The Society for the Protection of Ancient Buildings, 9, Buckingham Street, Adelphi, W.C.

2nd March, 1883.

[*The Suffolk Chronicle then added:*]
The following is the letter of the Revd H. Sykes, vicar of Walberswick, referred to in the last paragraph of the above letter:-[60]

63. Request for meeting. Thackeray Turner, SPAB, to Sir John Blois, Bt, 9 March 1883

9 March 1883

To Sir John Blois,
     13, Palace Gate, W.

---

[59] A copy of the draft by George Wardle is in SPAB I. See Correspondence 57 for the covering note to Thackeray Turner. The published version is also in RCMB and SROI 2, 2. An identical letter to the *Ipswich Journal* is in Brooke. Brooke wrote on this 'Blythburgh Church. See letter signed H. S(ykes.) in *The Athenaeum* 10 March 1883. pp. 319, 320.'

[60] See Correspondence 58.

Sir,

The committee of this society desires me to ask you if you will consent to meet a small committee, consisting of two gentlemen and myself, especially appointed to see you, to discuss the proposed restoration at Blythburgh?

Should you consent will you oblige me by saying what day and time would be most convenient for you to meet the committee here.

I am also directed to say that in consequence of your visit the committee have withheld this inclosed letter to the local papers.

I am, Sir,

Yours faithfully,

[*signed*]   Thackeray Turner

Secretary.

64. Newspaper cutting. Defence of Blythburgh and attack on SPAB. The Revd H. Sykes to *The Athenaeum*, 27 February 1883, published 10 March[61]

February 27, 1883.

My attention has been drawn to the letter of G.W. in your issue of the 17th;[62] and in defence of those who are engaged in the restoration of the church in question I feel called upon to reply. 'Degradation' and 'destruction' are strong terms to apply to the work the committee have undertaken; but what value is to be put upon such terrible words I will ask your readers to decide when they have read the other side of the question. G. W. speaks of a congregation of 'twenty' or 'thirty' to be accommodated by a 'modest repair' costing not less than 2,500*l.* Now I have been here four years, but in the depth of winter, when the congregation were shivering with cold, and when the minister and school children *needed* the 'protection of umbrellas' during the service, I never saw so small a number present as 'twenty' or 'thirty.' Your correspondent might have been *just*, if not *generous*. The congregation is *small enough,* without dividing the number of attendants by *four*. What shall we get in return for the outlay of 2,500*l.* on the plan laid down by the Society for the Protection of Ancient Buildings I will, as briefly as possible, set before your readers, though the picture can scarcely be realized except by those who are already acquainted with the unsightly appearance of the 'transomes,' the 'woodden mullions,' bricks, mortar, and whitewash, which disgrace the windows at present. Many of the windows are entirely bricked up, the mullions and tracery having been lost altogether, while others are partially filled in with wood, stone, and glass of every hue and quality. All these characteristics which disfigure the building at present are to be carefully preserved, and others that may need it are to be treated in like manner as heretofore. Transomes to be thrown across the windows inside to support what is left of the stonework, and when necessary these are to be removed and the spaces filled in with bricks, plaster, and whitewash. If any of the rich mouldings of the roof and wall-plates are decayed, we must insert plain oak beams or boards; by no means must these be worked to match the old carvings and mouldings. Where new tiles are required for the floor these must be the 'buff-coloured paving bricks' heretofore used. The old oak pews are to be preserved, and round the oak benches in the north aisle is to be hung, for the comfort of this *small* congregation, a heavy cloth or carpet, eight feet high, on

---

[61] Also in RCMB.

[62] See Correspondence 51.

what may be described as 'linen posts and lines.' Then to give the 'look of warmth and richness' to the north, south, and east walls of the chancel, 'a curtain of good but quiet colour' is to be hung, the same height as the other. Whether these hangings and their posts are to come out of the 2,500*l*., or whether they are *extras*, does not clearly appear. I beg to make one extract, which shall be from the *Proceedings* of the Suffolk Archaeological Institute, vol. iv., and your readers may consult such writers as Gardiner, Wake, and Suckling for a confirmation of what is stated. They will then be able to judge between us and our critics, whether their proposals for a 'modest repair' or ours for 'restoration' are more in accordance with the dictates of common sense. The writer concludes an interesting paper as follows:- 'At the present day, which has seen the restoration of so many of the houses of God in our land, the [*The cuttings end here. The remainder of the letter has been transcribed from a copy of The Athenaeum where it continued on another page.*[63]] condition of Blythburgh is a sore scandal. Here is one of the finest churches in Suffolk, in a place of historic note, and surrounded by fair estates, shorn of its architectural ornaments, and reduced to the lowest point of squalor; the nave fitted with rickety pews of the meanest deal; the windows, many of them blocked up with red brick and plaster; the flooring loose and broken; and the whole plentifully smeared with whitewash.

G.W. and his society would perpetuate this 'scandal,' and because our committee seek to remove it they must be held up to the odium of your readers as only capable of reducing 'a most precious work of art' to 'a vulgar parody of itself.' I have also to complain of the *dilatoriness* of G. W. and his associates. Not till Mr. Street's plans had been adopted by the committee, passed at a vestry meeting, sanctioned by the archdeacon, signed by the bishop, tenders invited and received, occupying about eleven months' time, did the society alluded to furnish our committee with their proposals, and they now seem aggrieved that we cannot accept their scheme in preference to the plans drawn up by G.E. Street, Esq., and his son. They would have us disregard the wishes of the parishioners, insult the congregation by utter disregard of their feelings, and represent the vicar of the parish and his churchwardens, the archdeacon of the county, the bishop of the diocese, together with the first architect of his day, as men whose judgement ought to be set aside for the superior scientific acumen of a London society. After reading G. W.'s estimate of his own and his society's superior knowledge, the words of Job struck me forcibly – 'No doubt ye are the people, and wisdom will die with you.'

H. S.

65. Proposed letter to *The Athenaeum*. George Wardle to Thackeray Turner, SPAB, undated but probably 13 March 1883

Dear Mr Turner,
Please send enclosed to the Athenaeum office tomorrow <u>Wednesday</u> as early as you can, with a short note to Norman McColl, the editor, asking him to insert it this week.
   Faithfully yours,
[*signed*]   George Wardle

---

[63]   Thanks are due to Mr Oliver Henderson Smith, of City University, London, for locating and copying this item.

66. Defence of SPAB position. Draft letter Thackeray Turner, SPAB, to the editor of *The Athenaeum*, 14 March 1883[64]

Blythburgh Church

14 March 1883

To the Editor of the Athenaeum.

Sir, In a letter you published last week about the restoration of Blythburgh church, H. Sykes accuses the Society for Protecting Ancient Buildings of dilatoriness in offering advice. He says 'not till Mr Street's plans had been adopted by the committee, passed at a vestry meeting, sanctioned by the archdeacon, signed by the bishop, tenders invited and received, occupying about eleven months' time, did the society furnish him with their proposals.'

The proposals of the society were furnished in September last and in August <thi> a deputation from the society met Mr Sykes, the vicar, in the church. At that meeting Mr Sykes gave no hint that any of the things detailed above had been done nor did he suggest that a <the> report <he understood would be made> at that stage would be too late. On the contrary, he seemed anxious to see it and when the report was sent in he said <he said> in acknowledgement, that it was laid before his committee but discussion deferred until another meeting 'and in the meantime the report will go round to the members of our committee for their private perusal.' < ??? > A quite useless formality if all that H. S. <says> describes had then been <then> done.

H. S. suggests that the eleven previous months had been lost by the society. The projected restoration was only heard of by the committee in January 1882 and in that month a survey of the church was made. Immediately after, the committee asked leave of Mr Street to discuss with him the best course to be taken for the repair. This discussion was avoided on the plea that the plans were not then matured. A second application was made <and new information was promised> and after some time an abstract of the architect's scheme was supplied to the society. This abstract was so imperfect that the society asked for a full copy, for which it offered to pay, and when this was received the summer was far advanced.

In this way the society was prevented from acting. However, when Mr Street's report was at last in the hands of the committee it had instant attention and <would be> the <report> recommendations of the society would have at once been made, but Mr Street's <report> proposals were so far from what the committee expected that a second inspection of the church was thought desirable before the opinions of the society were expressed. The second inspection was made in August and in the course of the next month the very full report of the society was completed and sent.

This is the reply of the committee to the accusation that it was both dilatory and too late. To <H. S.> the very grotesque description of <the> our report which H. S. has not thought it unbecoming of his position to make, the best answer will be the publication of the report itself. <The committee would be obliged if you would allow this next week.> If you <would> will kindly allow this, the committee thinks it would <be useful> not be without interest to all your readers who are interested in the preservation of ancient buildings, as showing what kind of repair the society rec- ommends <and when it could have> and how it would avoid that foolish competition

---

[64] Drafted by George Wardle.

with ancient workmen on their own ground which is complacently called <by its> 'restoration' <by those who>.

I have the honour to be,
Sir,
Your obedient servant,
[*To be signed*]   Thackeray Turner
Secretary

67. Concerning meeting. Telegram Sir John Blois, Bt, to Thackeray Turner, SPAB, 16 March 1883

[*From*] Sir John Blois, 13 Palace Gate.
[*Addressed to*] Thackeray Turner Esq., 9 Buckingham Street, Adelphi.

Much regret that a severe cold prevents my meeting committee today hope to meet early next week.

68. Concerning meeting. Thackeray Turner, SPAB, to Sir John Blois, Bt, 16 March 1883

16 March 1883

To Sir John Blois Bart.

Sir,
I beg to acknowledge the receipt of your telegram just received and to thank you for the same.

As my committee consider the affair of Blythburgh church very urgent I shall be much obliged if you will inform me, as soon as your present indisposition has left you (which I trust may be soon), what day and hour will be convenient for you to meet them.

As both the members of this subcommittee appointed to meet you are very much pressed by their businesses it would be a great convenience to them if you could make the hour of appointment either 4 or 5 o'clock in the afternoon. Will you forgive me for suggesting that if possible the day of meeting should be next Monday and if not on Monday then on Friday or Saturday.

I have the honour to be,
Sir,
Yours faithfully,
[*signed*]   Thackeray Turner
Secretary

69. Concerning meeting. Lady Eliza Blois to SPAB, 18 March 1883

13 Palace Gate, W.

Dear Sir,
Sir John wishes me to let you know that he is unable to leave the house as his cold still continues. He will write as soon as he is able and make an appointment.

I remain yours truly,

[*signed*]   Eliza Ellen Blois
18 March 1883

70. Draft notes on meeting with Sir John Blois, Bt, unsigned and undated

Sir John Blois Bart called here this morning and said that he had received my letter.[65] That he quite agreed with all <the views which he had seen as laid> the society's views as far as he seen them. That on the receipt of my letter he had seen the contractors and <I think he said that he> had visited the church. All that had at present been done was that one window had been taken out. That the parts which had been taken out were entirely of wood and that the wood was quite rotten. He could not see that the society could object to this being replaced by a stone window.

With the exception of the proposed use of cathedral glass instead of the old he did not know what there was that was going to be done that the society would object to.[66] He seemed to think that the old glass would be better than the new and thought that point might be got over. He gave me his address as 13 Palace Gate.

I said that I was glad that he sympathised with the society but that it seemed to me that judging from the vicar's letter there was no intention whatever of the society's views being complied with. He <said> answered quote: 'The vicar is no one. He is hopeless. He is only a commercial traveller. The bishop appointed him by mistake.'[67]

I think Sir John would attend the next committee meeting if asked. He gave me his London address unasked – 13 Palace Gate. When I named the London Blythburgh committee he said they were no use. He also said he did not wish <these letters> this correspondence in the local papers to go on as would stop subscriptions and that they had only received about £1,000 up to the present time.

I said that I was quite sure that the committee had no ill-feeling in the matter and that their only object was to save the church from being treated in the way in which so many churches have been treated and that they would do all in their power to help restoration committee if they would carry out the society's views.

71. SPAB report on Blythburgh church. Thackeray Turner, SPAB, to the editor of the *Suffolk Chronicle*, 19 March 1883

19 March 1883

To the Editor of the 'Suffolk Chronicle'
Sir, I am directed by the committee of the Society for the Protection of Ancient Buildings to forward to you the enclosed copy of the society's report upon Blythburgh church and to say that the committee trusts you will be able to do them the favour of finding room for it in your valuable columns, as it believes the report will be found of great interest to many of your readers.

Should the report be too long for insertion all at once, may I suggest that half should appear in one issue, and half in the next.

If you think fit to publish the report I shall be much obliged if you will send me a copy of the impression in which it appears, and also by your giving it the following heading in your columns.

---

[65] See Correspondence 63 and 68.
[66] On cathedral glass see Introduction n. 98.
[67] See Introduction n. 104 on Sir John's apparent neglect to exercise his right as patron.

Copy of the report made by the Society for the Protection of Ancient Buildings on the necessary repairs of Blythburgh Church.

I remain,

Sir,

Your obedient servant,

[*signed*]   Thackeray Turner

Secretary

72. London committee dissolved. S. Sutherland Safford to George Wardle, 21 March 1883

4 Garden Court ,
Temple, E.C.
21 March 1883

Dear Mr Wardle,

At a meeting of the committee of the Blythburgh Church Preservation Fund held here yesterday, it was resolved, on the motion of Mr Arthur Hill FSA, seconded by Mr Alfred Gaussen,

That inasmuch as the local committee is in full working order and has opened a general list of subscriptions, and as no money as been received by this (the London) committee, it be now dissolved.

Believe me,

Yours faithfully,

[*signed*]   S. Sutherland Safford

P.S.

I have been glad to see the publicity given to the report of the SPAB in the Athenaeum, but you see from the foregoing resolution that my late committee <u>as a body</u>, has been unable to claim any right to interfere in the matter.

[*signed*]   <u>SSS.</u>

73. Newspaper cutting. SPAB report on Blythburgh church. Report published in the *Suffolk Chronicle*, 24 March 1883[68]

WE publish to-day the report of the Society for the Protection of Ancient Buildings on Blythburgh Church. We have the authority of Sir Roger de Coverley that much may be said on both sides, and much certainly has been said on both sides of this controversy. Some of the statements of the Society for the Protection of Ancient Buildings strike the uninformed mind as a little extravagant. The object of this Society appears to be to make a patchwork of the buildings which may happen to be treated under their advice. There is a principle in this, without doubt, but it is the practise of this alone that would arouse our doubts. For example, we are told: 'Timber must not be considered perished so long as there is sufficient depth of heart wood unaffected. * * * Any new oak that may be inserted must be perfectly plain without moulding or ornament, though the part to which it be joined be finely moulded. It is possible that a great length of wall-plate may need removal, if the ornamental facia in that length

---

[68]   The Brooke papers include a cutting from the *Ipswich Journal* of the same article. Also RCMB.

is lost, or too much decayed to be repaired, it must not be reproduced or imitated with the new work.' The same advice runs through the whole of the report. We repeat that we are aware that much may be advanced in favour of this style of treatment of ancient buildings, but we almost tremble to think how much also may be said on the other hand. Even more should we fear to attempt to face the actual appearance of a building treated after this method in cases where the repairs shall be at all extensive.

COPY OF THE REPORT
MADE BY THE SOCIETY FOR THE PROTECTION OF ANCIENT BUILDINGS
ON THE NECESSARY REPAIRS OF BLYTHBURGH CHURCH.

The newspaper then printed the text of the letter, dated 27 September 1882, sent by the SPAB to Revd H. Sykes.[69]

74. Request for support. Draft letter Thackeray Turner, SPAB, to Sir John Blois, Bt, 31 March 1883

To Sir John Blois
    Sir,
I am desired by the committee to express the grave anxiety which it feels for the safety of Blythburgh church.

The committee has not replied to Mr Sykes's letter in the <Journal of> Ipswich Journal and has incurred the suspicion that the allegations were well founded. Meanwhile the work, against which the society so earnestly protested, are being pushed on.

Under this disadvantage the committee would <still> be much indebted for your advice but it feels that immediate steps must be taken to stimulate further opposition to the plans of the restoration committee and also for <the sake> putting itself right with the public. [*The draft continues in another hand*] I have been most anxious not to trouble you <I have the honour> <with this business> during your illness, and I only do so now in the hopes that you have sufficiently recovered <to be well enough> for this letter not to <trouble> cause you annoyance.

    I have the honour to be,
        Sir,
    Your obedient servant,
[*signed*]   Thackeray Turner

31 March 1883

75. Response from Sir John Blois. Lady Eliza Blois to SPAB, 3 April 1883

13, Palace Gate, W.
Dear Sir,
Sir John Blois went to Suffolk last week for change of air – and will call upon you on his return to London. In the meantime he hopes you will answer any letter in the papers – you may think fit.
    I remain yours truly

---

[69] For the SPAB report see Correspondence 35.

[*signed*]   Eliza Ellen Blois

3 April 1883

76. Newspaper cutting. SPAB position. Thackeray Turner, SPAB, to the editor of the *Suffolk Chronicle*, 5 April 1883, published 7 April[70]

BLYTHBURGH CHURCH
To the Editor of the Suffolk Chronicle
SIR, – Your readers and the subscribers to the Blythburgh Church Restoration Fund have now had an opportunity of considering the proposals made by the Society for the Protection of Ancient Buildings. We beg a little more space for the purpose of asking the subscribers, publicly, whether they have fully considered their duty towards the building which is now practically at their mercy? By the funds they have raised the subscribers have given to the Vicar and his committee the power of arresting[71] the present decay of the building, or of destroying its most beautiful features under pretence of restoring them. Subscriptions were asked on the ground that Blythburgh Church is an unusually noble and beautiful specimen of ancient architecture. If, on the contrary, this church had been the work of modern masons, its walls finished 'with a sanded face,' as Mr. Street specifies, its windows glazed with modern cathedral glass, and the floor laid with modern encaustic tiles, if this had been the case, and we had been told that the water was leaking through the roofs, we ask whether one spark of enthusiasm could have been got up for its preservation, and whether the funds now in hand could have been raised? Who will dare to say it could? Yet this may be the actual condition of the building when this fund has been spent!

We ask the subscribers to consider such a result before it is too late to change it. The result must rest with them whether what remains of the ancient Church of Blythburgh shall be preserved, or whether a practically new building shall be presented to the parishioners who have so little cared for the preservation of the old one.

Such as the old church was, on the day before this restoration began, it had won the admonition[72] of all who saw it, and chiefly of those best able to appreciate what is most beautiful in English architecture. The simple repairs that had been made, being modestly protective of work, much too valuable to be lost, were neither offensive to good taste nor injurious to what they protected. The church wanted nothing but the removal of the causes of decay and further repairs of the kind already begun. – I am Sir, etc.,
[*signed*]   THACKERAY TURNER, Secretary
    9, *Buckingham-street, Adelphi, W.C.,*
        5th April, 1883.

77. Newspaper cutting. Appeal for funds. The Revd H. Sykes to the *Ipswich Journal*, 10 May 1883, published 12 May[73]

BLYTHBURGH CHURCH RESTORATION.

---

[70]   There is a draft of this letter in SPAB I. A similar letter was sent to the *Ipswich Journal*. Also in Brooke.
[71]   'Averting' in the *Ipswich Journal*.
[72]   'Admiration' in the *Ipswich Journal*.
[73]   Also in Brooke and RCMB.

SIR, – Two or three years ago the restoration of Blythburgh Church was looked upon as a hopeless task. The parishioners, with aching hearts, beheld their 'holy and beautiful house, in which their fathers worshipped' falling into decay, and to their minds, into irretrievable ruin; while the crowds who, during the Summer season, visited the old church, wondered why such a noble building should be allowed to crumble away.

Often were the questions asked by astonished visitors, Who is the landlord? Who is the patron of the living? How is it that no effort is made to rescue this fine building from ruin?

In answer to this last permit me to inform your readers that the effort has been made, and with the help of those who sympathise with our work, we trust and believe that success will crown our effort.

Already truck loads of new mullions and tracery for the windows are on the spot. These are to take the place of the unsightly wood, bricks and mortar, which have so long disfigured the building. All the windows, except those which are entirely bricked up, are to be fully restored, and already the clerestory windows on the South side present a pleasing contract to the dilapidated condition of those in other parts of the church. The fine parapet on the South side is also to be restored, and the roof of the South aisle is being lifted, to be replaced by new oak timbers where the old ones are decayed, the new to correspond exactly with the carving and moulding of the ancient work.

All this has been contracted for, and is to be completed by the end of September. When completed, the subscribers to the fund will, we feel sure, be satisfied that their money is being well and wisely expended.

On reference to your advertising columns, it will be seen that the amount promised is £958, while the contract for this first portion of the work is £1,049 10s. The Committee feel confident that the balance will be cheerfully subscribed before the money has to be paid, and they now make an urgent appeal for funds to complete the work they have undertaken.

Permit me to remind your readers that 'He who gives at once gives twice.'

£5,000 now will accomplish what £10,000 would not do a few years hence. For this smaller sum we shall now be able to secure the building and render it again befitting the high and noble purpose for which it was erected, and for which for 400 years it has been used, viz., the worship of Almighty God.

Hoping this will be promptly and liberally responded to,

    I remain, yours respectfully,

        H. SYKES.

Walberswick Vicarage,

    May 10th, 1883.

P.S. – One clause in the advertisement needs explanation. Many have wondered why so much as one-third of the general fund should be devoted to the chancel. The reason is that all East of the screens, including two bays of the North and South aisles, are supposed to belong to the chancel, and form fully one-third of the entire building.

78. Newspaper cutting. Protest at nature of restoration. 'A' to the *East Anglian Daily Times*, 2 January 1884[74]

BLYTHBURGH CHURCH RESTORATION
TO THE EDITOR

SIR, – On visiting Blythburgh Church two days ago, I was very much impressed with the amount of work achieved by the Committee, as they had only a small sum to begin operations with (about £1,000).

At the same time there are details of this work which savour of mutilation rather than of restoration, and which possibly may be of a temporary nature. In this case a letter to you may draw out explanatory answers. When the public was invited to contribute funds, we were told that Mr. Street was in charge. Has Mr. Street sanctioned the carrying away of a portion of the beautiful carved 'chancel stalls' to construct about the most barbarous and frightful 'reading desk' one can imagine, which, by the way, has been placed in the body of the church?

Again, can Mr. Street be aware that panels have been abstracted from the 'rood screen,' the vacant spaces in which have been filled with common deal of the most trumpery description? It is said in the neighbourhood that these old panels were taken by accident, *and have gone into the roof! (sic)* If this be true, it is too late now to do more than protest, but it sounds incredible.

The first item may still be put straight, and the old 'stall-fronts' put back in the places they have occupied for centuries.

Assuming always that Mr. Street still directs affairs, one is bound to suppose these matters have escaped his observation. That they will pass with those who pay, and are prepared to pay again, is less probable.

Enclosing my card, I am, etc.,
   A.
St. James' Street, London, S.W.,
 2nd January, 1884.

79. Newspaper cutting. Progress of restoration. The Revd H. Sykes to the *Ipswich Journal*, 9 January 1884, published 12 January[75]

BLYTHBURGH CHURCH RESTORATION.

SIR, – Permit me to draw the attention of your readers to the advertisement in another part of your paper.

The restoration of this church, which a few years ago was considered hopeless, is steadily progressing. The new oak roof on the South aisle is all but complete. All the windows are expected to be fully restored by Easter, with the exception of a few in the chancel, now bricked up. The beautiful parapet on the South side will be secured and completed; 'the ricketty pews of the meanest deal,'* which were a great eyesore, have disappeared; the old oak benches, with their interesting 'poppy-heads,' have been restored to their original position, which will be a great gain by bringing the congregation nearer to the pulpit and reading-desk; the chancel stalls have been removed further apart, which has greatly improved the appearance; the pulpit and

---

[74] RCMB. A version published in the *East Anglian Daily Times* on 5 January is in Brooke and also in SROI 2, 2.
[75] RCMB and Brooke. This letter was incorrectly dated by Sykes.

reading-desk now occupy more appropriate positions, and the general effect as you enter that lately dilapidated edifice is simply marvellous, especially when you consider the cost (about £1,100).

In order to open the church at Easter free of debt, between £50 and £100 is needed. Is it too much to ask the admirers of this interesting and magnificent building to contribute this small sum in three months' time? I hope not; and if this can be done we shall be able to appropriate the proceeds of the opening services towards the restoration of the North aisle and nave roofs, which urgently need to be attended to.

I would take this opportunity of thanking most heartily those who have contributed to the restoration fund, and venture to hope that many of your readers will follow their example. I feel sure that all who visit the church will be more than satisfied that the Committee have well and wisely expended the funds placed at their disposal. -Yours truly,

H. SYKES.

Walberswick Vicarage, January 9th, 1883 [*sic*].

* Proceedings of the 'Suffolk Archaeological Society,' vol. IV.[76]

80. Newspaper cutting. Response to protest. The Revd H. Sykes to the *East Anglian Daily Times*, 9 January 1884[77]

BLYTHBURGH CHURCH RESTORATION.
TO THE EDITOR.

SIR, – I read the letter on Blythburgh Church which appeared in your issue of Saturday last with mingled feelings of indignation and pity – *indignation* that, under the guise of an inquirer, your correspondent should endeavour to cast odium upon those who are held responsible for the manner in which the restoration is being carried out – *pity* that such unfortunate people are still to be found, who, while they profess to be 'deeply impressed,' seem, to those who mark their conduct, annoyed more and more as the restoration proceeds. This impression has forced itself upon others as well as myself, and has been more than once expressed.

I have hesitated as to the course I should pursue, knowing that these 'irreconcilables' would misconstrue my conduct, whether I replied to the letter or allowed it to pass without notice. Leaving them therefore out of consideration, I will ask you to give me a little space in your next issue to correct some false impressions Mr. 'A's' letter is calculated to give to some of your readers, who do not happen to know the source from which it originated.

Had your correspondent been a sincere inquirer, and a genuine admirer of the restoration, he would have had no need to screen himself behind a *nom de plume*.

The information he professedly seeks would have been gladly rendered by the writer, had not 'A's' pride and self-importance prevented him from asking.

Mr. 'A.' would have your readers to understand that he is a casual visitor, who, only 'two days ago,' discovered the 'details' to which he applies the term '*mutilation*.' But what is the fact? These details were completed more than a month ago; and as 'A.' was residing within walking distance he has been a frequent visitor at the church, but up to last week has been quiet. This is accounted for easily. The feeling

---

[76] Raven, 'Blythburgh'.
[77] RCMB. The *East Anglian Daily Times* version published 11 January is in Brooke.

which has prompted the letter *now*, has been stirred by a recent event for which neither the Committee nor the vicar is responsible.

No part of the 'chancel stalls' has been 'carried away to construct a reading desk.' This was done some 15 years ago. Nor is there any change in the position, as the 'reading desk' has stood where it now does for years, *only* it has been moved about two feet nearer to the pillar. A similar change has been made with the 'chancel stalls.' They have occupied their present position in the chancel for many years, but the Committee thought they would look better to be placed a little further apart, and two of the 'heads' have been restored to their original position against the screen.

The improvement here has been greatly admired by all who have seen it, while in the nave the 'ricketty pews of the meanest deal' ('Proceedings of the Suffolk Archaeological Society,' vol. iv.) have disappeared, and the old oak benches, with their quaint but interesting poppy heads, have been restored to their original position.

The great improvement effected in the better arrangement of seats, stalls, reading-desk, and pulpit, at a trifling cost, must be seen to be appreciated, and I would earnestly invite all subscribers to visit the church and judge for themselves whether their money is not being well and wisely spent. The general effect of the alterations made, together with the substantial work to be observed on every side, is simply marvellous, and all who take an interest in this grand old church will feel gratified to see the vast improvement made with the funds placed at our disposal.

There is another subterfuge resorted to by your correspondent, which is as futile as his *casual visit*. His writing from St. James's Street, London, and the business-like phrase, 'I enclose my card,' do not preclude the probability that the letter was inspired from a house a hundred miles nearer Blythburgh than London.

With regard to the last clause of Mr 'A.'s' letter, I would ask, when the 'details' to which he alludes have been *passed* by the Building Committee, which includes the Vicar and churchwardens, the Rural Dean, the Lay Rector, a member of the Suffolk Archaeological Society, and a respected farmer of the parish, who are they that your correspondent refers to as not willing to 'pass' them? and what if they don't?

I can readily believe, after what I heard on Monday, that if the further restoration of the church could be indefinitely postponed, it would be a great relief to the party 'A.' represents, who evidently are and have been for some time, 'weary in well-doing.'

In conclusion, it gives me unfeigned pleasure to be able to assure your readers that those who have undertaken the restoration of Blythburgh Church have no notion of relaxing their efforts until their architect's proposals have been carried out.

On Monday the Building Committee gave instructions for plans and estimates to be prepared by Mr. Street for the next portion of the work to be undertaken, viz., the north aisle and the nave roofs.

I trust on Easter Sunday we shall be able to re-open our church *free of debt*, and thankfully raising our 'Ebenezer,' gird up our loins afresh to complete the work of renovation, and render this beautiful temple once more becoming the worship of God, for which it was first erected, and for which its restoration has been taken in hand.

When this 'consummation devoutly to be wished' has been achieved, these petty annoyances will, I feel sure, be lost in mutual congratulations, and in returning thanks to Him, whose are 'the silver and the gold,' that He has stirred the heart of His people to rescue this magnificent edifice from the ruin which was imminent. – Yours, etc.,

H. SYKES.

Walberswick Vicarage
Jan. 9, 1884

81. Newspaper cutting. Appeal for funds. The Revd H. Sykes to the *Ipswich Journal*, 26 November 1884, published 29 November[78]

BLYTHBURGH CHURCH

SIR, – Permit me to draw the attention of your readers to the advertisement in another part of your paper.

To all who have so kindly helped in the good work up to the present I wish to tender my heartfelt thanks, and if I earnestly solicit a repetition of their former kindness it is because the circumstances of the case are very pressing. I have also received great encouragement by the sums acknowledged in to-day's paper, and by the expressions of kindly interest which have accompanied the donations referred to. On reference to the list of subscriptions, it will be seen that friends of this grand old church have again and again come forward to assist in its preservation. I cannot but think that others will follow their noble example, and that many of those who have not yet come forward will come to our assistance when they find that the undertaking is a necessary one, and that the money subscribed is being well and wisely expended. Let me invite such to pay a visit to the church and they will need no proof from me that our work deserves their sympathy and assistance.

Funds are urgently required for putting the roofs of the church in a proper state of repair, that of the north aisle especially being in a dangerously defective state.

The roof of the south aisle has already been re-instated in oak, the lead re-cast, the parapet secured and replaced where missing, and a majority ($\frac{7}{8}$) of the windows in the church put into a state of permanent repair.

This has been done at an outlay of £1,065. A further sum of £1,000 is now necessary for the completion of the work. This will suffice to make good all the remaining roofs, re-open the windows which are blocked, and generally make weather-tight and ensure the lasting safety of this noble building.

In addition to the above, a small sum is still due on the first contract. I trust that friends and admirers will help us to clear this debt, and contribute liberally towards the remaining roof and windows.

I may just add, to show the urgency of our case, that since the re-opening at Easter a beam of oak has fallen from the north aisle roof, and other parts require immediate attention. I should be truly thankful if able to commence on this portion in the spring of next year, and £600 will enable us to enter upon the contract.

With your readers I hope I shall not plead in vain, and remain, yours very truly,
    H. SYKES.
Walberswick, November 26th, 1884.

[The SPAB file is then silent for nearly ten years until in 1894 a correspondent expresses concern about the condition of Blythburgh church.[79]*]*

---

[78]   Also in RCMB and Brooke.
[79]   See Correspondence 104 for the next involvement of the SPAB.

82. Grant from building society. Norwich Diocesan Church Building Society to the Revd H. Sykes, 17 April 1885[80]

The Close, Norwich
                17 April 1885

Dear Sir,
I have pleasure in informing you that the committee of the Diocesan Church Building Society have acceded to your request and I herewith enclose cheque for £25 0s. 0d. – the amount of the grant. I shall be obliged by your receipt.
    By this post I send you the plans – and I have sent the specifications to Mr Street.
        Yours faithfully,
            W. Moore

[The following documents **83–105** *are from Suffolk Record Office, Ipswich, FC185 E3 2 Part 1.]*

83. Reopening service. Sir Ralph Blois Bt to the Revd T.H.R. Oakes, 12 June 1890

/1890 Sir R. Blois 21 [*sic*] June/
Pirbright Camp,[81]
Woking.
                12 June 1890
Dear Mr Oakes,
I am very glad indeed to find from your letter that the work is almost if not quite finished at Blythburgh church; it will be most important now to collect the necessary funds to pay for this work.[82]

No doubt a reopening service would help and of course it would be as well that the service and the bazaar should not follow one another too closely. At the same time a great number of people who would be in the county and would attend in August have not yet arrived.

However Lady Blois is quite willing to come down to attend the service any day that you could arrange for it to be held although I am afraid I could not get away, so I will leave this matter entirely in your hands to arrange.

The bazaar will not be held till August but a great deal has already been done by Lady Blois and her friends and we are thinking of holding it at Cockfield but nothing is settled yet.

I should very much like to hear from you when anything further is settled about the reopening service.
    Yours very truly,
[*signed*]   Ralph B.M. Blois

---

[80] RCMB.
[81] Sir Ralph Blois was a captain in the Scots Guards.
[82] Repair of the roof and walls of the north aisle. See Appendix A 10.

84. Architect's expenses. A.E. Street to the Revd T.H.R. Oakes, 13 June 1890

Reply to this letter to be addressed

A.E. STREET ESQ.,
14A CAVENDISH PLACE,
CAVENDISH SQUARE,
LONDON, W.
13 June 1890

My dear Sir,
I have seen the work at Blythburgh church and have signed Mr Allen's account for £300. My own out of pocket expenses are

2 return tickets Great Eastern Railway	£1. 15s.	
2 do. Metropolitan Railway	<1. 6>	1s. 6d.
Church key		6

£1. 17.

Believe me,
    Yours faithfully,
[*signed*]   A.E. Street

Revd T.H.R. Oakes

85. Advice for work on tower. H.S. Patterson[83] to the Revd T.H.R. Oakes, 25 June 1890

25 June 1890

Dear Mr Oakes,
I have not had a moment since I left you and have posted over 250 letters in last two days.

I have consulted my factotum who advises a <u>steeplejack</u> for pointing and it would not be safe for any other man to attempt such risky work as outside the tower. The preparatory inquiry will save you 50 per cent and you must not think this other than legitimate and wise and best expenditure. I would most certainly advise you to engage such a man or 2 men to go down and see and report upon its cost. I could get an estimate from here <u>per foot</u>. The buttresses are all that needs to be done and if the long crack were '<u>grouted</u>' in with cement as it is – it is not much out of line it would be sufficient. You must 'cut your cloth according to the measure' – You can't do as you would '<u>but do as you can.</u>'

I will get you a probable estimate of the job but no man will be tied to it except he saw it -
With thanks and best wishes,
    Yours,
[*signed*]   H.S. Patterson

---

[83] In A.E. Street's office.

86. Ownership of drawings. A.E. Street to the Revd T.H.R. Oakes, 26 June 1890

Reply to this letter to be addressed
A.E. STREET ESQ.,
14A CAVENDISH PLACE,
CAVENDISH SQUARE,
LONDON, W.
26 June 1890

Dear Sir,

My source of information is identical with yours viz my own letters to Mr James.[84] It was subject to him paying me £5 that allowed to him to retain the drawings in his possession. But a payment of £5 does not make the drawings yours.

Since this time I have had to rewrite the specification practically and to do several full size designs for the roof, as well as writing a report on Walberswick church tower.

It does not encourage me to do <the> work for nothing, or about nothing, if the sole result is an abrupt 'Stand and Deliver' without a semblance of thanks.

The original drawings for south aisle etc. are the property of the committee for that work and they can have them: though, even in that case, I was not fully paid. My offer of \the/ loan of the drawings and specification holds good.

Yours faithfully,
[*signed*]   A.E. Street

Revd T.H.R. Oakes

87. Work on tower. The Revd T.H.R. Oakes to H.S. Patterson, 27 June 1890

Walberswick. 27 June 1890

Dear Mr Patterson,

You have indeed been busy. Many thanks for your kind letter to hand today. My first impulse was to take the responsibility at once according to your suggestions, and thus to write to you to send your man to me. But when my patron and churchwardens are only too ready to resent any neglect of their authority, as I know, on second thoughts, I write differently. <u>Now</u> I will say I hope to write soon to you to send your man. In the meanwhile I shall correspond with Sir Ralph Blois, or even, in case of necessity, follow him to Woking (where he is in camp, with the Scots Guards) and interview him.

Mrs O. and I were glad to know of your having made your long journey safely, and hope your health has no way suffered. With our best wishes etc.

[*unsigned copy*]

88. Ownership of drawings. The Revd T.H.R. Oakes to A.E. Street, 27 June 1890

<u>Copy</u>.   Walberswick. 27 June 1890
     My dear Sir,

---

[84] The Revd Henry James, Oakes's predecessor as vicar.

I delivered to you in good faith drawings and specification also contract, all which were undoubtedly my property. I must say your note of today surprises me. There was no more of an 'abrupt stand and deliver' in my response to your application for payment of your account than in your own letter. Indeed the comparison would rather show that <u>delivery</u> was demanded by you even to extravagance, for you admit that certain drawings, at any rate, are not your property. As to thanks, they were not withheld nor forgotten. Neither you nor Mr Allen have reported the work done yet. Mr Allen, when he called for payment of his account, said he had not finished. For all you have done for which you ask only thanks, which has been of advantage to me, I have \not/ only felt most grateful, but am ready to thank you. However, it is usual to express such thanks at the close of a transaction, and so this was deferred.

I regret your letter should thus impose upon me the defensive, but I trust this may serve the purpose of explanation and adjustment satisfactorily.

Mr Allen did not do his work to date (which has lost to us the opportunity for a reopening service and collection) nor preserved the old materials (which were not without value). So far as I can learn you have taken no notice of these delinquencies.

Yours faithfully,

[*signed*] T.H.R. Oakes.

89. Expenses and delays. A.E. Street to the Revd T.H.R. Oakes, 28 June 1890

Reply to this letter to be addressed
A.E. STREET ESQ.,
14A CAVENDISH PLACE,
CAVENDISH SQUARE,
LONDON, W.
28 June 1890

Dear Sir,

I don't know why my letter should surprize you. It is a truthful statement of the facts which are fully borne out by my letters and those of Mr James. You now appear to speak of things, such as the amended specification, contract etc. as undoubtedly your property which were not even done when I received what you are pleased to term the extravagant payment of £5. If you think the amount of the railway fares extravagant I can only say that I am not responsible for them.

While you have £200 in your hands you can, I imagine, recoup yourself for any real loss by failure on Mr Allen's part to hand over old materials. As you say explicitly yourself, the transaction is not yet closed. With regard to non completion by the promised date, if you had more experience in these matters you would be aware that some latitude has almost invariably to be allowed. Mr Allen is a man in a small way of business and possibly does not arrange that business well, but you have had the advantage of a very unusual arrangement by which Mr Allen has been for a long time out of pocket, an arrangement which no contractor would, in the usual course think of, and you must set the advantages of having employed him against the disadvantages. Mr Allen has a few shillings worth of work still to do. I had to call his attention to one or two things but I don't see how that affects matters. You have presumably not paid his <£> money in full. As far as the opening service, the date is usually arranged in conjunction with the contractor. You have said nothing to show that things were not going as you wished.

Yours faithfully,

[*signed*]   A.E. Street

Revd T.H.R. Oakes

90. Completion of work on north aisle and status of incumbency. The Revd T.H.R. Oakes to the Bishop of Norwich, 1 July 1890

Walberswick. 1 July 1890

Copy.

My Lord,

I have the honour to forward to you herewith the list of candidates confirmed by your Lordship at Halesworth yesterday, who came from this parish.

I have the honour also to report the completion of the restoration of the roof and walls of the north aisle of Blythburgh church. £500 is to be paid for this work, of which sum we have thus far obtained only some £300 (half of which Sir Ralph Blois or Lady Blois have either subscribed or secured). As your lordship was good enough to subscribe £20 (in July 1882, to be paid in two instalments) of which £10 was paid on the 14th April, 1883, and the remainder has not yet been received, may I take this opportunity to remind your Lordship of this, and respectfully beg in this moment of pressing necessity for its payment at your convenience.

Moreover, I would be glad to know, in view of my having never been inducted to 'the temporal possession of the goods and income amerced to the cure of souls' (Church Law, p. 229), or made the 'actual and lawful possessor of the freehold of the churches, churchyards, parsonage, glebes,' etc. (idem p. 243), whether, in the opinion of your Lordship, my position is open to question.

I have the honour to be, etc.

91. Request for payment. R.J. Allen to the Revd T.H.R. Oakes, 2 July 1890[85]

High Street,
Southwold.
2 July 1890
To Revd T.H.R. Oakes, Walberswick
Sir,
Sorry to trouble you. I hope you have the signature required for cheque, as I have some heavy a/c's to meet at this time. If you could send it by bearer it would greatly oblige.

  Yours obediently,
[*signed*]   Robert J. Allen

92. Expenses and ownership of drawings. The Revd T.H.R. Oakes to A.E. Street, 2 July 1890

/1890 <u>A.E. Street</u> 28 June/

<u>Copy</u>.

---

[85] See Correspondence 101 for evidence of shortage of funds when the payment was made.

Walberswick. 2 July 1890

My dear Sir,

What I said in my letter of the 27th June was 'There was no more of an "abrupt stand and deliver" in my response to your application for payment of your account than in your own letter. Indeed the comparison would rather show that <u>delivery</u> was demanded by you even to extravagance, for you admit that certain drawings at any rate, are not your property.' I submit it is clear that reference is made more particularly to the fact that it was extravagant to demand <u>drawings</u> and <u>documents</u> more than you were entitled to. I object to discuss your claim of £5 for drawings which was paid by Mr James, and am sorry you attempt to import this item in the manner you do. But the money was paid on the express terms of your own proposal and in your own handwriting that the incumbent should <u>keep</u> them. You required these to be delivered to you. In good faith, I delivered them to you. In bad faith and extravagantly enough you now demand their surrender. Of course, I must refuse (still only in the best spirit and good faith on my part), and I therefore request herewith that you will no longer dispute this point, but be good enough to return them.

Reference to my letter will also be sufficient to prove that there was no allusion either to railway fares. I said nothing during the progress of the work because all that I could <say> have said was already said, and ignored as it was, and the work under your superintendence, as I thought (though your letter now aims, it seems, to shift the responsibility), I considered it wisdom not to interfere.

> I am, my dear Sir,
>> Yours very truly,
>>> (*signed*) T.H.R. Oakes

A.E. Street, Esq.

93. Ownership of drawings. A.E. Street to the Revd T.H.R. Oakes, 3 July 1890

> *Reply to this letter to be addressed*
> A.E. STREET ESQ.,
> 14A CAVENDISH PLACE,
> CAVENDISH SQUARE,
> LONDON, W.
> 3 July 1890

Dear Sir,

It is hardly worth my while to follow you into your disquisitions or your own good faith, or into your particular application of the word extravagance. Neither of them affect the point at issue. This is a perfectly simple one and I must refer you to my previous letters for my view of this subject. I will only repeat that the £5 was payment for the actual making of the drawings and nothing more. If the church committee, through you or anyone else, ask for the original drawings they can have them as I have already said. They will be taking an unusual course in asking for them. That is all.

> Yours faithfully,
[*signed*]   A.E. Street

Revd T.H.R. Oakes

94. End of architect's involvement with Blythburgh and Walberswick. A.E. Street to the Revd T.H.R. Oakes, 4 July 1890

Reply to this letter to be addressed
A.E. STREET ESQ.,
14A CAVENDISH PLACE,
CAVENDISH SQUARE,
LONDON, W.
4 July 1890

Dear Sir,

Possibly my use of the word <to> 'keep' may have put me in a false position, and I have decided accordingly to send the plans. That it even entered my head for a moment to sell them outright is of course not the fact, though I neither ask nor expect you to credit it, since, while claiming the best of motives for your own doings you appear inclined to do just the reverse for others.

I suppose you are not aware of what is usually done and that is your excuse, but as a simple fact this is the first time in a ten years practice that I have even been asked to hand over drawings. That this first case should be one where I am actually out of pocket instead of having made a profit is odd.

Probably you will return me my report on Walberswick tower. I should have been glad to have helped to preserve it, but, under the circumstances, I think we had better have no <more> fresh business transactions. Your \last/ letter contained much that I might answer, such as my requiring you to deliver the plans to me etc. I simply followed the invariable course and could have done nothing without them. As for your reference to your silence during the work, and to my having ignored something you said, I am quite in the dark about it. If you were anxious to settle things yourself you might simply have said so: I had no reason for concerning myself with the thankless business except my feeling that Mr Allen would have made a considerable bungle of the work – the woodwork more especially – without some guidance. This I still feel.

 Believe me,
  Yours faithfully,
[*signed*] A.E. Street

Revd T.H.R. Oakes

95. Contribution to restoration fund and status of incumbency. Bishop of Norwich to the Revd T.H.R. Oakes, 5 July 1890

The Palace,
Norwich.
5 July 1890

My dear Sir,

I have referred to my correspondence with Mr Sykes 1882 and I find that I promised £10 towards the south aisle of <u>church</u> (not chancel) when £300 was collected, and also another £10 towards the north aisle of the <u>church</u> (not chancel) when £300 was collected.

I paid £10 April /83 in accordance with my promise.

If you can assure me that £300 has been collected for that part of the north aisle which is connected with <u>the church</u>, as distinct from the chancel, I will at once send you £10.

As your cure is a perpetual curacy, induction was not necessary. The improprietor holds the freehold of the church and churchyard, while you hold that of the glebe house, and any lands, tithes, and appurtenances belonging to the benefice.

I remain,

 Yours faithfully,

[*signed*] <u>John T. Norwich</u>

The Revd T.H.R. Oakes.

96. Arrangements for bazaar. Miss Alice Blois to Mrs Ada Oakes, 6 July 1890

Dear Mrs Oakes,

Thank you very much for your letter. My mother is writing to Mills to ask him to lend his meadow as he has done before; failing this can you suggest some other place to hold the bazaar? My mother hopes Mr Oakes will write to Lady Stradbroke, Lady Huntingfield, Lady Constance Barne, Honourable Lady Rose, Dowager Lady Crossley, Lady Crossley, <Lady Blois>, Miss Clara Blois, Mrs Cautley, Mrs Gaussen, Mrs Price, Mrs Roberts, Mrs Brooke, Mrs Price, Carlton Hall, Saxmundham, Mrs Parry Crooke, Mrs Lomax and Mrs Bence Lambert, asking them to be patronesses.

I enclose a programme of the Halesworth bazaar that may be a guide for the printing; as the circulars ought to be printed as soon as possible. Will you arrange to have them done. My mother is anxious we should have as many entertainments as possible, will you ask Mr Oakes to find a good conjurer. We will arrange concerts during the afternoon, and we think a magic lantern might do well. We hope you will have a stall and we are asking several friends to help. Perhaps Mrs Cooper will have a stall – Mrs Cooper of Southwold has always been most kind in helping us. We will settle the bazaar for Thursday and Friday the 7th and 8th of August if that will suit you.

We have heard from Mr Cautley asking us to fix our date, so the 2 bazaars will not interfere with each other. I hope your children are quite well. The baby must be getting quite big now.

 Believe me

  Yours sincerely,

[*signed*] <u>Alice Blois</u>

<u>6 July 1890</u>

97. Arrangements for bazaar. Mrs Ada Oakes to Miss Alice Blois, 8 July 1890

Copy

      Walberswick. 8 July 1890

Dear Miss Blois,

I thank you for your kind letter. I shall be pleased to supply a stall, but many things must be provided by purchase, the cost of which must be deducted from the proceeds.

Mr Oakes and I worked very hard for the bazaar last year. It was kept before the people by means of the parish magazine which was posted in every direction (at our own expense). Many letters were written and calls made besides. And the results were not encouraging. The sale of work was ignored and letters unanswered. It is evident <u>we</u> have no influence with the ladies you mention – at least, in the matter of church restoration. Under these circumstances would it not be again a mistake? We think it would be better if <u>Lady Blois</u> were to write to them this time. Again, it would be more appropriate in view of the fact that the freehold of the churches is Sir Ralph Blois's and not my husband's. It would follow that the printing had better be in the hands of Lady Blois as well, for correspondence would take time. When the answers to her letters might supply the information it might be sent by the same post which would bring it here to a London printer, who would return a proof for approval before we could even get it into the hands of a printer here. Perhaps Lady Blois might more readily hear of a good conjuror also. We shall be away from home during August, but will attend the bazaar. The children are very well thank you. Little Gracie is at a very interesting age. Mary apostrophised the rain this morning ending a long oration by 'Please rain, dear, do stop.'

Believe me, yours sincerely,

[*signed*] Ada Oakes

98. Architect's drawings. A.E. Street's clerk to the Revd T.H.R. Oakes, 8 July 1890

Reply to this letter to be addressed
A. E. STREET ESQ.,
14A CAVENDISH PLACE,
CAVENDISH SQUARE,
LONDON, W.
8 July 1890

Dear Sir,

<u>Blythburgh Church</u>

I am directed by Mr Street to forward per p.p. drawings Nos. 1. 2. and 7 and the specifications of the above church.

I am,

Dear Sir,

Yours faithfully,

per Arthur Edmund Street

[*signed*]   J.C.S.

Revd T.H.R. Oakes

99. Architect's drawings. Draft letter of the Revd T.H.R. Oakes to A.E. Street, 9 July 1890[86]

Walberswick. 9 July 1890

My dear Sir,

<The drawings which I sent you> I have the pleasure <now>, to acknowledge <ha> the receipt of drawings <with> and specification, and I thank you for the same. The contract, however, did not accompany them. Please be so good as to send me this also.

---

[86]   The document has a red line crossed through it.

I do not return your report <of> on Walberswick church tower, as you do not ask for it, and much regret you should so readily resolve to enter upon no fresh business transactions.

I quite understood at the time of my sending you the <plans> documents for Blythburgh that you could have done nothing without them, and so far did not think your request <it an> unusual <course>. <What> Your objection to return them, however, was a surprise; and I am very glad you have been good enough to withdraw it.

When I <said> wrote 'all that I could have said was already said'[87] I meant it was recorded in the <contract specification> documents above mentioned and <contract and the> the terms of the <contract> <specification> these documents have been ignored. <The> When <once> these were signed, whatever else, <I might said> <it was of no account> I might <say> have said would have been of no account. The written instrument was what was binding. To \have/ interfered would only have complicated matters. Now, the facts are perfectly clear and independent.

I am in no way anxious to settle things myself. <but as> no report of the completion of the work has come to hand (from either yourself or Mr Allen), and Mr Allen has presented a certificate of work done to the amount only of £300. As I see it stated in the specification that reference is to be made to you in case of complaint, I am perfectly in order. It is before the close of this transaction and you are the person to address. I am sorry you did not drop me a line and ask <me> the committee to view the work in company with you when you came down. For my own part, I must say with respect that I am obliged to consider Mr Allen's delinquencies more than the two simple points incidentally named in my letter of the 27 June.

[The draft ends there]

100. Architect's drawings. The Revd T.H.R. Oakes to A.E. Street, 9 July 1890

Copy

Walberswick. 9 July 1890

My dear Sir,

I thank you for the three drawings and specification to hand this morning. Please be so good as to send me the contract also.

I do not return your report on Walberswick church tower as you do not ask for it; and much regret you should so readily resolve to enter upon no fresh business transactions.

When I wrote 'all that I could have said was already said' I meant it was recorded in the documents relative to the work, in the discussion of which I had my full share and to which my signature was affixed.

I am, my dear Sir,
   Yours very truly,
      [signed] T.H.R. Oakes

---

[87] A reference to the letter of 2 July 1890, see Correspondence 92. The use of this phrase in the letter also dated 9 July to Street (Correspondence 100) suggests that Oakes settled for the short letter instead.

101. Bank account balance. F.E. Babington, Gurney's Bank, to the Revd T.H.R. Oakes, 15 July 1890

Gurney's & Co. Bank,
Halesworth.
15 July 1890

Dear Sir,
We beg to inform you that we have paid your cheque to Mr R.J. Allen for £100, and have placed it to the debit of the Blythburgh church a/c, but there is only £14 in our hands on this a/c to meet the cheque. Will you therefore be good enough to forward to us the deposit receipt for £100 which you hold, in order that we may place it, with the interest due, to the credit of the a/c.
    Yours faithfully,
    For Gurney's and Co.,
[*signed*]   F.E. Babington

102. Arrangements for bazaar. Lady Eliza Blois to the Revd T.H.R. Oakes, 24 July 1890

/1890 Lady Blois 24 July/

Dear Mr Oakes,
Can you arrange to have the Blythburgh church committee meeting next Monday at 11 'o clock at Blythburgh. My son hopes to attend if you can arrange it – and it will also suit me well. I hope to return to Cockfield tomorrow.
    We have engaged the Southwold band for the 7th and 8th and Mr Cooper is arranging about the tents. Trust it will be a success. Perhaps Mrs Oakes will be able to attend the meeting on Monday so it would enable me to arrange with her the details of the bazaar.
    I remain
    Yours sincerely,
[*signed*]   E.E. Blois
          24 July 1890

103. Architect's account. Lady Eliza Blois to the Revd T.H.R. Oakes, 16 January 1891

/1891. Lady Blois. 16th January/
 Cockfield Hall,
Yoxford.

Dear Mr Oakes,
I much regret that I have not been able to arrange to meet you at Blythburgh – and now we are moving to London on Monday. Have you received Mr Street's certificate that he considers the work of the contract completed?
    At our last meeting I find from Sir Ralph's notes that you hold £28 11s. 1d. (after paying the £30 to clear the last account) and I have £66 10s. 2d. at the Beccles bank. The first week in March I will gladly give £25 0s. 0d. Therefore we have £120. 1s.

– and have only £80 to raise. Perhaps you may have received a little more since the meeting. I remain

Yours sincerely,

[signed]   E.E. Blois

16 January 1890

Sir Ralph will often be here. You had better write and tell him exactly how the account stands. Possibly the new Southwold vicar may be interested in the church.

104. Concern about condition of Blythburgh church. Oliver Baker to Thackeray Turner, SPAB, 12 August 1894

101 Gough Road,

Edgbaston, Birmingham.

12 August 1894

My dear Turner,

[*The writer first refers to proposals to restore or rebuild three buildings of current or potential concern to the SPAB, quoting 'a friend' in relation to Enfield Court House. The letter continues:*] He [*the unnamed friend*] also goes on to say 'There is a church close by Walberswick at a village called Blythburgh. It is a splendid church having both internal and external beauties of a unique character. There is an open stone work parapet over the south aisle extending over the south porch also, such as I have never seen before anywhere. It is in good order saving over the said porch where it is very dilapidated. The porch is the one part of the church needing repair. It is one of those porches with a room above. The vaulting supporting the latter is gone, so that one can see right up into said room. The part in need of repair is the arch to the entrance to the porch from the churchyard. It is being crushed in by the above structure and very little more <more> settlement or giving will mean mean [*sic*] the whole of the front of the porch falling in. Very little would make it sound. Sir Ralph Blois is lord of the manor I think, or else Lord Stradbroke, but this is easily ascertainable. Micklethwaite would be sure to know. There is also a leakage in the nave roof, a splendid piece of work with flying <buttresses> angels retaining their ancient coloured decoration. In other respects the church is perfect. It has also the old wash on the walls, a beautiful old brick and tile floor, two or three beautiful Purbeck tombs, two old oak screens in entrance to chapels either side of chancel, stalls and a lot of loose oak carving which was taken away to make room for a tin pot organ but which ought to be put up again before it gets broken. This latter was a screen dividing the chancel from the south chapel.

Perhaps you can do something through Mr Micklethwaite or otherwise. [*The letter continues, dated 15 August 1894, with information about other buildings.*]

Sincerely yours,

[*signed*]   Oliver Baker

105. Request for information about situation at Blythburgh. Thackeray Turner, SPAB, to J.T. Micklethwaite, 14 September 1894

14 September 1894

in re

<u>Blythburgh Church Suffolk.</u>

My dear Micklethwaite,
A correspondent informs us that parts of this church are in need of repair and that it is an 'unrestored' building. We were under the impression that the church had been thoroughly restored.

The committee thought that as Blythburgh is near to Walberswick you may have seen the church and could give us some information?

Yours very truly,
[*signed*]   Thackeray Turner
                   Secretary

J.T. Micklethwaite, Esq.

106. Condition of Blythburgh church. J.T. Micklethwaite to Thackeray Turner, SPAB, 17 September 1894

[*SPAB annotation*] /Other half with Thryburgh church/

15 DEAN'S YARD,
WESTMINSTER, S.W.
17 September 1894

Dear Turner,
I am just back here and find your letter about Blythburgh church. I have never had time to visit the church when I have been at Walberswick, but I believe it was much 'restored' by Street and that the present Street has been at work there since his father's death. I can answer for it not being quite 'unrestored' from what I have seen on passing it by the railway.
[*The rest of the letter is in another SPAB file.*]

107. Concern about Blythburgh church. Evacustes A. Phipson to SPAB, 22 October 1894[88]

3 Sussex Road, Southsea.
22 October 1894

Gentlemen,
I have orderd 10 large drawings and a sechbook to be forwarded to you as requested and herewith send another small book. This with a few more large ones \and another book/ which i shal hav to send from Southsea make up my summer's wurk, and i hope it wil meet with your aproval. As i shal be in London in a few days i can call for the skeches if don with.

I had another exampl ov the queer uses made ov the good wurd 'restoration' when at Eye. In 1861 a fine fresco in almost perfect preservation representing the last judgment was discoverd over the chancel arch. The church was being 'restored' and therefore, wun woud supose, this fresco woud be just tuched up where necesary and left. Insted ov this it was again whitewashed over. Can this be truthfuly calld 'restoration'? I also, at Troston, came across a good exampl of Mrs Sparling's contention

---

[88]   The idiosyncratic spelling in this letter has not been changed.

that it is not the brihtness ov colors, but the bad taste with which they ar aplied, that causes them to apear tawdry.[89] For, while ancient colord screens, such at that at Attleboro or that at Eye, ar perfectly chaste, tho only primary colors ar used, the screen at Troston, which was newly painted in the Jubilee year in 'esthetic' tints such as maroon, pink and olive, has only a vulgar efect. The parson at Troston was quite surprised when i informd him that the pulpit was ornamented with inlaid woods, (a very rare ocurence) he had suposed it was only painted! When there is such ignorance among educated men what can you expect from the unlernd?

You wil be pleasd to hear that the vicar of Yaxley near Eye, a gentleman ov great taste and erudition, has very carefuly colected all the fragments ov ancient staind glas, which wer left in the varius windos ov the church, and aranged them together in the east window. There are specimens ranging from 1190 to 1549 and later. Another alteration which you may perhaps not so hihly aprove is the taking down of the Jacobean \pulpit/ canopy which was much dilapidated. Those parts of it not decayd hav all been utilised in panel work for the surplice presses which ar handsom and entirely composed of the old carving displaced at the restoration of the church in 1868, before which event the interior was fotografd.

In lamentabl contrast to this i hav to inform you that at the restoration of Blythboro church (now in progress) a large number ov painted glas windows, of the hihest interest, hav been taken out so carelessly that now the contractors do not no how to replace them, and such of them as hav not been stolen ar at this moment lying about in confusion. The services ov Mr Watling, the distinguishd antiquary of Ipswich, hoo alone is abl to rearange the fragments, have been declined, and the consquence is that a large number of the most valuabl and interesting windos wil unles your society intervenes at once, be utterly dispersed and destroid. Mr Watling has been engaged for 40 years in making most careful and exact facsimiles ov sculptures, stained glass, frescoes, etc from churches and other bildings all over Suffolk, and his colection, which is priceless, and he believs unique, shoud certainly be aquired by som public institution before it is too late. There is no time to lose as he is alredy ov very advanced age, and i trust your society wil memorialise the British or South Kensington Museum to make overtures for its aquisition. It woud be an irreparabl loss to the nation if the volumes were to fall into private hands. I do not supose Mr Watling requires any exorbitant sum for them but it is not fair to expect a poor man to part with a lifetime's work for nothing. His adress is 41 Pearce Rd, Derby road, Ipswich.

I presume you ar aware that Christ-church manor house, Ipswich, is thretnd with demolition. This fine Elizabethan bilding, nearly in the center of the town, with a grand park stretching out for more than a mile was offerd to the boro at a very moderate price but refused. Most of the park with the mansion was then sold to a bilding sindic who boht it with alacrity and now propose to drive a new road riht thru it. Now the town is going to purchase a part of the worst portion of the park, for a sum not much less than they coud previusly hav obtaind the hole for, and hav spent £10,000 in erecting a new museum and library when they coud hav had this splendid historic mansion, much larger and admirably adapted in every way for the purpose, absolutely for nothing, seeing it was thrown in with the land only to pull down. I am

---

[89] St Mary's Church, Troston. Restored generally in 1869. Bettley and Pevsner, *West Suffolk*, p. 542. St Mary's, Yaxley, was restored 1867–8 with the almost complete rebuilding of the chancel. Bettley and Pevsner, p. 574.

afraid with folkes who sho such pig-heded stupidity as this, any arguments your society might bring forward woud be ov litl avail, stil you miht induce the sindic to delay the destruction of the hall for a time, in order to see if it miht not be used for a scool, asilum, or somthing of that kind. I do not say that Christ-church is a particularly fine specimen ov architecture, still it is handsom, picturesk and venerabl, and at any rate infinitly superior to anything likely to be put up in place of it.

Respectfully,

[*signed*]   Evacustes A. Phipson

108. Request for information. Thackeray Turner, SPAB, to the Revd T.H.R. Oakes, 26 October 1894

26 October 1894

in re,

Blythburgh Church Suffolk

Revd and dear Sir,

We have received letters from two or three different quarters calling attention to the restoration of Blythborough church. It is said that the work is now in progress and that 'a large number of painted glass windows of the highest interest, have been taken out so carelessly that now the contractor does not know how to replace them, and such of them as have not been stolen are at this moment lying about in confusion.'

The committee thinks its right course is to write to you at once and repeat to you the rumour which has reached here.

We trust that you will forgive us for troubling you and we hope that you may be able to entirely contradict the statement.

I remember when I was down inspecting the tower of your other church that you then mentioned Blythburgh to me. Is the work still in the hands of Mr Street, also have you a copy of the report which the society made in 1882? If not we shall be pleased to lend you a copy.

I remain, Revd and dear Sir,

Yours faithfully,

[*signed*]   Thackeray Turner, Secretary

Revd T.H.R. Oakes

109. Situation at Blythburgh. The Revd T.H.R. Oakes to Thackeray Turner, SPAB, 27 October 1894

Walberswick, Southwold.
27 October 1894

Dear Sir,

Blythburgh church: I feel much interested by your courteous letter received this morning. I should be glad to know who may have been the authors of the several letters which have been addressed to you. There is, I regret to say, no work in progress beyond my personal efforts to obtain funds; in which efforts I have met with so little encouragement that it seems likely to be long before any plans for further work can be carried out. I presume the work to which your correspondents refer was work not now in progress; but done some ten or twelve years ago; and which, with them, I can but partially approve; but it was done long before I was incumbent. The fragments of painted glass 'at this moment lying about in confusion', to which they refer, would be \perhaps/ some fragments which I found in the belfry, which were spread on sheets for the purpose of examination one day in July last, which I have now, carefully preserved, in my own house, and can but suppose somebody visiting the church during the operation, <u>supposed</u> \they/ were neglected. The facts are entirely to the contrary. They were never in my time lying about in confusion, unvalued and neglected. I hope you will be so good as to contradict a 'rumour' likely to be so adverse to the success of my endeavours to engage the sympathies and secure the confidence of antiquarians, and their <u>pecuniary</u> <u>assistance</u> in the protection of so worthy an edifice. The south porch is rapidly falling into ruin, and I feel most anxious to do something for its salvation; but without funds am utterly at a loss for any expedient. I have a copy of the report of your society of 1882. If any work was further undertaken I think Mr Street would would [*sic*] have charge of it.

I remain, dear Sir,

Yours faithfully,

[*signed*] T.H.R. Oakes

110. Request for more information. Thackeray Turner, SPAB, to the Revd T.H.R. Oakes, 2 November 1894

2 November 1894

in re,

<u>Blythburgh Church</u>

Revd and dear Sir,

The committee thanks you very much for your letter, and it will take care to contradict the false rumours which are afloat, and will have very great pleasure in doing so.

Should we be trespassing too much upon your good nature if we were to ask for a description of the works which have already been done so <as> that we may compare them with our report of 1882, and see how far the work we recommended should be done has been carried out, and how far work contrary to our advice has been done.

Of course we have always been fully alive to the fact that Mr Street does not agree with this society, and this puts a difficulty in the society's way.

[*?Words*] can assure you that the society fully appreciates your efforts, and it will gladly do all it can to save the building from ruin.

I remain, Revd and dear Sir,

Yours faithfully,

[*signed*] Thackeray Turner

     Secretary

Revd T.H.R. Oakes

111. Request for names of SPAB informants. The Revd T.H.R. Oakes to Thackeray Turner, SPAB, 3 November 1894

Walberswick, Southwold.

3 November 1894

Dear Sir,

<u>Blythburgh church</u>: I shall be pleased to render your excellent society any service in

my power; but before doing what I can I should wish to know the names of the three persons who have lately written to the society, for which I asked.

I remain, dear Sir,
    Yours faithfully,
[*signed*]   T.H.R. Oakes

112. SPAB position on divulging names. Thackeray Turner, SPAB, to the Revd T.H.R. Oakes, 5 November 1894

5 November 1894

in re,

<u>Blythburgh Church</u>

Revd and dear Sir,

I did not notice the request in your previous letter for the names of our three informants or I should certainly have replied.

It is a hard and fast rule of the society never to divulge the names of our informants. I think you will see how impossible it would be for the society to obtain information if it had not such a rule.

I may say I am very sorry that I cannot depart from the rule in this case, as I feel sure that if I gave the names, you would not know our informants. They have nothing to do with the parish and do not live near it.

Thanking you for your letter.

    I remain, Revd and dear Sir,
      Yours faithfully,
[*signed*]   Thackeray Turner
          Secretary

Revd T.H.R. Oakes

113. Advice on restoration. Thackeray Turner, SPAB, to the Revd T.H.R. Oakes, 12 November, 1894

12 November 1894

in re,

<u>Blythburgh Church</u>

Revd and dear Sir,

I had the pleasure of laying your letter of the 6th inst. together with the specifications before the committee of this society at its last meeting.[90]

The committee desires me to thank you for your letter and also for your courtesy in allowing the society to see the specifications which I now return, by parcel post.

The committee [*damage*] that much 'restoration' work has been carried out at the church. This of course the society [*damage*] not approve of, for it holds most strongly that ancient buildings should be altered as little as possible, and that no new work should be in imitation of the work it replaces.

It must be remembered that the more modern work you put in an ancient building

---

[90] Neither the letter nor the specifications are in the SPAB file.

the more you disturb the quiet and restful appearance which gives to such buildings their charm; i.e. the new work overpowers the old.

With regard to the proposal to lay down tiles in the sacrarium, and to put an extra step and altar pace [*sic*], the committee cannot without seeing the building form a just opinion upon the merits of the case, but it holds very strongly that all alterations to our old buildings are a mistake if they can reasonably be avoided.

With regard to putting down new tiles, we should say at once, that the use of any glazed or machine made tiles would be a mistake, for whenever they have been used in an old building they have always [*damage*] themselves to be out of keeping with it.

If the matter is pressing and you would wish it, we can probably arrange to visit the church some time next [*damage*] and meet you there and discuss the matter.

I remain, Revd and dear Sir,

Yours faithfully,

[*signed*]   Thackeray Turner
                Secretary

Revd T.H.R. Oakes

114. Request for SPAB advice. The Revd T.H.R. Oakes to Thackeray Turner, SPAB, 13 November 1894

Walberswick,
Southwold.
13 November 1894

Dear Sir,

I have received your letter of yesterday's date and also the specifications of the work done, thus far, in the restoration of Blythburgh church, and thank you for them. I cordially assent to all that you have said concerning the avoidance of disturbance of the ancient plan and appearance of such an edifice. Thus I shall be very glad of your advice as to any improvement of the desolate appearance, as now manifest, of the sacrarium, which is, of course, not consistent with the ancient grandeur and profuse decoration of the whole edifice. I may say, perhaps, that the matter is not 'pressing'; yet it is the desire of those kind friends who propose it that the work should be undertaken as soon as funds can be obtained; and it is in asking for subscriptions that the necessity of definite plans and aims intrudes itself. I shall be thankful, therefore, for your kindly promised aid at your earliest convenience, that is as soon as it may be arranged with least trouble to yourself or your committee, and I may add with <u>least</u> expense.

I am, dear Sir,

Yours faithfully,

[*signed*]   T.H.R. Oakes

Thackeray Turner, Esq.

115. Proposal for visit by William Morris. Thackeray Turner, SPAB, to the Revd T.H.R. Oakes, 16 November 1894

16 November 1894

in re Blythburgh Church Suffolk

Revd and dear Sir,
I beg to thank you for your letter of the 13th inst:
    I am glad to say that Mr William Morris has expressed a desire to see the church and has said that he will accompany me, but that it will be useless to go at the present time of the year when the days are so short.
    Under these circumstances I shall try and fix a day as soon as the days are longer for I feel sure you would be sorry to lose the advantage of having so good an opinion as that of Mr William Morris.
    I will of course let you know as soon as the date is fixed.
        I remain, Revd and dear Sir,
            Yours faithfully,
[*signed*]   Thackeray Turner,
                Secretary

Revd T.H.R. Oakes

116. William Morris visit. Thackeray Turner, SPAB, to the Revd T.H.R. Oakes, 5 July 1895

5 July 1895

in re <u>Blythborough Church Suffolk</u>

Revd and dear Sir,
I have just heard from Mr William Morris that he hopes to be able to visit Blythborough church with me on Wednesday July 17th.
    If however we have to defer the visit I will let you know.
    Trusting that the day will be convenient for you.
        I remain, Revd and dear Sir,
            Yours faithfully,
[*signed*]   Thackeray Turner,
                Secretary

<u>Revd T.H.R. Oakes</u>

117. William Morris visit. The Revd T.H.R. Oakes to Thackeray Turner, SPAB, 13 July 1895

Walberswick,
Southwold.
13 July 1895

Dear Sir,
I have been in Yorkshire for a month and find your letter of the 5th inst. awaiting my return. I am glad you will be able to visit Blythburgh and bring with you Mr William Morris on next Wednesday. I presume you will leave Liverpool Street by the 10.15 (a.m.) train, reaching Walberswick at 2.[*0*]2 (p.m.). If you will come on to <u>Walberswick</u> (passing Blythburgh), it will afford you the opportunity of seeing Walberswick after the repair of the tower and lunching with me at the vicarage, and

I will drive you to Blythburgh afterwards. I shall be very pleased if this arrangement will suit you.

I am, dear Sir,

Yours very truly,

[*signed*]   T.H.R. Oakes

Thackeray Turner, Esq.

118. William Morris visit. SPAB to the Revd T.H.R. Oakes, 15 July 1895

15 July 1895

in re Blythburgh Church

Revd and dear Sir,

I am desired by Mr Turner to acknowledge the receipt of your letter of the 13th inst. and to thank you for the same.

Mr Turner wishes me to inform you that he has already arranged with Mr William Morris to leave Liverpool Street by the 8.[*0*]5 a.m. train which arrives at Blythburgh at 11.20 a.m. and to return to town by the 2. [*?37*] p.m. train.

Mr Turner therefore thinks it might be impossible for them to visit Blythburgh church and then drive to Walberswick, see the tower and return by the 2.23 p.m. train from there.

It is important to them that they should return by this train.

I remain, Revd and dear Sir,

Yours faithfully,

[*signed*]   [*?John Wardle*]

Revd T.H.R. Oakes

119. Report of William Morris visit. Thackeray Turner, SPAB, to the Revd T.H.R. Oakes, 19 July 1895

19 July 1895

in re, Blythburgh Church

Revd and dear Sir,

At our committee meeting held here yesterday the report upon your church by Mr William Morris and myself was received.

After the subject had been fully considered I was desired to write to you and say that this committee fully approves of the advice we gave you when visiting the building on the 17th inst.

Such a noble building as your church is naturally known to the members of my committee and a lively interest is felt for its preservation.

It is agreed that with reference to the special question upon which you consulted us, viz, the treatment of the chancel, that it would be a mistake to repave the space within the railing as no modern tiles are made which would be in keeping, and as a more satisfactory result could be obtained by retaining the present paving and buying an oriental carpet – an old one by preference – and laying it down over the existing paving.

The altar rail is so inconveniently high and the standards are so offensively ugly, that it seems worth while to remove the standards and put plain square oak posts of the right height in their place. The altar table might with advantage be lengthened but should not be raised by any additional step.

The wall panelling would be greatly improved by being painted white and a further improvement would be to put up a good hanging the whole width and height of the panelling behind the altar.

The church is so light already that nothing would be gained by opening out any of the blocked-up windows. In the opinion of my committee the church would suffer by so doing.

Having said this much upon the question on which you consulted us, the committee cannot refrain from saying that it hopes these suggestions will not be carried out until the [*damage*] most urgently necessary [*damage*] are done.

The lead work of the roof is in most urgent need of repair and unless done great expense will shortly be needed in renewing decayed timbers.

The door and doorway from the tower on to the nave roof are both in crying need of repair as well as the north east buttress of the tower at the roof level.

A few slight repairs are needed at the base of the wall and buttress on the north side of the church.

Again the south porch should be attended to and without delay. It is possible that the south west buttress should have new foundations but in any case a tie rod should be introduced in the inside, running from east to west, [*damage*] against the south wall [*damage*] cracks [*damage*] with liquid [*damage*] and sand. This needs careful doing. The crack should be thoroughly washed out with clean water so as to wash away all dust and damp the work to enable the cement to get a firm hold. The face of the crack should then be covered with clay to about two feet in height at a time, and the cement grout composed of one of cement to three of clean sharp sand should then be pressed in and if necessary some of the facing flints may be removed to facilitate this operation. When this has been done the facing stones can be reset where necessary.

We trust that you will be able to raise sufficient funds to have these repairs carried out and also to make the improvements in the chancel and to replace the flagstaff upon the tower and the screen which has been removed in the chancel, but my committee desires most strongly to urge the importance of doing all the necessary structural work before attempting decorative improvements.

We cannot close this letter without expressing our satisfaction at finding the interior of this beautiful ancient building kept so clean.

I remain Revd and dear Sir,

Yours faithfully,

[*signed*]   Thackeray Turner,
Secretary

Revd T.H.R. Oakes

[*The following documents are in SPAB box Blythburgh II. Another six years have passed.*]

120. Newspaper cutting. Restoration fund appeal. *The Times*, 12 October 1901

The Rev. A.W. Woodruff writes from Walberswick Vicarage, Southwold:-
Archaeologists and visitors to East Anglia will readily recall the ruined churches of
Dunwich, Walberswick, and Covehithe. Within the last year one side of the tower of
Dunwich has fallen. Prints of 1876 show Walberswick church with most of the south-
east wall intact; the greater part is now in ruins. The larger and more interesting
church of Blythburgh, adjoining Walberswick, is at the present moment in peril. A
portion of the roof shows signs of danger, and the beautiful south porch may collapse
at any moment. It cannot be the nation's wish that these splendid monuments of
the past should be allowed to disappear; and therefore as vicar of Blythburgh and
Walberswick – parishes which must look outside for help – I hope that you will allow
this appeal in your columns. Donations should be sent to Messrs. Barclay's Bank,
Southwold, to the Blythburgh or Walberswick Church Restoration Fund, or to me.

121. Condition of south porch. The Revd A.W. Woodruff to SPAB, 26 October 1901

October 26 1901   Walberswick Vicarage,
Southwold.

To the Secretary, Society for the Protection of Ancient Buildings

Dear Sir,

Blythburgh Church

In reply to yours of this morning,[91] I have been warned that the south porch of
Blythburgh is in a dangerous condition, the front (south) having cracked considerably and bulged outwards. Consequently a notice and barrier have been put up and
the main entrance to the church temporarily closed. Besides this, one of the main
beams shows serious signs of weakness in the nave and centre aisle. I am expecting
an architect to visit and report upon both these defects in the course of a week or two
and I shall be pleased to let you know later on what he reports after examination.

I am yours faithfully,

[*signed*]   A.W. Woodruff

122. Architect's examination of church. Thackeray Turner, SPAB, to the Revd A.W. Woodruff, 1 November 1901

1 November 1901

in re,

Blythburgh Church, Suffolk

Revd and dear Sir,

I read your letter of the 26th ulto. to the committee of this society at its meeting held here yesterday, and I was desired to thank you for the same, and for your
kindness in promising to allow the society to know the result of your architect's
examination.

---

[91]   This letter is not in the file.

I remain Revd and dear Sir,
　Yours faithfully,
[*signed*]　　Thackeray Turner
　　　　　　Secretary

Revd A.W. Woodruff

123. Architect's examination of church. Thackeray Turner, SPAB, to the Revd A.W. Woodruff, 27 February 1902

27 February 1902

in re,
　Blythburgh Church, Suffolk

Revd and dear Sir,
　In your letter of the 26th October last you were good enough to inform this society that you expected an architect to examine your church in a week or two and you kindly promised to inform the society of the result of his examination.
　May [*three words damaged*] you have received the report and if so whether you can inform us of its contents?
　Apologising for thus troubling you.
　　I remain Revd and dear Sir,
　　Yours faithfully,
[*signed*]　　Thackeray Turner
　　　　　　Secretary

Revd A.W. Woodruff

124. SPAB reaction to architect's reports. Thackeray Turner, SPAB, to the Revd A.W. Woodruff, 14 March 1902

/encl. 2 Reports and papers/

14 March 1902

re, Blythburgh and Walberswick churches

Revd and dear Sir,
The committee of this society desires to thank you very much for the two reports[92] which you have kindly allowed it to see and which I read at our meeting held here yesterday.
　The committee directs me to say that it is absolutely astonished and taken aback by these reports, which might have been written 15 or 20 years ago, and in its opinion, if they were carried out, they would involve the destruction, from an artistic and historical point of view, of the work which they deal with. Indeed we have not seen such drastic and thorough-going restoration advocated for many a year.
　I wish you could have been present at our meeting, for I find my task of expressing

---

[92]　These reports are not in the file. See Introduction, n. 155.

the committee's views to you most difficult, and I fear you will feel that what I have written is an over-statement although I can assure you it is not so.

I think it is true, that nearly every architect, at any rate, has given up the idea of attempting to complete ancient work by making new work in imitation of it.

The committee sincerely hopes that you will reconsider the question, and that your architect will see his way to abandon 'restoration' and consider how he can repair the building in the simplest possible way.

Blythburgh church is of wide-world reputation and the committee feels it almost unthinkable that it should be treated in such a way.

Should you feel that your hands will be strengthened by a report from the society, the committee would try to arrange to send an architect down to \enable/ it report to you as to what ought to be done.

I enclose one or two papers which will explain more fully than I can in a letter our attitude with regard to ancient buildings.

I remain Revd and dear Sir,
    Yours faithfully,
[*Unsigned*]
            Secretary

Revd A.W. Woodruff

125. Response to SPAB criticism. The Revd A.W. Woodruff to SPAB, 17 March 1902

                                        Walberswick Vicarage,
                                                Southwold.
                                            March 17 1902

To Secretary, Society for the Protection of Ancient Buildings
Dear Sir,

I beg to acknowledge yours of 14th with numerous enclosures. As regards the society's views I was not at all surprised as I am fully acquainted with the position taken up by the society, but this attitude towards ancient buildings is evidently not shared by all people, including architects and FSAs. However it will probably be satisfactory to your society to hear that nothing shall be done as long as I am vicar. I cannot bind my successor who will probably come into office in July or August, but your society might address an urgent appeal to him, say in the course of July next.

As one who is himself so much interested in the protection and preservation of ancient ruins, may I humbly ask where was the society when \a great portion of/ Dunwich tower[93] fell last year?

    I am yours faithfully,
[*signed*]   A.W. Woodruff

126. Request for name of new incumbent. Thackeray Turner, SPAB, to the Revd A.W. Woodruff, 21 March 1902

/encl./

---

[93]   The abandoned church of All Saints, Dunwich, was a victim of coastal erosion, eventually falling into the sea between 1904 and 1919.

21 March 1902

re, Blythburgh and Walberswick churches

Revd and dear Sir,
I read your letter of the 17th inst. to the committee of this society at its meeting held here yesterday, and I was desired to thank you for the same and for the courteous manner in which you have received the society's representations.

The committee would be greatly indebted to you if you would kindly inform it, on the enclosed postcard, of the name of the new incumbent, so that it may address him at the proper time.

Trusting that you will forgive the society for again troubling you.

I remain, Revd and dear Sir,
    Yours faithfully,
[*signed*]   Thackeray Turner
          Secretary

Revd A.W. Woodruff

127. Request for name of new incumbent. Thackeray Turner, SPAB, to Sir Ralph B.M. Blois Bt, 11 April 1902

re, Blythburgh and Walberswick churches

    To Sir R.B.M. Blois Bart.
Sir,
The Society for the Protection of Ancient Buildings ventures to address you as patron of Blythburgh and Walberswick, as it has been informed that during the course of the next few months you will be making a fresh presentation to these livings.

The committee of the society will be greatly indebted to you if, when the appointment has been made, you would kindly allow the society to know the name and address of the new incumbent, as it is anxious to address him upon the subject of the preservation of these two buildings, which have for many years passed received the society's closest attention.

Trusting that you will forgive the society for making this request.

      I am, Sir,
    Your obedient Servant,
[*signed*]   Thackeray Turner
          Secretary

11 April 1902

128. Protection of south porch. Thackeray Turner, SPAB, to the churchwardens of Blythburgh Church, 19 September 1902

To the churchwardens of Blythburgh, Suffolk
Gentlemen,
The late incumbent of Blythburgh informed us that he was leaving, and the society has been waiting to hear who is the newly appointed incumbent, in order that it might write to him on the subject of the church.

It has lately learnt from an architect who has visited the building that the porch is in actual danger, and it has desired me to write and ask you whether you cannot in your capacities as churchwardens, direct that temporary support be given to the porch by means of shores so as to avoid a catastrophe?

The committee is convinced that the porch can be repaired and made substantial without rebuilding, and it hopes in due course to be allowed to report upon it.

I remain, Gentlemen,

Yours faithfully,

[*signed*]   Thackeray Turner
                Secretary

19 September 1902

129. Response to SPAB proposal. Claude F. Egerton to Thackeray Turner, SPAB, 29 September 1902

Blythburgh,
Suffolk.

29 September 1902

Dear Sir,

Their [*sic*] is no incumbent appointed as yet and I am in charge of the 'Restoration Fund'. The porch in my opinion will bear no touching without coming down, and though it is only my opinion, still I consider the porch in its present condition would be better than a mass of supports round it, even if they would be effectual. This is a very poor parish and it is difficult to get money. We have however about £200 in hand or promised. Is your society in the habit of helping with pecuniary assistance as if so it might be possible to put the porch right. The roof also is in bad repair in places though I am going to try to get that done. In any case we shall be glad if a competent man reported on the church, needless to say without expense to us which we cannot afford.

Yours truly,

[*signed*]   Claude F. Egerton

130. Protection of south porch. Thackeray Turner, SPAB, to Claude F. Egerton, 3 October 1902

3 October 1902

re, <u>Blythburgh Church, Suffolk</u>

Dear Sir,

I beg to thank you for your letter of the 29th ulto: which I laid before the committee of this society at its meeting held here yesterday.

The committee desires me to explain that the shoring which it suggested should be put to the porch, it intended should only be put as a temporary support which would be removed after the porch had been repaired.

We are convinced that a small sum spent in this way now would save many pounds, and what is of still greater importance, much valuable ancient work.

The committee gathers from your letter that nothing is likely to be done until the new incumbent is appointed, and therefore it feels that to report now would be premature, but if the committee is wrong in its conclusion, perhaps you would kindly inform it.

The committee directs me to add that it will gladly, at the proper time, try to make arrangements for the building to be visited and reported upon.

Again thanking you.

    I remain, dear Sir,
        Yours faithfully,
[*signed*]   Thackeray Turner
            Secretary

Claude F. Egerton, Esq.

131. Introduction of SPAB to new incumbent. Thackeray Turner, SPAB, to the Revd R.P. Wing, 25 April 1903

/Enc/

25 April 1903

re, <u>Blythburgh Church, Suffolk</u>

Revd and dear Sir,

For many years past this Society has given advice respecting the upkeep of Blythburgh church, and it has surveyed the building on more than one occasion.

We heard that further works were contemplated and wrote to your predecessor who forwarded to us the architect's report. My committee was absolutely shocked at his drastic proposals, and it wrote urging that they should not be carried out.

In reply he informed us that he would not have them carried out as he was resigning the living.

My committee begs that you will allow it now to approach you and to ask that you will not countenance the proposals then contemplated and that you will treat the building in accordance with this society's principles.

The committee will gladly give you every help should you be willing to do this.

I am taking the liberty of enclosing some of the society's papers.

    I remain, Revd and dear Sir,
        Yours faithfully,
[*Copy not signed*]
           Secretary
Revd R.P. Wing

132. Concern about condition of Blythburgh church. Joseph E. Southall to Thackeray Turner, SPAB, 1 July 1903

c/o Mrs Palmer,
11 South Green,
Southwold,
Suffolk.
1 July 1903

Dear Sir,

I went, the other day, to see the fine church at Blythburgh (about 4 miles from Southwold) and found that the beautiful carved and painted roof there has been badly neglected so that rain comes through and the timbers are beginning to give way – and the caretaker tells me that a thorough overhauling is in prospect, with the possibility of <u>repainting</u>. \ As already done at Southwold ./ If you know this large church (with fine Perpendicular roof and clerestory) you will know that its painted roof is of great beauty and the timbers contain almost completely through nave and choir the old painting with \carved/ angels, and lovely patterns <on the timbers> on the mouldings. The whole effect is remarkably beautiful and sweet in colour, and so I write to ask whether you are at present aware of what is going on – and if not whether anything could be done in the way of advice to those responsible.

The \south/ porch and tower are in a bad way also.

I am,

Yours faithfully,

[*signed*]   Joseph E. Southall

Thackeray Turner, Esq.

/By same post I send you circular about restoration proposed. JS./

133. Justification of SPAB's use of press publicity. Thackeray Turner, SPAB, to Joseph E. Southall, 3 July 1903

3 July 1903

re, <u>Blythburgh Church, Suffolk</u>

My dear Sir,

I am very glad that you have written to us about this case.

I read your letter to my committee and it desired me to say it hoped very much you would be willing to assist it by calling on the parson. In the hope that you will consent to do this I will tell you how matters stand.

The case has been before the society for many years past and it has been visited on more than one occasion.

In October 1901 an appeal appeared in the Times[94] for funds to restore the church and, after some correspondence with the vicar, he kindly allowed the society to see the reports made by the architect whose name appears on the appeal you sent.

The works proposed were of a most drastic nature, and the society wrote to the vicar to the effect that it was astonished and taken aback at these reports (one referred to Walberswick church) which might have been written 15 or 20 years ago, and if carried out would in the opinion of the society involve the destruction from an historical and artistic point of view, of the work which they deal with. The society begged the vicar to reconsider the question, and expressed a hope that the architect would see his way to abandon restoration, and consider how he could repair the building in the simplest possible way. It further offered to visit and report.

The vicar replied that he was leaving and that nothing would be done so long as he was there.

---

[94] See Correspondence 120.

In September 1902 we wrote to the churchwardens to the effect that an architect who had visited the building about that date reported that the porch was in actual danger and asking whether they could not direct that tempory [*sic*] support should be given to it, as we were convinced it could be repaired without rebuilding.

To this letter a very unsatisfactory reply was received from Mr Egerton.

In April of the present year we wrote to the new incumbent informing him of the facts of the case, and asking him not to countenance the proposals contemplated in 1901 but to treat the building in accordance with the society's principles. So far we have not received a reply from him.

The committee feels that Blythburgh church is such a well known building that if it is their determination to adhere to their destructive proposals, we must appeal to the public through the press.

It may be that you could let the parson know that the society has no other

[*letter incomplete*]

134. Report of visit to church. Joseph E. Southall to Thackeray Turner, SPAB, 7 July 1903

Re Blythburgh Church

11 South Green,
Southwold.

7 July 1903

Thackeray Turner Esq.

My dear Sir,

In accordance with the request contained in your letter I went yesterday to see the vicar of Blythburgh and Walberswick and found him not at all hostile to the views of the society but not <u>very</u> much interested in the artistic or historical aspect of the church. Having only recently come to the living he felt that the restoration question was not altogether in his hands and suggested that he and I should go over to Blythburgh to see Mr Egerton the churchwarden. This we have done this morning and I hope that the result will prove to be fairly satisfactory.

I found Mr Egerton (who is a racing man, fond of horses and dogs) to have no particular views on the matter in hand but wanting to collect money for the restoration and disappointed to find that this was not to be helped by the society. He appeared to have an easy faith in such an architect as the \recent/ restorer of Peterborough cathedral whom he proposed to call in when funds permit (which luckily is not yet); meanwhile they are only doing certain repairs to the roof I believe.[95]

I tried to shew him that the society was most anxious for the due repair and preservation of the fabric but differed from restoring architects when it came to such work as putting up new tracery or other ornament over the porch and pointed out to him the needless expense upon such work. He appeared to appreciate both the principle involved and also the saving in expense (especially the latter) and first hesitated and

---

[95] This is probably a reference to George Frederick Bodley (1827–1907), who worked on the west front of Peterborough cathedral, 1898–1902. There is no evidence that Philip Johnston, the architect eventually chosen for Blythburgh, ever worked at Peterborough. Personal communication from Julian Limentani.

at last even agreed with my contention and expressed perfect willingness to consult with any-one whom the Society might send.

He fully agreed as did also the vicar that the roof must not be re-painted – he had not heard it suggested but Mr Wing confessed that the contractor had proposed it to him – making it 'exactly like the old work.' On this point (a most important one) at any rate I think we ought to succeed and Mr Egerton said he should be glad if it were really not necessary to rebuild the porch. I hope I may say that Mr Egerton did see and appreciate the fact that new ornamental work is both out of place and out of harmony in an ancient building – though the idea was new to him apparently. This being so I hope a beginning is made and if one of our society expert in such matters could be sent here great good may result. I fear I can do no more but perhaps you will let me know what turn things take <from>. If I <could> can give any further information I shall be glad. I will send you some photographs of the roof and porch taken last week as soon as I get prints.

I am yours faithfully,
[*signed*]   Joseph E. Southall

135. Arrangement of visit by SPAB's architect. Thackeray Turner, SPAB, to the Revd R.P. Wing, 10 July 1903

10 July 1903

re, <u>Blythburgh Church, Suffolk</u>

Revd and dear Sir,
Our member, Mr Joseph E. Southall, has reported to the society his interview with you and Mr Egerton, and the committee at its meeting held here yesterday decided to endeavour to arrange for the building to be visited on behalf of the society.

As soon as we are able to definitely arrange for one of the society's architects to visit, we will communicate with you.

I remain Revd and dear Sir,
Yours faithfully,
[*signed*]   Thackeray Turner
Secretary

Revd R.P. Wing

136. Request for advice from SPAB. Claude F. Egerton to Joseph E. Southall, 26 July 1903

Blythburgh,
Suffolk.

26 July   1903
Dear Sir,
I am very much obliged to you for your letter and for the cheque, for which on behalf of the restoration committee I thank you. You may rest assured that we shall only repair what is necessary to prevent falling down, and if you could find an expert who would suggest what ought to be done to the porch, we should be very grateful.

Yours very truly,
[*signed*]   C.F. Egerton

137. Concerning visit by SPAB's architect. Joseph E. Southall to Thackeray Turner, SPAB, 27 July 1903

Blythburgh Church

13, Charlotte Road,
Edgbaston,
Birmingham.

27 July 1903

My dear Sir,

Thank you for your last letter. On returning home I sent Mr Egerton a cheque of one guinea towards the repair – not restoration – of the church and have just received from him the reply which I enclose for your committee to see.[96] It seems as though the present moment was the time for the expert member of the society mentioned by you, to go and advise if possible at once while the Blythburgh people are in this mind about the matter. I have not told Mr Egerton that he is coming.

Believe me,

Yours sincerely,

[*signed*]   Joseph E. Southall

Thackeray Turner, Esq.

138. Concerning visit by SPAB's architect. Thackeray Turner, SPAB, to Joseph E. Southall, 28 July 1903

28 July 1903

re, Blythburgh Church, Suffolk

My dear Sir,

Many thanks for your letter and for the letter from Mr Egerton.

We wrote to the vicar on the 10th inst. saying the society was trying to arrange to visit, and that as soon as we had done so we would write again.

A professional member has promised to visit, but he has not yet named a day but when he does so we will at once inform the vicar.

Yours sincerely,

[signed]   Thackeray Turner
            Secretary

Joseph E. Southall, Esq.

139. Concerning visit by SPAB's architect. Telegram Alfred H. Powell to John Kent, SPAB, 30 July 1903

Cambridge, 10.13 a.m. 30 July 1903
To Kent c/o Turner, 10 Buckingham Street, Strand, London.
Train due Blythburgh 1-48 Saturday. Powell.

---

[96] Correspondence 136.

140. Concerning visit by SPAB's architect. Thackeray Turner, SPAB, to the Revd R.P. Wing, 30 July 1903

30 July 1903

re, <u>Blythburgh Church, Suffolk</u>

Revd and dear Sir,

I have much pleasure in informing you that the society has arranged for one of its architects, Mr Alfred H. Powell, to visit your church, and he has promised to do so on Saturday next, the 1st of August, coming by the train due to arrive at Blythburgh at 1.48.

I very much regret that I am unable to give you longer notice, but I trust the date will be convenient to you.

I may add that Mr Powell has had considerable practical experience in the repair of ancient buildings.

     I remain Revd and dear Sir,
   Yours faithfully,
[*signed*]   Thackeray Turner
     Secretary

Revd R.P. Wing

141. Note by Thackeray Turner, SPAB, undated

Should you wish to communicate with Mr Powell his present address is Queens' College, Cambridge.
[*signed*]   Thackeray Turner

142. Selection of SPAB architect for Blythburgh. Alfred H. Powell to Thackeray Turner, SPAB, 5 August 1903

Queens' College Cambridge.
August 5 1903

My dear Turner,
Your postcard just to hand.

They are pulling down the old Falcon Inn[97] [*?said*] here the brutes, with its old galleries. Am going to try and raise the wind. Brandon church lantern was down when I got there. I'm sure I could have mended it in situ. I sent you Blythburgh report. Please find somebody to go there. Is Weir impossible. Would it do for Wells? I believe he'll be free soon but I'm not sure if Pryor[98] doesn't want him. Then there is Stallybrass whose address is B.T. Stallybrass, Ridge, Chilmark, Salisbury. He's

---

[97] The Falcon Inn, Petty Cury, Cambridge. In the nineteenth century the yards of the city's ancient inns became the worst of its slums. The inn and its galleries were demolished in 1903 at the insistence of the Medical Officer of Health. Cambridge Historic Core Appraisal (Cambridge City Council, 2006).

[98] Edward Shroeder Prior.

quite sound SPAB as also is Wells of course. But the trouble is <u>money</u>. Sir R. Blois the patron talks of getting money 'next year'. He ought to be hurried up.

Must send this to post. I note your hours of arrival and will see about a meal for you.

Yours ever,

[*signed*]   Alfred H. Powell

I think we shall be all safe with the cement.

143. Visit expenses. Alfred H. Powell to Thackeray Turner, SPAB, 7 August 1903

Queens' College Cambridge.

August 7 1903

My dear Turner,

I forgot to enclose my bill of expenses for Blythburgh which comes in all to 23s. 8d.

Yours ever,

[*signed*]   Alfred H. Powell

144. SPAB advice. Thackeray Turner, SPAB, to Claude F. Egerton, 11 August 1903

11 August 1903

<u>Blythburgh Church.</u>

Dear Sir,

When I saw Mr Alfred Powell last week, he told me that you were very much interested in Blythburgh church, and therefore I am taking the liberty of forwarding a copy of a letter which I am today addressing to the vicar and churchwardens.

As I do not know the address of your co-churchwarden I regret that I cannot send him a copy. Perhaps you will kindly explain this to him?

Yours faithfully,

[*signed*]   Thackeray Turner

Secretary

C.F. Egerton, Esq.

145. SPAB advice. Thackeray Turner, SPAB, to the Revd R.P. Wing, 11 August 1903

11 August 1903

re, <u>Blythburgh Church.</u>

Revd and dear Sir,

In forwarding the enclosed letter to you I am writing to tell you that, with a view of saving you trouble, I have sent a copy to Mr Egerton, but I have been unable to send a copy to your other churchwarden not knowing his address.

I may add that should you wish for the society's support in appealing for funds, I have no doubt the committee would be willing to assist you by writing a letter which you could publish, if satisfied that the work would be properly done.

I remain, Revd and dear Sir,

Yours faithfully,
[*signed*]   Thackeray Turner
             Secretary

Revd R.P. Wing

146. Recommendation of architect. Thackeray Turner, SPAB, to the vicar and churchwardens of Blythburgh, 11 August 1903[99]

/Copy/

re, Blythburgh Church, Suffolk.
To the Revd the vicar, and
the churchwardens.

Gentlemen,

We have received Mr Alfred Powell's report on your church, but unfortunately there is no meeting of my committee until next month.

I gather however, from what Mr Powell says, that you are anxious to hear from the society. Therefore I am writing to say that I feel sure the committee will fully approve of his report, and be very glad to hear that you are acting on his advice in having the porch shored up, for his report only confirms a report which we had received from a member of the society, an architect,[100] who stated that the porch could certainly be repaired without rebuilding, thus retaining its authentic character.

I feel sure, from long experience, that you will find the only satisfactory way of dealing with your church, will be to get an architect who will remain at Blythburgh during the progress of the work, and if you will follow the course which many custodians of ancient buildings have recently adopted on the advice of the society, and have the work carried out in this manner, you will find that not only will you preserve the exceptionally valuable qualities of your church, and put it into a sound state of repair, but that you will do this at considerably less cost than if you employed an architect and contractor in the usual way.

Architects who have been working for us in this way have employed labour and bought materials on behalf of the custodians, who have paid for the labour and materials as the work has progressed, thus avoiding unnecessary profits passing into contractors' hands.

Mr Powell has done work of this sort for the society to its entire satisfaction. He is at present engaged in repairing the president's lodge at Queen's [*sic*] college, Cambridge, and I should suppose that he would be willing to undertake the work at your church at a later date, should you desire it, but I understand that at present you are in the unfortunate position of having to collect funds.

Please understand that I am writing this letter, as you will see, without the instructions of my committee, and I have undertaken the responsibility of doing so, with the sole object of assisting you in preserving one of the most valuable buildings in the county, and I may add that I shall at all times be only too glad to give you any assistance which lies within my power.

I remain, Gentlemen,
     Yours faithfully,

---

[99] Also in SROI 2, 2.
[100] The member was Joseph E. Southall. See Correspondence 132. For Powell's report see Appendix A 11.

93

[*signed*] Thackeray Turner
　　　　Secretary
11 August 1903

147. Photographs of Blythburgh. Thackeray Turner, SPAB, to Joseph E. Southall, 4 September 1903

4 September 1903

re, <u>Blythburgh Church, Suffolk</u>

My dear Sir,
I laid the interesting photographs[101] before the committee at its meeting held here yesterday and I was desired to thank you sincerely for the same.

The church has been visited on behalf of the society and we understand that the porch <has been> is to be shored up in accordance with the advice given by our member on the spot.

We have written to the vicar and churchwardens on the subject of the best method to adopt in supervising the repairs to the building, but so far have not heard from them.

Yours very truly,
[*signed*]　　Thackeray Turner
　　　　　　Secretary

Joseph E. Southall, Esq.

148. Comment on Blythburgh individuals. Joseph E. Southall to Thackeray Turner, SPAB, 6 September 1903

13, Charlotte Road,
Edgbaston,
Birmingham.

6 September 1903

Dear Sir,
Thank you for your letter. I am very pleased to hear that Blythburgh has been visited and good progress made. I fear they have not even money for the proper repairs yet. I hope the roof may be saved as it is I think the really notable part of the church even more than the porch. The vicar seemed to me to be a mere nobody compared to the churchwarden Mr Egerton who had the restoration under his care before the present parson came there.

I am,
　Yours faithfully,
[*signed*]　　Joseph E. Southall

Thackeray Turner, Esq.

---

[101] Southall's photographs are not in the SPAB's collection.

149. Report of SPAB's architect. Thackeray Turner, SPAB, to the vicar and churchwardens of Blythburgh, 25 September 1903

25 September 1903

re, Blythburgh Church, Suffolk.
To the Revd the vicar, and
the churchwardens.

Gentlemen,

At the last meeting of this society Mr Alfred Powell's report on your church was carefully considered. <It> The committee desires me to inform you that the report confirms the opinion expressed by other architects who have seen the building.

He is of opinion that the roofs of the building are in need of careful inspection and repair, that he could see sufficient to convince him that the nave must be attended to but that any detailed report upon its condition could only be made by having a scaffolding underneath it, and that such scaffolding would necessarily have to be erected before the work was undertaken.

The methods of repairing ancient timber roofs have greatly improved in recent years, and many roofs which at one time would have been removed, have recently been thoroughly repaired in situ.

Mr Powell further says that he considers the lead on the nave roof ought to be recast and relaid. He also reports that the tower is in urgent need of repair, that it is very high and has been struck by lightning, not long ago, that the eastern wall at the level of the bell cage is split and bulged badly, and that the springing stones of the window arch have fallen out and others seem to be coming loose. He also says that part of the <tower> parapet is hardly safe at the south west corner, and that to repair the tower would mean a scaffolding, and he thinks it would have to be strong enough to shore from.

With regard to the south porch, he gives a long and close description of its present condition and concludes by saying:- 'I am confident that the porch, if they will keep it standing, (and they promise to set about shoring at once,) can be mended securely without being taken down even partially.'

This gives my committee great satisfaction, for a medieval building which has been rebuilt, no matter how carefully, has not the same historical interest as one which has been repaired without rebuilding.

The committee desires me to add that if you gentlemen find yourselves in sympathy with the society it will be glad to assist you should you desire it, by writing you a letter, for publication, calling attention to the exceptional value of your church and the pressing need for funds.

I remain, Gentlemen,
Yours faithfully,
[*signed*]   Thackeray Turner
Secretary

150. Situation at Blythburgh. Claude F. Egerton to SPAB, 4 October 1903

Blythburgh,
Suffolk.

4 October 1903

Sir,

95

I am in receipt of your letter of the 25th ult. The porch has been securely shored and is at present safe from falling. As our funds in hand do not amount to more than £200 at present, I fear it is useless to start on the roof. Perhaps the letter you suggest might be written and I should be glad to receive it.

Yours very truly,
C.F. Egerton
Churchwarden

151. Assurance sought about adherence to SPAB principles. Thackeray Turner, SPAB, to Claude F. Egerton, 9 October 1903

9 October 1903

re, <u>Blythburgh Church</u>

Dear Sir,

I had the pleasure of reading your letter of the 4th inst: to the committee of this society at its meeting held here yesterday.

The committee was greatly pleased to learn that the porch has been securely shored, but before writing the letter which it offered to write, it wishes to point out to you that it has its duty to its members to remember, and that it would be severely blamed if it assisted works which were not done in accordance with the principles of the society. Therefore it feels bound first to ask you whether you can give it your assurance that the work will be carried out in accordance with the society's views, as this will enable it to write a much stronger letter?

If you could see your way to deciding whom to employ to carry out the work, this would probably be the best assurance which could be given to the committee.

Trusting that you will forgive me for again troubling you.

I remain, dear Sir,
Yours faithfully,
[*signed*]   Thackeray Turner
Secretary

C.F. Egerton, Esq.

152. Blythburgh restoration philosophy. Claude F. Egerton to SPAB, 11 October 1903

Blythburgh,
Suffolk.

11 October 1903

Dear Sirs,

In reply to your letter I beg to inform you that the idea of the council here is to put the church in good order, that is to say to make the roofs safe and <u>watertight,</u> and the tower also in a safe condition. They wish to do this without altering in any way the ancient character of the building and in fact to do nothing to the church except what is necessary to prevent further decay. We should be quite willing for the repairs to be carried out under the personal supervision of Mr Powell or any one else the society would recommend, but as we know that it is an expensive business, and as I said in my letter we are at present not justified in commencing, perhaps your letter may help and if you can give me a copy I think I can get it into the Daily Mail, <whose> the editor of which I know.[102]

Yours very truly,

[*signed*]   Claude F. Egerton
        Churchwarden

153. Help in raising money. Thackeray Turner, SPAB, to Claude F. Egerton, 16 October 1903

/Enc./

16 October 1903

re, <u>Blythburgh Church, Suffolk</u>

Dear Sir,

I beg to thank you for your letter of the 11th inst: which I read to the committee of this society at its meeting held here yesterday.

I enclose a letter which was approved by the Committee, and which we trust will be helpful to you in raising the necessary funds. If the society can give you any further help, it will gladly do so.

I remain, dear Sir,

Yours faithfully,

[*signed*]   Thackeray Turner
        Secretary

P.S. We will tell Mr Alfred Powell that you intend engaging his services.
                T.T.

Claude F. Egerton Esq.

154. Restatement of SPAB position. Thackeray Turner, SPAB, to Claude F. Egerton, 16 October 1903

16 October 1903

<re, Blythburgh Church, Suffolk>

Dear Sir,

The committee of the Society for the Protection of Ancient Buildings desires me to thank you for your letter and to say how glad it is to learn that the vicar and church-wardens have already taken the urgently necessary step of supporting the south porch by temporary shoring until sufficient funds have been obtained to put it in substantial repair without rebuilding.

Your church is a building of such exceptional value, and of such great size, that the committee realises the impossibility of the parish providing sufficient funds to carry out the expensive repairs which are needed both to the western tower and the beautiful medieval decorated roofs, as well as the porch, and it feels sure that when the public realises that you have decided to make an effort to get this much needed

---

[102] Thomas Marlowe (1868–1935) was editor of the London newspaper *The Daily Mail* from 1899 to 1922. Obituary, *The Times* 6 December 1935.

97

work done, and that it is your intention not to countenance 'restoration', but to do the work substantially and soundly with the least possible alteration to the present aspect of the building, that you will receive the financial support which you may reasonably expect, and this society will gladly assist you with advice at all times.

I remain, dear Sir,

Yours faithfully,

[*signed*]   Thackeray Turner
        Secretary

Claude F. Egerton, Esq.
Churchwarden

155. Request for information about work at Blythburgh. Thackeray Turner, SPAB, to Claude F. Egerton, 30 September 1904

30 September 1904

re, <u>Blythburgh Church, Suffolk</u>

Dear Sir,

The committee of this society will be much indebted to you if you will inform it how matters are progressing with regard to Blythburgh church.

It has much pleasure in informing you that owing to the appeal which we put in our annual report one of our members has paid to the society the sum of £50 (fifty pounds) towards the work of repair on condition that the work meets with the society's approval.

I remain, dear Sir,

Yours faithfully,

[*signed*]   Thackeray Turner
        Secretary

Claude F. Egerton, Esq.

156. Fundraising but no work. Claude F. Egerton to SPAB, 1 October 1904

Blythburgh,
Suffolk.

1 October 1904

Dear Sir,

I am in receipt of your letter of the 30th inst, and am much gratified to hear of the donation you mention. Beyond shoring up the porch as advised, we are doing nothing but collect funds. The account now stands at £325 or with the £50 you mention £375. Mr Lucas RA is arranging with Mr Thomas of the 'Graphic' for a series of pictures with an appeal which may do some good.

Yours very truly,

[*signed*]   Claude F. Egerton

157. Request for professional opinion on adequacy of protection for porch. Thackeray Turner, SPAB, to Alfred H. Powell, 7 October 1904

7 October 1904

re, <u>Porch Blythburgh Church</u>

My dear Powell,

A question has been raised by a member of the committee as to whether the shoring to the porch at Blythburgh is sufficient to secure it until the repairs can be taken in hand, and the committee would much like to have your opinion upon the subject. I should add that our member has not seen the shoring.

    Yours very truly,

[*signed*]   Thackeray Turner

        Secretary

158. Report on porch. Alfred H. Powell to Thackeray Turner, SPAB, 14 October 1904

Tyrley Castle, Market Drayton

    Salop.

October 14 1904

re Blythburgh

My dear Turner,

I enclose you the sketch[103] I made at the time for the shoring of the porch here.

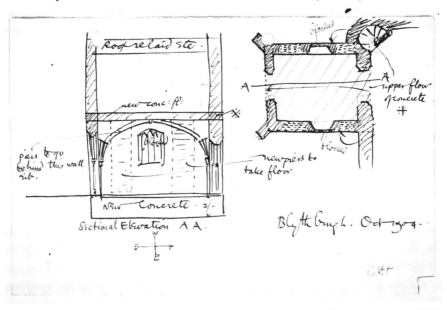

Plate 7. The south porch. A sketch by Alfred H. Powell for proposals for repair, October 1904. Correspondence 158. © SPAB Blythburgh, Box II

---

[103] See Plate 7.

I think it ought to be strong enough, if it don't squash the walls in by its weight. I fear 'twas but poorly designed on my part and I think the correction in chalk is your own! The top of the south west buttress looks dangerous rather, on the drawing but I should not think it would fall if they can begin in reasonable time.

I <u>have not seen</u> the shoring myself – so I don't really know how it has been carried out.

Yours always,
[*signed*]   Alfred H. Powell

Please let me know if there are any buildings in this neighbourhood you would like me to look up for you.

159. Request to visit Blythburgh. Thackeray Turner, SPAB, to Alfred H. Powell, 21 October 1904

21 October 1904
re, <u>Blythburgh Church</u>

My dear Powell,
Many thanks for your letter and the sketches which I return herewith.

The matter was considered by the committee at its meeting yesterday and it desired me to write to you and say it considers it to be of the utmost importance that the shoring to the porch should be efficient, for, were it to fail, it would damage the society's \reputation/ considerably.

Under these circumstances the committee would be grateful to you if you would visit Blythburgh, at the society's expense, and assure yourself that the shoring is efficiently doing its work.

We are afraid it will inconvenience you but as you have the case in hand we could not ask any one else to go.

Thanks, we will bear you in mind, if there should be any buildings in the Market Drayton neighbourhood we want visiting.

Yours sincerely,
[*signed*]   Thackeray Turner
Secretary

160. Request not to delay work. Thackeray Turner, SPAB, to Claude F. Egerton, 28 October 1904

28 October 1904

re, <u>Blythburgh Church</u>

Dear Sir,
I laid your letter of the 1st inst:[104] before the committee of this society at its meeting held here yesterday when I was desired to thank you for the same, and to ask you whether you do not think it will be possible to take the porch in hand next spring?

The committee considers that the sum you have collected will be more than

---

[104] See Correspondence 156.

sufficient to carry out the works needed to repair and strengthen the <u>porch,</u> and, considering its critical condition, it is undesirable to delay repairing it for longer than is absolutely necessary.

    I am,

      Yours faithfully,

[*signed*]   Thackeray Turner

          Secretary

Claude F. Egerton Esq.

161. Church south porch. Thackeray Turner, SPAB, to Alfred H. Powell, 28 October 1904

28 October 1904

re, <u>Blythburgh Church</u>

My dear Powell,

First, let me say how much the committee is indebted to you for your promptness in visiting Blythburgh church. It is a relief to find that you and Mr Wells consider the shoring adequate.[105]

    The committee quite agrees with you in thinking that the repairs should be taken in hand at the earliest possible date, but it thinks it would be too risky to begin them before the spring.

    Mr Egerton, the churchwarden, informed us, on the 1st October, that they have collected £325 and in addition to this a member of the society has given £50, which we hold, towards the repair fund. We are writing to ask Mr Egerton whether the porch cannot be taken in hand in the spring, as they have in hand more than is necessary for its repair.

    Please let us know what we owe you for travelling expenses.

      Yours sincerely,

[*signed*]   Thackeray Turner

          Secretary

162. Visit expenses. Thackeray Turner, SPAB, to Francis W. Aplin, 4 November 1904

/Enclosures/

4 November 1904

re, <u>Blythburgh Church, Suffolk</u>

Dear Sir,

The committee will be much indebted to you if you will kindly forward with the enclosed letter a cheque payable to Alfred H. Powell, Esq. for £2 16s. 5d. (two pounds, sixteen shillings and five pence) in settlement of his account for expenses in visiting Blythburgh church.

    The cheque to be drawn on the general account.

---

[105] For Powell's report see Appendix A 12.

Yours faithfully,
[*signed*]   Thackeray Turner
                    Secretary

Francis W. Aplin Esq.
Honorary Treasurer

163. Visit expenses. Thackeray Turner, SPAB, to Alfred H. Powell, 4 November 1904

/Enclosure/

4 November 1904

re, <u>Blythburgh Church, Suffolk</u>

Dear Powell,
I am desired by the Committee to forward to you the enclosed cheque value £2 16s. 5d. in payment of your travelling expenses.
   Will you please return the account receipted?
   Yours sincerely,
[*signed*]   Thackeray Turner
                    Secretary

164. Visit expenses. Thackeray Turner, SPAB, to Francis W. Aplin, 11 November 1904

/Enclosures/

11 November 1904

re, <u>Blythburgh Church, Suffolk</u>

Dear Sir,
The committee will be much indebted to you if you will kindly forward with the enclosed letter a cheque payable to Alfred H. Powell Esq. for £2 16s. 5d. (two pounds, sixteen shillings and five pence) in settlement of his account for expenses in visiting Blythburgh church.
   The cheque to be drawn on the general account.
       Yours faithfully,
[*signed*]   Thackeray Turner
                    Secretary

Francis W. Aplin Esq., Honorary Treasurer

165. Visit expenses. Thackeray Turner, SPAB, to Alfred H. Powell, 11 November 1904

11 November 1904

re, <u>Blythburgh Church, Suffolk</u>

My dear Powell,

Owing to an error at the bank the cheque for your travelling expenses was not sent to you last Friday, but it has been forwarded to you today.

    Yours sincerely,

[*signed*]   Thackeray Turner

        Secretary

P.S. Your china had not arrived when I left home this morning but I am looking forward to seeing it. I was just about to reply to your previous letter when I realised you [*? words*] until I saw your handywork.[106]

    T. T.

166. Meeting with patron. The Revd R.P. Wing to Thackeray Turner, SPAB, 27 January 1905

                                      27 January 1905

Dear Sirs,

Will you please, at once communicate with

Sir R.B.M. Blois Bart

    Cockfield Hall

        Yoxford, Suffolk.

He desires an interview re Blythburgh church.

[*signed*]   R.P. Wing, vicar of Blythburgh

P.S. Sir R.B.M. Blois is lord of the manor and patron of the living.

167. Meeting with patron. Thackeray Turner, SPAB, to Sir Ralph B.M. Blois, Bt, 28 January 1905

                                      28 January 1905

re, Blythburgh Church, Suffolk

Sir,

I have been informed by the Revd R.P. Wing, the vicar of Blythburgh, that you are desirous of seeing me with reference to Blythburgh church, and he has asked me to communicate with you with a view to arranging an interview.

    If convenient to yourself I could arrange to keep an appointment here on Thursday or Friday next at 3 oclock p.m.

    Will you please let me know if either of these days will suit you?

        I am, Sir,

      Your obedient Servant,

[*Unsigned*]

          Secretary

To Sir R.B.M. Blois Bart.

---

[106] Both Turner and Powell were accomplished ceramic painters, Powell and his wife Louise becoming pottery designers for Wedgwood. William Whyte, 'Turner, Hugh Thackeray (1853–1937)' *ODNB*; Michael Drury, *Wandering architects* (Stamford, 2000), pp. 45–61.

168. Meeting with patron. Thackeray Turner, SPAB, to the Revd R.P. Wing, 28 January 1905

28 January 1905

re, <u>Blythburgh Church, Suffolk</u>

Revd and dear Sir,

I beg to thank you for your letter of yesterday's date, and to inform you that I have written to Sir R.B.M. Blois Bart. with a view to arranging an interview.

   I remain, Revd and dear Sir,

  Yours faithfully,

[*Unsigned*]

    Secretary

Rev. R.P. Wing

169. Meeting with patron. Sir Ralph B.M. Blois, Bt, to Thackeray Turner, SPAB, 31 January 1905

31 January 1905

Dear Sir,

I shall be very pleased to come and see you next Thursday 2nd at 3 p.m.

  Yours truly,

[*signed*] Ralph Blois

To Thackeray Turner Esq.

170. Patron's concern about south porch and nave roof. Sir Ralph B.M. Blois, Bt, to Thackeray Turner, SPAB, 3 February 1905

3 February 1905

Sir,

I was in Blythburgh church a short time back and I think it is absolutely necessary that steps should be taken to repair both the south porch and the angel roof before further damage is done. I should be very much obliged if your society would let me know whether they consider the porch should be repaired first or the roof; it appears to me that the porch is in a most dangerous condition as if any of the timber used in shoring it up gave way a great disaster for the church must result. On hearing from you a meeting of our committee shall be called.

  Yours truly,

[*signed*] Ralph Blois

To The Society for the Protection of Ancient Buildings.

171. Availability of work for architect. Alfred H. Powell to Thackeray Turner, SPAB, 6 May 1905

Mill Hill
 Brandsby, Easingwold,
 York. 6 May 1905

My dear Turner,
I want to get some more building work and wonder if you've anything on you would like me to look after for you and give me a chance to remember everything this time!

I hope you enjoyed your holiday before Easter. I have just got back from a very enjoyable week in France (Paris and Rouen) with W.R.L. and others.[107]

Yours always,
[*signed*]   Alfred H. Powell
Love to you all.

172. Request for cost estimate. The Revd R.P. Wing to Thackeray Turner, SPAB, 8 May 1905

8 May <u>1905</u>

Dear Sir,
    Blythburgh Church
    South Porch
I am requested to apply to your society for an estimate of cost of restoring <above> above (or preserving same) that steps may be taken for setting the work in hand.
[*signed*]   R.P. Wing
            <u>Vicar</u>

173. Cost estimate. John Kent, SPAB, to the Revd R.P. Wing, 12 May 1905

12 May 1905

re, <u>Blythburgh Church</u>

Revd and dear Sir,
In the absence of the secretary from town I beg to acknowledge the receipt of your letter of the 8th inst, and to inform you that a reply shall be sent to you within the next few days.

    I remain, Revd and dear Sir,
    Yours faithfully,
[*signed*]   John Kent
            Assistant Secretary

Revd R.P. Wing

174. Cost of repair of porch. Alfred H. Powell to Thackeray Turner, SPAB, 20 May 1905

Mill Hill
Brandsby, Easingwold
York. 20 May 1905

My dear Turner,
I think we did mention a price for the porch at Blythburgh. I should imagine £200

---

107 W.R. Lethaby.

ought to cover it fairly well. I will write to Wells who was with me there and see what he thinks. I don't know <u>when</u> (and I suppose you can't give me a date) I should have to go to Blythburgh if I undertook to look after it. My plans at present are that I am full up till the end of June or till the 20th of June say – I should want £6 6s. 0d. a week from them. I imagine it would take 3 months to do. Please let me know if you can what the alternative you suggest might be.

Yours very truly,

[*signed*]   Alfred H. Powell

I am here till Monday and then at Cambridge from 25th to 31st where a letter to Newnham College, Cambridge will find me.

Yours, AHP.

175. Cost of repair of porch. Thackeray Turner to Randall Wells, 26 May 1905

26 May 1905

re, <u>Blythburgh Church etc.</u>

Dear Mr Randall Wells,

Many thanks for your letter about Swardeston church, which I will lay before the committee at its next meeting.

I believe Mr Powell has written to you with regard to giving an estimate of the cost of repairing the porch of Blythburgh church. The matter is very pressing, and we shall be glad therefore if you will let us know direct the amount of your estimate so as to save time.

Yours very truly,

[*signed*]   Thackeray Turner
              Secretary

176. Cost of repair of porch. Randall Wells to Thackeray Turner, SPAB, 28 May 1905

/From Mr Randall Wells/

45 Trinity Road,
Wimbledon S.W.
28 May 1905

Dear Mr Turner,

    <u>Blythburgh Church</u>

From my present knowledge I am afraid that I can be of no help to you in this matter – I <u>accompanied</u> Mr Powell down there one Sunday but I took no notes or measurements that would justify <the> my making the roughest estimate of cost. I think Mr Powell's recollection of the occasion must be at fault.

    <u>Croydon palace chapel</u>

[*The rest of the letter, not concerned with Blythburgh, was detached and filed elsewhere by the SPAB.*]

177. Request to visit Blythburgh. Thackeray Turner, SPAB, to William Weir, 2 June 1905

2 June 1905

re, <u>Blythburgh Church, Suffolk</u>

Dear Weir,

The committee will be much indebted to you if you will kindly visit Blythburgh church and furnish it with an estimate as to the cost of repairing the porch.

If you can give us this help will you please write to the parson and name a day for your visit?

His address is:-

Revd R.P. Wing,
   Walberswick,
     Southwold.
   The matter is somewhat pressing.
   I enclose some papers for your perusal.
   Yours very truly,

[*signed*]   <u>Thackeray Turner</u>
       Secretary

178. Cost of repair of porch. Thackeray Turner, SPAB, to the Revd R.P. Wing, 2 June 1905

2 June 1905

re, <u>Blythburgh Church, Suffolk</u>

Revd and dear Sir,

We have made enquiries and find that it is impossible to give an estimate of the cost of repairing the porch without making an examination of it in its present condition.

The committee has therefore asked one of its architects, who has had exceptional practical experience in the repair of ancient buildings, to visit the building at an early date.

We have asked him to write to you and arrange a date.

   I remain, Revd and dear Sir,
   Yours faithfully,

[*signed*]   Thackeray Turner
       Secretary

Revd R.P. Wing

179. Cost of repair of porch. The Revd R.P. Wing to Thackeray Turner, SPAB, 2 June 1905

/I have written to Mr Weir today about this. John Kent/
2 June 1905

<u>Suffolk</u>

The Revd R.P. Wing, vicar of Blythburgh and Walberswick will esteem it a favour if the secretary of S.P.A.B. will supply him with an estimate of the cost of restoring

or preserving Blythburgh church south porch – Mr Wing made a similar request on May 8th 1905.
[*Unsigned*]

180. Delay in providing cost estimate Thackeray Turner, SPAB, to the Revd R.P. Wing, 5 June 1905

5 June 1905

re, <u>Blythburgh Church</u>

Revd and dear Sir,
I beg to thank you for your letter of the 2nd inst, received this morning.
    I wrote to you last Friday, and our letters no doubt crossed in the post.
    I deeply regret that there should have been any delay in supplying the estimate, but we will press the matter forward and let you have it as soon as we possibly can.
    I remain Revd and dear Sir,
[*Unsigned*]
        Secretary

Revd R.P. Wing

181. Urgency of visit to Blythburgh. John Kent, SPAB, to William Weir, 5 June 1905

5 June 1905

re, <u>Blythburgh Church</u>

Dear Mr Weir,
We have received another letter from the vicar asking for the estimate of the cost of repairing the south porch.
    As his previous letter was dated 8th of May you will see there has been some delay in the matter. Therefore if you could kindly arrange to visit at an early date the committee would be deeply grateful.
    The church is such a valuable building that the committee is \the more/ anxious that the repairs should be done in accordance with the society's principles.
    Yours faithfully,
[*signed*]   John Kent
        Assistant Secretary

182. Date for visit to Blythburgh. William Weir to Thackeray Turner, SPAB, 5 June 1905

Morningside, Station Road,
Winchmore Hill, N. 5 June 1905

Dear Mr Turner,

re Blythburgh Church Porch
Many thanks for your letter. I have written the parson and propose to visit on Wednesday the 7th inst. and hope to have the information for your meeting on Thursday.

Yours truly,
[*signed*]   William Weir

Thackeray Turner, Esq.

183. Visit to Blythburgh. Thackeray Turner, SPAB, to William Weir, 16 June 1905

16 June 1905

re, <u>Blythburgh Church</u>

Dear Weir,
This matter seemed to me to be so pressing that I wired to the vicar this morning as follows:-
   'Have you written Weir. Kindly write how the matters stand.'
   I will let you know if I receive a reply.
      Yours very truly,
[*signed*]   Thackeray Turner
            Secretary

184. Visit to Blythburgh. Thackeray Turner, SPAB, to the Revd R.P. Wing, 16 June 1905

16 June 1905

<u>Blythburgh Church</u>

Revd and Dear Sir,
I wired to you today:- 'Have you written Weir, how do matters stand.'
   There seems to have been some misunderstanding.
   We put Weir into communication with you and when I asked him what he had done, said you had asked him to wait and has not heard further.
   Trusting I may hear from you. I remain,
      Revd and dear Sir,
      Yours faithfully,
[*signed*]   Thackeray Turner
            Secretary

The Revd R.P. Wing

185. Visit to Blythburgh. John Kent, SPAB, to Thackeray Turner, 17 June 1905

/Encl./

17 June 1905

re, <u>Blythburgh Church</u>

Dear Sir,
I enclose a post card from the vicar and letters to Sir R. Blois and Mr Weir.
   I have written the P.S. to the letter to Sir R. Blois on a separate piece of paper, in case you decide not to send it.

Yours faithfully,
[*signed*]   John Kent
P.S. Receipt enclosed for signature.

Thackeray Turner, Esq.

186. Visit to Blythburgh. Thackeray Turner, SPAB, to William Weir, 17 June 1905

17 June 1905

re, Blythburgh Church

Dear Weir,
We have received a post card from the vicar asking us to apply to Sir Ralph Blois Bart. the patron.

We have written to him and said you could no doubt visit next week if matters could be arranged. We have given him your address.

Yours very truly,
[*Unsigned*]

Secretary

187. Request for help with visit. Thackeray Turner, SPAB, to Sir Ralph B.M. Blois, Bt, 17 June 1905

17 June 1905

re, Blythburgh Church

Sir,
We received a letter from the vicar of Blythburgh dated the 8th May in which he asked the society for an estimate of the cost of restoring or preserving the south porch of Blythburgh church.

We at once made enquiries, but owing to the absence of the gentleman who had visited the building on behalf of the society there was some unavoidable delay. It was found that owing to the lapse of time no reliable estimate could be given without a further survey of the porch being made. The committee therefore arranged for one of its architects, Mr Weir, to visit the building and prepare an estimate.

On the 2nd June we wrote and informed the vicar, and Mr Weir wrote naming a day for his visit. But the vicar telegraphed to Mr Weir saying 'do not visit, will write' or words to that effect. However, as he did not receive a letter, Mr Weir again wrote to the vicar, but no reply was received. I therefore wired to the vicar yesterday 'Have you written Weir, kindly write how matters stand', and we have received a post card from the vicar, this morning, as follows:-

'Please apply Sir R. Blois Bart, Cockfield Hall, Yoxford, Saxmundham, Suffolk.'

We are very reluctant to trouble you, but the matter is somewhat pressing owing to Mr Weir having to start some works in Wales next week.

Mr Weir has had such exceptional \practical/ experience in the repair of ancient buildings that the committee is anxious he should make the estimate.

I have no doubt Mr Weir could arrange to visit Blythburgh next week if you could kindly make it convenient for matters to be arranged to permit of his doing so.

His address is:-
William Weir Esq.,
  Morningside,
    Station Road,
      Winchmore Hill, N.
  I am, yours faithfully,
[*Unsigned*]
         Secretary
To Sir Ralph Blois Bart.
P.S. As the society is anxious to see the porch repaired, it will pay Mr Weir's expenses, and the estimate will be provided free of cost.

188. Visit to Blythburgh. John Kent, SPAB, to William Weir, 21 June 1905

21 June 1905

re, Blythburgh Church

Dear Mr Weir,
I enclose a copy of a letter just received from Sir Ralph Blois.
  Yours faithfully,
[signed]   John Kent
      Assistant Secretary

189. Visit to Blythburgh. William Weir to John Kent, SPAB, 21 June 1905

Many thanks for letter. Have arranged to visit Blythburgh on Saturday.
  Yours,
[signed]   William Weir
21 June 1905

190. Arrangements for visit to Blythburgh. Sir Ralph B.M. Blois, Bt, to Thackeray Turner, SPAB, 25 June 1905

Hyde Park Hotel,
Albert Gate,
London, S.W.
25 June 1905

Dear Mr Turner,
I am extremely sorry the vicar of Blythburgh has been so very slow in answering your letter. I have written to Mr Weir asking him to meet me at Blythburgh church at 3 p.m. next Saturday, the first moment I can possibly be there.
  Yours truly,
[signed]   Ralph Blois

191. Report on church porch. William Weir to Thackeray Turner, SPAB, 26 June 1905[108]

Morningside, Winchmore Hill, N.
26 June 1905

Dear Mr Turner,

   re: Blythburgh Church, Suffolk

I enclose herewith my report \with plan and photographs/ on the south porch of this church, for the consideration of your committee.

   I regret not being able to fall in with the suggestions previously made, for several reasons which I shall be glad to explain at the meeting on Thursday.

   I return herewith the papers which you kindly sent for reference.

   Yours truly,

[*signed*]   William Weir

Thackeray Turner, Esq.

192. Copy of report sent to Blythburgh. Thackeray Turner, SPAB, to Sir Ralph B.M. Blois, Bt, 30 June 1905

/Enclosures/

30 June 1905

re, <u>Blythburgh Church</u>

Dear Sir Ralph Blois,

The committee of this society has now considered the report made to it by Mr William Weir upon the south porch of Blythburgh church, and it desires me to forward to you the enclosed copy of the report, together with an estimate, and to inform you that the suggestions contained therein and works of repair recommended, meet with the society's entire approval.

   I am,

   Yours very truly,

[*signed*]   Thackeray Turner
              Secretary

P.S. May I add that my committee was unanimous in its hope that it might be possible to have the work done at once or at any rate before the winter comes on. T. T.

193. SPAB report to be laid before Blythburgh committee. Sir Ralph B.M. Blois, Bt, to Thackeray Turner, SPAB, 2 July 1905

/As far as Mr Weir can judge £200 would be the cost./

2 July 1905

Dear Sir,

I received and thank you for Mr Weir's report; it shall be laid before the committee

---

[108] For Weir's report see Appendix A 13.

meeting next Saturday July 8th. I hoped and expected Mr Weir would be able to form anyhow an approximate estimate of the necessary repairs to the roof, it would help me very much if you could let me have this before July 8th as if the cost is likely to be below what the committee expects to have to spend I feel quite certain you can get the work to the south porch started at once. I hoped from what Mr Weir said we should not have to recast the lead on the main roof but in his report he says this must be done.

Please let me hear from you at this address before July 8th.

Yours truly,

[*signed*]   Ralph Blois

To Thackeray Turner, Esq.

194. Request for committee's decision. Thackeray Turner, SPAB, to Sir Ralph B.M. Blois, Bt, 21 July 1905

21 July 1905

re, Blythburgh Church

Dear Sir,

I trust you will forgive me for again troubling you, but we shall be glad if you will let us know what decision the repair committee has come to with reference to the porch?

It is important that arrangements should be made as to the order in which the works that Mr Weir is to supervise should be taken in hand, and we should therefore be grateful to you if you would kindly inform us whether the work at Blythburgh church is to be taken in hand at an early date?

I am, dear Sir,

Yours faithfully,

[*Unsigned*]

Secretary

Sir Ralph Blois Bart.

195. Opposition to SPAB from Archdeacon. Sir Ralph B.M. Blois, Bt, to Thackeray Turner, SPAB, 26 July 1905

26 July 1905

Dear Mr Turner,

I am very sorry I cannot yet write definitely about the south porch at Blythburgh church for the simple reason that at a meeting last Saturday Archdeacon Lawrence of Suffolk said he would not allow your society to touch the church; he would give no reason. Perhaps you can suggest some reason. At present matters are at a deadlock and the porch should be commenced before the autumn. I have written to ask for his reason and have received no reply.

Yours truly,

[*signed*]   Ralph Blois

196. Archdeacon's opposition. Thackeray Turner, SPAB, to Sir Ralph B.M. Blois, Bt, 28 July 1905

28 July 1905

re, <u>Blythburgh Church, Suffolk</u>

Dear Sir Ralph Blois,
Thank you very much for your letter of the 26th inst.
    We are quite in the dark as to Archdeacon Wilson's [*sic*][109] reason for objecting to the society but we will at once make enquiries.
        Yours truly,
[*signed*]   Thackeray Turner
                Secretary

197. Request for help with Blythburgh committee. Thackeray Turner, SPAB, to Prince Frederick Duleep Singh, 28 July 1905

/1 Enc:/

28 July 1905

re, <u>Blythburgh Church, Suffolk</u>

Dear Prince Frederick,
The committee will be deeply grateful to you if you will kindly peruse the enclosed press copy[110] of a statement with reference to the above named building, and help it if you possibly can.
    Do you happen to know Archdeacon Lawrence or anybody who can influence him, or find out why he objects to the society as we are entirely in the dark as to his reason?
    The church is magnificent and in pressing need of repair.
    Please forgive us for troubling you.
        Yours very truly,
[*signed*]   Thackeray Turner
                Secretary

198. Request to influence Princess Louise. Thackeray Turner, SPAB, to Philip Norman, 28 July 1905

/1 Enc:/

28 July 1905

re, <u>Blythburgh Church, Suffolk</u>

Dear Norman,
The committee will be deeply grateful to you if you can kindly help the society with reference to the above named building.
    If you will kindly read the enclosed statement you will see how the matter stands.

---

[109] Archdeacon Lawrence.
[110] 'Press' is a reference to the document copying process.

Now, we gather from the public press, that H.R.H. Princess Louise[111] is interested in the church and is patronesss of a bazaar and fète to be held shortly.

The committee [*?thus feels*] that the princess would [*?like*] to know how the matter stands (presuming [*?the press*] statement to be correct) and it thought you [*?might*] be willing to help it in writing to Captain Probert[112] and asking him to lay the facts before H.R.H.

We feel sure H.R.H. would not wish to help in bringing about a 'restoration' of the building and might be willing to use her influence in favour of the repairs being carried out under the auspices of the society.

We are quite in the dark as to Archdeacon Lawrence's reason for objecting to the society.

Yours very truly,
[*signed*]   Thackeray Turner
          Secretary

199. Statement by the SPAB reviewing the matter of the repair of Blythburgh Church, July 1905

The Society for the Protection of Ancient Buildings,
20 Buckingham Street, Adelphi, W.C.

Blythburgh Church, Suffolk

The subject of Blythburgh church has been before the society for many years past and it has given advice from time to time.

In <1902> 1901 the vicar appealed in the 'Times' for funds to repair the building and the society applied to him for information. He very kindly \(in 1902)/ allowed the society to see reports upon Blythburgh and Walberswick churches, and the committee was alarmed at the nature of the proposed works. If the works proposed to be carried out at Blythburgh church had been accomplished, a large portion of artistic and historical value of the building would have been destroyed.

The society pointed this out to the vicar, and he replied that nothing would be done by him as he was leaving the parish.

In 1903, as a result of the good offices of a member of the society, after some correspondence with the vicar and Mr Egerton (the churchwarden), the church was visited by a professional member of the society, and, acting on the advice given by it, the beautiful south porch (which it was proposed to rebuild) was shored up with a view to its repair at a later date.

An interview with the patron (Sir Ralph Blois) took place at the society's office in January 1905, and in June, in compliance with a request made by the repair committee, an estimate (entailing another visit to the building) was provided, for the repair of the porch. The estimated cost was £200.

The society now learns from Sir Ralph Blois that Archdeacon Lawrence of Suffolk said \at a recent meeting of the repair committee that/ he would not allow the society to touch the church, but he gives no reason for this decision. The matter is now at

---

[111] *The Times*, Ecclesiastical Intelligence, 2 August, 1905, reported that the princess would open an art exhibition and fancy fair at Cockfield Hall, Yoxford, on Saturday, 5 August, in aid of the preservation fund of Blythburgh Church.

[112] Captain William Probert, the princess's equerry.

a standstill although there is enough money in hand to repair the porch, which is in most pressing need of attention.

It should be added that a member of the society has promised to contribute £50 towards the cost of the work, and that the patron and others interested are in favour of the society's recommendations being carried out.

July 1905

200. Request to influence Princess Louise. Philip Norman to Thackeray Turner, SPAB, 2 August 1905

2 August 1905
45, Evelyn Gardens,
South Kensington.

Dear Thackeray Turner,
    In reply to your letter on the subject of <u>Blythburgh Church</u>.
I had an opportunity last night of talking to the duchess of Argyll's equerry and delivered to him your paper for the princess's perusal and your covering letter to me for his own. He is \always/ very much inclined to accept our views with regard to anti-scrape matters, and she seems anxious to do the right thing.

I am in hopes that she will put in an effective 'word in season' next Saturday, when she is to open the art exhibition and fancy fair at Cockfield Hall in aid of the Blythburgh church preservation fund. She has been pressed to open it by people who honestly believe that they are helping to preserve. Perhaps she will be able and willing to direct them into the right path, but of this I cannot be sure. At any rate I have done my best, and she will be thoroughly informed.

    Yours very truly,
[*signed*]   Philip Norman

201. Princess Louise. John Kent, SPAB, to Philip Norman, 2 August 1905

2 August 1905

re, <u>Blythburgh Church</u>

Dear Sir,
In the absence of Mr Thackeray Turner from town, I beg to acknowledge the receipt of your letter of today's date, and to thank you sincerely for your action in the matter.
    The meetings of the committee are now adjourned until the 21st September.
    I am,
    Yours faithfully,
[*signed*]   John Kent
            Assistant Secretary

Philip Norman F.S.A.

202. Concerning Archdeacon's opposition. Prince Frederick Duleep Singh to Thackeray Turner, SPAB, 5 August 1905

Old Buckenham Hall,

Attleborough,
Norfolk.
5 August 1905

Dear Mr Turner,

I have made enquiries from a person who knows <Ca> Archdeacon Lawrence but can make nothing out as to his objection to the society re Blythburgh. I am now writing to Sir Ralph Blois whom I know.

Yours sincerely,

[*signed*]   Frederick Duleep Singh

203. Withdrawal of opposition by Archdeacon. Prince Frederick Duleep Singh to Thackeray Turner, SPAB, 17 August 1905

Old Buckenham Hall,
Attleborough,
Norfolk.
17 August 1905

Dear Mr Turner,

I have had a very satisfactory letter from Sir Ralph Blois. He tells me the archdeacon has 'climbed down' about the S.P.A.B. and never meant that he objected to its being connected.

Sir Ralph <has> intends calling a meeting of the committee <if he> for the repair, towards the end of next month (I presume that is when he gets back from Scotland). He has asked me to become a member of the committee, which I will do certainly if I am eligible, and he wants to move a resolution that the services of the society be engaged \immediately/ for the repair of the porch – by which I suppose he means that the society is asked to have the work done by someone like Mr Weir. He says if, having become a member of his committee I wrote or otherwise explained my views about the porch (and repairs in general) being done by the society, it would help him very much.

I am returning the press copy you sent me but if you would send me the part referring to the porch again, as well as the views of the society about Blythburgh church as a whole, I would try and do what he wants. Will you let him know if there is anything else you want him to do in the matter before the committee meeting above referred to is called.

Yours sincerely,

[*signed*]   Frederick Duleep Singh

/P.T.O./ The pastoral play I organised at Norwich at St Peter's Hungate has brought in about £28 net. I see no prospect of raising anything more so as soon as the accounts for the play are made up I will go into the matter thoroughly and see how much we have in the bank and promised, and we shall then know if there is <u>any</u> chance of repairing the church.

204. Addition to Blythburgh committee. Thackeray Turner, SPAB, to Prince Frederick Duleep Singh, 21 August 1905

21 August 1905

Dear Prince Frederick,

Thank you very much for your letter. I am glad to learn that you have consented to go on the Blythburgh committee.

I enclose an extract which is I suppose what you ask for, but if it is not please let me know.[113] Perhaps I ought to say that the committee always states that it does not undertake repairs, for if it did, it might be held pecuniarily responsible. It does, however, when asked, recommend an architect who it requires to submit his proposals and refer all doubtful questions to the society.

It is very satisfactory that the archdeacon has climbed down and I am sure my committee will be pleased.

I shall be much interested to hear how much money you have been able to collect for St Peter's Hungate.

I wonder whether you know Isleham church[114] close to Mildenhall and about 15 miles from Cambridge? I want very much to get information about it. A correspondent wrote saying that it is a very interesting Norman church consisting of nave and chancel and that it is now used as a barn. If his impression is correct it is certainly a case the society ought to look into.

 Yours very sincerely,

[*signed*] Thackeray Turner
   Secretary

205. Rejection of SPAB by Blythburgh committee. Sir Ralph B.M. Blois, Bt, to Prince Frederick Duleep Singh, 19 February 1906

Cockfield Hall,
Yoxford.

19 February 1906

Dear Duleep Singh,

I am sorry to say the Blythburgh church restoration committee have opposed <my> our wishes and my mother's wishes with the result that a lot of money has been withdrawn including £50 I promised. I am enclosing your kind donation as its conditions are not being complied with. Whether this action will have the desired effect I don't know but as matters now stand the beautiful porch is to be left as it is while an attempt is to be made to repair the roof with the money in hand and under no circumstances is the society to be employed. I am very much annoyed about this as with the society's aid the porch would have been made perfectly safe last autumn and the roof would have been finished before Easter, added to which a great deal of money would have been given. Absolutely no work has been done up to the present. [*Some fifty further words have been crossed out by the writer and cannot be read.*]

 Yours ever,

[*signed*] Ralph Blois

---

[113] An extract from Correspondence 199: 'In 1903, as a result of the good offices of a member of the society ... an estimate (entailing another visit to the building) was provided, for the repair of the porch. The estimated cost was £200'.

[114] Isleham Priory church, now an ancient monument in the guardianship of the state.

206. Rejection of SPAB by Blythburgh committee. Prince Frederick Duleep Singh to Thackeray Turner, SPAB, 22 February 1906

22 February 1906

Dear Mr Turner,

I have received the enclosed from Sir Ralph Blois which <u>don't</u> return about Blythburgh. It is most unsatisfactory is it not? and a <u>great</u> pity. He has sent back my small cheque, as I said it was only to be used if the people were sensible. I am just off for 3 or 4 weeks to south of France. I am sorry I have been able to do nothing about that church (Norfolk) you wrote about. If not too late when I get back I will try.

Yours sincerely,

[*signed*]   Frederick Duleep Singh

207. Withdrawal of financial support. Thackeray Turner, SPAB, to Sir Ralph B.M. Blois, Bt, 2 March 1906

2 March 1906

re, <u>Blythburgh Church, Suffolk</u>

Dear Sir,

Prince Frederick Duleep Singh has very kindly informed the committee of this society of the contents of your letter to him concerning the above named building.

The committee deeply regrets the position of affairs, and it will be glad if you will kindly inform the restoration committee that the society has £50 in hand to be given or witheld at its discretion, and that under the circumstances it does not feel justified in handing the money over to the restoration committee.[115]

The building is in crying need of repair, and the committee considers that a portion, at least, of the necessary works could easily have been accomplished by this time had better counsels prevailed.

Thanking you for the support you have given the society in the matter.

I remain, dear Sir,

Yours faithfully,

[*signed*]   Thackeray Turner
       Secretary

To Sir Ralph Blois Bart

208. Request to influence Princess Louise. Thackeray Turner, SPAB, to Philip Norman, 2 March 1906

/2 Enclosures/

2 March 1906

re, <u>Blythburgh Church, Suffolk</u>

Dear Norman,

---

[115] See Correspondence 155. Sir Ralph Blois's £50 and Prince Frederick Duleep Singh's donation were also withdrawn. See Correspondence 209 for Sir Ralph's estimate that more than £120 had been lost.

I am desired by the committee to forward to you the enclosed letter from Prince Frederick Duleep Singh, and a letter to him from Sir Ralph Blois.

You will see that matters are in a most unfortunate state, and the committee will be grateful to you if you can arrange things so that the Princess Louise may be informed of the position of affairs.

We have £50 in hand to be given at the discretion of the society, but of course under the circumstances the committee would not feel justified in handing the money over.

Will you kindly return the letters in the enclosed envelope when you have quite finished with them?

Yours very truly,

[*signed*]   Thackeray Turner
                    Secretary

209. Patron's annoyance with Blythburgh committee. Sir Ralph B.M. Blois, Bt, to Thackeray Turner, SPAB, 8 March 1906

Cockfield Hall,
Yoxford.

8 March 1906

Dear Sir,

Many thanks for your letter. Both Lady Blois and myself and the members of my family who saved the church from ruin in the early eightys are very much annoyed at the ill advised action of this restoration committee, a committee most of whose members were elected only because they were able to give professional help to raise money. I can only hope that under the circumstances your society will hold the £50 for the benefit of Blythburgh church until such a time that your society is called in to restore portions of the building. I may mention this committee is losing upwards of £120 by its action. I will inform the committee of the sum you hold and I know that if my advice had been taken last June the south porch would now be safe and the roof would have been finished certainly before the end of the summer. Nothing has yet been done.

Yours truly,

[*signed*]   Ralph Blois

To Thackeray Turner, Esquire

210. Princess Louise. Thackeray Turner, SPAB, to Philip Norman, 9 March 1906

/1 Enclosures/

9 March 1906

re Blythburgh Church, Suffolk

Dear Norman,

I enclose a copy of a letter which I have just received from Sir Ralph Blois, as I think you ought to see it before calling upon Captain Probert.

Yours very truly,

[*signed*]   Thackeray Turner
                    Secretary

211. Statement of SPAB position. Thackeray Turner, SPAB, to Sir Ralph B.M. Blois, Bt, 9 March 1906

9 March 1906

re, <u>Blythburgh Church</u>

Sir,

I will lay your letter of yesterday's date before the committee of this society at its next meeting.

The subject was under discussion at our meeting yesterday, and as the opinion had been expressed by our architect that the porch could not be considered safe in its present condition, as the shoring was put up under the impression that it was only of a temporary nature to save the work for a few months until the repairs were completed, considerable anxiety was felt.

It was thought inadvisable for this committee to communicate direct with the restoration committee. At the same time it was felt that if a catastrophe occurred the society might be held to be in fault.

Under these circumstances I trust that by making this statement to you, Sir, we may be considered to have put our opinion on record, and that you will inform the committee of the society's statement, or not, as you think advisable.

This letter shall be read at our next meeting.

I am, Sir,

Yours faithfully,

[*signed*]   Thackeray Turner
                    Secretary

To Sir Ralph Blois Bart

212. Influencing Princess Louise. Philip Norman to Thackeray Turner, SPAB, 28 April 1906

28 April 1906
45, Evelyn Gardens,
South Kensington.

Dear Thackeray Turner,

In re Blythburgh Church

I did not think it was worth while to take any steps about this until the return of the Princess Louise, who has now either just arrived in London or will do so immediately. After reading the correspondence carefully I came to the conclusion that the best thing for me would be to send extracts of it including everything of importance, marked <u>private and confidential</u> to Captain Probert, and asking him to lay \the points of/ them before the princess. The difficulty is that he is a Suffolk man and I have a sort of half suspicion that he may have taken the side of the committee; however if he has done so it would have been through ignorance, as he is a gentleman and a fairminded man.

I have therefore copied out all the essential parts of the letters and am sending them to him by this post. At any rate he and she will then no [*sic*] how matters stand. I now return the correspondence.

I am sorry that I have not been able to attend your meetings of late, I have been so very busy. Moreover I am now going abroad for a month, and shall probably work my way to the north east corner of Spain where (mirabile dictu) there is (at Gerona) a cathedral nave with a span of 73 ft; that of Chartres being 50 ft, York 52, Canterbury 43, and Westminster Abbey 38. I shall be back in London at the beginning of June.

Yours sincerely,

[*signed*]   Philip Norman

I told Probert (in my letter) that according to the report of Mr Weir, in whom SPAB thorough believes, the porch at Blythburgh is in a most dangerous state.

213. Request for meeting from patron. Sir Ralph B.M. Blois, Bt, to Thackeray Turner, SPAB, 26 June 1906

25, Bruton Street, W
26 June 1906

Dear Sir,

A meeting of the committee for the restoration of Blythburgh church will take place at Blythburgh on Monday July 9th and before this date I am very anxious to have an interview with you as the committee has not yet definitely decided into whose hands the work shall be entrusted. Will Thursday next June 28 at 11am suit you for me to see you at your office?

Yours truly,

[*signed*]   Ralph Blois

To Thackeray Turner, Esq.

214. Meeting with patron. Telegram John Kent, SPAB, to Thackeray Turner, 27 June 1906

To Turner Westbrook [*Godalming*]

Please wire Sir Ralph Blois 25 Bruton Street W. whether you can see him at office Thursday at eleven about Blythburgh.

[*John*] Kent

215. Request from Blythburgh for cost estimates. Sir Ralph B.M. Blois, Bt, to Thackeray Turner, SPAB, 9 July 1906

Cockfield Hall,
Yoxford.

9 July 1906

Dear Sir,

At a meeting of the Blythburgh church restoration committee held today I was asked to write and ask you to let me have a report from Mr Weir giving me the cost of the work necessary to the south porch with and without the vaulted roof, also to the roof and all other necessary repairs. This report and cost will be closely compared with Mr Johns[*t*]on's report a copy of which I enclose.[116] Please let me have this before July 25.

---

[116] For Johnston's report see Appendix A 15.

Yours truly,
[*signed*]   Ralph Blois

To Thackeray Turner, Esq.

216. Request to produce cost estimates. Thackeray Turner, SPAB, to William Weir, 10 July 1906

10 July 1906
re, <u>Lilbourne Church, Rugby</u> etc

Dear Weir,
Many thanks for your letter of the 7th[117] which I will read to the committee on Thursday.

re, <u>Blythburgh Church</u>
I enclose a letter etc from Sir Ralph Blois.
Will you please let us have the report \and estimates/ asked for by him, as soon as possible?
<u>re, Potter Heigham church</u>
I enclose letters from Mr Carter.
If the work has to be done this year could you supervise it?
The church is a most valuable building.
Yours very truly,
[*signed*]   Thackeray Turner
            Secretary

217. Preparation of cost estimates. William Weir to Thackeray Turner, SPAB, 11 July 1906

c/o Revd G.W. Turner,
Madley Vicarage, Hereford.
11 July 1906

Dear Mr Turner,
Sir Ralph Blois in his letter asks for the 'cost of the work necessary to the south porch <u>with and without</u> the vaulted roof.' 'Also to the roof and all other necessary repairs.'
I don't suppose you wish me to give a price for <u>restoring the vaulted roof</u> and I am afraid from the notes I have it will be impossible to give an estimate for the repairs of church and roofs generally. If this is required it would be necessary for me to visit the building and go into the matter.
I shall be glad to know what to do? I am returning to West Stow on Monday.
I will write you about Potter Heigham church later on.
Yours truly,
[*signed*]   William Weir

Thackeray Turner, Esq.

---

[117] Not in the SPAB Blythburgh file.

218. Basis of cost estimate. Thackeray Turner, SPAB, to William Weir, 13 July 1906

13 July 1906

re, <u>Blythburgh Church</u>

Dear Weir,

The committee feels that you will know best whether or no you ought to visit the building again, but it will gladly pay the cost of so doing if it is necessary.

With regard to the question of the vaulting, is it not a fact that some of the ancient stones of the vaulting are in existence? If so, putting them back in place would be true restoration.

It is a difficult question, which we must leave to your judgement. But the committee feels that if they have a strong wish to have the vaulting replaced, we ought to give way and do it in such a way as to cause no offence to the society's principles, and this might perhaps be done by erecting it in oak, not following the old mouldings, of course.

The committee is very anxious that you should do the work as the building is of such exceptional value, and we believe that the sum of money asked for by the architect is probably considerably in excess of what you would feel to be necessary, and that this would probably carry the point. At the same time it does not wish you to run your price fine in consequence.

As to what you say on the subject of employing additional help, the committee sympathises with you. At the same time I think its feeling is that it would be more satisfactory that you should have, say, 3 jobs going on at one time with 3 men under you, than that you should have one job on your own account and \that/ your two men should each have a job on their account.

Yours very truly,

[*signed*]   Thackeray Turner
           Secretary

219. Request for information from SPAB. Sir Ralph B.M. Blois, Bt, to Thackeray Turner, SPAB, 16 July 1906

16 July 1906

Dear Sir,

I should be much obliged if you could let me have an answer to my letter of last Monday 9th re Blythburgh church. Prince Frederick Duleep Singh has joined our committee and at a meeting to be held about August 1st we hope to be able to decide to ask your society to do the necessary work.

Yours truly,

[*signed*]   Ralph Blois

To Thackeray Turner, Esq.

220. Provision of cost estimates. Thackeray Turner, SPAB, to Sir Ralph B.M. Blois, Bt, 17 July 1906

17 July 1906

re, <u>Blythburgh Church</u>

Dear Sir,
Upon the receipt of your letter of the 9th inst. we at once communicated with Mr Weir, and he has promised to make the report and estimates, and I hope to forward them to you at an early date.
   I am glad to learn that Prince Frederick Duleep Singh has joined the committee.
      I am,
      Yours faithfully,
[*Unsigned*]
            Secretary

To Sir Ralph Blois Bart

221. Visit to Blythburgh. William Weir to Thackeray Turner, SPAB, 17 July 1906

From Mr Weir
17 July 1906

re, Blythburgh Church
'Many thanks for your letter of the 13th inst. I will visit the building tomorrow <on> and Thursday and send on the particulars as early as possible'.

222. Report on Blythburgh church by William Weir. Thackeray Turner, SPAB, to Sir Ralph B.M. Blois, Bt, 23 July 1906

23 July 1906
re, Blythborough Church

Dear Sir Ralph Blois,
I have just received Mr Weir's report[118] and as you say time is pressing I send it to you before it has been laid before my committee. However, I have read it carefully through and feel that it will meet with the committee's approval.
   Yours very truly,
[*signed*]   Thackeray Turner
            Secretary

To Sir Ralph Blois, Bart

223. Report on Blythburgh church. Sir Ralph B.M. Blois, Bt, to Thackeray Turner, SPAB, 24 July 1906

24 July 1906
Dear Mr Turner,

---

[118] For Weir's reports see Appendix A 16–17.

Many thanks for sending Mr Weir's report and approximate cost of work. I conclude I should be quite safe in saying the cost could not exceed £50 in addition to the sum stated. Will you please return Mr Johns[t]on's report that I sent you. The committee meeting is fixed for August 8th and Prince Frederick will attend.

Yours truly,

[*signed*]   Ralph Blois

To Thackeray Turner, Esquire

224. Comments on Blythburgh architect's report and estimates. Thackeray Turner, SPAB, to Sir Ralph B.M. Blois, Bt, 28 July 1906

/1 Enc./

28 July 1906

re, Blythburgh Church, Suffolk

Dear Sir Ralph Blois,

I beg to thank you for your letter of the 24th inst and to return Mr Johnston's report herewith.

With regard to the question of cost, the only doubtful points in connection with the proposed works are the roof timbers and the weight of the cast lead. It is impossible to say definitely what their condition is until the lead is removed, but there is every reason to believe they are no worse than Mr Weir anticipated.

I think you would be quite safe in saying the cost is not likely to exceed the approximate estimate provided the roof timbers and the lead are in as good a condition as anticipated and that an extra sum of £50 should be ample to cover any extra cost which may be found necessary.

I think I should point out that Mr Johnston's estimate for repairing the main roof is £426 2s. 6d. (main roof £179 2s. 6d., carpenters work £120, roof timbers £127), and if the lead is recast there would be an extra of £230, bringing his estimate up to £656 2s. 6d.

Mr Johnston's estimate for the repair of the tower is only £27. The estimate for the porch is equally misleading, £35 only being allowed for the repair of the walls, while £75 is proposed to be spent on the vaulting, which would soon thrust the walls out again.

There is a considerable amount of repair required to the walls generally, and the tower is also much worse than it appears to be before close examination.

Should you require any further information I will gladly do my best to supply it.

Yours very truly,

[*Unsigned*]

Secretary

225. Recommendation of William Weir. Thackeray Turner, SPAB, to Sir Ralph B.M. Blois, Bt, 2 August 1906

2 August 1906

re, Blythburgh Church, Suffolk

Dear Sir Ralph Blois,

I think I ought to inform you that Mr Weir's estimate <u>includes the cost of supervision</u>.

I give below a list of some of the buildings which have been repaired under the superintendence of Mr Weir, in consultation with the society, as I think it may possibly be of use to you.

Exeter guildhall
Eglwys Brewis, Glamorganshire
Eglwys Cummin, Caernarvonshire
North Stoke church, Oxon.
Sandon church, Staffs.
Wilby church, Norfolk.
Sutton Courtenay church, Berks.
West Ham church tower, Essex.
Coln St Denis church tower, Glos.
Denton church tower, Lincs.
Onibury church, Shropshire.
St Oswald's church, Widford, Oxon.
Hough church, Lincolnshire.
Church of St Peter Hungate, Norwich
Uttoxeter church tower, Staffs.
Wroughton church tower, Wilts.

Yours very truly,
[*signed*]   Thackeray Turner
Secretary

226. SPAB uncertainty about prospects at Blythburgh. Thackeray Turner, SPAB, to Philip Norman, 2 August 1906

/1 Enclosure/

2 August 1906

re, <u>Blythburgh Church, etc</u>

Dear Norman,
Many thanks for your letters and also for your cheque value £1 1s. 0d. (one guinea) for which I enclose a formal receipt.

With regard to Blythburgh – Mr Weir recently visited and reported upon the church for the society at the request of Sir Ralph Blois, the patron, and the matter will be considered by the restoration committee at a meeting on the 8th inst when Sir Ralph Blois and Prince Frederick Duleep Singh will be present.

We hope Mr Weir's report and estimate will be adopted, but it is very uncertain as to what will happen.
Yours very truly,
[*signed*]   Thackeray Turner
Secretary

227. Selection of architect by Blythburgh committee. Sir Ralph B.M. Blois, Bt, to Thackeray Turner, SPAB, 8 August 1906

8 August 1906

Dear Mr Turner,

I am sorry to say at a committee meeting held today it was decided to employ Mr Johnston as architect for Blythburgh church if he will undertake to work with your society's advice and will reduce his estimate leaving out certain work, [*?words*] which the committee approved. I need hardly say this was against both Prince Frederick's and my advice and I offered to guarantee the money if <your estimate should> your society should have to spend more than your estimate of £800. I sincerely hope under your society's advice the work will be well done by Mr Johnston and think if he agrees to work under this condition all will be [*?word*] without friction. Thanking you very much for all you have done for me.

    Believe me,

      Yours very truly,

[*signed*]   Ralph Blois

228. Blythburgh architect. Thackeray Turner, SPAB, to Sir Ralph B.M. Blois, Bt, 9 August 1906

9 August 1906

re, <u>Blythburgh Church, Suffolk</u>

Dear Sir Ralph Blois,

I beg to thank you for your letter of the 8th inst which I will lay before the committee of this society at its next meeting, but, owing to the vacation, this will not be held until late in September.

    Yours very truly,

[*Unsigned*]

        Secretary

229. Conditions for SPAB support. Thackeray Turner, SPAB, to Sir Ralph B.M. Blois, Bt, 5 October 1906

5 October 1906

re, <u>Blythburgh Church, Suffolk</u>

Dear Sir Ralph Blois,

I laid your letter of the 8th August before the committee of this society, and I was directed to write to you and say that as the work is to be carried out in accordance with the society's principles, the committee thinks it essential in the interests of the society, that the work being done should be inspected on its behalf, from time to time, in order that if the principles of the society are being departed from, we may try and persuade the architect to conform, or, if this cannot be, that we may inform the restoration committee.

I am therefore desired to ask you (1) Whether the works have begun? (2) If so, how far have they progressed? (3) Whether the society has permission to send its representative down?

The committee also desires me to say that it makes this suggestion with reluctance. It is obvious that it will be an expensive course of action for the society to adopt. On the other hand, it feels that it is unsatisfactory to the society for the statement to be made that the work is being carried out on the society's lines, without the society being able to assure itself that this is a true statement of the case.

Yours very truly,
[*signed*]   Thackeray Turner
             Secretary

P.S. Before writing to you the society informed Prince Frederick of its proposed action and it has met with his Highness's approval.

230. Opinion of Blythburgh committee member. John Seymour Lucas, RA, to Thackeray Turner, SPAB, 9 October 1906

Priory Place,
Blythburgh,
Suffolk.
9 October 1906

Dear Sir,

Mrs Egerton has forwarded your letter to me, as Mr Egerton is away from home.

I feel sure I am expressing the feeling of the whole committee in saying we should be very pleased if your representative would inspect the work now in progress at Blythburgh church. The committee at the last meeting in passing a vote of thanks to your society, expressed a wish that it would still continue to watch the work as it progressed.

Living on the spot[119] I have continually watched the workmen, and as far as I can judge they leave nothing to be desired. They are most careful, and disturb as little as possible.

Believe me,
     Faithfully yours,
[*signed*]   Seymour Lucas

To Thackeray Turner, Esq.

231. Request to visit Blythburgh. Extract of letter from Thackeray Turner, SPAB, to William Weir, 12 October 1906

12 October 1906

[*The letter first deals with Little Washbourn church, Worcestershire, and The Ley, Weobley.*]

re, <u>Blythburgh Church</u>

We wrote to Blythburgh about inspecting the work as it proceeds, and I now send you the reply.

The committee hopes you will kindly visit the work at our expense. Whether you meet the architect there or not is for you to decide.

Yours very truly,
[*signed*]   Thackeray Turner
             Secretary

---

[119] Seymour Lucas bought three old cottages in Priory Road, Blythburgh, in 1901. He remodelled them to create Priory Place (now The Priory). The house is 100 metres from the church.

232. Visit to Blythburgh. Thackeray Turner, SPAB, to John Seymour Lucas, RA, 12 October 1906

12 October 1906

re, <u>Blythburgh Church, Suffolk</u>

Dear Sir,

I read your letter of the 9th inst to the committee of this society at its meeting held here yesterday.

The committee desired me to thank you for your courteous letter, and to inform you that it is trying to arrange for Mr Weir to visit the church on behalf of the society, whose opinion will carry great weight with the committee.

I am,

Yours faithfully,

[*signed*]   Thackeray Turner

Secretary

Seymour Lucas, Esq. R.A.

233. Meeting with Blythburgh architect. Thackeray Turner, SPAB, to William Weir, 18 October 1906

18 October 1906

re, <u>Blythburgh Church</u>

Dear Weir,

The address of Mr Philip M. Johnston, the architect, is 21 De Crespigny Park, Denmark Hill, S.E.

He called here last Tuesday, and said he would be willing to meet you at the church the next time he visited it. He was at the building last Friday and he told the authorities he hoped to visit again in a fortnight. He however promised to write and let us know when he proposed to visit. But I think it would be well for you to write to him and arrange a day.

Yours very truly,

[*signed*]   Thackeray Turner

Secretary

234. Meeting with Blythburgh architect. William Weir to Thackeray Turner, SPAB, 24 October 1906

[*Extract of letter*] From Mr Weir
24 October 1906

re Blythburgh Church 'I have arranged to meet Mr Johnston and go over the work on Monday 29th inst.' (For letter see Marston church)

235. Report on visit to Blythburgh. William Weir to Thackeray Turner, SPAB, 5 November 1906.[120]

Extract from letter from Mr Weir, 5 November 1906.
re, Blythburgh Church 'I enclose a report on the result of my visit to the work at the above, which I am sorry to say appears hopeless.'

236. Disassociation of SPAB from work at Blythburgh. Thackeray Turner, SPAB, to Sir Ralph B.M. Blois, Bt, 9 November 1906

/Enc/

9 November 1906

re <u>Blythburgh Church, Suffolk</u>

Dear Sir Ralph Blois,
In accordance with arrangements which had been made, Mr William Weir, representing this society, met the architect, Mr Johnston, at Blythburgh church, on the 29th October.

My committee has now received and carefully considered Mr Weir's report, a copy of which I enclose.

The committee feels that, on the face of it, the report is true, and it has therefore reluctantly come to the decision that it is in duty bound to disassociate the society with the work, as being contrary to the society's principles.

I think when you read Mr Weir's report you will see that the society can take no other possible action, and it desires me to say it is a matter of deep regret and disappointment to the committee that things have turned out as they have.

I am sending a press copy of the report to Prince Frederick Duleep Singh.

    I am,
  Yours very truly,
[*signed*]   Thackeray Turner
        Secretary

237. Report on work at Blythburgh. John Kent, SPAB, to Prince Frederick Duleep Singh, 10 November 1906

/2 Enclosures/

10 November 1906

re <u>Blythburgh Church, Suffolk</u>

Sir,
I am directed by the committee to forward to your Highness a press copy of a report which it has received from Mr Weir, together with a copy of a letter which it has addressed to Sir Ralph Blois.

    I am Sir,
  Your Highness' obedient servant,
[*signed*]   John Kent

---

[120] For Weir's report see Appendix A 18.

Assistant Secretary

H.H. Prince Frederick Duleep Singh

238. Patron's regret at Blythburgh decision. Sir Ralph B.M. Blois, Bt, to Thackeray Turner, SPAB, 12 November 1906

November 12 1906

Dear Mr Turner,

I am sorry to hear from you about Blythburgh church, but I quite understand the reason why your society can do nothing further to help with the work. I need hardly tell you how extremely sorry I am at the way the business has been managed.

Yours truly,

[*signed*]   Ralph Blois

To Thackeray Turner, Esq.

239. Regret at Blythburgh decision. Prince Frederick Duleep Singh to Thackeray Turner, SPAB, 12 November 1906

Breckles,
Attleborough,
Norfolk.
12 November 1906

Dear Mr Turner,

I am exceedingly sorry to hear what you tell me about Blythburgh. I am writing to Sir Ralph at once. I trust there may be time to stop the 'restoration' and other waste of money proposed. But the work already done is most unfortunate.

Yours sincerely,

[*signed*]   Frederick Duleep Singh

240. Attempt to influence Blythburgh committee. Thackeray Turner, SPAB, to Prince Frederick Duleep Singh, 23 November 1906

23 November 1906

re Blythburgh Church

Dear Prince Frederick,

I am sorry I was not here when you called.

With regard to Blythburgh church, although you can fairly say you cannot speak on questions of construction, nevertheless the report shews that the tie-beams have been improperly scarfed, milled lead instead of cast lead has been put on the roofs, and imitative work introduced.[121] I should have thought that you could point out to

---

[121] The SPAB preferred sand cast lead to the cheaper milled lead. The latter was regarded as less reliable, the stretching in milling rendering the structure porous and spongy, leading to shrinkage and cracking in use. Peter Nicholson, *An Architectural Dictionary* I (1819), p. 210. This empirical finding has an explanation in the rearrangement of the crystalline structure in rolling, leading to discontinuities in the form of laminations or folds, increasing the susceptibility to deterioration.

the committee that, as the society is advised by a number of professional gentlemen, who have allowed the report to go out, that they \(the committee)/ cannot continue to allow the architect to proceed without, at any rate, calling in another opinion.

I say this much, because I understand that you wished for advice, but really how far it is possible to do any good, I feel very doubtful.

re, Mildenhall Church, Suffolk
We hear that £1,000 has been given towards the restoration of Mildenhall church. I think you know the building. Do you think anything can be done?

    Yours very truly,
[*signed*]   Thackeray Turner
        Secretary

241. Attempt to influence Blythburgh committee. Prince Frederick Duleep Singh to Thackeray Turner, SPAB, 28 November 1906

                    Breckles,
                    Attleborough,
                    Norfolk.
              28 November 1906

Dear Mr Turner,
I am much obliged for your letter. What I meant was that I could not discuss technicalities with Mr Johnston (I hope to have an interview with him at the church) tho' I can urge him as to preserving and not restoring. I do not think it is any good calling a committee meeting till I have seen the church and Mr Johnston, and know exactly what to say to the committee. It appears most of them (even Mr Lucas!) is quite content with what is being done externally. When we have the meeting I will certainly urge what you say. It is a grievous pity that it ever got into the hands of such a man. Mildenhall is such a very 'thoroughly restored' church including such things as a fancy turret on the tower that I really don't think there is much left to harm except the beautiful roof. I know all the people connected with the church and will make enquiries.

    Yours sincerely,
[*signed*]   Frederick Duleep Singh

[*William Weir prepared three further reports on Blythburgh Church dated 1926, 1933 and 1947, ref. SPAB/Blythburgh/Additional. See Appendix A* **19–24**.]

242. Advice on contracting for work on church. William Weir to the Revd A.D. Thompson, 17 July 1933[122]

17 July 1933
Dear Mr Thompson,

                Blythburgh Church
Thank you for your letters of the 11th and 15th inst. in regard to likely builders for the proposed work.

---

[122] Correspondence 242–3 and 245 are from BCP 28.3.4 and 6, 28.4.1.

I will prepare a specification and would suggest asking tenders from a couple of builders for carrying out the work on a percentage basis, whereby the builder is paid an agreed percentage for his profit on the nett cost of the work undertaken.

A separate contract should be arranged for the leadwork, based on an agreed price per cwt: for recasting and relaying the lead.

I enclose herewith my report (3 copies) on the building, with an approximate estimate of the cost of the proposed repairs, which I trust will meet with approval.

I should be pleased to give you any further particulars that may be desired in regard to the proposed work.

> Yours truly,
[*signed*]   William Weir
The Revd A.D. Thompson,
The Vicarage, Walberswick,
Suffolk.

243. Concerning lead and architect's fees. William Weir to the Revd A.D. Thompson, 19 July 1933

19 July 1933
Dear Mr Thompson,

> Blythburgh Church

Thank you for your letter of the 18th inst. to answer to the two points mentioned.
(a)   The lead of the south aisle should be included in the first work to be undertaken and the lead on the north aisle, which is not so bad, left until funds are available. The approximate cost of the south aisle would be £35-ish or half the estimate for the two aisles.
(b)   The estimated cost is exclusive of architect's fees, which together with travelling expenses would be about 10 p.c.

> Yours faithfully,
[*signed*]   William Weir
The Revd A.D. Thompson,
The Vicarage, Walberswick,
Suffolk.

244. Work at Blythburgh Church. The Revd A. D. Thompson to William Weir, 26 February 1934[123]

/March 1st/

> The Vicarage,
> Walberswick,
> Suffolk.
> 26 February 1934

> Blythburgh Church

Dear Mr Weir,
I return your sketch with the measurements marked. Drake was not there this morning but the bricklayer and I measured them between us and cross checked the

---

[123] SPAB Add.

measurements and also compared the overall measurements with the sum total of the parts.

Thank you for going to Addington. I will convey your opinion to Miss Candy.

I have held up the making of the altar stand for the chapel although I cannot see much point in it and I think the Advisory Board would be very foolish to raise any objection. I have postponed the making entirely out of respect for you and not for any feelings of regard for the Advisory Board in this matter. You will remember that you yourself personally approved of the scheme and I am sure your opinion must carry very great weight with the board. Besides, I have a faculty authorising me to carry out the refurnishing of the altars.

It seems to me that the Advisory Board only consider one point of view and have no respect for local sentiment and feeling or for local associations and I am not going to allow an altar top (even if it is only pine) which has for many years been used for the most sacred service of the church to be scrapped. The board can take proceedings against me, but if you would rather be out of the row, I would wait until you were finished or do it in spite of your formal disapproval, although I would rather have a friend by my side in this matter than be left to fight alone. I am rather hurt. Also, if the altar top is not put there, the candlesticks and war memorial will have to come back into the sanctuary and chancel respectively as local feeling is very strong on both these and I cannot let them become things of complete insignificance. Neither can I outrage local sentiment so completely. The Advisory Board would hate to see these things back and they will raise a hornet's nest if they express any opinion which suggests side-tracking them. My scheme is surely the lesser of two evils and it satisfies all local feeling and my own scruples.

I am prepared to give my pledge to the bishop (who, in my opinion is really the only stumbling block in this matter) that I will not furnish the chapel without a further faculty (which I shall not be contemplating) and that I will only use the altar once a year (i.e. on Remembrance Sunday).

Why don't you say 'carry on' or at least come down earlier than we proposed? I would like to see the church finished by the early part of April when I hope to have the rededication service.

> Yours sincerely,
[*signed*]   A.D. Thompson

245. Report on Blythburgh church. William Weir to the Revd A.D. Thompson, 25 July 1947

25 July 1947

> The Beeches,
> Wilbury Hill Road,
> Letchworth, Herts.

Dear Mr Thompson,
Blythburgh Church
Enclosed is my report on the condition and repairs to the building, which I hope will meet with approval.

I am very glad the fabric escaped serious damage from enemy bombs and I hope the damaged window glazing will be renewed before the colder weather sets in.[124] It was a great pleasure to meet you again and go over the building. There was plenty of room in the trains and I had a comfortable journey.

Yours sincerely,

[*signed*]   William Weir

---

[124] The clerestory windows were damaged by the explosion over Blythburgh of a United States Navy Liberator bomber on 12 August 1944, when Joe Kennedy Jnr, elder brother of President John F. Kennedy, was killed. See Mick Muttitt, 'Witness to the first Kennedy tragedy' and 'Joe Kennedy Jnr's last mission' in Alan Mackley (ed.), *The Poaching Priors of Blythburgh* (Blythburgh, 2002), pp. 52–5.

BLYTHBURGH CHURCH RESTORATION COMMITTEE MINUTE BOOK[1]

Front cover

Blythburgh Church Restoration Minute Book October 1881
Haggai I. 14[2]

Minutes and memoranda

1. Names of the members of the restoration committee, no date[3]

Names of the restoration committee
The Revd H. Sykes, vicar and chairman

| Robinson Briggs | Esq. } | churchwardens |
| Charles Youngs | " } | |

Arthur Cooper	"	Mrs	Sykes
George Mills	"	"	Cooper
Thomas Tuthill	"	"	Briggs
Thomas Rawlinson	"	"	Youngs
Chas. A. Bicker	"	Miss	Sainty
Revd G.I. Davies		Mrs	Tuthill
S. Wilton Rix,	Esq.	Lady	Blois

Architect <George> \Arthur/ Edmund Street Esq. R.A. \M.A./
    14 Cavendish Place,
      Cavendish Square,
        London W.

2. Parishioners' meeting, 7 October 1881, minutes

7 October 1881

---

[1] Suffolk Record Office, Ipswich, FC198 E2 1, Church Restoration. Compiled by the Revd Henry Sykes from 1881 to 1884. In addition to the minutes of restoration committee meetings, it contains printed notices, newspaper cuttings and lists of people. These are reproduced in the relevant appendix.

[2] 'And the LORD stirred up the spirit of Zerubbabel the son of Shealtiel, governor of Judah, and the spirit of Joshua the son of Josedech, the high priest, and the spirit of all the remnant of the people; and they came and did work in the house of the LORD of hosts, their God.' *The Bible, Authorised Version.*

[3] This list includes additions to the committee up to August 1882. See Appendix D, 'Notes on People'.

A meeting of parishioners was held in the national school <room>⁴ on the above date, convened by circular, (see inside cover), when the following proceedings took place.

'The Church's one foundation' was sung; a portion of Holy Scripture read, (1 Chron. XXIX.) and prayer was offered by the vicar, including the Collect 'Prevent us O Lord' and the Lord's prayer. After some remarks by the chairman on the necessity of the work to be undertaken, and the privilege of working for God, Mr Briggs proposed and Mr Youngs (churchwardens) seconded –

I. 'That it is desirable an effort should be made at once towards raising funds for the restoration of our church'.

II. 'That the following persons form a committee for the purpose of carrying out the foregoing resolution, with power to add to their number, viz. –

The Revd H. Sykes, vicar
Robinson Briggs Esq. }   churchwardens
Charles Youngs   " }
Arthur Cooper   "   Mrs Cooper
George Mills   "   "   Briggs
Thomas Tuthill   "   "   Youngs
Thomas Rawlinson   "   "   Sykes
                              "   Tuthill

III. That the committee meet for the first time on Monday Oct. 10. 1881. in this school at 6.30 p.m.

After singing the Doxology the meeting was brought to a close by the vicar pronouncing the Benediction.

    Signed,
        H. Sykes, chairman

3. Restoration committee meeting, 10 October 1881, minutes

10 October 1881

At the first meeting of the committee held on this date, all the members being present, with the exception of Mrs Sykes, who was too ill to attend, the following resolutions were adopted

I. That the vicar write to G.E. Street Esq. R.A. Cavendish Square, London, to ascertain his fee for an inspection and report upon the state of the church and if his charges do not exceed 10 guineas and travelling expenses, Mr S. have authority to engage him for the purpose named above.

II. That 100 small cards be printed for the use of those who are willing, to collect small sums.

III. That Miss Sainty and Mr C.A. Bicker be added to the committee.

    H. Sykes, chairman.

4. Restoration committee meeting, 10 November 1881, minutes

10 November 1881

---

4 Blythburgh school for 145 pupils opened in 1875 in Dunwich Road.

A meeting of the committee was held in the school-room on this date (for attendance see register) when the minutes of the previous meeting were read and the vicar informed the meeting that he had engaged Geo. E. Street Esq. R.A. in accordance with the resolution of Oct. 10th that his fee would be ten guineas and that Mr. Street had visited the church on the 3rd inst. <and> would send his report in a few weeks and give an estimate of the cost of each part of the undertaking.

The subject of holding the church services in the school-room was also considered and recommended; the organ to be removed from the church and additional forms brought to the school when the bishop's consent had been obtained to the holding of the services in the school.

The next meeting to be held after notice.

 Signed,

  H. Sykes, chairman.

5. Memorandum, no date

Geo. E. Street Esq. who had been appointed architect to the restoration committee died in the interval of the meetings held on 10 November 1881 and the one held on 21 January 1882. See scrap on the preceding leaf.[5]

  H. S.

6. Restoration committee meeting, 21 January 1882, minutes

21 January 1882

A meeting of the committee was held in the classroom of the national school on the above date (for attendance see register) when the vicar reported that he had received the architect's report and estimates (see copy) and had forwarded them to the bishop without delay. The bishop had written to say he should be most happy to meet Mr. Sykes on the 23rd with reference to the report and the plans proposed for raising the money.

Lady Blois kindly consented for her name to be added to the committee; Miss Cooper was also placed on the committee.

A bazaar in aid of the restoration fund was determined upon to be held during the summer in the parish.

The next meeting of the committee was fixed for Friday the 27th at 3 p.m. to receive the report of the <bishop's> vicar's interview with the bishop.

7. Restoration committee meeting, 27 January 1882, minutes

27 January 1882

At the meeting held on this date the vicar stated he had had an interview with the bishop on the 23rd when his lordship went over the architect's report and estimates seriatim and suggested that all the works contemplated should be divided into three classes, viz – those that were <u>urgent</u>, those that might be <u>postponed,</u> and those which might be considered <u>questionable</u>. His lordship then suggested that if the committee agreed with him the architect should be asked to give separate estimates of the three

---

[5] A newspaper report of the death of George Street. See Appendix C 5.

divisions so as to ascertain what amount of funds would have to be raised for the various portions of the work required to be done.[6]

The bishop also kindly offered to go over the report etc. with the venerable archdeacon Groom during the week and then return the papers to the vicar afterwards.

His lordship in answer to a question said we could not expect any help from the Ecclesiastical Commissioners as they had no property in the parish. They would meet a benefaction for the improvement of the living, but not for the restoration of the buildings.

The bishop also expressed his satisfaction with the appointment of Mr Arthur Street in conjunction with Mr Blomfield to carry forward the work begun by the late George Street Esq.

After the above report the meeting asked Miss Sainty if she would try and get up an entertainment in the school for the benefit of the funds. Miss Sainty kindly promised with assistance, to get up an entertainment with the school children and others for Friday 10 February 1882.

The meeting was then adjourned till further notice.

Signed,
H. Sykes, chairman

8. Memorandum, no date

The architect's clerk came down on the following Monday to inspect the windows and to report how many were in a dangerous state. The vicar went over with him deciding which should be undertaken at once and which should be postponed.

9. Restoration committee meeting, 31 March 1882, minutes

31 March 1882

At a meeting of the committee held in the classroom of the national school on this date (for attendance see register) it was unanimously resolved

I. That the restoration of Blythburgh church be proceeded with as <u>one</u> work (including <nave> church and chancel) and that the funds be invested in the name of the vicar and churchwardens \for the time being/ and their successors in office.

II. That the architect be instructed to prepare plans and specifications for a new \roof/ for the south aisle, including nave and chancel, the parapet over the south aisle, and for those windows which are considered to be in a dangerous condition.

Signed,
H. Sykes, chairman

10. Restoration committee meeting, 14 April 1882, minutes

14 April 1882

At a meeting of the committee held in the classroom of the national school on this date (see register) a letter was read from the archdeacon stating that the resolutions passed at the last meeting could not be carried \out/ on the terms proposed.[7] Another

---

[6]   See Appendix A 1.
[7]   The authority to take such decisions rested with the Vestry. See Introduction n. 57. The Vestry minutes are in SROI FC198 A1 1, Vestry Minute Book (1884–1902).

letter was read from the managers of the Halesworth bank stating that the rate allowed upon deposits at 14 days \notice/ would be 2 per cent. No resolution was proposed with respect to the investment of funds but the following was adopted

I. That an advertisement be inserted in the 'Ipswich Journal' and 'East Anglian' announcing a bazaar to be held at Blythburgh in the month of August 1882 and stating where contributions would be gratefully received. Also circulars.

II. The plans of the architect for the work to be undertaken, in the first instance, were shewn to the committee and adopted.

III. The plans were ordered to be returned and the architect instructed to draw out specifications for the same. Such plans and specifications when completed were to be submitted to a vestry meeting to be duly convened for that purpose.

Signed,

H. Sykes, chairman

11. Memorandum, no date

The letter referred to on the opposite side (April 14) is dated the 15th April which must be a mistake probably 13th.[8]

12. Note. Closure of church for Sunday services, no date[9]

The church was closed for the Sunday services by the bishop's permission.

13. Memorandum, no date

The vestry meeting alluded to on the other side[10] was duly called when the plans and specifications were passed without dissentients and after the notice had been posted on the church and school doors for two Sundays stating that the vestry meeting had been held, the plans, specifications, and notice were sent to the archdeacon and by him forwarded to the bishop for his sanction and approval.

These plans were 'approved' by the bishop and signed by him 7 July 1882.

14. Restoration committee attendance register

		1881		1882			
	Restoration Committee	Oct10	Nov10	Jan21	Jan27	Mch31	Apr21
1.	The Revd H. Sykes	/	/	/	/	/	/
2.	Mr R. Briggs	/	/1	/	a	/	a
3.	Mr Chas. Youngs	/	/2	/	/	a	a
4.	Mr A. Cooper	/	/	a	/	/	/
5.	Mr Mills	/	/3	/	a	a	a

---

[8] The letter from the archdeacon discussed at the committee meeting on 14 April.

[9] Written after the insertion of a newspaper cutting dated 19 May 1882.

[10] RCMB 10 above.

6.	Mr Thos. Tuthill	/	/4	/	a	a	a
7.	Mr Thos. Rawlinson	/	/5	a	a	a	a
8.	Mr C.A. Bicker		a	a	a	a	a
9.	Mrs Sykes		/	a	a	a	a
10.	Mrs Cooper	/	/6	/	/	/	/
11.	Mrs Briggs	/	/	/	a	/	a
12.	Mrs Youngs	/	a	a	a	a	a
13.	Mrs Tuthill		/	a	a	a	a
14.	Miss Sainty			/	/	/	a
15.	Lady Blois			/	/	/	/
16.	Miss Cooper					/	a
17.	Miss Sykes					/	a
18.	Miss Goodram						/

[*The meaning of the numbers against some members at the 10 November 1881 meeting is not known.*]

15. Restoration committee meeting, 3 July 1882, minutes

3 July 1882

At a meeting of the committee held in the classroom of the national school on this date the following members were present, viz – The Revd H. Sykes, Mrs Cooper, Mrs Briggs, Miss Sykes, Messrs R. Briggs, C. Youngs, Geo. Mills and A. Cooper.

The chairman read two letters from Lady Blois and the committee requested him to write proposing to divide the funds collected in the following proportions provided that the archdeacon and the bishop approved viz 2/3 to the church 1/3 to the chancel.[11]

For want of time the investment of funds was left over to another meeting.

Signed,
    H. Sykes, chairman

16. Restoration committee meeting, 24 July 1882, minutes

24 July 1882

At a meeting of the committee held in the classroom of the national school on this date the following members were present, viz The Revd H. Sykes, Mrs Cooper, Miss Goodram, Miss Sykes, Messrs R. Briggs, Geo. Mills, and A. Cooper.

The Chairman read the minutes of the preceding meeting and read the correspondence which was approved and was then desired to supply the bishop with a list of subscriptions and the plan of operations.

---

[11] See Introduction n. 59 on patron's responsibility to maintain the chancel.

Lady Blois having signified that Monday the 31st would be convenient, a meeting was arranged for that date at 4 o'clock.

Signed,
    H. Sykes, chairman

17. Restoration committee meeting, 31 July 1882, minutes

31 July 1882

At a meeting held in the classroom of the national school on this date the following members attended, viz Lady and Miss Blois, The Revd H., Mrs and Miss Sykes, Mrs Briggs, Mrs Cooper and <Mr A. Cooper>, Mrs Youngs, Mr Mills and Miss Goodram. A 'Free and easy' was the result, and a protest by the vicar against raffling.[12]

18. Report of bazaar, 9 August 1882

9 August 1882

The first day of the Bazaar opened with most favourable weather and the attendance numerous, more than <£50> <£25> £25 being taken at the entrance 1s. each.
First days receipts £170 19s. 3d.

19. Report of bazaar, 10 August 1882

10 August 1882

Second day the weather was all that could have been desired, but the attendance not so numerous as on the previous day. Taken at the entrance £5 or £6 at [?]6d. each.
Receipts second day £57 0s. 2d.
For particulars see printed reports

Total   £227 19s 5d.

20. Report on the restoration of Blythburgh church and bazaar, *The Halesworth Times*, August 1882

[*In the margins of this cutting Sykes added corrections at various places.*]

RESTORATION OF BLYTHBURGH CHURCH.
GRAND BAZAAR AND FANCY FAIR.

This beautiful, ancient, and historic church has for a long series of years gradually been falling more and more into decay and ruin, any repairs which have been done have only been in patches with niggard hand, and consequently as far as outward appearance has gone, everything has conspired to make it as unsightly as human hands could make it. Its restoration has been mooted time after time, but the task appeared so formidable a one, on account of the size and delapidation of the church,

---

[12] A 'Free and Easy' was an informal gathering of people more or less known to each other, providing their own songs and recitations. Kerry Powell, *The Cambridge Companion to Victorian and Edwardian Theatre* (Cambridge, 2004), p. 167.

that even the bravest feared to undertake so onerous a work, and had it not been that the parishioners were afraid longer to worship in it, and had to adjourn to the school-room for Divine service, it might have been many years longer before any attempt would have been made to restore any of its ancient glory.

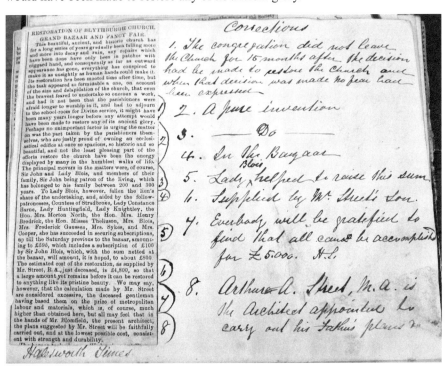

Plate 8. Restoration committee minute book. Criticism by the Revd Henry Sykes of a newspaper report on the 1882 bazaar. August 1882. © SROI, FC198 E2 1

[*Sykes*] Corrections. 1. The congregation did not leave the Church for 15 months after the decision had be[*en*] made to restore the church and when that decision was made no fear had been expressed.

Perhaps no unimportant factor in urging the matter on was the part taken by the parishioners themselves, who are justly proud of owning an ecclesiastical edifice at once so spacious, so historic and so beautiful, and not the least pleasing part of the efforts [*to*] restore the church have been the energy displayed by many in the humblest walks of life.

[*Sykes*] 2. A pure invention.

The principal movers in the matters were, of course, Sir John and Lady Blois, and members of their family, Sir John being patron of the living, which has belonged to his family between 200 and 300 years.

[*Sykes*] 3. A pure invention.

144

To Lady Blois, however, [*has*] fallen the lion's share of the undertaking,

[*Sykes*] 4. In the Bazaar.

and, aided by the following patronesses, Countess of Stradbroke, Lady Constance Barne, Lady Huntingfield, Lady Knightley, the Hon. Mrs. Morton North, the Hon. Mrs. Henry Brodrick, the Hon. Misses Thelluson [*sic*], Mrs. Blois, Mrs. Frederick Gaussen, Mrs. Sykes, and Mrs. Cooper, she has succeeded in securing subscriptions, up till the Saturday previous to the bazaar, amounting to £595,

[*Sykes*] 5. Lady \Blois/ helped to raise this sum.

which includes a subscription of £100 by Sir John Blois, which, with the sum netted at the bazaar, will amount, it is hoped, to about £800. The estimated cost of the restoration, as supplied by Mr. Street, R.A., just deceased, is £4,800, so that a large amount yet remains before it can be restored to anything like its pristine beauty.

[*Sykes*] 6. Supplied by Mr Street's son.

We may say, however, that the calculation[*s*] made by Mr. Street are considered excessive,

[*Sykes*] 7. Everybody will be gratified to find that all could be accomplished for £5,000. H.S.

the deceased gentleman having based them on the price of metropolitan labour and materials, which is, of course, much higher than obtained here, but all may feel that in the hands of Mr. Blomfield, the present architect, the plans suggested by Mr. Street will be faithfully carried out, and at the lowest possible cost, consistent with strength and durability.

[*Sykes*] 8. Architect A. Street, M.A. is the Architect appointed to carry out his father's plans etc.

21. Restoration committee meeting, 21 August 1882, minutes

21 August 1882

At a meeting of the Committee held in the National School on this date the following members were present The Revd H. Sykes, and Miss Sykes, Lady Blois, Mrs Cooper, Mr A. Cooper, Mrs Briggs, Mrs Youngs, and Miss Goodram.

Mr Sykes presented his cash a/c to the meeting and gave copies to those present. Cash in bank £101 11s. 0d.

The bazaar account was presented by Lady Blois which shewed the total receipts £230 18s. 0d. the expenses – £19 3s. 10d, net proceeds £211 14s. 2d., a result which exceeded all that <that> the committee had expected.

It was agreed with Lady Blois' consent, that the whole amount collected for the 'Restoration of Blythburgh Church' up to the 5th day of August, together with the proceeds of the bazaar and £10 due of the promised subscriptions shall go to the <u>general</u> fund and be divided in the proportion advertised – viz two-thirds to the <u>church</u>

145

and one-third to the <u>chancel</u> fund. Lady Blois undertaking to give two-thirds of the money she has invested at Beccles and Mr Sykes to give one-third of the money he has invested at Southwold to the <u>church</u> and <u>chancel</u> funds respectively.

The Revd G.I. Davies, rural dean (who was present) and Mr Rix of Beccles <be> were added to the committee.

A vote of thanks was accorded to Mrs F. Gaussen for getting up the concert in London whereby the sum of £54 was realized for the restoration fund (see report).

Signed,
    H. Sykes, chairman.

22. Restoration committee meeting, 21 September 1882, minutes

21 September 1882

At a meeting of the committee held at the 'White Hart' inn[13] on this date the following were present – viz The Revd H. Sykes, Sir John Blois, Lady Blois, R. Briggs Esq., Chas. Youngs Esq., Mrs Cooper, Geo. Mills, A. Cooper, Chas. A. Bicker, S. Wilton Rix, Esq.

Moved by Sir John Blois and seconded by R. Briggs Esq., that the minutes of the last meeting be confirmed.

Signed,
    H. Sykes, chairman.

Proposed by Sir John Blois and seconded by Chas. Youngs that a building committee be appointed to consist of the following persons The Revd H. Sykes, Sir John Blois, Messrs R. Briggs, Chas. Youngs, Mr. Rix, Revd G.I. Davies and Arthur Cooper, three to form a quorum.

Proposed by Sir John Blois and seconded by Mr Briggs that that [*sic*] the meetings of the committee be held at the 'White Hart' Blythburgh on the first Monday in each month.

That the chairman write to Mr Street and ask him how to divide the work so as to bring the estimates down to the sum actually in <viz £700> in hand or available for present use (£730).

H. Sykes, chairman.

Moved by Sir John Blois and seconded by R Briggs Esq., that the minutes of the last meeting be confirmed.

Signed,
    H. Sykes, chairman.

23. Building committee meeting, 2 October 1882, minutes

2 October 1882

---

[13] The White Hart, London Road, Blythburgh.

146

A meeting of the building committee was held on this date at the 'White Hart' when the following members were present The Revd H. Sykes, vicar, Revd G.I. Davies, Sir John Blois, Messrs S.W. Rix, R. Briggs and Chas. Youngs.

I. A letter from Mr Street and another from Mr Allen were read with reference to curtailing the expenditure within the limits of the cash in hand.

II. The cash in hand and the funds available for building purposes were found to be £808 10s. 0d. and it was agreed upon to wait another month before any further action was taken with respect to the contracts.

III. The Revd G.I. Davies promised the handsome sum of ten pounds towards the £241 required; the subscription to be called for when £230 has been raised.

IV. Sir John Blois proposed that all the funds be invested at Beccles in the names of the vicar and churchwardens provided they are willing to sign the contracts, at the same time he gave the committee to understand that he should not sign a separate contract for the chancel as a dispute had been raised as to what part of the building really belonged to the chancel and for which he is legally responsible.

V. It was agreed that the a/c for advertizing etc. should be called in, and that the advertisements should be curtailed as far as possible and confined to the two papers already employed viz 'The Norfolk Chronicle' and 'The Ipswich Journal'.

VI. The monthly meeting to be held at 12.30 instead of 12 o'clock.

H. Sykes, chairman.

24. Building committee meeting, 6 November 1882, minutes

6 November 1882

At a meeting held on this date the following members were present The Revd H. Sykes, vicar, Sir John Blois, Messrs S.W. Rix, R. Briggs, Chas. Youngs and A. Cooper.

I. The <meeting> minutes of the preceding meeting were read and agreed to with the exception of nos IV, V, & VI.

II. As a dispute had arisen as to the exact limits of the chancel it was agreed that this point must be settled before a division of the funds, in proper proportion, could take place. Information to be collected from churches similarly constructed to Blythburgh with a view to this dispute being amicably settled.

III. That the following bills be paid by the vicar and churchwardens as soon as the funds in the account current at the bank <would> will permit viz –

Henry Stevenson and Co	£9	15s. 0d.
F.S. Jackson and others	7	6s. 0d.
Wells Gardner and Co.	3	19s. 0d.
Peter Carcova [?]		17s. 0d.

IV. That the monthly meeting shall be altered to meet the convenience of distant members.

H. Sykes, chairman.

25. Memorandum, 6 November 1882

Resolved that the list of subscriptions be inserted once a month instead of weekly, the advertisement to be sent to the papers after each meeting of the building committee.

26. Building committee meeting, 4 December 1882, minutes

4 December 1882

At a meeting of the building committee held at the 'White Hart' on the above date the following members were present viz The Revd H. Sykes, chairman, Messrs Rix and Youngs.

The minutes of the preceding meeting were read and the list of subscriptions presented; after which the time was passed in hearing from Mr Rix his opinion upon the subject of restoration and this opinion being <rebutted> \replied to/ by the chairman the meeting adjourned.[14]

1 January 1883
Signed,
H. Sykes, chairman

27. Building committee meeting, 1 January 1883, minutes

1 January 1883

At a meeting of the building committee held at the 'White Hart' on this date the following members were present viz Revd H. Sykes, chairman, Sir John Blois, Messrs R. Briggs, C. Youngs and A. Cooper.

After due consideration it was agreed that the chancel question should remain an open question, Sir John Blois agreeing to sign the contracts for the chancel as set forth in the specifications, but upon protest that he should not in consequence be held responsible for the N. and S. chapels in the future unless it could be <legally> proved that he was liable by the law.

The chairman was requested to ask Mr Street's terms for his professional services as architect.

The <estimates> tender of Mr Allen of Southwold, for s. aisle roof and the windows specified for £1,049 10s. 0d. was formally accepted and the chairman was authorised to communicate with the architect and the contractor with a view to the contracts being drawn up and signed as soon as the funds in the bank amounted to the above sum.

In the meantime Mr Allen was requested to make all the preparation possible so as to commence the actual work in the early spring, or as soon as the weather permit.

The chairman was requested to ask Mr Allen if he would sign an agreement not to press for payment till the whole amount was collected, the committee in the meantime to use every action to collect the amount required.

Signed 5 February 1883
    H. Sykes, chairman

---

[14] Samuel Wilton Rix (1806–94), a Beccles solicitor and local historian. A nonconformist and one-time member of Beccles corporation, serving as mayor. He opposed the drastic restoration of Beccles church tower in 1891, proposed by the architect Sir Arthur Blomfield. Rix questioned whether it was absolutely necessary that anything should be done. The proposal would destroy the most interesting monument in the town and replace it with a model. His position was therefore closer to that of the SPAB than to Sykes, hence the reference to the latter's rebuttal. Thanks are due to David Lindley for this information.

28. Building committee meeting, 5 February 1883, minutes

5 February 1883

At a meeting of the building committee held at the 'White Hart' on this date the following members were present – viz – Revd H. Sykes, chairman, Sir John Blois, Messrs R. Briggs, C. Youngs, S.W. Rix and A. Cooper.

The monthly statement of accounts was presented by the chairman and the minutes of the preceding meeting read.

The contracts drawn up by the architect and signed by the contractor were read and considered.

Sir John Blois objected to two clauses and desired another clause to be added by which the contractor should agree not to demand the <fu> balance of account till the whole amount was collected.

The chairman was requested to communicate Sir John's wishes to the architect and to request him to make the above alterations.

Signed, 5 March 1883
   H. Sykes, chairman

29. Building committee meeting, 5 March 1883, minutes[15]

5 March 1883

At a meeting of the building committee held at the 'White Hart' on this date the following members of the committee were present, viz. – The Revd H. Sykes, chairman, Messrs R. Briggs, <F> S.W. Rix, and A. Cooper.

The <meeting> minutes of the previous meeting were read and the cash account for the month presented, with a statement of the receipts and payments from the first.

With regard to auditing the accounts it was the opinion of all present that it would be desirable that the auditor should be a competent accountant and not a member of the committee. Chas. Lenny, Esq. of Halesworth was mentioned as a suitable person to employ.

Signed,
H. Sykes, chairman.

30. Building committee meeting, 2 April 1883, minutes

2 April 1883

At the meeting held at the 'White Hart' on this date the treasurer received from Mrs. Cooper the sum of £11 15s. 6d.

No further business could be transacted as no members of the building committee were present besides the chairman.

   H. Sykes.

---

[15] A duplicate entry of the introduction to this minute: 'At the meeting of the building committee … and A. Cooper.' was deleted.

31. Memorandum, no date

The chancel contract was sent to the architect for alteration 5 February and was returned to Sir John Blois with the alterations and addition on Thursday 8 February, but from a letter received from the architect's clerk dated 29 March the contract had not been returned to Mr. Street.

32. Building committee meeting, 7 May 1883, minutes

7 May 1883

At the monthly meeting of the building committee held on this date the only members in attendance were Mr C. Youngs and Mr A. Cooper.

The chairman was too ill to be present, but sent in the monthly cash statement and the general statement shewing the receipts and payments from the first so far as the vicar's accounts are concerned

Amount at Beccles	£264	3s. 4d.
-do- Halesworth	549	6s. 3d.
In treasurer's hand	3	9s. 8¼d.
		£816 19s. 3¼d.
Total promised		£958 12s. 7d.
Cash in hand		816 19s. 3¼d.
Not paid		£141 13s. 3¾d.

33. Building committee meeting, 4 June 1883, minutes

4 June 1883

At a meeting of the building committee held at the 'White Hart' Inn on this date the following members were present, viz the Revd H. Sykes, chairman, Messrs R. Briggs, Chas. Youngs, <F> S. Rix and A. Cooper.

The cash account for the month was presented and the general statement of funds.

Certificates from the architect were presented by the contractor for the payment of £75 for the <u>church</u> portion and £75 for the <u>chancel</u>.

The £75 on account of the church portion was ordered to be paid and the chancel certificate was forwarded to Sir John the same date.

The chairman asked for a cash book and some boxes for the old painted glass which were granted.

Signed,
    H. Sykes, chairman.

34. Building committee meeting, 2 July 1883, minutes

2 July 1883

The Chairman and S. Wilton Rix Esq. were the only members of the building committee who attended the meeting on this date and no business was transacted.

Signed,
    H. Sykes, chairman.

35. Building committee meeting, 6 August 1883, minutes

6 August 1883

The chairman, Sir John Blois, and Mr Briggs attended the meeting on this date when the accounts were considered and the vicar was requested to apply to the Church Building Society.

The audit of accounts to be postponed till the present contract be completed.

H. Sykes, chairman.

36. Building committee meeting, 3 September 1883, minutes

3 September 1883

The chairman and Chas. Youngs, Esq. attended and Mr Allen applied for another advance, £450 0s. 0d. which was referred to the architect.

No other business transacted.

    H. Sykes, chairman.

37. Building committee meeting, 8 October 1883, minutes

8 October 1883

At a meeting held at the White Hart, the following <were> were present – The Revd H. Sykes, Lady Blois, Mrs Cooper and Mr Briggs.

The accounts for the month were presented and the following business transacted.

Drip stones under the clerestory windows were recommended by the architect and the cost £8 5s. 0d. was allowed as an extra.

A plan for re-seating the church was suggested by the vicar and with some alteration allowed. Mr Allen was empowered to take down the old square pews and requested to give an<d> estimate for re-arranging the benches and stalls according to \a/ plan considered.

Mr. Allen was empowered to examine the leads on the nave and north aisle and repair them where needed.

38. Meeting of vicar and churchwardens, 23 October 1883, minutes

23 October 1883

The vicar and churchwardens met at the church on this date and after examination of the plan and estimate referred to decided for Mr Allen to re-arrange the old benches, stalls etc. and to repair the flooring with brick where absolutely required and to send his account when completed.

39. Building committee meeting, 5 November 1883, minutes

5 November 1883

At the monthly meeting held on this date at the 'White Hart' the following were present The Revd H. Sykes, Lady Blois, Miss Blois and Mr Youngs, and at the church were joined by Mrs Cooper and eventually by Mr A. Cooper.

It was suggested that the 'East Anglian' should be the only paper for acknowledging subscriptions. Agreed to <u>nem</u>. <u>con</u>.

H. Sykes, chairman.

40. Building committee meeting, 3 December 1883, minutes

3 December 1883

At a meeting of the building committee held at the 'White Hart' on this date, the Revd H. Sykes, Mr Chas. Youngs and Mr A. Cooper being present, the architect's certificate for £75 to the contractor was agreed to and ordered to be paid.

H. Sykes.

41. Building committee meeting, 7 January 1884, minutes

7 January 1884

At a meeting of the building committee held on this date the following members were present – the Revd H. Sykes, S.W. Rix, Esq., Messrs Chas. Youngs and A. Cooper. Lady Blois, Mrs Gaussen and Mrs Cooper also attended.

Resolved that the window sill for the inside of the east window proposed by the architect <should> be inserted provided that the contractor's estimate for the same be <were> approved by Mr Street. (cost £6 15s. 0d. entered 8 November)

2nd. That the architect be instructed to prepare plans and estimates for the north Aisle and nave roofs.

3rd. That the subscriptions be inserted in the 'Norfolk Chronicle' and 'Ipswich Journal' as usual.

Signed,
H. Sykes, chairman.

42. Building committee meeting, 3 February 1884, minutes

3 February 1884

That the account of Mr Allen for re-seating the church be paid.

2nd. That communion cushions be re-covered with the same material as before.

3rd. That book rests be affixed to the bench rails.

4th That the panelled lining to the chancel be grained oak to match the communion rail.

5th. That one pillar and the arch be scraped as a sample.

Members present Mr Briggs, Mr Cooper and
H. Sykes, chairman.

43. Building committee meeting, 24 March 1884, minutes

24 March 1884

At a special meeting of the building committee held at this date, at the 'White Hart' the following members attended, Mr Briggs, Mr Youngs, Mr Cooper, and the Revd H. Sykes, vicar.

1st The accounts were received and referred to \Mr Lenny/ to be audited.

2nd The plans, specifications, and estimates, for the north aisle and nave roofs were produced and sanctioned as a whole, the details to be further considered.

3rd The above plans etc. were ordered to be sent to the archdeacon and the bishop with a Form of Application to the 'Diocesan Church Building Society' for their approval and signature previous to their being presented to the Church Building Society.

Signed,
    H. Sykes, chairman.

44. Building committee meeting, 7 April 1884, minutes

7 April 1884

At a meeting of the building \committee/ held on this date at the 'White Hart' the following were present. The Revd H. Sykes, vicar, Messrs R. Briggs, and Chas. Youngs, churchwardens, Sir John Blois, lay rector, and Mr A.B. Cooper. [*Three vertical lines have been inscribed against the word 'lay'*]

The auditor's report was received and ordered to be entered upon the minutes:

'Halesworth 31 March 1884.
The churchwardens and committee for the restoration of Blythburgh church.

Gentlemen, I beg to inform you that I have this day examined these accounts and find the balance in your favour at the bank to be £83 5s. 3d. and in the treasurer's hands 12s. 2½d. The architect's fees are not included.

It is but a simple act of justice to your vicar to add, that the funds appear to have been carefully utilized, and the accounts kept with scrupulous accuracy.

Yours truly,
    Chas. Lenny
P.S. My charge for the audit is £2 2s. 0d. for which I send a receipt and shall be glad if you will place the amount to your restoration fund.'

Sir John expressed his satisfaction at the manner in which the business had been conducted hitherto <and> also with the care taken in keeping the accounts and did not consider the expenses excessive in proportion to the funds collected. Having made this statement Sir John intimated that he and Lady Blois would retire from the committee on the completion of the present contract. [*three vertical lines have been scored against this statement*]

The arrangements for the re-opening of the church at Easter were considered and approved of and advertisements ordered to be inserted in the 'East Anglian' for 3 days also in the 'Ipswich Journal' and 'Norfolk Chronicle' for the Saturday following.

Mr Briggs offered to send for the seats from Southwold, and Mr Cooper to take them back again.

H. Sykes, chairman.

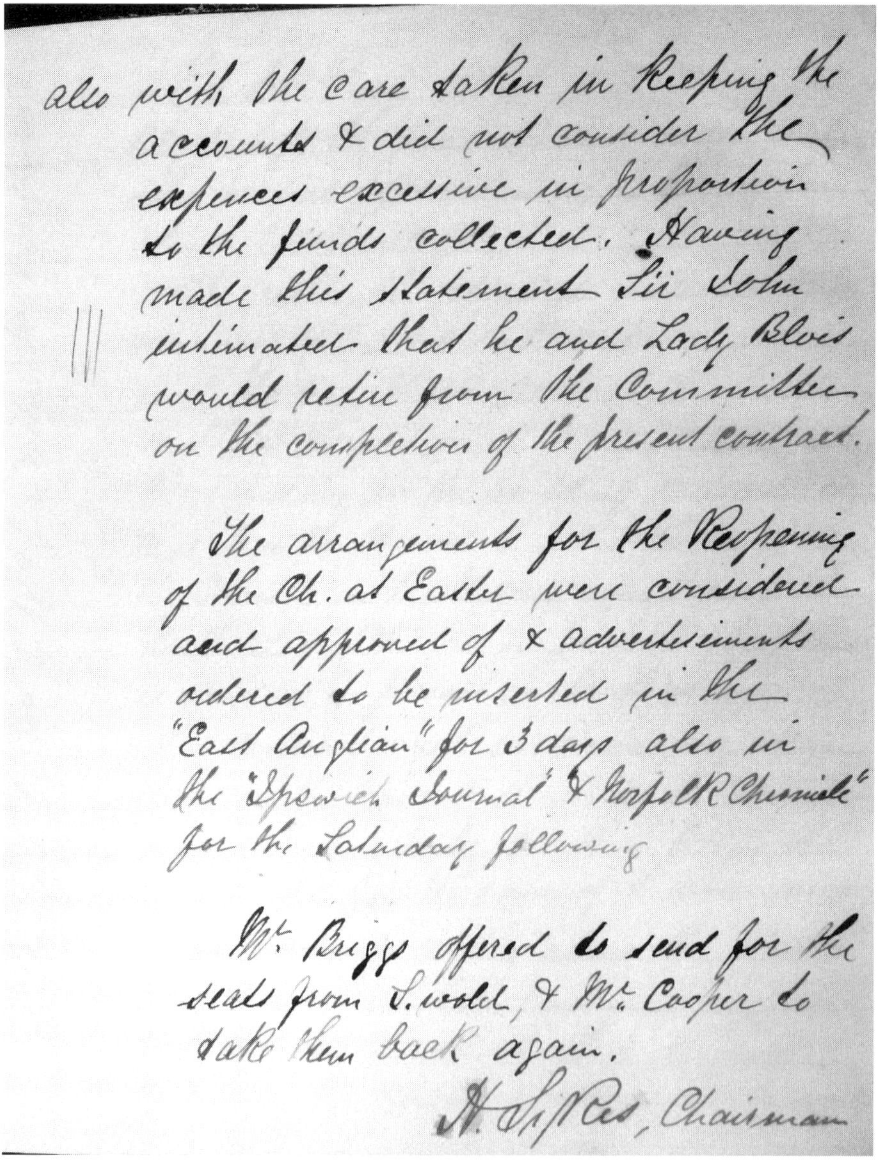

Plate 9. The restoration committee minute book entry recording the retirement of Sir John and Lady Blois, emphasised by the insertion of three vertical lines in the margin by the Revd Henry Sykes, 7 April 1884. © SROI, FC198 E2

45. Summary of restoration work done and details of reopening service, Easter Day 1884

Blythburgh church was re-opened on this date after partial restoration after having been closed for nearly 2½ years.

The restoration effected consisted of a new roof of English oak on the south aisle with the lead thereon re-cast; the parapet on the south aisle secured and completed; all the windows in the building restored, except 2 in the chancel, 6 in the clerestory over the chancel on the north side and 1 near the north door (this last one provided for *) /*promised by Mrs Cape and her sister Mrs Braithwaite/ these 9 windows are at present bricked up. The contract, with two extras, viz drip-stones on the south aisle and stone sill to east window was entered into by Mr R.J. Allen of Southwold for the sum of £1,064 10s. 0d.

In addition to the above the old deal pews had been removed and the oak benches restored to their original position, the pulpit and reading desk had been made to occupy <the> <a> more appropriate positions, the stalls in the chancel removed further apart and the two half poppyheads restored to their original position against the screen, the floor, where absolutely required, had been levelled and paved with light coloured bricks at a cost of £43 18s. 9d. (paid).

Repairs of the leads on the nave and north aisle roof, with the lining of the chancel and sundry items had not yet been charged for, but had been done by Mr Allen in day work.

The ancient coloured glass in the windows had been cleaned and \with new leads/ repaired by Messrs Bell and Beckham of London at a cost of £25 (not paid) and six coloured emblems had been placed in the south windows at a cost of £3 12s. 0d. defrayed by Roland T. Cobbold, Esq. of Debham [sic] Lodge, Essex.

For particulars of the services on Easter Day, 13 April 1884 and the following Wednesday 16 April see printed account.

Easter Day

Morning	Hymns	214	Ps. 122	296	272
"	Tunes	182	201	199	180
Afternoon	Hymns	221	216	368	Ps. 117
"	Tunes	185	64 Bath	285	226
Evening	Hymns	219	47	391	245
"	Tunes	226	Maidstone	160	253

Wednesday

Morning	Hymns	Ps. 100	99	533	230
	Tunes	490	108	239	116
Afternoon	Hymns	739	45	368	574
	Tunes	180	204	285	200
Evening	Hymns	295	47	545	11
	Tunes	200	Maidstone	101	13

Tunes from the 'Hymnal Companion' except Bath \source unknown/ and Maidstone from 'Hymns Ancient & Modern'

Total amount collected at all the services £30 17s. 0d. for particulars see cash book.

46. Building committee meeting, 5 May 1884, minutes

5 May 1884

At a meeting of the building committee held at the 'White Hart' Blythburgh the following were present – the Revd H. Sykes, Lady Blois, Miss Blois, Messrs Briggs, Youngs and Cooper.

A desultory conversation on the propriety of applying to the 'London Incorporated Church Building Society' for a grant, and the holding a bazaar, both of which were declined.

The following bills were ordered to be paid, viz –

Mr Norman, Organ Builder	2	7s.	0d.
* S. and J. Ashford, Cushions	2	4s.	2d.
* Eaton W. Moore, Lamps	5	0s.	0d.
* H.J. Debney, Carpets	1	12s.	5d.
Ipswich Journal	1	1s.	6d

* churchwardens account

H. Sykes

CHURCHWARDENS' ACCOUNTS

[*A summary of the churchwardens' annual income and expenditure for the whole period covered by this volume. Full accounts are shown for the year 1880–1, the last complete accounting year before closure, and for 1884–5, the year after the reopening.*[1]]

1. Summary of accounts, 1879–1907

Year	Opening balance			Income[2]			Expenditure			Balance carried forward		
	£	s.	d.									
1879–1880	18	13	8	31	10	0	14	9	10 ½	35	13	9 ½
1880–1881				31	10	0	22	14	4 ½	44	9	5
1881–1882				25	0	0	33	2	9 ½[3]	36	6	7 ½
1882–1883				25	12	3	8	9	9[4]	53	9	1 ½
1883–1884				23	0	0	56	1	7[5]	20	7	6 ½
1884–1885				26	18	4	27	3	9 ½	20	2	1
1885–1886				25	0	0	28	1	1[6]	17	1	0
1886–1887				25	0	0	41	6	11	14	1	
1887–1888				25	0	0	16	9	9 ½	9	4	3 ½
1888–1889				25	0	0	27	2	5 ½	7	1	10
1889–1890				25	0	0	18	4	3	13	17	7
1890–1891				10	1	0	24	2	6 ½	(3		11 ½)

---

1   SROI FC185 E 1 1. The funds for church restoration were kept separately and the accounts do not seem to have survived. Regular reports were made to the restoration (building) committee. For an example see RCMB 33.

2   The church received rent for two fields adjoining Wenhaston Lane, 'Penny Pightle' and 'Thistley Meadow'. Between 1879/80 and 1905/6 the combined annual rent fell from £26 10s. 0d. to £17 10s. 0d. A rent charge on the Southwold Railway, which cut through church property, was £2 per annum. In addition £3 per annum was received from Neale's Charity. Thistley Meadow was sold in 1953 by the vicar and churchwardens as vendors for £200 to Captain John Hill. Letter dated 13 May 1953 from the Revd A.D. Thompson to John Hill. BCP 28.1.5. Penny Pightle (2.149 acres, OS 1904, field 210) remained in the church's hands. A review of the documentation in 1969 showed that the minor part of the field occupied by the Southwold Railway was not leased to them, but ownership had been conveyed to them in the late 1870s with a permanent rent charge. Letter dated 24 June 1969, from Falck & Co., solicitors, to R.I. Collett, churchwarden. BCP 15.38.

3   Includes £10 10s. 0d. paid to Arthur E. Street, architect.

4   The church was closed for part of 1881/82 through to 1883/84.

5   £36 6s. 7d. to restoration fund.

6   £15 0s. 0d. to restoration fund.

1891–1892	23	19	9	27	3	5	(3	17	7 ½)
1892–1893	23	16	0	28	0	7 ½	(4	4	7 ½)
1893–1894	26	6	0	22	11	0		(9	7 ½)
1894–1895	18	11	0	15	0	4 ½	3	10	7 ½
1895–1896	68	19	9 ½[7]	72	10	5[8]		nil	
1896–1897	209	11	4[9]	209	18	8[10]		(7	4)
1897–1898	32	12	2[11]	25	14	5	6	10	5
1898–1899	35	6	11[12]	24	9	5 ½	17	7	10½
1899–1900	34	18	0[13]	26	12	6 ½	25	13	4
1900–1901	35	16	1[14]	36	6	5	25	3	0
1901–1902	33	10	6[15]	29	19	5	28	14	1
1902–1903	57	10	9 ½[16]	37	18	6 ½	48	6	4
1903–1904	13	4	1 ½[17]	33	0	4	28	10	1 ½
1904–1905	39	16	0 ½[18]	44	7	11	23	18	3
1905–1906	28	13	3 ½[19]	46	2	9	6	8	9 ½
1906–1907	11	8	1 ¾[20]	17	10	9 ½	6	3	3 ¼[21]

2. Churchwardens' accounts, 1880–1

	£	s.	d.
Expenditure for the year 1880			
Archdeacon's fees visitation	18		
Mr. C. Young's attendance	5		
Harvey cleaning paths /omitted 1879/	15		
½ doz wine	8		
Elmy Ben ½ year tolling bell	9		
Hatcher Mrs. do cleaning church	18	6	
Organ repaired	1	15	
Hatcher Mrs. ½ yr ending 18 April 1881	1	8	6
Fisk Jas. windows	1	14	8
Allen Mr. inspection of church roof	1	10	
Income tax on Thistley Meadow	1	2	
Brunning repairs	10		

---

[7] Includes £43 13s. 11d. church collections and donations. Not entered in earlier years.
[8] Includes £45 6s. 10½d. to restoration fund.
[9] Includes £152 17s. 10d. for the restoration fund and 4s. 11d. from vicar.
[10] Includes £150 17s. 10d. to restoration fund.
[11] Includes £14 1s. 2d. collections in church. £100 9s. 1d. held in restoration fund not included.
[12] Includes £15 5s. 11d. collections in church.
[13] Includes £14 17s. 0d. collections in church.
[14] Includes £16 5s. 1d. collections in church.
[15] Includes £13 3s. 10½d. collections in church.
[16] Includes £23 18s. 6½d. collections in church.
[17] Includes £ 6 12s. 10½d. collections in church.
[18] Includes £ 4 10s. 5d. collections in church.
[19] Includes £ 9 3s. 3½d. collections in church.
[20] Includes £ 5 8s. 1¾d. collections in church.
[21] 1½d. owing to churchwardens in the 1905–6 account has not been carried forward.

Aldis do	1	15	1 ½
Burton lighting etc.	1	10	4
Elmy tolling bell	9	6	
Bicker coals	1	3	
Harvey cleaning paths	15		
Teas to tenants	6		
Paid to treasurer of Blythburgh school board[22]	3		
Income and land tax on church land	5	4	
Mr C. Bicker for attendance at church to the children	3		
Balance in the hands of the churchwardens at this date 20 April 1881	44	9	5
	£67	3	9 ½

1879	By balance	35	13	9 ½
	" rent Thistley Meadow	21	10	0
	" " Penny Pightle	5		
	" " charge on Penny }			
	Pightle due 1 March 1881 }	2		
	From \Southwold/ Railway Company }			
	By Neales' charity	3		

20 April 1881
Audited and found correct
[*signed*] H. Sykes   } auditors
      E.G. Tuthill }

£67	3s.	9 ½d.

3. Churchwardens' accounts, 1884–5

17 April	Pd to Revd H. Sykes on a/c }			
	of church restoration fund }	13		
18	Crawford W. cleaning church			
	and church paths 7 days		14	
	Treasurer school board	2	10	
	Mrs Cooper bibles		10	
	Archdeacons' visitation fees		18	
	Churchwardens fees		10	

---

22   From Neale's charity for school books.

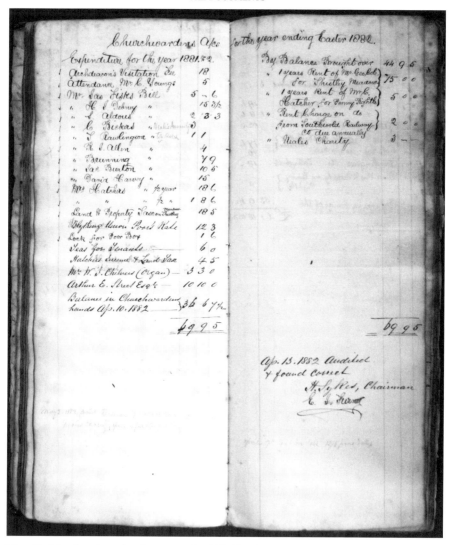

Plate 10. The churchwardens' accounts for 1881/82, the year in which the church was closed. The annual income at the disposal of the church was just £22, when the estimated cost of church restoration was £5,000. © SROI, FC198 E1 1

Bill for wine (Foreman)			7	3
do	padlock	Barker		7	6
do		Aldous	1	3	2
do		Hatcher, Mrs		18	6
do		do	1	8	6
do		Fuller		12	

	Rates on Thistley Meadow			16	1
	Taxes on Penny Pightle			4	7
Apl 21	Bill	Debney	1	12	5 ½
	Rawlingson, Thomas	tolling bell		18	
	Bill	M. Pendry	12	11	
			27	3	9 ½
	Balance in hand		20	2	1
			£47	5	10 ½

1885				
April	By balance	20	7	6 ½
1885				
	By rent charge on Penny Pightle from Southwold Railway Co. (less income tax ⅛) for year ending April 1884	1	18	4
Apl.	By rent charge on Penny Pightle from Southwold R. C. (due annually) for year ending April 1883.	2		
	By Neales' charity	3		
	" rent of Penny Pightle	5		
	By rent 1 year on Thistley Meadows	15		
		£47	5	10 ½

<Mar> 9 April 1885

[*signed*] H. Sykes, chairman

APPENDICES

APPENDIX A

ARCHITECTS' AND CONTRACTORS' REPORTS AND COSTS, 1881–1950

[*Unless otherwise referenced, documents nos. 2–10 are from SPAB I, nos. 11–19 from SPAB II, and nos. 20–4 from SPAB Add.*]

1. Proposals and estimates for the restoration of Blythburgh church by A.E. Street, architect, 31 December 1881[1]

[*Layout of original followed*]

(Copy)
       14 Cavendish Place,
        London W.
         31 December 1881

  My dear Sir,
     I should have sent you an approximate estimate of the cost of the repairs necessary in the very interesting church of Blythburgh but for the great press of work of all kinds involved by my late loss.

/Chancel √==/ The roof of the chancel will require to be <u>releaded</u>.
       { Six angels will have to be renewed, and the modern
/postpone/ { timbers decorated.
  /?/   The six clerestory windows on the north side are blocked and must be re-opened. Two windows
/postpone/ in the eastern bay to be opened and have new tracery inserted. <u>The east window</u> will require
 /√/   opening and also new tracery.
 /√/   On the south side of the chancel there are six of the clerestory windows requiring repair.
/Nave==/ The nave <u>roof</u> is less altered than that of the chancel. The four eastern bays are old and in fair condition. The new bays at the west end
/<u>postponed</u>/ should be entirely renewed.
       { The <u>roof of the south aisle</u> lets in a great deal of
       { water, and the timber will probably be found to be

---

[1] SROI 2, 2. This includes annotations by the bishop of Norwich. A copy was sent to F.C. Brooke with a letter from the Revd Henry Sykes, 27 February 1883. See Correspondence 56.

/√/	{ most seriously decayed. The roof of the <u>north aisle</u>
	{ also requires considerable repair.
	{ Many of the <u>windows</u> in the south <u>chancel</u> and south
/postpone/	{ nave aisles are blocked up and in a bad condition.
	{ I should propose to repair and restore them.

The nave columns and arches seem to be all in good
condition and require no repair at all. I should
restore the <u>stonework and glass of the twenty-four nave</u>
<u>clerestory windows,</u> also <u>clean the stonework, and</u> plaster
/√/ <u>the walls of the nave</u> and <u>restore the \?/ west</u> window of the
tower.

A great many of the monumental stones remain in the
floor. These should be relaid. The church seems to have
been originally paved with glazed tiles of a dark colour
some 5″ some 7″ square. I propose to pave the church with
/?/ <u>glazed and encaustic tiles,</u> but if <u>simpler tiles</u> are used
/√/ a considerable saving could be effected.

	{ There are 23 old and small seat ends in the nave
/√/	{ some of them blocked up in pews. These should if possible
/postpone/	{ be used: I have allowed for the accommodation of 250
	{ persons.

I have allowed a separate sum for <u>the restoration of the</u>
/postpone/ <u>screens.</u> They are covered with whitewash and all the
mouldings are gone, but there is sufficient remaining in
the tower to restore them from. It seems that some
of the <u>rood screen</u> has been taken to Walberswick
/?/ within the last few years. <u>This might possibly be</u>
<u>reused and replaced.</u> A church like this suffers
terribly from the loss of its screens. They form an

/?/	{ integral part of the design, and should be if possible
	{ restored to their original state.
/postpone?/	{ The piscina in the chancel should be restored, and I
	{ have provided for a new altar.
	{ There is a great deal of the old stained glass in the
	{ heads of windows which should be carefully preserved
/<u>mention</u> √/	{ and replaced in its old positions. I have provided for
	{ new stancheon and saddle bars to the windows.
	{ The monument which forms an arch between the chancel
	{ and north aisle has its roof supported with piers of
/postpone?/	{ brick.[2] If these are needed which seems probable, it
	{ will be necessary no doubt to turn an arch in the
	{ wall over it.

The east end of the north aisle is now cut off and
used as a vestry and perhaps might remain so.

	{ The south porch should have its groining restored,
/Mention/	{ also the parvis above and the roof floor doors etc.

---

[2]   The tomb of John Hopton. See Introduction n. 39.

/postponed/   {   renewed.
              {   The parapet of south aisle wants considerable restoration
/√/   {   but otherwise the aisle is in good condition.
              {   The plinths round the church must be repaired, also
                 the three panels in chancel buttresses.
              {   The parapet of the tower is all bricked up and in
              {   part destroyed. I propose to restore it and also the
/postpone/   {   belfry windows, \)/and <u>external walls of the church</u>
/√/   should be <u>made good</u> and <u>repaired where necessary</u>.

I estimate the cost of the works as follows

Works to the chancel	£ 745.	/(a)/
Works to the nave and aisles	£3140.	/(b)/
Works to the tower	330.	/(c)/
Total	£4215.	

For the restoration of the screens not included in the
above estimate. £<u>450</u>. There would also be the
warming arrangements and heating with warm air including
the channels apparatus and apparatus chamber would not be
less than £<u>200</u>.

               I am
                 Dear Sir
               Yours faithfully,
               Arthur Edmund Street.

/1.   Schedule of <u>works to</u> be
   undertaken at once in

(a) and (b) – with estimates	330	745
2. Schedule of <u>works postponed</u>	450	3140
in a. b. c. with estimates.	200	
		3885
	980	___/

The Revd H. Sykes.

2. Report on the state of Blythburgh church by Philip Webb, January 1882[3]

/Mr Webb's draft report/

Notes on the present state of the church of <u>Holy Trinity, Blythburgh</u>, Suffolk.
  On no account should the repairs be let on contract for the whole: a responsible

---

[3]   This report was not sent to Blythburgh, although its views were incorporated in the report sent in
    September 1882. See Correspondence 35.

experienced clerk of the works[4] should be appointed with instructions as to letting portions of the different trades to local or other men under his direction, and for obtaining schedules of prices for the supply of materials scaffolding tarpaulins etc. The works should be done piecemeal so that but few men need be engaged at one time and over which the clerk of works would be able to watch and superintend, and protect each uncovered part from the weather. The scaffolding, which should be a good one, to be removed from time to time as work is finished thus allowing the church to be used for service during the repairs. The foundations of the work should be carefully examined all round, particularly at the <south> north east end of chancel, where \is/ the only \visible/ crack of importance in the body of the church.

As there must be an underground chamber or crypt under the east end of north chancel aisle (under vestry) it should be opened, as from the floor of this chamber the foundation under the abovementioned crack could best be got at.[5]

Repair all roofs in preference to any other work, after the foundations have been looked to, and in no case should a roof be lifted if it is possible to avoid doing so. The removal of an aisle roof would be sure to affect the stability of the clerestory: At present the north arcade and clerestory seem to be perfectly upright, but those on the south look to have a slight set outwards, and should, therefore, not be exposed to change of bearing or support.

It is evident that it would be better not to remove the wooden mullions which have been inserted in several windows, but such of them as have decayed in parts should be repaired in \those/ parts. As the building is evidently subject to very strong winds, it would be unwise to remove the wooden transomes which have been placed across the mullions on the inside of \some of/ the aisle windows. Indeed, it would be well, where any of the mullions shew a tendency to lean, to <supply> apply to them the same kind of support supplied by such transomes. By this means it would be possible to avoid removing the tracery of any of the windows (a point of great importance) and such repairs of broken mullions as would be necessary could be reduced to the smallest amount.

The plastering of the walls of the church is, on the whole, in a good state, and should certainly not be disturbed or removed. Where, from neglect, the water has come in and run down the walls the decayed and rotten plaster should be taken off and renewed with thin, tough, common hair plaster plainly and neatly trowelled but not in the modern fashion of leaving it with a sandy surface. This plaster should not be a thick coat. When the plaster is quite dry it can be whitened to match the rest of the church.

The pavement is too good in appearance to be interfered with in any wholesale way. Such parts as have sunk over <[word?]> graves or vaults or elsewhere would have to be lifted, levelled up with concrete and the paving renewed with the local buff paving-bricks, such as now compose the greater part of the floor. The matrixed flags, \of which there are many,/ should not be displaced, but in one case (and per-haps more) what remains on the stone in the way of memorial should be protected, with matting or rug, from passing feet.

Stained glass. The great beauty of the few remains and the brittleness of much of the lead-cames would make the removal of the glass very dangerous, therefore \the

---

[4] For a discussion of the role of a clerk of the works see Alan Mackley, 'Clerks of the Works', *The Georgian Group Journal*, VIII (1998) pp. 157–66.

[5] The vestry was, and is still, at the east end of the south aisle.

repairs of/ its setting should be done in its place by strengthening in the best ways possible, \adding only as much new lead as would be necessary/ and the work should only be intrusted to an ingenious workman, \who would do it/ piece by piece: Where quarries of the ordinary glazing are more than cracked or are gone they should be replaced with some of Powell's strong 'antique' white glass:[6] Many old quarries \ and even bits of stained glass/ could be collected about the church and put back. Sometimes a cracked quarry could be mended with a <strip> length of new came. No new coloured glass should be added.

Seating. The bench ends which are framed into original sills should not be removed. Where there are deal floor boards these might be removed to allow of getting to the damp earth <[*?word*]> below which should be dug out and the space filled in with concrete and the boarding made good with oak or elm boards. These seats are chiefly on the north side of the church. On the south side parts of the oak sill and bench ends remain.

Founder's Chapel.[7] The oak choir seats and fronts should be replaced in their original position in the chapel (the man who removed them is alive and active).

Replace the chancel screen now in the tower on S side of choir front as far as it will go without addition (don't understand this. P.W.). The 4 square deal pews on the north side of nave gangway might be removed. At the back of third pew west of screen is a piece of another screen with its end in line with the pier on which is the remains of a bracket. This piece of screen might be kept in its place and plain \ new/ oak benches put eastward of it. As there will be sufficient old seats on the north side of church perhaps it would be well to screen these sittings with a heavy cloth or carpet hanging (as marked on plan) say 8 feet high. This could be hung to a strong oak rail supported on oak posts and strutted bases set down the north aisle. /*Sketch of screen support*/

The deal pews on the south side of central gangway might also be removed leaving the remains of old oak seating as they stand; the congregation could use this seating at will.[8]

After the removal of the stall work now in the choir to its <right> original position in the north chancel aisle, the space might be occupied with some new choir seats of the simplest possible construction in solid oak, set quite clear of the bases of pillars.

It will be seen that the plastering at the east end of chancel has suffered from the usual reckless use of nails driven in to support the usual so-called decoration, this injury should be repaired without removing the plaster, and the east wall could be hung with some heavy good coloured hangings supported on oak posts and rails (moveable) standing quite clear of the wall, to the height of the sill of the east window. It would be well also to remove the injurious and incongruous altar rail and substitute a plain moveable one of solid oak to stand clear of the north and south walls, making good the injury caused by the insertion of the ends of the present rail in the walls.

Outside. Upon carefully looking to the lead covering of the south aisle roof it was quite plain that it would be necessary to renew the lead but, as before noted

---

[6] The firm of Powell and Sons, founded in 1834 by James Powell (1774–1840) when he bought the Whitefriars Glass Company, established in the seventeenth century. Their machine-produced quarry glass was used by Philip Webb in designs for William Morris. Wikipedia article accessed 9 April 2015.

[7] A reference to John Hopton (see Introduction n. 39) and the east end of the north aisle.

[8] These box pews were removed. See RCMB 37 and 45.

this should be done piece-meal, bay by bay from scaffoldings set up on the inside and outside of the church: Upon the lead and boarding being lifted under a carefully constructed tarpaulin roof each bay of the woodwork below could be examined piece by piece and the perished timbers replaced with new oak, this oak work to be left perfectly plain without moulding or ornament: The probability is that a great part of the wall plates would have to be renewed \(this would not include moulded and embattled facia on the inside)/ but it is evident that it would not be necessary to renew a great part of the exposed woodwork which has chiefly decayed in the sap parts. In any case it would be injurious to remove any part of the roof bodily. After renewing as above advised, it would be well to lay on the top of the present outside face of common rafters some oak rafters of small scantling \(say 3″ x 4″)/ 12 inches apart, running lengthways from west to east, and on this to lay <the> new boarding with stout wood rolls 2 feet apart to receive the lead. \Should any of the principals require strengthening this could be done by putting new oak at top of them and bolt-ing through./ This would raise the the [*sic*] roof under \sills of/ clerestory windows, but there would be room enough for this, and the damaged walling here should be carefully repaired and prepared for receiving the lead curtain. Perhaps it would be well to consider if one drip could not be got in the length of rafter so as to shorten the length of lead sheets. Of course a plumber would be engaged to recast the old lead, either in the churchyard or close to the church, and he would preserve the dates of repairs which are cast on the sheets, adding that of the present renewal. \The new cast lead should not be of less weight than 8 lbs to the foot./ /Great care should be taken in dealing with the nave roof not to injure the carpentry or carving and at the time of repair any ornamental part which has fallen off and answers and then should be retained./ Portions of the lead spouting from the nave roof on to aisle roof would have to be repaired or renewed but of this as little as possible should be done: Preparation should be made for guarding the outlets to the spouts from the aisle roofs by wire covers in addition to the lead roses and sinks.

One of the most serious causes of mischief to the nave roof has been <that there was no> <has been> \from the want of a/ ridge roll, <so that> the water has been driven by the wind under the lap of the lead, and the plumbers, to stop this, have most unwisely soldered the joint at the lap and this has helped to pull the lead and crack it, under the contraction and expansion from cold and heat. The nave and north aisle roofs should be treated in the same way described to the south aisle roof, and an intermediate drip in the length of rafter in the nave roof be of more importance than <in> to the aisle roofs.

The clerestory window glazing should be <dealt> dealt with as described to other windows.

It will easily be understood that, to remove and reset the pierced and crested stone parapet to the south aisle would be most injurious. The jointing has been secured with iron dowels and cramps and to separate the stones would shatter them: Any parts quite loose should be lifted and reset, but the greater part should have most painstaking attention to avoid the evil of removal. After cleaning out the joints as far as possible without disturbing the stones or lichens the outside faces should be stopped with stiff clay and liquid \Portland/ cement with a small quantity \(say one third or one half of sand)/ of fine sharp sand should be poured into the beds and joints, the same being worked in with the aid of wires and hoop iron. The success of this operation will depend on the patient skill of the clerk of works and workman \ employed/ and the quality and measured quantity of the cement and sand. The cement should be of the slower setting kind, and the joints well wetted before application. Even when this work has been done it should be watched every year, and weak spots attended to as they re-appeared.

Plants growing on the parapets and elsewhere should be cut off, but no disturbance should be allowed in rooting them out. In no case should the lichens be removed as they are the best protective of the stone.

Where any window mullions and tracery are too much decayed or too instable to be remedied by slight though carefully done repairs, it would be well to brick them up (there being an excess of light in the church) as has been done to the south (north?) window of chancel, making the brickwork flush with the outside.[9]

Only small portions of the other parapets to the roofs would have to be lifted and reset including, perhaps, the north pinnacle of chancel, but the coping stones should be run with cement as before described. Neither should the outside facings be repointed. Where there are loose parts of facings they should, if shallow, be refixed, and if deep should be run in behind with liquid cement and sand. Repointing, beyond being injurious to the appearance of an old building, generally comes away bodily after a short time.

From the above remarks it will be seen that the committee of this society believes that after the foundations have been attended to the repairs and recasting and relaying of the lead of all the roofs should follow next in order. These works would be done at considerable cost, but they are of vital importance to the security of the church and should not be delayed. The church generally \otherwise/ being in a [?]substantion condition and its present appearance being most dignified and uninjured by the restorer the money subscribed for its repair need not be used for any other purpose.

/It is evident that the nave roof should be that first taken in hand so that the new work when done to the nave may not be disturbed or injured by the later opening on the nave./

/Mr Webb's report./

3. Report on condition of the roof of Blythburgh church by Philip Webb, January 1882

<u>Blythburgh</u>

Present condition of the roof. January 1882

First balk. S. end. new, rough, with clumsy brackets

2nd ,, do. do.

Space between is a half bay over the altar. Without side windows

3rd ,, New, rough, etc.

Full bay between 2 and 3. Half the rafters are new and the boards are placed across the rafters.

4th balk New with old boss and angels (imperfect). Rafters in place except at either side of the balk. The boards on S. S. are wanting and are replaced by cross boards.

5th balk As 4th but with one angel only left.

---

9 The south window of the chancel was bricked up and remains so. The SPAB view that 'the church is light enough as it is' was to be repeated in several documents. See for example Correspondence 35 and 119.

6th balk   Old. The paint on the sides almost washed off. Pattern cannot be made out. Angels and bosses in their places. Rafters and boards nearly all in place.

7th balk   Much the same as 6th and the bay also.

8th and 9th   " " " "   but more boards missing.

10th and 11th   New with new rafters and boarding.

4. Extract of specifications for work to be done on Blythburgh church, A.E. Street, no date[10]

Blythburgh
Extract of Specification
Blythburgh Church Suffolk

Extract of <u>Specification</u> of certain works required to be done in the restoration of the windows and the south aisle roof of the church of Blythburgh in the diocese of Norwich and county of Suffolk, from the plans and under the superintendence of Arthur Edmund Street of 14 Cavendish Place, London, W., architect, and Mr Blomfield, MA.

Materials   The materials for the several works throughout will require to be perfectly good and sound to the satisfaction of the architect.

Cement   All cement specified for any of the trades is to be of the best Portland and to bear the test of setting under water when gauged neat, and all sand used with it is to be carefully washed before mixing.

Workmanship   The workmanship for each trade is to be of the strongest and best description and is to proceed and to be carried on at such times and in such portions at a time as the architect may direct, and the whole is to be done to his complete satisfaction. The iron window casements to be executed at contractor's own expense by a tradesman specially selected by the architect.

Renewal of Stonework   The windows of the north and south nave aisles coloured red on the ground plan are in a dangerous condition and require immediate restoration.[11] The contractor to state a separate price for these four windows. These windows will require to be almost entirely new. /<u>Separate estimate</u>/

Chancel   The contractor to give a separate tender for works to the chancel and chancel aisles, viz for all works east of the screen both to the windows and the roof. Not any work is proposed to be done to the central /x/ roof or to the north aisle roof of either chancel or nave at present.

Windows of the South Nave Aisle   The first window west of the screen is to have the wooden mullions taken out and the window completely restored with new stone mullions and new tracery copied from the other window. The second and third windows are in a dangerous state and will have the jambs, mullions and tracery entirely taken out and restored. The fourth window requires new tracery and the mullions

---

[10] A copy in unknown hand of the original received by the Revd Henry Sykes at Blythburgh in January 1882. See Correspondence 24.

[11] The ground plan is one of three of Street's drawings in SROI FC185 E3 3, Blythburgh church plans.

restored. The fifth window to have the wooden mullions taken out, the tracery restored.

North Nave Aisle   The first window west of screen requires general restoration. The second do. is dangerous, requires new mullions and the tracery reset and restored. The third window must have new mullions and the tracery and jambs restored. The fourth window requires the central part of tracery renewed and the mullions and jambs restored.

The window of south aisle is dangerous. The tracery requires renewal above one light and the mullions and jambs require to be new. The west window of north aisle to have the wood mullions removed and new stone mullions inserted and tracery.

The west window of tower to have new stone mullions and tracery.

Chancel   The two windows in the aisle east of screen are in a dangerous state and require new jambs and mullions. Some of the tracery can be re-used. The other four windows in the chancel aisles require new mullions in the place of the wooden mullions and the heads opened out and tracery renewed.

The east window will require to be entirely new and must be copied from the old portions remaining visible. The whole restoration of the windows to be carried out in strict accordance with this specification and in the manner hereinafter directed.

Mortar   The mortar to be composed of one part of good fresh stone lime and two parts of clean sharp drift sand. No sea sand to be used in any part of the work.

Stone   The new stone required to be of the same kind as in the existing work, selected hard and even in quality and in sizes suitable for the particular character of the work required. To be good weather <sand> stone, free from sand or clay holes, vents and other defects, to be laid on its natural quarry bed in good strong fine mortar, finished with the same face as the old work, to be well bonded together and secured with all necessary slate or iron dowels lead or stone plugs, galvanised iron or copper clamps etc complete as directed by the architect. <The> The whole of the masonry to be worked in every part most carefully and strictly in accordance with the old work and the directions given by the architect from time to time.

Old Stone Work /removal of/   The old stonework requiring removal to be very carefully taken down, pains being taken to disturb no portion beyond what is absolutely necessary and to leave proper projections and indents for tying in with new work.

Bedding hollow   Window sills to be bedded hollow between jambs and monials and to be pointed up under where the work has settled.

Monials[12]   Stone for monials to be specially selected of the best cleanest and strongest which the quarries afford, and <the dowels> to be dowelled in every joint with one inch square slate dowels four inches long set in cement, entering half into each stone.

---

[12]   Mullions.

Tracery	The stone for tracery to be selected as for monials and worked so as to ensure its greatest strength lying in the direction of the chief pressure, to be plugged in all joints.
Lead plugs	Where needful or directed, with plugs of cast lead ½ inch square and 1¼ inch long. All tracery joints to be formed on the true radius line of all curves whether of main tracery lines or of 'cusping' which they may cross.
Centering	All arches to be turned on proper centres which are not to be eased or struck except as ordered or permitted by the architect or the clerk of works.
Grooving	The whole of the jambs, monials and tracery to be carefully grooved for the new glazing and the sills channelled to receive lead troughs for carrying off the condensed moisture.
Inner jambs	The jambs of new windows inside or <of> restored jambs, to be worked to stand ¾ inch in front of walling face to stop plaster. Inside arches the same.
Decayed parts	The decayed portions of stonework of windows to be carefully removed and replaced with new of the same stone as the old, worked accurately to the original section of old work and well bedded back into the walling.
Parapet	The parapet along south wall to be carefully taken down and repaired and reset, the decayed, split or broken portions removed and replaced with new stone work of the old form, which is to be strictly followed, the whole carefully dowelled where needful or directed with inch square slate dowels, 3″ long, set in cement. The whole parapet to be carefully pointed in fine mortar including the diaper flint and stonework, and provide all requisite copper cramps etc.
Tracery	The external tracery of windows to be carefully repaired as specified above, all parts decayed removed, new worked to old forms, jointed and plugged to lead as before specified. This may be done by cutting back stonework to line of glass where inside stone work is sound.
Pointing	All masonry dressings to be carefully pointed in fine mortar as the work proceeds.
Rough arches	Rough discharging arches of walling stone to be turned over, all <as> new external openings or openings altered.
Monials	All monials of windows which are shaken or decayed to be renewed with monials worked to the old sections.
Ironwork	All ironwork connected therewith being most carefully cut out of the jambs and sill and refix properly, new ironwork being provided where the old is unfit for re-use.
Chases etc	All chases, grooves, sinkings and the like require to be carefully executed, and all ironwork carefully leaded in and well caulked up.
Making good	All pointing to be examined and made good, the new work cleaned down. All jobbing in this branch to be duly performed and the work left perfect and complete.
South aisle wall	Hack off the old plaster from the walls of south aisle, and prepare for new plastering as specified in Plasterer, make good any defects in the walling.

174

Clerestory windows   A separate price to be given for restoring the clerestory windows. The stonework etc to be restored precisely in the same way as
described herein for the aisle windows.

Separate estimate   These windows had an inside bar at springing and halfway up
with [*diagram*] eyes and pins, and two smaller outside bars intermediate. The glass put in in three panels. This ironwork is to be
renewed. Any defect in the clerestory walls is to be re-instated.

Tenders to be divided as follows

1st   For the work specified to the windows coloured red on plan.
2. For the remaining windows specified.
3. For the restoration of clerestory windows in same.
4. For the South Aisle roof.
5. For the works to the Chancel, ie all works to windows, roofs etc east of Screens.

5. Comments by SPAB on extract of specifications, no date[13]

Blythburgh
Abstract of specification as submitted to us
viz
Tenders are asked for the work in five parts
No 1   For the work specified to the windows coloured red on plan
    2   The remaining windows specified
    3   The restoration of the clerestory and windows in same
    4   The south aisle roof
    5   The works for the chancel, i.e. all works to windows, roofs etc east of screen
No description of the work proposed to the south aisle roof or to the <roof and win-
dows> works in chancel comprised under the etcetera have been given to us.

The specification submitted to the society is but an abstract and seems to have been
taken capriciously. It relates chiefly to the <repair> restoration of the windows
    5   Windows of the north aisle of nave
    6   "   south   " "
        All the windows of the clerestory
        The principal window of tower
    6   Windows of chancel aisles
        The east window
        are specified as needing <u>almost</u> complete renewal and there is a general
direction <that all monials of windows> under which any window not specified may
be as completely restored. The east window would be entirely new and probably the
two blocked windows either side. The windows in [*?two words*] are described as
'dangerous' and needing immediate restoration. Among the directions for restoring
windows are these:
        <old stone work> Window sills to be bedded hollow and to be pointed up under
where the work has settled. Stones for monials to be well selected and to be dowelled
at all the joints with slate dowels set in cement. Tracery joints to be plugged when

---

[13]   Probably July 1882. Unsigned, but seems to be in same hand as Philip Webb's report, Appendix A 2
    above.

needed with lead plugs. Certain arches to be turned in proper centres which are not to be eased or struck except as ordered by the architect or clerk of works. The whole of the jambs, monials and tracery to be grooved for the new glazing and the sill channelled to receive lead troughs.

The jambs of new windows inside to be worked to stand ¾″ in front of walling face, to stop plaster inside. Arches do do.

All decayed parts of tracery to be carefully removed and new stone worked to the old form. This may be done by cutting back stone work to line of glass, when inside stone work is sound.

Rough discharging arches of walling stone to be turned over all new external openings on monials of windows which are shaken or decayed to be renewed with monials worked to the old sections.

All iron work connected therewith being most carefully cut out of the jambs and sills and refixed properly. New iron work being provided when the old is unfit for use.

The stone work of the clerestory windows to be restored precisely as described for the aisle windows. The iron work to be renewed. Any defects in clerestory walls to be made good.

Beside the work to the windows, which is the bulk of that described, the following things are to be done.

The parapet along south wall to be carefully taken down and repaired and reset. The decayed, split or broken portions removed and replaced by new stonework, the whole carefully dowelled, dowels to be set in cement. The whole parapet carefully pointed in fine mortar, including the flint and stone diaper. Copper cramps to be used.

Old stonework must be very carefully taken down (this appears to be a general direction) pains being taken to disturb no portion beyond what is absolutely necessary and to leave proper projections and indents for new work.

All masonry dressings to be carefully pointed in fine mortar as the work proceeds – again –'all pointing to be examined and made good, the new work cleaned down.

The old plaster on south wall to be hacked off and new plaster as specified (specification not given).

No work is proposed to be done to the central roof or to the north aisle roof at present.

6. Report on Blythburgh church. Memorandum by J. Henry Middleton and George Wardle to the restoration committee of the SPAB, no date[14]

To the Restoration Committee of SPAB
Blythburgh Church

Gentlemen,

Blythburgh Church, Suffolk, is a very fine and, on the whole, well preserved specimen of the grand type of church, so common in Norfolk and Suffolk. It consists of nave, with western tower, and two aisles, which extend eastwards, on both sides along a great part of the chancel, into which they open by an arcade of 2 arches, both on north and south: on the south of nave there is a 2 storied porch.

The outside is very richly ornamented with flint inlay, flush with hard yellow

---

[14] This report of a visit made in August 1882 was sent to Blythburgh on 27 September and acknowledged by Sykes. See Correspondence 35 and 36.

limestone ashlar. This traceried inlay increases in richness towards the chancel. There are elaborate moulded battlements \parapets/ along both aisles. Those on the south have well sculptured figures of saints and animals at intervals along the whole length. \That on the S. aisle is pierced and has a crest of trefoils interrupted by more sculptures etc./

Over the east gable of the chancel there is a carved representation of the Trinity, to whom the church is dedicated.

The whole of the external stonework is in good condition, and needs no repair, except that some of the battlement stones are loose, and need fixing with copper <or> cramps.

Many of the windows, especially towards the east, have lost their tracery, and are now blocked up with brickwork. There is a good deal of old painted glass remaining \in the small lights of the tracery./

The roofs are very magnificent. There is no chancel arch, and the nave roof runs on to the extreme east. It is very flat in pitch: the principals have a curved wall-piece, and are richly moulded, as are also the ridge piece and 2 purlins on each side. At the intersection of ridge and principals there are figures of angels \east and west/ with long wings, holding shields. The small rafters are very wide and close together. The whole is decorated with (well preserved) contemporary (i.e. 15th century) painting. There are flowers and IHS in red and green, on white, blue and red grounds. In the chancel all the ground is white. In the nave the rafters have a white ground but the boarding between is <alternately> blue and red \in alternate bays./ The aisle roofs are even \more/ richly \moulded/ than that of the nave. The principals, steeper in pitch, have beautiful curved wall-pieces, pierced with rich open tracery. \There are no signs of colour./ The colour is all gone, owing to rain leaking in.

The wood-work of all the roofs appears sound, but probably the feet of the timbers are decayed and need strengthening with iron plates. \Some of the principals and many of the common rafters of the nave r[*oof*] are new and of unpainted deal./ The whole of the lead probably needs recasting and relaying with new oak 2 inch rolls, and many new battens. The very low-pitched roof of the nave should have 2½ inch drips, as the water is evidently soaking in at the laps of the sheets.

Screens. There are fine oak screens across east ends of nave aisles, and part of the old screens remain at the west and south of the chancel. The rood-loft, which ran across the whole width of the church, is gone.

In the choir there are some fine oak stalls, with return stalls complete. These have been lately moved out of the north-east chapel, and should be lifted back into their place, which they are made to fit. They do not fit in the choir and look very much out of place there: they are very gorgeous, with figures of the apostles etc under canopies, cut out of solid blocks of oak.

Pews. A great number of the original oak pews remain in situ in the nave. They are low, and without backs, well moulded, and have poppy-heads richly carved with human figures, animals and foliage. The place of the missing old seats is occupied by mean modern high pews of deal – in some places set on the old oak curb.

The Pavement is chiefly composed of bricks of a good red colour, and looks extremely well. In some places a few old tiles remain, worn down to their red earthen-ware ground.

There are a number of tomb-stones – one very curious 15th century priest's tomb, in hard limestone, let into the pavement flush, in the form of a cross, it has a chalice and inscription incised upon it.

Font. There is a fine octagon 15th century font on a platform of 2 steps, with a \ separate/ stone stool on the west and south for the priest, and his clerk to stand upon. An incised inscription runs along the tread of the upper step.

The north door has fine oak panelled tracery.

The Porch has had an upper room, with access by a winding stair. The floor of this upper room, with the stone vaulting below it, has fallen in, and is missing.

The west tower is very stately, it has no external doorway. It once had a lead-covered spire, but that was destroyed by lightning. Its belfry windows have lost their mullions, which should be replaced in order to support the tracery. The whole church appears to have been completely rebuilt in the 15th century.

We are, Gentlemen,

Yours faithfully,

[*signed*]J. Henry Middleton

and George Wardle

7. Tenders for restoration, received 7 September 1882[15]

---

15 Brooke and SROI 2, 2.

Blythburgh Church. Tenders for Restoration Received 7 September 1882

Builder	No. 1. Estimate to restore 2 windows In N. and 2 do. in S. aisle marked red on plan	No. 2. 3 windows S. aisle. Window in tower. 2 windows N. aisle. W. windows S. aisle. 8 windows in all.	No. 3. Restoring clerestory windows and walls	No. 4. To take off old roof and fix new roof on S. aisle plastering walls restoring parapet	No. 5. Restoring chancel		Total of aisle and clerestory £686 10s.
Messrs. Dowsing and Sons Norwich	£ 220	£ 395	£ 261	£ 324	£ 621	£ 1821	
Messrs. Bardell and Bros. Kings Lynn	£71 2s.6d.	£212 10s. 3d.	£196 18s. 6d.	£468 0s. 11d.	£584 0s. 2d.	£1532 12s. 4d	
Bartram Aylsham	146	296	148	528	240	1358	
Messrs. Grimwood and Sons. Sudbury	Items not given in detail					1235	
Mr R.J. Allen Southwold	55	137	£119 10s. 0d.	375	363	£1049 10s. 0d.	

8. Estimate of cost of the restoration of Blythburgh church by Robert J. Allen, builder, September 1882[16]

Copy

Restoration of Blythburgh Church

No. 1 Estimate to take old stonework to restore to reglaze with cathedral glass the two windows in south aisle and two windows in north aisle marked red on plan, completing the same for the sum of fifty five pounds.

£55 0s. 0d.

No. 2 Estimate for three windows in south aisle, west window, window in tower, two windows in north aisle, west window. These eight windows to be restored and reglazed with cathedral glass and casements for the sum of one hundred and thirty seven pounds.

£137 0s. 0d.

No. 3 Estimate for restoring clerestory windows and walls re-glazing with old glass, casements, etc. for the sum of one hundred and nineteen pounds ten shillings.

£119 10s. 0d.

No. 4 Estimate to take off old roof and to fix new as per specification on south aisle using what wood the architect may deem fit, cutting down all the old plastering off walls, restoring same, restoring parapet wall and diaper work for the sum of three hundred and seventy five pounds.

£375 0s. 0d.

No. 5 Estimate for chancel comprising east window restored and reglazed as before described. Two windows east end of north and south aisles. Two windows each side of aisles cutting down old plaster and stuccoing walls in south aisle. New Bath stone parapet fixed on east end of south aisle restoring parapet front two bays also clerestory wall and window east of screen for the sum of three hundred and sixty three pounds.

£363 0s. 0d.

Summary

No. 1	Estimate	£ 55 0s. 0d.
No. 2	do.	£137 0s. 0d.
No. 3	do.	£119 10s. 0d.
No. 4	do.	£375 0s. 0d.
No. 5	do.	£363 0s. 0d.
Total		£1,049 10s. 0d.

(signed)   Robert J. Allen.
Builder
Southwold.

9. List of restoration works, January 1883, unsigned

January 1883.

---

16 SROI 2, 2.

Roof etc. of nave, chancel and north aisles

Windows south nave aisle	Windows generally restored.
" north "	ditto
Chancel windows	2 windows in aisle east of screen restored and 4 other windows ditto.
Parapet along south wall	\<to\> restored
North aisle wall	Old plaster \<stuc\> struck off and replastered.
N \<S\> aisle roof	Restored
Glazing	Cathedral glass.

Walls and parapet of north chancel aisle and north aisle of church

10. Payments to R.J. Allen, builder, 1883–92[17]

Extracts from ledgers of R.J. Allen, Builder and Mason, Southwold.

Restoration Committee Blythburgh Church.
188[?][18]

Jan 27.	For materials supplied and work done according to Plans and Specifications. As per estimate. Chancel and Nave.	1049. 10. 0
Oct	Worked stone for dreep under Clerestory Windows fixed as per estimate	8. 5. 0
1884		
Jan 31.	Bath stone sill to East Window, moulded and fixed all complete as per estimate	6. 15. 0
		1064. 10. 0

1883
Nov 29

	Mens time taking down old seats, preparing for and laying old joists and flooring etc, letting pieces in old sills, bench ends and seats. Preparing old panel work under seats, and fixing same, taking down old screen. Making new panels, fixing new joists and floor in Chancel. Altering and refixing old stalls. Making platform and fixing Reading Desk. Making steps and fixing pulpit, preparing new backs, rails and stays to seats etc. Taking up old marble ledgers, etc.	26. 11. 6
	Materials	5. 0. 1 ½
	R.J. Allen's time	5. 0. 0
	To train fares	2. 6. 8
		38. 18. 3 ½

1883

April 20 R.J.A. and man relaying lead on Main roof				6. 6

Oct 1   2 men looking too and soldering roof of Nave,
and North Aisle   3. 11. 8

Cleaning and restoring moulded Bases, Columns,
Caps and Arches, complete   2. 10. 0

    <Man and labourer fitting and fixing flint stones in Wall of Church>

           6. 8. 2

1883
Nov 30   2 men laying new and repairing old brick floor in Church.   1. 8. 6

1200 white floor bricks   3. 12. 0

           5. 0. 6

1884.
Mar 1   Men preparing and fixing panel work in Chancel and
Fixing Communion Rail and preparing and fixing Book
Boards, fixing Lamps etc.   3. 2. 7½

1889.
Oct 11.   Agreed to provide all materials and to fix on North Aisle
Oak Roof and Walls restored, Inside stuccoed, etc
according to plans and specifications, including drip stone,
all work to be carried out exact as old and finished by
May 1st 1890.   £500. 0. 0

July 19.	Received cheque	Rev Oakes		100.	0.	0	
Aug 4	Received cheque	Sir Ralph Blois		100.	0.	0	
" "	" "	Lady Blois		70.	0.	0	
Oct 2	" "	Rev Oakes		30.	0.	0	
							300. 0. 0[19]

1891[20]

Ap. 7	Cheque.	Mr Youngs		10.	2.	11	
	"	Lady Blois		85.	0.	0	
	Queen Annes Bounty[21]			11.	19.	7	
	Rev Oakes. Penny Bank			12.	17.	6	
							120. 0. 0
Dec 30	Cheque	Lady Blois		10.	0.	0	
1892							
Jan 14	"	Rev Oakes		20.	0.	0	
Mar 18	"	Lady Blois		25.	0.	0	
							55. 0. 0

---

19   The style of this typed document has not been altered. The various sources of the payments confirm that there was no single restoration account, with the Revd Thomas Oakes and the Blois family keeping their funds separately. 'Mr Youngs' is presumably the churchwarden Charles Youngs, but 'Allen's bill £3 4s. 9d.' is the only reference in the churchwardens' accounts for 1890–1. Between 1880 and 1891 the total paid by the churchwardens to Allen was £17.18s. 1d. CWA.

20   '1' typed over '0'.

21   Queen Anne's Bounty was created in 1704 for the augmentation of poor benefices. The significance of this payment is not known. It may relate to the parsonage and not the church.

11. Report on visit to Blythburgh church by Alfred H. Powell, 1 August 1903[22]

<u>Blythburgh Church Suffolk</u>
To the Society for the Protection of Ancient Buildings

The church, which stands on a small hill overlooking the marshes, consists of a tower (a landmark for several miles round) nave, north and south aisles, and south porch. The south porch I found in such a ruinous condition that I have advised <them> the vicar and churchwarden to shore it up at once, and have given them a drawing explaining how it should be done. The work is to be entrusted to an old mill-wright who lives in the village.

The porch is built of flint, round pebbles for the core and inside of the walls, and faced with blue squared flints on the outside. The parapets and weathering etc of wrought stone as usual in East Anglian churches.

The east wall has entirely parted from the wall of the south aisle (a). The gable front I enclose a pencil sketch of – \[*sketch plan*]/ It is very badly cracked and a slight pressure or movement might, and probably would, bring a good deal of it down. The arch of the porch is crushed and split parallel with the wall face, against the left shoulder of the said arch and the flint work above that point is bulged out some 3 or 4 inches. The side walls have spread slightly at top so that the archway is wider at the level of the capitals than at that of the bases. The front wall of the porch appears to me to have sunk, causing the separation above mentioned between the east wall and the aisle. I showed on my drawing, three shores against the upper part of gable wall, and one against the flint bulging above the crushed arch. One shore on each flank just behind the angle buttresses, and a seventh against the east wall of porch near the crack between porch and south aisle.

Also I showed a centreing for arch, to be supported independently of the building. I hope the society will think I did right in ordering this to be done at once. I am confident the porch, if they will keep it standing, (and they promised to set about shoring at once) can be mended securely without being taken down, even partially.

The vaulting has fallen long since, and I <suggested> pointed out that it would be quite a mistake to revault it and that if the room over was necessary a wooden floor could be put in. The lead <work on> roof will have to be taken up and the timbers examined.

I find it difficult to explain here any method of mending the flint wall, which is so bad that it will be a work requiring a great deal of care.

I impressed upon the churchwarden and the vicar that they could not possibly get the work done satisfactorily without the personal supervision of someone recommended by the SPAB, to which they assented and I said that I would ask the society to endeavour to find someone to do this work of supervision, as early as possible.

Next in importance, from a repairs point of view, is the nave roof. This, as the society probably knows, is a very remarkable work. It has been painted richly from end to end and decorated with great wooden winged angels, two at the centre of every tie-beam. As I could see clearly from the ground, the timbers are in some cases broken, in many cases wet through and probably rotten, and the lead covering is in a bad

---

22 See Correspondence 139–49.

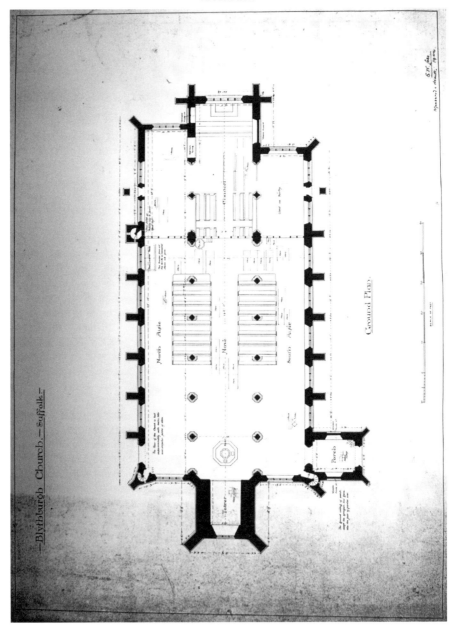

Plate 11.
Measured plan of
Blythburgh church,
after stalls had been
moved from the
north-aisle chapel
to the chancel, and
the removal of box
pews from the nave
by E. W. Lees, 1900.
BCP, Drawings 1

184

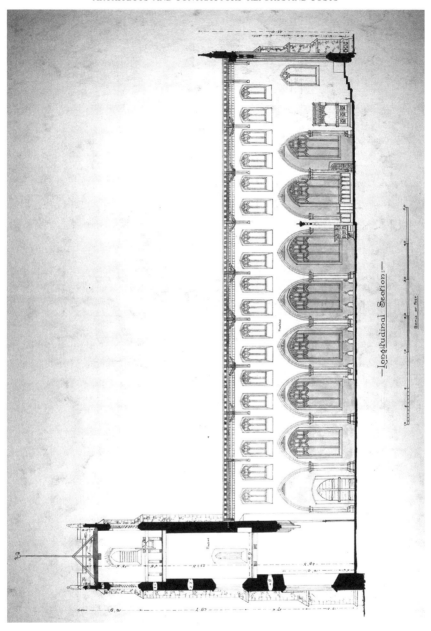

Plate 12.
Blythburgh
church elevation.
Measured
longitudinal section
from the south by
E.W. Lees, 1900.
BCP, Drawings 4

condition throughout. The urgent thing to be done here is to scaffold and examine. This could be done, as Mr Egerton (churchwarden) himself suggested, viz. by putting ledger poles across through clerestory windows, and scaffolding from them to any required height.[23] These ledgers would have to be supported by uprights from the nave floor approaching from over the aisle roof as sketch. \[*sketch of cross-section of nave and aisles*]/ This scaffolding I said ought not to be put up without supervision by someone as above mentioned and they agreed to wait; but it is highly desirable that they should not have to wait long.

Only four of the original painted beams remain but about 10 angels I think. The west two bays of the roof \(which contains 8 in all)/, have at some time been stripped and the rafters replaced on edge, so that their flat painted surfaces do not now show. The lead ought to come off the whole roof of nave and be recast bit by bit, but at present they have only £250 collected which will not go very far. I expect £150 would go on the Porch including the turret stair and lead roof.

The floor of the church, at west end – is very pretty – broken and sunk but patched all over with bricks and stones.

The tower is cracked down the centre of each face. It is very high, and has been struck by lightning once not long ago. The eastern wall at level of <ringing flo> bell cage is split and bulged badly and the springing stones of the window arch have fallen out \[*sketch of window arch*]/ and the others seem loosening. The springing stones in the opposite side of the arch are broken and loose.

The parapet of tower is hardly safe on the south west corner.

To repair the tower properly would mean a scaffold and I believe it would have to be strong enough to shore from.

\[*sketch plan of church*]/ (very) sketch plan

There are original XVth century seats in nave, finely carved – also in chancel, and few that are not original.

Yours faithfully,

[*signed*] Alfred H. Powell

12. Report of visit to Blythburgh. Alfred H. Powell to Thackeray Turner, SPAB, 25 October 1904[24]

Tyrley Castle, Market Drayton,
      Salop.
Monday 25 October 1904
My dear Turner,

I started at once on receipt of your letter and went to Blythburgh where Wells joined me and together we made a careful examination of the porch. The shores, though a little cumbrous, are doing their work well apparently, and not overdoing it. The porch does not seem to have moved at all since I was there. The vicar Mr Wing told me they have collected £400 (<I think> I understood him today over £400) and I don't see why they should not make a start, either <u>at once</u> (if not already too late) or certainly first thing in spring. We feel sure the porch work could be done for £300. Wells, who is, as you know, now an experienced builder, suggests (and I entirely agree with him) that the foundations should be examined from inside the porch and

---

[23] As a professional civil engineer Egerton was qualified to give such advice. See Introduction n. 158.
[24] See Correspondence 157–61.

that a raft of \cement/ concrete should be laid under the whole of it 2'. 0" thick, including possibly the portion of the south aisle wall forming the north side of the porch. From this base it would then be possible to recore – almost rebuild – the walls from the inside on the east and west (see sketch plan and elevation) forming four piers of new work, flush with the wall faces, up to the level of the old floor above the now fallen vaulting. At this level by the insertion of an armoured concrete floor, supported on the four new piers, an efficient and permanent tie would be secured between all the four walls sufficient also to hold the bulged south gable wall from further movement at this level. The rest of the necessary work would then consist of coreing the walls from the inside out to the flint facing as usual. In this way we think the porch could be made perfectly sound with only the slightest interference with the external flint face. The parapet – or what remains of it, could be steadied securely, the fallen angel pinnacle of the south-east corner, be replaced – the roof taken off, good timbers of it reused – lead recast if necessary and relaid – the turret stair mended and if desirable the communication from it to the upper chamber be reopened. Finally relay a brick floor in porch, as at present, covering up the new concrete foundations. Your difficulty will I suppose be finding someone suitable to carry out the work. I am myself very fully occupied now until well on in the spring of next year. I don't know if you could get Wells to take it up if his work here for Prior is finished in time – I think I should write and ask him if I were the committee as his visit interested him very much in the place and he has a very wide knowledge of building and would, if he undertook it, take his own men and be there himself. However you may know someone at liberty now. The church altogether is sadly in need of looking to, tower and all.

Yours always sincerely,
[*signed*] Alfred H. Powell

13. Report on the condition of Blythburgh church by William Weir, 26 June 1905[25]

re: Blythburgh Church, Suffolk.

To the Secretary,
The Society for the Protection of Ancient Buildings, London.
Dear Sir,
I visited this Church on the 24th inst. and was kindly met by Sir Ralph Blois and the vicar.

The structural condition of the fabric is sound with the exception of the south porch, the roofs of the nave and chancel, and the walls of the tower. The south porch calls for attention before the other portions which I have named in relation to their condition. The shores which were placed to support it about two years ago, on the advice of your society, appear to have arrested the movement in the walls, but <their> condition \of the walls/ is so serious that no delay should be made in setting about the work of repair.

The mischief appears to have been caused by the thrust of the vaulted roof over the ground floor, which gradually forced the walls outwards and caused the cracks in the

---

[25] See Correspondence 177–94. A draft version is in SPAB Add.

east and south faces. The vaulting has fallen long since and only the wall ribs and the springing of the diagonals remain. The weather which has penetrated into the cracks has gradually increased them and displaced the flint facing.

The east and west walls are about 2ft 6inches in thickness, built with flints pointed on the outside and plastered on the inside faces.

Both walls are in sound condition with the exception of a crack close against the aisle where the east wall has been thrust outwards. The crack extends from the ground upwards through the thickness of the wall. Windows exist at the centre of each wall at the ground and the first floor levels. They are blocked up on the outside faces and most of the mullions and tracery are missing.

The south wall is only 1ft 7inches in thickness. It is faced with squared flints on the outside. The archway, which is wide and pointed, is crushed and thrust outwards, and the wall over is badly cracked on the west side and to the east of the centre.

Portions of the pierced stonework of the parapet are missing, and the angel pinnacle at the south east angle has fallen and is stored in the church.

The roof is constructed with oak timbers, resting on two bearers against the east and west walls, the latter appear to be in bad condition. It is covered with cast lead, dated 1769, very uneven and patched in places. There is no lead flashing at the junction of the roof with the parapets to prevent the wet penetrating into the walls.

The stone steps of the turret staircase are in bad condition near the top. The walls appear to be in good condition. In place of the original finish on the top of turret a brick arch is turned over and plastered on the outside.

There is no appearance of any settlement in the foundations of the walls, nevertheless it would be well to examine them and if found to be unsatisfactory they should be underpinned on a good bed of cement concrete.

The crack in the east wall close against the aisle, would require to be cut out and the solid portion of the wall bonded into the aisle wall.

The stones of the pointed arch at the entrance would require to be repaired, and the joints cleaned out and well grouted with blue lias lime and sand. The cracks in the wall over would then be made good by bonding together the solid portions, from the inside face, as described in the case of the east wall.

As the walls have already proved insufficient to withstand the thrust of a vault it is quite evident that it must not be replaced. At the same time the walls require bracing together at the first floor level, which could best be done by means of oak beams resting on the east and west walls, with iron bolts taken through the walls and secured to S pieces on the outside faces. A floor could be constructed with oak joists framed into the beams and boarded on the top. Such a floor would give the necessary stiffening to the walls without any risk of thrust.

In dealing with the roof two new oak beams should be inserted under the present bearers, and resting on the east and west walls. The existing timbers would then be repaired and the oak boarding refixed and covered with deal boarding to receive the lead. The lead would require to be recast and laid to proper falls to the exiting outlets.

The stone steps of the staircase where displaced and broken would be made good and the windows to the upper chamber reopened.

The built up windows at the ground level should not be opened up, as it would necessitate the renewal of the stone mullions and tracery.

The parapet would require to be carefully refixed and the south east angle pinnacle with the angel figure set up again.

The outside pointing has perished and vegetation and weeds are growing on the surface of the walls. The joints would require to be thoroughly cleaned out to allow of sufficient key for the new pointing, which would be finished flush with the face of flintwork. The mortar being composed of ground blue lias lime and sharp coarse sand in the proportion of 1 to 4 respectively.

The plaster where perished on the inside of walls would require to be carefully repaired.

The approximate cost of the necessary work for the repairing and strengthening of the porch, including personal supervision, would amount to the sum of £200.

Scaffolding and plant	£	10
Making good walls[26]		50
work on roof		
recasting and relaying lead[27]		25
new timber		5
First floor		20
General work on porch and pointing		
walls – plasterers		25
		135
Supervision		50
	£	185
Say	£	200

Yours truly,
[*signed*]William Weir
      London, 26 June 1905

14. Report on the condition of Blythburgh church by Philip M. Johnston, 1906[28]

To
    The Committee for the Reparation of Blythburg [*sic*] church.

Gentlemen,
After a careful inspection of Blythburgh Church in July last, I drew up on the spot a short report on its structural condition, and made certain general recommendations as to the repairs urgently needed by the main Roof, the Porch and other parts of the fabric. In concluding this report I stated that 'eight or nine hundred pounds would do all that is urgently necessary' in the different sections of the work.

Upon receiving your invitation to act as Architect for the proposed work, I made another visit to the Church, during which I examined the whole building very thoroughly, took notes for the specification, and made a careful plan to scale.

I was accompanied on this last occasion (Dec. 1905) by Mr John Rayner, a well-known Contractor, of East Hanningfield, Essex, who has been carrying out work for

---

[26] Representing two months work by a mason and labourer.
[27] Requiring an estimated one ton of lead, including new lead for £5, £10 for casting and £10 for laying.
[28] SROI 2, 2. The style of this typewritten document has been retained. See Introduction n. 191.

me in that County, and who has undertaken several church contracts in the eastern counties.[29] The Estimate which I now beg to submit was drawn up as the result of our joint inspection. It has been corrected by the quantities since obtained by Mr Rayner, and it may therefore be regarded as his definite detailed Estimate for the work.

I am acting upon the proposal made some time ago, that I should write and illustrate a pamphlet on the Church, the cost of which has been generously offered by my friend the Revd H.L. Randall, rector of Cocking, Sussex. I will not therefore anticipate this by dealing with the history and architecture of the building in the present report, but will confine myself to the practical side of the proposed reparation.

Annexed to this is a copy of Mr Rayner's estimate.

If the work is intrusted to Mr Rayner – a course which I venture strongly to recommend to the Committee – it can be taken in hand at once, either in sections, as funds are available, or all together. Mr Rayner has offered to place the work in charge of a thoroughly competent foreman who has acted as clerk of the Works in a Suffolk Church restoration under the late Sir Arthur Blomfield, and who has recently been employed as foreman in a work executed under my own superintendence. I can personally recommend him as reliable and competent.

I will now describe the nature of the works proposed.

SECTION I. Main Roof.

A second survey of the fabric has confirmed the view that I put forth after my first inspection, viz: that the main roof of nave and chancel is not in as bad a state as it appears to be when seen from below. Practically all of the principal timbers, rafters, and the boarding over them, with its interesting and beautiful painted decoration, can be saved. To effect this repair I propose scarfing the decayed ends of rafters and principals, and, if necessary, using wrought iron straps and other ironwork to strengthen weak places. All the carved angels and shields, for which the roof is so famous, are to be carefully examined and securely re-fixed. The large collection of parts of these figures and shields now preserved in the Vestry can be replaced in the positions they originally occupied.+ A judicious use of iron straps etc. will assist in holding together weak or broken parts, and it may be found advisable to try some chemical treatment for stopping the spread of decay and the worm that has attacked much of the carving. But in any case care will be taken to save every scrap of the old colouring.

Happily the roofs of the aisles have been thoroughly repaired and are in excellent order.

The best well seasoned English oak only will be used in these repairs, but for the external boarding, on which the lead work rests, pitch pine may be suitably employed at a saving of cost. I propose to replace the missing oak cornice-moulding at the junction of walls and roof, and a sum has been provided for this in the Estimate (Item II). It would, however, be attempting too much to restore the angels and shields which probably formed the original terminations to the wall-brackets of the principals.

A good deal of the lead-work of the main roof is in a very bad state: although, taken as a whole, the roof is not as bad as might be expected. I propose to take it bay by bay, as it has been taken in preparing this estimate, and to renew and repair as each part requires. An alternative estimate, prepared at my request by Mr Rayner, for entirely renewing the lead roof proves this to be the more economical plan.+

---

[29] No other information about Rayner has been located and his involvement with the work at Blythburgh cannot be confirmed.

Happily the aisle roofs are already in a sound state, having been renewed about 25 years ago, under the late Mr G.E. Street, R.A.

+ I hope that this good work of their 'restoration' will be greatly facilitated by the help of careful drawings to scale made on the spot by an eminent Archaeologist many years ago.

+ Mr Rayner's alternative price for an <u>entirely new</u> lead roof over nave and chancel gives an <u>extra</u> cost of £250.

SECTION II. The Porch.

The critical state of the beautiful South Porch is only too painfully evident, but I have every hope of being able to restore it to a sound and sightly condition at a comparatively small cost. In doing so it will be necessary to take down the facing at any rate on the upper part of the south wall and to rebuild the crown of the arch. The stones will be numbered, and the knapped flint-work replaced with them exactly in the old positions, and when the walls have been underpinned and a good concrete bottom inserted, the stability of the whole will be well assured. It is probable that bad drainage and the digging of vaults and graves up to and below the footings have caused a good deal of the mischief. Probably such things led to the fall of the vaulting in the ground storey in the eighteenth century. This I propose, if funds permit, to replace, using in the many moulded stone vault-ribs now lying in the churchyard. The similar vaulting at Southwold affords a very good model.

Also it is desirable that the beautiful quatrefoil cresting which is such a character-istic feature here should be restored, together with the angel that formerly stood at the south east angle now preserved in the Church.

The roof and floor of the parvise chamber are other items in this section; and some repair to the floor must be allowed for. Also I think it highly desirable that the beau-tiful windows, niche and stoup should be unblocked and the missing parts restored; and, similarly, that the battlemented finish of the Porch-turret, now represented by an ugly dome-shaped mass of brickwork, should be replaced on the old lines. Here, again, Southwold porch furnishes a safe pattern to go by.

Every care will be taken in all this to preserve every scrap of the old work.

SECTION III. <u>Repairs to Clerestory aisle and other walls and to the Tower</u>.

A good deal of repair of a general character is needed to complete the scheme. This includes the drainage of roofs and walls, as well as repairs (happily slight) to the latter. Settlements in the Tower walls call for careful repair, and the replacement of the missing window tracery is to be desired.

The execution of the proposed works would probably occupy three to four months, but during part of that time the services of the Church need not be interrupted.

I may add that I should give my own personal supervision to the work and should do all in my power to preserve every feature of interest in the building.

I have the honour to be, Gentlemen,
Your obedient servant,
(Sgd). PHILIP M. JOHNSTON.

15. Estimate of cost of work recommended by Philip M. Johnston, 26 June 1906[30]

Mr Rayner's Estimate.

	£	s	d
Repair and renewal of leadwork to main roof	£ 179	2	6
Carpenters work to same	120	0	0
Repairs to parapets and main walls	35	0	0
Repairs to tower	15	0	0
Repairs to clerestory windows and other stonework and to the glazing and lead down-spouts north and south sides	50	0	0
Repairs to drains etc north side and to down spouts on both sides and to north and south walls of aisles and drainage	54	0	0
East end repairs – to walls	2	10	0
Paved dry area round walls about 62 ft run and extras	40	0	0
Tower roof and battlements repairs and laying of lead and flashings	12	0	0
Woodwork of nave and chancel roofs in oak – making good to plates to 4 old principals (scarfing end etc) provision for repairing old carved work and providing all scaffolding	127	0	0
260 ft run of moulded oak cornice in nave and chancel	25	0	0
Cleaning and colouring walls and repairing internal stonework and repairs to brick paving etc	105	0	0
Porch opening and restoring blocked windows – Image niche and stoup	55	0	0
Repair of walls, involving partial rebuilding of south front and refixing face flints – replacing the missing angel and the open cresting of parapet	35	0	0
Renewing the roof and leadwork	30	0	0
Restoring the battlemented termination of stair turret	15	0	0
Restoring the vaulting over the porch and the floor of parvise over Same	75	0	0
	£ 975	2	6[31]

16. Review of Philip Johnston's report on Blythburgh church. William Weir to Thackeray Turner, SPAB, 21 July 1906

West Stow Hall,
Bury St Edmunds. 21 July 1906
Dear Mr Turner,

re: Blythburgh Church

I return Mr Johnson's [*sic*] report. Perhaps it might be well to point out the estimated cost of the repair of main roof as shown on enclosed extract – viz. £426 2s. 6d. To recast the lead would entail an extra cost of £230 making a total of £656 2s. 6d. The items for repair of tower amount to only £27. The porch is equally misleading – £35

---

30 Copy in William Weir's hand in SPAB Add.
31 The total is incorrect. The items add up to £974 12s. 6d.

is only allowed for the repair of the walls, and £75 is proposed to be spent on the vaulting, which would soon thrust the walls out again.

I enclose my report on the general building and trust it will meet with your committee's approval. If there are any items you would wish to alter, please do so. I have kept the cost as low as possible, but I find there is a lot of repairs wanted to the walls generally. The tower is also much worse than it appears to be, unless closely examined.

I hope \soon/ to send you the report which I was unable to do <last> this week.

With reference to the Compton church I think the beginning of October would be the earliest date possible. The new Vicar of St Mary Coslany at Norwich is making an effort to get funds to repair the tower at any rate, before the winter sets in, and if he is successful I should like to be able to take the work on hand, as another winter may prove fatal to the tower. Would it be possible to keep the question of doing the work at Compton open for some time, until I hear definitely about St Mary's?

re: Potter Heigham Church

I wrote to Powys, who is finding work in London very slack, and I think it could be arranged for him to take Potter Heigham in hand, if it would help you out of the difficulty?

Yours truly,

[*signed*]William Weir

Thackeray Turner Esq.

[*Extract by William Weir of Philip Johnston's estimate of cost for repairing Blythburgh church*]

Repair of lead

Main roof	179 .	2 . 6
Carpenters work?	120	
Roof timbers	127	
	£ 426 .	2 . 6
Parapets and main walls	35 .	0 . 0
Clerestory windows etc,		
glazing and down pipes	50 .	0 . 0.
	85 .	0 . 0.
Repairs to tower	15 .	0 . 0
Roof and battlements and		
repair of lead	12 .	0 . 0
	27 .	0 . 0
East end repairs	2 .	10 . 0
Porch		
Repairs	£ 35 .	0 . 0
Renewing roof and leadwork	30 .	0 . 0
	65 .	0 . 0

Opening and restoring 4 blocked

windows etc   <u>55 . 0 . 0</u>

re Blythburgh church.
   July 1906.

17. Report on Blythburgh church by William Weir, 21 July 1906

re: Blythburgh Church, Suffolk.

To the Secretary
The Society for the Protection of Ancient Buildings

Dear Sir,
In accordance with your request I made a second visit to the above named church on the 19th inst: and carefully examined the fabric with a view to the repairs necessary, to make it sound and weatherproof.

The church consists of the chancel about 46 ft: long by 20 ft; 3 inches wide internally, with north and south aisles 15 ft: 3 inches wide. The nave 84 ft: long by 20 ft: 3 inches wide, with north and south aisles 15 ft: 3 inches wide. The south porch with parvise over and the western tower.

The whole church appears to have been built in the 15th century, and to have escaped any structural alteration or addition. The walls are built of flintwork with stone dressings for the openings, buttresses, and parapets. The original roofs, of flat pitch, remain and in the case of the chancel and nave retain a good deal of their original colour decoration. Unfortunately the two westmost bays of the nave roof have been reconstructed. Oak has been used for the main timbers, the old rafters, originally framed flat, have been cut in two and used on edge, which has hidden the colour decoration. The tie beams to the chancel roof have been renewed with oak and pitch pine bolted together in an unsatisfactory manner. They are not strong enough for the weight of the roof and the length of bearing, and are badly sagged. Both roofs are covered with cast lead.

In the case of the chancel several portions of the lead have been renewed with cast lead, fixed on wood rolls, and a lead capping put at the apex where the sheets have crept away and allowed of the wet penetrating. The gutters behind the parapet have not sufficient fall and would require to be taken up and the lead recast and relaid on deal boarding constructed with proper falls to the existing outlets. The cover flashing also requires to be refixed and pointed to prevent the wet penetrating behind the leadwork.

In dealing with the lead on the roof of nave which is in fair condition, with the exception of the apex and the gutters behind the parapet and a few sheets which have cracked at the rolls. The gutters would require to be recast and relaid as described in the case of the chancel, and a new lead capping, similar to the one on the chancel, fixed at the apex. The defective sheets would require to be recast and refixed. The lead is dated 1739, 1752, and 1766 and should last for many years to come, if carefully repaired, at the same time it would be more satisfactory to have it recast and relaid on deal boarding.

As regards the woodwork of the roof, the two westmost bays, which have been reconstructed, appear to be in sound condition. The other four bays of the nave, are

194

not so satisfactory. The ridge piece at apex, is broken close against the 2nd westmost tie-beam, and the four old tie-beams are perished at the ends, and do not appear to have much bearing on the walls. The eastmost one unfortunately is broken close against the south end, over the shaped bracket which bears on the wall underneath. It would be necessary to examine the wall plates on the north and south sides and if found sound new ends would require to be scarfed to the tie-beams and well secured to the wall plates. The ridge piece and tie-beam where broken would require to be repaired and strengthened in an effectual manner. The other main timbers and rafters appear to be sound. Great care would require to be taken in refixing the shields, bosses, and carved angels, as well as the portions, carefully stored in the vestry, which have fallen from time to time.

It would be well to examine the tie-beams of the chancel roof, with a view to strengthening them if possible.

The aisle roofs appear to be in good repair; unfortunately the wet is getting in behind the lead gutter at the back of parapet, owing to the cement pointing having bulged away from the wall.

In dealing with the walls of the chancel, nave, and aisles, the stone copings of the parapets, and the foundations of the buttresses call for special attention. Most of the joints of the copings are open and admit of the wet soaking into the walls, and in several places the copings are displaced and require to be refixed. The angle pinnacles over the east end of the chancel are very loose and require to be refixed, the one on the north side is in danger of falling, owing to the wall underneath being very loose. The masonry of the windows generally is sound, and only requires the beds and joints repointing in places. The flint facing on the south side of clerestory requires repointing. Near the east end of the chancel a portion of the parapet is repaired with brickwork and the flint facing of the wall underneath, down to the string course is very loose and bulged. It would require to be reset. The stone staircase in the north west angle of the north aisle has settled outwards, and cracked the walls from the ground upwards. It would be necessary to rebond the solid parts of the walls together.

The lead heads and down pipes around the building require special attention. The water at present discharges close against the foundations, and in some instances on top of them. It would be necessary to refix the whole lot in a proper manner and provide gulleys and drainpipes to carry the water away from the building.

The glazing of the clerestory windows, especially on the south side, requires attention. It would be necessary to renew the lead in cases, but generally if they were restopped, outside and inside, and saddle bars provided where required it would be sufficient to meet the case.

In dealing with the interior, the repair of the plaster on the walls and the cleaning down and limewashing of same, as well as some slight repairs to the brick and tile paving around the Font is all that appears necessary – with the exception of the Hopton tomb on the north side of the chancel – which calls for attention. The canopy, which has a bearing of 7 ft, supports the wall above; unfortunately the weight has fractured the Purbeck marble. It would be necessary to strengthen the lintel over in order to take the weight of the wall and repair the fractured canopy.

The condition of the tower is by no means satisfactory. The walls are strongly built of flint with stone dressings to the angles, buttresses, and openings. Access is gained to the ringing chamber on first floor, and the belfry, and roof, by means of ladder inside the tower. Unfortunately serious cracks exist at the centre of each face of the tower, which have evidently been caused by a defective bellframe in years past. The cracks are visible on the outside, and the inside of the walls and extend from near the ground level to the parapet. It would be necessary to repair them by cutting out the loose portions at the sides of cracks and rebonding the solid portions together. The condition of the parapet on the top of [*the*] tower also calls for attention. Two of the angles are held together with iron bands and ties. Most of the stone coping is missing and is renewed with brick, all of which requires to be rebedded. Heavy stone figures occur at the angles which are by no means safe at present. The flintwork on the south face of [*the*] parapet has mostly dropped out and allows of the wet penetrating. The other sides are loose and require the flints rebedding and pointing. The belfry windows have lost their mullions and tracery and in places the stone jambs are loose and in a dangerous condition. The openings are fitted with deal frames and louvres, which should be renewed with oak in a substantial manner to strengthen the openings. The joints of the various string courses, and weatherings of buttresses, are open and require repointing. The angle buttresses on the east side over the lead roof of [*the*] nave require attention – they appear to be corbelled out from the wall under the roof, and have become loose and displaced at the roof level.

The floor of the ringing chamber is sound with the exception of the boarding, part of which would require to be renewed. The bellframe is constructed of oak. It requires to be repaired and strengthened, and the one bell remaining, dated 1608, rehung. The roof is covered with cast lead, dated 1777, with gutter on the east and west sides. The lead is cracked in places and allows of the wet penetrating. It requires to be repaired and a cover flashing of lead, fixed on the back of the parapet. The flagstaff rests on the beam at the centre of the roof and is stayed against the parapet by means of wood struts, which shake the parapet. The wet has penetrated at the junction of lead and flagstaff and rotted the beam. The better position for the flagstaff would be at the north west angle of the tower, where it could be securely fastened without any fear of doing harm to the tower. The windows of the ringing chamber, at present blocked up, should be opened and reglazed with leaded lights and casements for ventilation.

I have dealt with the repair of the south porch in my report of June 1905 and estimated the approximate cost of its repair at the sum of £200. In the event of the work being undertaken in conjunction with the general repairs, there would be a saving on the cost of supervision and labour to the extent of £25. With reference to your question of reinstating the vaulting I failed to find any of the missing portions. I would suggest that the vaulting be replaced, if desired, in such a way as would not destroy the authenticity of the portions that fortunately exist.

I annex a summary of the approximate cost of the various works of repair as set forth in the above.

Yours truly

[*signed*]William Weir   London, 21 July 1906.

Blythburgh Church. Summary of the approximate cost of the various works of repair as set forth in the accompanying report.
Nave and chancel roof
The renewal of the lead gutters as described, and the repairs to
 the lead covering   £115. 0. 0
The extra cost of recasting the whole of the lead, and relaying
 on deal boarding – £155.
The repair and strengthening of the roof timbers etc including

scaffolding	120. 0. 0	
Rebedding and repointing the parapet and copings of the chancel, nave, and aisle roofs. Underpinning the buttresses and general repairs to the walls	95. 0. 0	
Refixing the lead heads and down pipes, and providing gulleys and drains around the building	45. 0. 0	
Repairing and restopping the leaded lights of clerestory windows	15. 0. 0	
Repairing plaster on inside of walls, cleaning down and limewashing anew, also repair to floor around Font and strengthening wall over Hopton tomb	50. 0. 0	
Repairing the crack in the tower, refixing the parapet where unsafe and pointing facing where necessary	125. 0. 0	
Providing oak frames and louvres to belfry windows, repairing bell frame and refixing flagstaff	55. 0. 0	
Providing lead flashing to tower roof and repairing leadwork	5. 0. 0	
Repairs to porch as estimated 1905 £200. less saving in supervision etc if undertaken with general work £25.	175. 0. 0	
Additional cost of replacing vaulted roof as described £40.		
	£800. 0. 0	

William Weir,
London, 21 July 1906

18. Report on work in progress at Blythburgh church by William Weir, 3 November 1906[32]

re: Blythburgh Church, Suffolk.

To the Secretary,
The Society for the Protection of Ancient Buildings.
Dear Sir,
In accordance with your request I met Mr Johnston at Blythburgh Church on the 29th October and went over the work now in progress.

The repair and strengthening of the nave roof is completed, and the lead covering nearly so. The ends of the main beams were found, in most cases to have perished, and new pieces of English oak have been spliced and bolted to the sound portions of same, as well as an additional piece, 5″ x 13″ being put on the top, to which the beams have been bolted. The purlins, which are framed into the main beams, have also been strengthened with a 4″ x 3″ piece of oak on top and bolted together at intervals. The wall plates on which the rafters bear have been renewed, and the various shields and angels have been strengthened where necessary with a new backing of oak. The old painted boarding on the top of the rafters, where disturbed, has been carefully replaced. The deal boarding on the top has been fixed above the new bearers and the gutters formed behind the north and south walls, to carry the water to the old outlets.

The weakest point in the work appears to be the manner in which the new ends are

---

[32] A draft version is in SPAB Add.

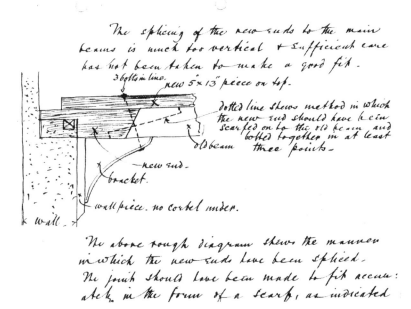

Plate 13. A sketch by William Weir explaining his criticism of the way new ends had been spliced to the old roof beams. The joints were too vertical and fitted badly, November 1906. Appendix A 18. © SPAB, Blythburgh Box II

spliced on to the old beams. As the roof now is, it all depends on a few bolts to hold up the main beams on which the whole roof is supported. The splicing of the new ends to the main beams is much too vertical and sufficient care has not been taken to make a good fit.

/Diagram of attachment of main beams to new ends/

The above rough diagram shews the manner in which the new ends have been spliced. The joints should have been made to fit accurately in the form of a scarf, as indicated by the dotted lines on the diagram and bolted together at various points.

The new ends to the beams are built into the walls without a space being left at the sides for ventilation, which will result in their early decay.

The roof was formerly covered with cast lead of good substance and in fair repair. It has unfortunately been removed and replaced, with milled lead, weighing 6 lbs to the foot super, dressed over wood rolls and ridge piece.[33] The old lead has been used for the gutters and 2 or 3 sheets on the roof. The roof is almost flat and where the sheets are not in one length the laps are deficient, some only having 6 inches. There is no excuse for using milled lead, as the old cast lead was with the exception of a few sheets, in good condition and infinitely better than the milled lead which has been used.

The south porch has been dealt with in the following manner. The east and portion of west wall has been underpinned on a concrete foundation. The outer arch at

---

[33] On sand cast versus milled lead see Correspondence n. 121.

entrance has been rebuilt and several new stones inserted, with 'Monk's park' stone. The flint facing of the <Tympanums> spandrels over the arch have been rebedded, and the niche over, opened out, and being refixed. Where the wall was broken and displaced over the west side of arch, the inside of the crack has been filled up and some iron bonds inserted in the wall. Sufficient bond has not been obtained between the solid portions of the wall, and what is obtained with the iron bonds is very superficial. The other crack at the junction of the east wall with the wall of aisle, has been filled up in a similar manner and iron bonds inserted. I should consider any attempt to replace the stone vaulting, in the present weak condition of the walls, extremely dangerous. The timbers of the roof of porch have been repaired and strengthened with some new pieces – unfortunately the two beams which support the whole roof rest on the wall of aisle and south wall of porch, which is only 1 ft 7 inches in thickness. Cross beams should have been inserted under the existing beams, resting on the east and west walls, in order to tie them together, and prevent the roof from thrusting them outwards. The cast lead has been removed and replaced with milled lead.

The four built up windows in the east and west walls, have been opened out and it is proposed to restore the missing mullions and tracery, which will further weaken the walls.

It is proposed to remove the brick vault over the top of the turret staircase, and restore the battlemented termination which is supposed to have existed.

It appears a very great misfortune that the funds, which are not sufficient to undertake the necessary repairs, in order to make the fabric weatherproof, should be spent in useless 'restoration' as proposed in the case of the turret staircase and the windows of the porch; and \that/ such work as the repair and refixing of the lead heads, and down pipes, and the pointing of the parapet and walls etc, should be overlooked. The interior of the nave is in a most neglected condition; the wet which has been running down the walls has perished the plaster, which should certainly be repaired and limewashed, before the scaffolding is removed.

Yours truly
[*signed*]William Weir
London, 3rd November 1906.

19. Report on the condition of Blythburgh church by William Weir, 6 February, 1926[34]

The Beeches,
Stotfold Road,
Letchworth.
6th February 1926.

<u>Holy Trinity Church, Blythburgh.</u>

Report on the condition of the building for the Advisory Committee of the Diocese of St. Edmundsbury and Ipswich.[35]

The Church consists of the Chancel about 46 feet long by 20 feet 3 inches wide, with North and South Chapels, 15 feet 3 inches wide, dedicated to the St. Anne and

---

[34] Typewritten. A handwritten draft version is also in SPAB Add.
[35] See Introduction p. liii for Diocesan Advisory Committee.

the Blessed Virgin respectively. The Nave 84 feet long by 20 feet 3 inches wide, with North and South aisles, 15 feet 3 inches wide. The South Porch and the Western Tower.

The walls are built of flintwork with stone dressings to the openings, buttresses and parapets.

The Chancel and Nave retain their original roofs constructed to a flat pitch with substantial tie beams, purlins and rafters. The two westernmost bays of the Nave roof have been reconstructed with new oak for the tie beams and purlins dated 1782, and the old rafters, which were originally framed flat, have been cut into two narrow sections and fixed on edge. The two bays are covered with cast lead dated 1759. The spire, which was struck down by lightning in 1577, is supposed to have destroyed these two bays, but the dates do not uphold the theory.

The remaining four bays of the Nave roof were repaired in 1906, when the timbers were strengthened with additional pieces of oak on top. Unfortunately, milled lead was used for the covering instead of recasting the old lead. This portion of the roof retains the original colour decoration to a large extent and is of considerable interest.

The Chancel roof consists of four bays, and with the exception of the tie beams it retains the original timbers and colour decoration. The eastmost tie beam has been renewed or strengthened with oak and the other four with deal. The latter have sagged considerably at the centre. The roof is covered with cast lead dated 1739.

The roofs of the aisles have modern oak roofs, without any colour decoration, and covered with cast lead. They are probably the work of Sir G.E. Street, who restored the Church in 1882–4. The leadwork on the south aisle is dated 1769 and it is probable the date was refixed when the roofs were renewed.

The south porch was repaired in 1906 and the roof covered with milled lead. The top of the turret staircase on the west side of the porch was rebuilt with a battlemented parapet during the work to the porch.

The tower arch which is much less ornate than the rest of the Church, is soundly built of flintwork and stone dressings to the buttresses and openings. Access is gained by ladders to the ringing chamber on the first floor, and the belfry and roof.

The belfry contains one bell, dated 1608, hung in an oak frame which originally contained four bells. The belfry windows have lost their mullions and tracery and are fitted with deal frames and louvres. The roof is constructed of oak and covered with cast lead. There is a flagstaff at the centre of the roof, supported with wood struts against the parapets.

The Church is supposed to have been built between 1442 and 1473, but the arcades of the Nave and Chancel, the south porch, the doorway in the north aisle, and the tower all appear to belong to the fourteenth century.

The condition of the building is sound and in good repair with the following exceptions:-

The tie beams to the roof of the Chancel are considerably sagged in their bearing and do not appear strong enough for their purpose. They should be examined and strengthened as necessary.

The wet appears to penetrate in places through the leadwork of the Chancel roof, and the lead requires attention. The pointing to the lead flashing at the parapets on most of the roofs is defective and allows of the wet soaking into the walls. It should be renewed with Mastic cement wherever defective.

The four bays of the Nave roof that were repaired in 1906 appear sound. The ridge pieces in two of the bays have been strengthened with iron straps, fixed on the underside where cracks recently occurred.

The two westmost bays which were reconstructed appear sound, and the leadwork in fair repair.

The question of reinstating the rafters to show the colour decoration in these two bays would entail a considerable amount of work, and as each rafter has been cut in two and made to serve for two rafters, there would only be sufficient to replace one bay. The other bay would need <two> new rafters.

The roofs of the aisles and chapels appear sound. The lead in the gutter of the north aisle is laid in long lengths, two of which are cracked and require repairing.

The parapet of the north Clerestory is displaced near the centre, and the joints require repointing in several places.

The leaded glazing in the westmost window of the Clerestory is boarded up and needs releading. The lead heads and down pipes require refixing in places.

The joints of the quatrefoil parapet of the south aisle are in need of repointing. A portion of the flint facing at the east end of the south Clerestory has bulged outwards and needs rebuilding in position. The stone coping to the parapet above is perishing in places and needs attention.

The flint facing at the ground level of both the aisles is loose in places, and requires to be rebedded and pointed with good mortar.

The walls of the tower are cracked at the centre of each side, probably caused by early settlement. There appears to be no recent movement, but it would be advisable to point the surfaces and grout in the cracks.

The louvres of the belfry windows need repair and the inside covering with wire netting to prevent the birds getting in.

The bell should be rehung and put in ringing order.

The leadwork on the roof of the tower appears sound, but the gutters are choked with vegetation and need cleaning out from time to time. The pointing round the lead flashing is loose and the wet is soaking into the walls. The flagstaff is perishing from want of paint and the wet is getting through at its junction with the roof. Two of the wood struts supporting the flagstaff are displaced and the others are a danger to the parapet. An oak support should be fixed to the centre beam supporting the roof and carried up about 6 feet above the roof, to which the flagstaff should be secured with wrot [*sic*] iron holdfasts.

In the interior of the building the walls of the Nave and Clerestory retain the old plaster in bad repair. The masonry of the arches and piers of the arcades are covered with several coats of limewash. The Masonry should be exposed by the removal of the limewash and the plaster cleaned and repaired.

The plaster on the walls of the Chancel has been renewed in modern times and has a hard mechanical surface that contrasts badly with the old plaster. The masonry of the two bays of the arcades should be cleaned of the limewash.

There is a built up window on the north and south aisles of Sanctuary of which the Mullions and tracery appear to be missing. The large five-light window in the east wall gives ample light to the interior, and if the opening up of the side windows involves new tracery and mullions it would be better not to do it.

The Chapels are enclosed with oak screens across the aisles. The one on the south side cuts across the piscina and it should be moved further east. Portions of the ornamental work are missing from the tracery of both screens, and there are some pieces stored in a chest which should be compared and refixed in position.

The Chancel screen unfortunately has been very much restored.

The position of the Altar rails cuts into the Sedilia and should be moved to their original position further west.

The three stone seats of the Sedilia are fixed on the same level and they should be reinstated in their original positions.

The Sanctuary is paved with nine inch square red quarries. There are two steps within the Altar rails and a foot pace at the Altar. The arrangement is somewhat cramped and it would be an improvement to remove the foot pace and rearrange the Altar and the hangings.

The Hopton tomb in the north wall of the Chancel is constructed of Purbeck marble through the thickness of the wall, and the canopied head is broken and displaced by the weight of the wall over. The head is temporarily supported with brick piers resting on the Altar tomb.[36] The wall above should be supported with a tile lintel, and the canopy carefully repaired and fixed in position. The Surface of the Purbeck marble is perishing in places and should be dressed with beeswax dissolved in turpentine.

The Altar tomb to the Swillington family in the north aisle, which is also of Purbeck marble, should be dressed with beeswax where perishing.

The Nave is seated with interesting old benches with carved poppy ends. Modern oak backs and book boards have been added to the seats.

The Chancel seats are modern with the exception of the front desks of fifteenth century workmanship with finely carved ends and fronts.

The floors are boarded at the seats and paved with bricks and tiles otherwise.

There is an interesting Font at the west end of the Nave on a high base with two steps.

The Clerestory windows are glazed with old crown glass in diamond shaped panes, and there are portions of stained glass in some of the windows of the aisles, otherwise the windows have been glazed with modern Cathedral glass of bad texture and colour.

[*signed*] William Weir

20. Estimated cost of repairs to Blythburgh church by William Weir, June 1929

/Copy/
The Beeches,
Stotfold Road,
Letchworth, Herts.

Blythburgh Church. June 1929.
Approximate cost of the following works of repair:
1. North and South aisles.
   Recasting and laying leadwork on both roofs, on new
   foundation of deal boarding.   £700
2. Chancel roof.
   Strengthening the three main cross beams including
   \the/ relaying \of the/ disturbed leadwork.   £ 70
5. Repairs to leaded glazing of Clerestory windows

---

[36] This 'temporary' support had been there since at least 1808. Sylvanus Urban, *The Gentleman's Magazine.*

and elsewhere.	£ 50	
3. The repair and repointing of parapets and <surfaces of walls> exterior surface of walls \and buttresses/ at ground level X	£150	
7. Repair and strengthening of wall over the Hopton tomb and \the/ removal of the temporary brick <piers> supports <to the vault>		£ 75
6. Repair of louvre boards to Belfry windows and fixing wire netting on the inside. \£40/ Repair to bellframe and rehanging the bell. \£35/		£ 75
4. Repair and refixing of Rainwater heads and down pipes and overhauling the drains		£ 50
		£1170
Architect's fees etc		115
		£1285

/Lead gutters Nave roof. 30' x 2'
2

$\overline{60}$
7

$\overline{112}$) 420 (4 cwts. 2 times = 8 cwts./

On completion of the repairs to the fabric the following
works should be undertaken.

<7.> The repair and strengthening of wall over the Hopton tomb and the removal of the temporary brick supports.	£ 75
Strengthening the bellframe and rehanging the bell	£ 35
Cleaning and limewashing the plaster throughout the building.	£ 50
Cleaning the limewash from the piers and arches of Nave and Chancel.	£ 25
The reinstatement \on the screens/ of the portions of carved enrichment at present stored in the Church.	£ 15
The refixing of the South Chapel screen to its original position further east and clear of the piscina.	£ 10
The refixing of Altar rails to their original position further west and clear of the Sedilia.	£ 5
The reinstatement of the stone seats of the Sedilia to their original positions.	£ 10
The question of the removal of the foot pace in the Sanctuary and the furnishings of the Altar.	£ 50
The cleaning and preservative treatment of the Purbeck marble of the Hopton and Swillington tombs.	£ 10

The cost of the repairs to the fabric should not exceed

/Fabric
works.
  £700
    25
   100
    25
    50
   200
_____
£1100
_____

other works
 £ 75
  35
  50
  25
  15
  10
   5
  10
  50
  10
_____
£ 285

1100
 250
_____
£ 750 /
_____

21. Report on the condition of Blythburgh church by William Weir, 11 July 1933[37]

Letchworth, Herts.
11th July 1933.

Report on Holy Trinity Church, Blythburgh
The Rev. A.D. Thompson,
The Vicarage,
Walberswick,
Suffolk.

Dear Sir,
As requested at our recent interview I have made a careful examination of Blythburgh Church and have pleasure in reporting as follows:-

    In February 1926 I made a report on the building for the Advisory Committee of the Diocese of St. Edmundsbury and Ipswich, of which I append a copy for reference.

---

[37] Typewritten.

Some works of repair were undertaken in 1928–29 to the exterior of the walls and the leadwork on the roofs of the aisles, together with repairs to the plaster on the interior of the Nave clerestory. Since when the lead glazing of the South Clerestory windows has been repaired and releaded.

The condition of the fabric is much the same as I found it in 1926, with the exception of the leadwork on the roofs of the North and South aisles and the lead gutters at the West end of the Nave roof. On commencing to repair the lead it was found to be badly perished on the underside and too thin to deal with. The oak boarding on which it is laid having set up a chemical action and eaten away the surface. Temporary repairs were carried out and new pieces of lead inserted to make the roofs weather proof until the lead could be recast.

The lead gutters behind the parapets at the West end of the Nave roof are laid with badly constructed strips, which allow of wet penetrating, and the plaster over two of the Clerestory windows is badly stained in consequence.

Of the works of repair still to be done to the fabric I consider the following are the most important:-

1. North and South aisles – Recasting and relaying the leadwork on both roofs on a new foundation of deal boarding, approximate cost £700.

2. Nave roof – Recasting and relaying the leadwork of the gutters at the two westermost bays behind the parapets on deal boarding reconstructed with drips and falls to the existing outlets. Refixing and pointing the lead flashings throughout the roof, approximate cost £25.

3. Chancel roof – strengthening the four main cross beams where badly sagged, including the relaying of the disturbed leadwork. Refixing and pointing the lead flashings of the roof, approximate cost, £100.

4. The repair or releading of Clerestory windows on North side of Nave and Chancel, including the renewal of saddle bars as necessary, approximate cost £25.

5. The repair and fixing of lead rainwater heads and downpipes and overhauling the drains, approximate cost £50.

6. The repair and repointing of parapets and masonry and the exterior flint facing of the walls, approximate cost £200.

On completion of the fabric repairs the following work should be undertaken:-

The repair and strengthening of the wall over the Hopton tomb and the removal of the temporary brick supports.

Strengthening the bell frame and rehanging the bell.

Cleaning and lime washing the plaster throughout the building.

Cleaning the lime wash from the piers and arches of Nave and Chancel.

The reinstatement on the screens of portions of carved enrichments at present stored in the Church.

Refixing the South Chapel Screen in its original position further east and clear of the Piscina.

Refixing the Altar rails in their original position further west and clear of the Sedilia.

Refixing the stone seats of Sedilia in their original positions.

The question of removing the footpace in the Sanctuary and the furnishings of the Altars.

The cleaning and preservative treatment of the Purbeck marble of the Hopton and Swillington tombs.

The approximate cost of the work to the fabric as stated amounts to a total sum of

£1,100, and for the other work as outlined the cost should not exceed an additional sum of £300.

In carrying out the work with the funds in hand I would advise following the order stated with the exception of the leadwork on the North aisle, which should be omitted until further funds are obtained.

I am,

Yours faithfully,

[*Copy not signed*]

22. Review of work on Blythburgh church by William Weir, undated[38]

Blythburgh Church, Suffolk. Repairs 1933–34.

The chancel roof was in a dangerous condition owing to the sagging of the main cross beams supporting it. The original beams had been replaced with modern ones made up of sections of oak and deal, insecurely bolted together and in danger of collapsing.

The work of strengthening the beams has been done with 'T' shaped steel joists, cambered to the pitch of the roof and fixed over the beams and bolted through their depth at intervals. Sections of the lead covering had to be removed to set at the beams and where necessary it has been repaired or recast before relaying.

The leadwork on the westernmost bays of the nave roof was in a dilapidated state and it has been recast and relaid on deal boarding.

The timbers have been put in good repair and the rafters, which had been refixed upright instead of flat, and spaced too far apart when the bays were reconstructed, have been refixed in their original positions showing the painted soffits and supplemented with new ones to make out the deficiency.

The vault of the south porch, of which only the springings remained in situ, has been reinstated with portions of the stone ribs stored in the church and supplemented with cast concrete ribs where necessary. The filling between the ribs was done with a thin bed of concrete inserted in position on a centre of sand supported between the ribs. In order to guard against any thrust on the walls, a stout copper tie was fixed across the middle of the vaults, with the ends turned down in the walls and embedded in concrete.

A floor has been constructed with deal joists and boarding bearing on the east and west walls, clear of the vault. A door of English oak has been fitted to the upper chamber and the plaster on the walls repaired and twice limewashed. At completion the underside of the vault and the walls of the porch were brushed clean and given two coats of limewash of a warm white tone.

The canopied head of the Hopton tomb in [*the*] north wall of [*the*] chancel was broken and displaced and was supported with brick piers resting on the altar tomb. On examination the flint wall above the canopy was found roughly shaped in the form of an arch, in contact with the ends of [*the*] canopy and broken under the apex.

The wall has been rebounded and cut away to clear the canopied head, which has been repaired, and strengthened, and suspended in position from the wall above with copper rods.

---

[38] BCP 28.3.3. A draft of the section on the Hopton tomb is in SPAB Add.

23. Note on repairs to Blythburgh church by William Weir, undated[39]

Blythburgh Church.
Repairs since 1933.
Repairing roofs N. and S. aisles and S. porch and recasting leadwork.
Repairing and strengthening timbers of chancel roof and recasting lead gutters and ridge.
Recasting lead on two westernmost bays of nave roof and repairing timbers.
Repairs and repointing to the exterior of the building.
Cleaning down interior plaster and limewashing.
Installation of electric light. Welding and rehanging bell in tower.

24. Report on the condition of Blythburgh church by William Weir, July 1947

[*William Weir's draft*]
Letchworth, Herts. July 1947.

The Parish Church of Blythburgh, Suffolk.
Report on the condition and repair of the building.
   North aisle. The N.W. angle buttress is in need of repointing to the offsets where wet penetrates through the wall. The \offsets of the/ other buttresses should be examined and repointed, including those of [*the*] south aisle. The old plaster facing on \lower portions of/ [*the*] west and north walls of [*the*] tower is perished and wet penetrates. It should be removed and the walls repointed \with cement gauged mortar flush with the surface./ The heads of rainwater pipes \of aisles/ get choked with rubbish from the gutters. They should be protected with wire balloons fixed into the top of the pipes and the heads and gutters cleaned out at intervals.
   The coping of [*the*] parapet at [*the*] east end of [*the*] chancel roof is broken at its projection and should be repaired. A portion of the string course under [*the*] parapet at [*the*] east end of [*the*] south aisle is broken away, and should be renewed.
   Roof of nave. A portion of the lead covering, about 70 [*feet*] in length, midway in the roof retains the old lead. It was not recast when <the lead> \the other portion/ was recast in 1935. The lead is not in very bad condition but should be recast and the timbers repaired as necessary, in course of time.
   Tower. The coping and string course of [*the*] parapet is in need of repair and repointing in several places. The lightning conductor should have a terminal point provided, and its earth contact examined. It is proposed to add five bells <underneath> to the existing bell, \to be hung underneath/ and rung from the ground floor, at present used for the storage of coke. A space underneath the ladder against the south wall can be partitioned off for the coke leaving sufficient room for <the> ringing. The floor is of concrete <covered over a portion> \partly covered/ with boards in bad repair. The boards should be removed and a screed of cement mortar put over the concrete and covered with bituminous mastic and boarding.
   Nave arcade. A large patch of plaster has fallen <from above> \away at/ the 6th window of [*the*] clerestory from the west end, and needs renewing. Close against this

---

[39] BCP 28.4.2.

the wall is badly stained by wet that had penetrated through the roof. The stain needs removing and the limewash touching up.

[*signed*]   W[*illiam*] W[*eir*]

\If desired a/ <A> chapel could be arranged at \the/ east end of north aisle, <if desired and furnished with suitable> with suitable furnishings and chairs.

[*signed*]   W[*illiam*] W[*eir*]

Copy sent to vicar, 26 July 1947[40]

25. Report on the condition of Blythburgh Church, unsigned and undated[41]

To: The Vicar and Churchwardens,
of Holy Trinity, Blythburgh.
Having inspected the church on the 8th July I beg to report on its condition. I would mention that in making my survey and report, I have been greatly assisted by access to records dating back to 1881, in the possession of the S.P.A.B. These contain original drawings and specifications by A. Street of 1881–1883; reports by Wm. Morris and Thackeray Turner, and also by Wm. Weir who saw various works in progress from 1905 onwards, even though he was not Architect to the church until about 1926.
  The roofs are of lead.
  The building was extensively repaired and reconditioned by Mr A. Street and on his death by Mr A. Blomfield between 1881–4.[42] At this time the aisle roofs were re-constructed and the windows largely renewed. A list of the works described in Mr Street's specification is attached in Appendix 1.[43]
  The two westernmost bays of the nave roof were reconstructed in 1782. The remaining four bays of the nave roof, and also the roof of the south porch were repaired in 1906. At this time, the top of the south turret stair was rebuilt, and the east and west walls were underpinned, and generally repaired as the porch had pulled away from the church.
  In 1935, under the direction of Mr Weir, the south porch vault was rebuilt; this having fallen some long time previously, no doubt due to the movement of the porch. At the same time the chancel roof was strengthened and the leadwork repaired or renewed as described later.
Detailed description of the condition of the Fabric.
Exterior. Roofs.
  The leadwork of the north and south aisles was re-cast and re-laid with hollow rolls in 1933 under the direction of the late Mr Wm. Weir. The four western bays of the main roof were re-cast and re-laid in 1935 and the leads over the chancel re-laid

---

[40] The letter received by the vicar is dated 25 July 1947. The report sent refers incorrectly to the arrangement of a chapel at the west end of the north aisle. Blythburgh church papers.

[41] The reference to the late William Weir dates this document after 1950. Although incomplete, this typewritten report is useful as a review of restoration work, and demonstrates the importance of the SPAB archive to architects concerned with Blythburgh.

[42] The writer confuses George Street, who died in 1881 after preparing proposals for Blythburgh, with his son Arthur, who supervised the work.

[43] The appendix is not in the file.

(without re-casting) about the same time. The centre section of the roof was re-laid after the repairs to the roof timbers in 1906, when this section was raised above the general level to accommodate strengthening members fixed about the original timbers. The work done in 1933 and 1935 is still satisfactory, but the lead which has not been re-cast should be done in the near future. The few splits which exist in this old lead, and the defective pointing to the flashings in two bays on the south side of the main roof, should be attended to at once.

Interior. Roofs.

Unfortunately, the ladders available at the time of my survey were not long enough to reach up to the main roof timbers, but I was able to make a general examination from the top of the ladders and with the aid of a pair of field glasses. The four east-ernmost bays of the nave roof repaired in 1906 were strengthened by the addition of pieces of oak on top, bolted through. Mr Weir reported at the time that he had seen the work (for which he was not the architect) and considered that some of the joints had not been made carefully enough, and that the ends of the beams had been built into the walls without leaving sufficient space for ventilation. However, he reported again in 1926 that the roof was sound. The chancel roof beams were strengthened by Mr Weir, by the addition of steel members, in 1935.

So far as I could ascertain, the roof timbers generally are now sound, though I could not examine the ends of the beams where they rest in the walls, to ensure that no decay or active beetle attack is taking place. The south wall post of the first truss in the nave (next the chancel) is worm eaten and rather soft, but I could not get close enough to see whether this was an old condition (as is very likely) or not. Before long it will be necessary to strip the lead [*the rest of the document is not in the file*].

APPENDIX B

APPEALS AND DONATIONS[1]

I. PRINTED APPEALS

1. Restoration fund appeal leaflet, August 1882[2]

BLYTHBURGH CHURCH RESTORATION

In answer to some enquiries, the late Mr. Street, R.A., wrote October 13th, 1881 – 'I should be only too glad to have any hand in rescuing so singularly interesting a church from further decay and ultimate ruin.'

Mr. Street was engaged up to the time of his illness and death in preparing a report and estimates, which have been completed by his son, and the Committee now urgently appeal to all lovers of the grand and beautiful in architecture to help them in raising funds for the preservation of this noble edifice from the ruin which is imminent.

Contributions may be given to the Chancel Fund, or to the Church Fund as distinct from the chancel, but where neither is specified all sums received will be placed to the General Fund, which will be divided in the proportion of two-thirds to the Church and one-third to the Chancel Fund.

£4,865 is required, and towards this sum the following subscriptions etc. have already been received or promised:-

	£	s.	d.
Sir John Blois	100	0	0
Concert in London	54	6	6
Rev. E. Hollond	50	0	0
Churchwardens' Fund	42	0	0
The Hon. Mrs. H. Brodrick	25	0	0
Mrs. F. Gaussen	25	0	0
Rev. H. Sykes, vicar	25	0	0
The Hon. and Right Rev. the Lord Bishop of Norwich for roof (Church Fund)	20	0	0
Concert at Yoxford	18	10	0
Sir William Rose	15	0	0
Mrs. Cooper	15	0	0
Robinson Briggs, Esq.	15	0	0

---

[1] See Introduction pp. xxxviii–xli for a discussion of the source of donations and the rate of donation over time. Persons appearing only in subscription lists are generally not referenced. For others see Appendix D, 'Notes on People'.

[2] SROI 2, 2.

Lady Huntingfield	10	0	0
Collected in church and church box	8	6	0
Miss Gaussen, collected by	6	2	6
Mrs. Braithwaite	6	0	0
Right Rev. the Lord Bishop of Sodor and Man	5	5	0
Mrs. Cape	5	5	0
The Ven. Archdeacon Broome for S. aisle roof, (Church Fund)	5	0	0
Dowager Lady Huntingfield	5	0	0
Mrs. Savill Onley	5	0	0
Miss Tatlock	5	0	0
Mrs R. Trevor Still	5	0	0
Mrs. Attoe, collected by	5	0	0
C.H. Bousfield, Esq.	5	0	0
D.B. Chapman, Esq.	5	0	0
Miss Gaussen	5	0	0
Miss Wollage	5	0	0
Mrs. J.G. Cooper	5	0	0
Miss H. Stanford	5	0	0
Miss A. Stanford	5	0	0
Lady Blois' children, collected by	4	14	0
The Hon. Mrs. H. Brodrick, collected by	4	7	6
Mrs. Blois, collected by	3	11	0
Mrs. Hatcher, collected by	3	9	6
Mrs. Cooper, collected by	3	8	0
Entertainments in School	3	0	0
Miss C. Cooper	2	10	0
Miss E. Cooper	2	10	0
Mrs. Youngs, collected by	2	5	0
Lady Brassey	2	2	0
W. Longman, Esq.	2	2	0
H.S.R. Stanford, Esq.	2	2	0
N.W. Lavers, Esq.	2	2	0
H.J. Debney, Esq.	2	2	0
Mrs. R. Blois	2	0	0
Mrs. Unthank	2	0	0
F.E. Babington, Esq.	2	0	0
Anonymous, per Mrs. Cooper	2	0	0
Miss Sainty, collected by	1	16	0
Mrs. J. and E. Garrod, collected by	1	11	6
Mrs. A.E. Baker. (Canada) collected by	1	5	0
Miss C. Barmby, collected by	1	2	0
Rev. C.H. Lacon	1	1	0
Rev. H. Bartram	1	1	0
Mrs. Robert Flick	1	1	0
E.H. Barker, Esq.	1	1	0
W.G. Ling, Esq.	1	1	0
Mrs. E. Macnaghten	1	0	0
Mrs. Dobree	1	0	0

Mrs. Gwillym	1	0	0
Mrs. R. Barclay	1	0	0
J. Hewitt, Esq.	1	0	0
W.H. Pars, Esq., U.S.	1	0	0
Mr. R. Prance	1	0	0
Miss C. Bickers, collected by	1	0	0
Miss Ling, collected by	0	19	0
Miss Goodram, collected by	0	17	0
Mrs. Braithwaite, collected by	0	15	0
Mr. E. Cooper, collected by	0	15	0
Miss M.A. Hatcher, collected by	0	14	2
Mr. George Mills, collected by	0	13	0
Miss Palmer, Morewood	0	12	0
Miss Cooper, collected by	0	12	0
Miss Emily Smith, collected by	0	12	0
Mrs. Briggs, collected by	0	10	6
Mr. S.S. Higham	0	10	6
Mrs. S.S. Higham	0	10	6
Miss Strickland	0	10	0
Mrs. Heran, collected by	0	10	0
Mrs. A.D. Chapman	0	10	0
Miss Chapman	0	10	0
Miss Dodd	0	10	0
Miss Grace Turner	0	10	0
Mr. Richard Flick	0	10	0
Mrs. Mickle	0	10	0
Mr. A.A. Baker	0	10	0
Mrs. A.E. Baker	0	10	0
Miss Elizabeth Elliot	0	10	0
Mr. George Elliott	0	10	0
Miss. C. Elliot	0	10	0
Messrs. Roe and Hall	0	10	0
Mrs. H. Athill	0	10	0
Mr. James Fryett	0	10	0
Mrs. Prance	0	10	0
Miss Elizabeth Adams, collected by	0	9	0
	£594	19	2

Subscriptions will be gratefully received by Lady Blois, Cockfield Hall, Yoxford; the Rev. H. Sykes, vicar, Walberswick, Southwold; R. Briggs, Esq., Bulcamp, Wangford; and Charles Youngs, Esq., Hinton Hall, Saxmundham, churchwardens; also by Messrs. Gurney and Co., Norwich, Yarmouth and Lowestoft.

Collecting cards may be had on application to the Vicar.

2. Appeal leaflet, 15 August 1882[3]

[p.1, An illustration of Blythburgh Church, seen from the south-east]

[p.2] The Parish Church of Blythburgh is one of the most noble ecclesiastical fabrics in the county of Suffolk; the unity of its design, the extent of its dimensions, and the exact symmetry of its parts, being alike remarkable. It was originally raised under the auspices of the Prior and Brethren of the adjoining Convent, by one of whom the plan of the building is supposed to have been drawn. It comprises a nave, chancel, two aisles, and a south porch, together with a square tower at the western end, of inferior proportions, and, most probably, of anterior date. The style of the architecture, and the bequests towards its erection, contained in many ancient wills, prove that it was founded in the middle of the fifteenth century. The interior was richly furnished in ancient days, many images of saints having formed part of its decoration. The octagonal font was raised by John and Katherine Masin, and its *Arca Domini*, or poor-box, of the same age as the church, is one of the most interesting illustrations of the harmony of design between the general structure and its minor parts. The reading-desk, of carved oak, is one of the finest in any parish church in the kingdom. The iconoclasts did much injury to the church in 1643–4, the journal of William Dowsing recording that his deputy, who visited the church, took down twenty superstitious pictures and twenty cherubims; and he adds, 'I brake down three 'orate pro animabus,' and gave order to take down about 200 pictures within eight days.'[4] The fine stalls in the Hopton chantry escaped this havoc, but have been injured in more recent days by the use of the chantry as a parish school.

'The roof of the nave, which is of oak, was originally painted and gilded with monograms and figures of angels. At the east end of the chancel is a well-executed crowned figure in stone, intended to represent the Trinity. The records of the church are very interesting, and an inventory, made in 1547, shows that the church possessed many sets of eucharist vestments and copes, which were sold after the Reformation, the prices obtained being also recorded by the churchwardens. In the ancient Saxon church which occupied the site of the present building were interred the remains of Anna, king of the East Angles, who was killed in 654. His bones were subsequently removed to Bury.'

Church Bells, May 8, 1880.

'Few ecclesiastical structures in this kingdom possess a juster claim to unqualified admiration than Blythburgh Church. Unless a speedy and thorough restoration be here effected, this stately fabric must shortly sink into irretrievable ruin.'

Extract from *History and Antiquities of Suffolk*, Rev. A. Suckling. [5]

'It is painful to Christian eyes to see this venerable and beautiful temple so wasted by the encroachments of time and weather. Efforts to save this beautiful edifice are now being made, and if these pious endeavours are seconded, as indeed they ought to be, it may be preserved.'

Extract from *Blythburgh Church*, by Jane Margaret Strickland.

'In answer to some inquiries, the late Mr. Street, R.A., wrote, October 13th, 1881:

---

3 Brooke. This is a more elaborate version of document I.1, Restoration fund appeal leaflet, August 1882.
4 Cooper, pp. 299–300.
5 Suckling, p. 150.

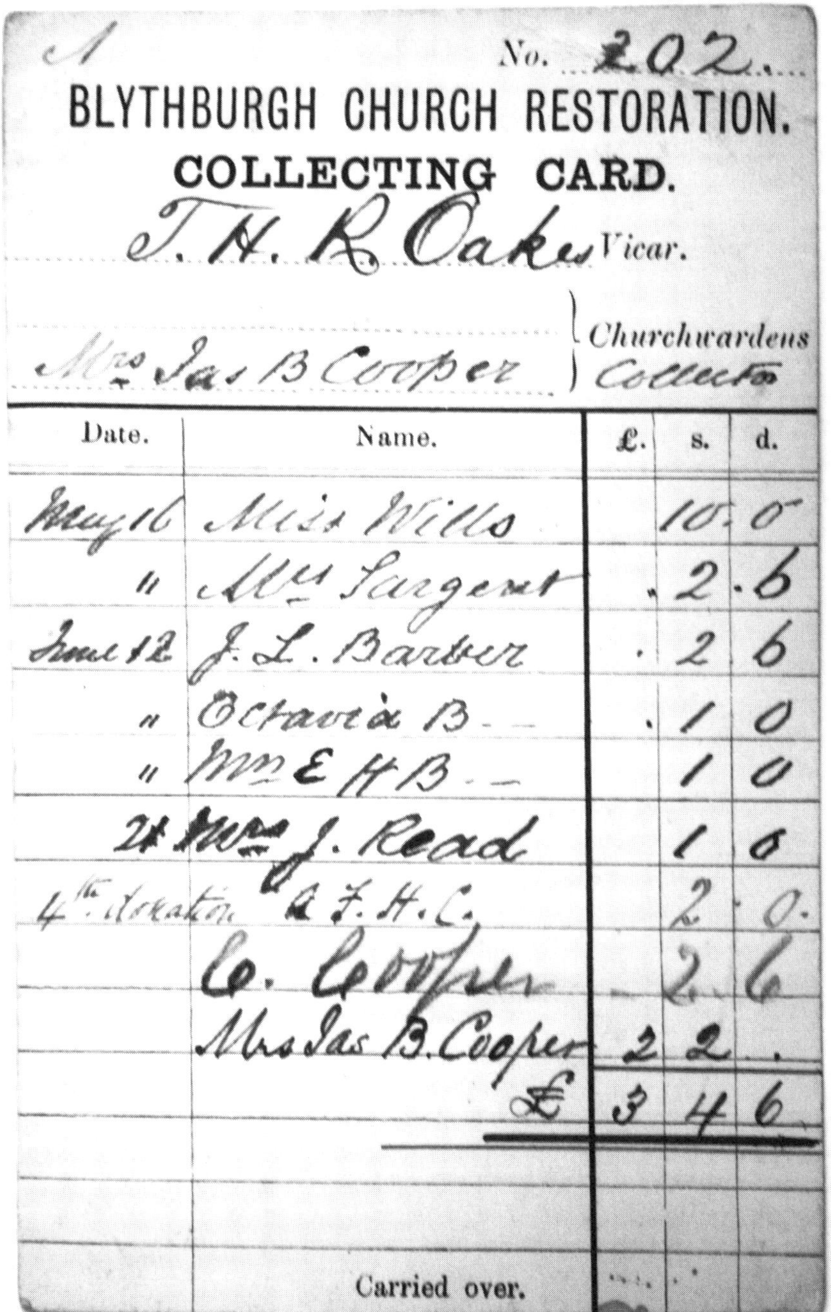

1

		No. *202*

BLYTHBURGH CHURCH RESTORATION.
COLLECTING CARD.

T. H. R. Oakes Vicar.

Mrs Jas B Cooper } Churchwardens
} Collector

Date.	Name.	£.	s.	d.
May 16	Miss Wills		10	0
"	Mrs Sargent		2	6
June 12	J. L. Barber		2	6
"	Octavia B. —		1	0
"	Mm E H B. —		1	0
21	Mrs J. Read		1	0
4th donation	& F. H. C.		2	0
	Co. Cooper		2	6
	Mrs Jas B. Cooper	2	2	
	£	3	4	6
	Carried over.			

Plate 14. The printing of cards for the collection of small sums was agreed by the restoration committee at its first meeting in October 1881. This example dates from the incumbency of the Revd T.H.R. Oakes, 1888–96. © SROI, FC185 E3 2 pt1

215

– 'I should be only too glad to have any hand in rescuing so singularly interesting a church from further decay and ultimate ruin.'

Mr. Street was engaged up to the time of his illness and death in preparing a report and estimates, which have been completed by his son, and the Committee now urgently appeal to all lovers of the grand and beautiful in architecture to help them in raising funds for the preservation of this noble edifice from the ruin which is imminent.

[*p.3*] The plans and specifications for the repair of the S. aisle roof have been prepared by Mr. Street, and tenders are to be sent in Sept. 4th; estimated cost, 600*l*. The next portion will be the N. aisle roof, and then those windows which are considered to be in a dangerous condition. The probable cost of these will be about 1800*l*. Other portions will be commenced as funds come in.

The Church has been closed, with the Bishop's permission, for eight months, and cannot be opened for the Sunday Services till the roof and windows have been secured.

The total sum required to preserve the building, and render it fit for Divine Service, is estimated by the Architect, A.E. Street, Esq., at 4865*l*.

A Bazaar was held at Blythburgh on the 9th and 10th August, under the immediate patronage of –

THE COUNTESS OF STRADBROKE.
THE LADY CONSTANCE BARNE.
THE LADY HUNTINGFIELD.
THE HON. MRS. MORTON NORTH.
THE HON. MRS. HENRY BRODRICK.
THE HON. MISSES THELLUSSON.
LADY BLOIS.
LADY KNIGHTLEY.
MRS. BLOIS.
MRS. FREDERICK GAUSSEN.
MRS. SYKES.
MRS. COOPER.
[*names printed in three columns*]

Which realised over 200*l*., and the following sums have been given or promised, viz.:-[6]

Contributions may be given to the Chancel Fund, or to the Church Fund as distinct from the Chancel, but where neither is specified all sums received will be placed to the General Fund, which will be divided in the proportion of two-thirds to the Church and one-third to the Chancel Fund.

Subscriptions will be gratefully received by Lady Blois, Cockfield Hall, Yoxford; the Rev. H. Sykes, vicar, Walberswick, Southwold; R. Briggs, Esq., Bulcamp, Wangford; and Charles Youngs, Esq., Hinton Hall, Saxmundham, churchwardens; also by Messrs. Gurney and Co., Norwich, Yarmouth, and Lowestoft.

---

6   The list of contributions is repeated from document I.1 above but individual contributions below £5 are grouped together as 'Sums under 5*l*. each', equalling £75 18s. 4¾d. The final total is £596 13s. 4¾d., but this appears to be £10 too high. Sums under 5*l*. and the total have been crossed out.

COLLECTING CARDS may be had on Application to the Vicar.

[*Signed*] H. SYKES, VICAR.
WALBERSWICK, August 15th, 1882.

3. Addition to appeal leaflet and list of subscriptions, 19 December 1882[7]

ADDENDA. – The *Chancel* in the accompanying circular is to be understood as including two bays of the N. and S. aisles, *i.e.* all of the Church E. of the screens and equals one-third of the entire building.[8]

Tenders have been received for the S. aisle roof and for the restoration of all the windows, except those which are entirely bricked up. The cost of this portion will be £1,049 10s. 0d.

As soon as this amount has been raised the contracts will be signed and the work of restoration proceeded with.

Walberswick, Dec. 19*th*, 1882.   H. SYKES.

ADDITIONAL SUBSCRIPTIONS, ETC.[9]

[*printed in two columns in original*]

	£	s.	d.
Amount brought forward [*total donations above £5*]	510	15	0
Proceeds of Bazaar	211	14	2
James Harvey, Esq	10	10	0
Rev. G.I. Davies, R.D.	10	0	0
B.A. Wilcox, Esq	5	5	0
Rev. Canon H. Howell	5	0	0
Rev. S.B. Turner	5	0	0
Rev. T.D. Turner	5	0	0
Rev. E.J. Moor, R.D.	5	0	0
Rev. J.N.F. Ewen, (Ch. Fund)	5	0	0
F. Cross, Esq.	5	0	0
T. Percy Borrett, Esq.	5	0	0
E.G., per Lady Blois	5	0	0
[*Smaller donations brought forward and listed individually*]	78	9	8
Mrs. Hatcher, collected by	4	10	0
Rev. A.S. Ormerod (Ch. Fund)	4	0	0
Mrs. Braithwaite, collected by	3	6	9
Rev. J.B. Pelham	3	3	0
″ George Hamilton	3	3	0

---

[7] Brooke.

[8] See RCMB 23–4. The patron, Sir John Blois, questioned whether the two aisles were part of the chancel for which he was responsible.

[9] The £510 15s. 0d. brought forward is the sum of earlier contributions above £5 in doc. 1.1, 'Printed appeal, 1, "Restoration fund appeal leaflet, August 1882"'. Smaller earlier donations under £5 were listed individually but are not repeated here. £3 9s. 6d. collected by Mrs Hatcher in the earlier list is now shown as £4 10s. 0d. Revd Bartram's donation has increased from £1 1s. 0d. to £2 2s. 0d. Nine shillings collected by Miss Adams are not shown again. There are some differences in the spelling of names.

Miss Cross	3	0	0
Mrs. John Crowfoot	2	2	0
Rev. E. Bartrum	2	2	0
" P.L. Cautley (Ch. Fund)	2	2	0
" R. Gathorne	2	2	0
" J. Lancaster	2	2	0
W. T. Bensly, Esq., L.L.D.	2	2	0
Anonymous, per Lady Blois	2	2	0
Collected in Church Box	1	13	0
Rev. John Thorp	1	1	0
" J.J. Raven, D.D.	1	1	0
" J.H. White	1	1	0
" W.H. Sewell	1	1	0
" T. Chambers, D.D.	1	1	0
Mrs. A. Crampin	1	1	0
A.J. Harvey, Esq, M.A.	1	1	0
Jas. Garrould, Esq	1	1	0
J Turner, Esq	1	1	0
Lady Constance Barne	1	0	0
Mrs. F. Farrer	1	0	0
Rev. W. Blyth	1	0	0
" G. Watson	1	0	0
Mr. C.A. Bickers, collected by	1	0	0
Miss E. Smith ditto		17	0
Rev. A.G. Adamson ditto		13	0
A.H. Aldous, Esq.		10	6
Rev. J.R. Turnock		10	6
" R.H. King		10	0
Thos. Reid, Esq., London		10	0
Mrs. Godfrey		10	0
Railway Box		10	0
Small sums	2	19	9
Total	£926	3	4

/Additional[10]

Amount brought over	926	3	4
Lord Rendlesham	5	0	0
Rev. R.W. Kennion	2	2	0
Miss Stone	2	0	0
Ven. Archdeacon Blakelock	1	0	0
Rev. Canon Hankinson	1	0	0
" H.T. Deacle	1	0	0
Leut. Colonel St. John Barne	1	0	0
Miss M.E. Thorp, collected by	1	1	0
Rev. F. Hildyard		10	0
A Friend		3	0

---

[10] These additional subscriptions were entered by hand.

218

A Card	2	0
Total 15 February 1883.	£941 1	4 /

4. Draft of notice. Bazaar, 7–8 August 1890[11]

/1890. <u>Miss Blois</u>. 6th July/

<u>Blythburgh Church Restoration</u>.

A Grand Bazaar in aid of the above fund under the patronage of

The Countess of Stradbroke
The Lady Huntingfield
The Lady Constance Barne
The Honourable Lady Rose
Dowager Lady Crossley
Lady Blois
Miss Clara Blois
Mrs Price
Mrs Brooke
Mrs Parry Crooke
Mrs Lomax
Mrs Oakes
Mrs Gaussen
Mrs Bence Lambert
Mrs Hollond
Mrs Cautley
Mrs Roberts
will be held in

on Thursday and Friday 7th and 8th August, 1890.

<Admission – Thursday 1s. after 6 – 3d. Friday>
Admission 1s. after 6. 3d.

5. Appeal for funds, 1905[12]

[*p.1*]   Concerning Blythburgh Church
One of the Finest Specimens of Gothic Architecture in the County falling to pieces
for want of £3,000.

[*Sketch of Blythburgh church by Ernest Crofts, R.A. 'BLYTHBURGH CHURCH.
BUILT A.D. 1460.'*]

RESTORATION COMMITTEE

Patroness: H.R.H. THE PRINCESS LOUISE, DUCHESS OF ARGYLL
The Bishop of Norwich

---

[11] SROI 2, 1.
[12] BCP Blue Scrap Book, p. 43. 1.

The Archdeacon of Suffolk
Rev. Canon Raven, R.D.
The Vicar of Blythburgh
Lady Blois
Mrs. Seymour Lucas
Mrs. Egerton
Mrs. Hamilton
Sir Ralph Blois, Bart., Lord of the Manor
Sir Caspar Purdon Clarke, G.S.I., F.S.A.
Sir Augustus Helder, M.P.
E. Crofts, Esq., R.A., F.S.A.
Luke Fildes, R.A.
C.F. Egerton, Esq.
J. Seymour Lucas, Esq., R.A., F.S.A.
Carmichael Thomas, Esq.
Norman Graham, Esq.
Hon. Secretary: Sir Ralph Blois, Bart.
Cockfield Hall, Yoxford, Suffolk.
Hon. Treasurer: C.F. Egerton, Esq.
Bulcamp, Wangford, Suffolk.

[*p.2*] The ARCHDEACON OF SUFFOLK has visited this Church and has reported
as follows:
BLYTHBURGH CHURCH, Date 1460. Proposed work to
be carried out to preserve this interesting Building:
ROOF. – It is the intention to introduce new timber only
where it is absolutely necessary to replace principals and
rafters that are in a dangerous state. Care will be
especially taken with all coloured portions.
SOUTH PORCH. – The walls are at present shored up
and a large proportion of them must be rebuilt. The
Stone and Flint Work will be taken down and carefully
replaced in their original position.
Much of the Flint Work needs pointing outside the
fabric and some making good on the walls inside. The
present Flooring will be left untouched, and there is
no intention of introducing new seating or interfering
with the immense interest attached to the building.

Quotation from Suckling's 'Suffolk.'
Few ecclesiastical structures in this kingdom possess a juster
claim to unqualified admiration than Blythburgh Church.[13]
Quotation from 'Highways and Byways in East Anglia.'
It is a building which no one interested in Church Architecture
can afford to miss seeing.[14]
Quotation from 'Gardner's Antiquities.'

---

[13] Suckling 1848, p. 150.
[14] BCP Blue Scrap Book, p. 43.1.

The Church, both inwards and outwards, is adorned with many figures and devises, the various decorations thereof affording much speculation to the curious, do attract the admiration of the beholders.[15]

[p.3]

AN ART EXHIBITION AND FANCY FAIR
Will be held with the object of
Raising £3,000 for the Preservation of Blythburgh Church
ON SATURDAY, AUGUST 5th, 1905, at
COCKFIELD HALL,
By the kind permission of Sir Ralph Blois, Bart., and Lady Blois.
/To be opened at 3 o'clock by the Marchioness of Bristol
Entrance 1/- after 5 6d/
Under the immediate Patronage of
H.R.H. THE PRINCESS LOUISE, DUCHESS OF ARGYLL,
/who has previously promised to be present/
AND
The Marchioness of Bristol
The Countess of Stradbroke
The Lady Beatrice Pretyman
The Lady Evelyn Cobbold
The Hon. Mrs. William Lowther
The Hon. Mrs. William Vanneck
The Hon. Mrs. Walter Vanneck
The Hon. Anne Vanneck
Lady Gooch
Lady Crossley
Lady Quilter
Dowager Lady Blois
Mrs. Barne
Mrs. Bence-Lambert
Mrs. Kendal Brooke
Mrs. Clarke
Mrs. Egerton
Mrs. Hollond
Mrs. Leverett Scrivener
Mrs. Long
Mrs. Milner Gibson
Mrs. Price
Mrs. Wentworth
/Mrs Parry Crooke/

[p.4]   AN ART UNION[16]
Will be held during the afternoon for which Tickets may now be obtained from

---

15   Gardner 1754, p. 122.
16   The art union was a lottery inspired by organizations established to support art and artists. The London Art Union was founded in 1837 with the encouragement of the government and had 20,000 members by 1876. Subscribers paid one guinea and received an engraving of a famous painting by an English

SIR RALPH BLOIS, COCKFIELD HALL, YOXFORD, SEYMOUR LUCAS, R.A., NEW PLACE, WOODCHURCH ROAD, WEST HAMPSTEAD.

FIRST DRAWING.
The Prize consisting of a Sketch graciously contributed by
H.R.H. THE PRINCESS LOUISE, DUCHESS OF ARGYLL
TICKETS 10/6 EACH.

SECOND DRAWING.
The Prizes consisting of Sketches contributed by the following
Eminent Artists among many others:
Luke Fildes, R.A., Seymour Lucas, R.A., Ernest Crofts, R.A.,
Sir Ernest Waterlow, R.A., David Murray, R.A., and W. Goscombe John, A.R.A.
TICKETS 5/- EACH.

Stalls will be devoted to the following objects:
Fine Arts, Millinery, Flowers and Fruit, Confectionery, Toys, Provisions,
Needlework,
Books and Publications.

It is earnestly hoped by the Committee that those who are interested in the preservation of this beautiful building will either send a donation to the Hon. Treasurer or Hon. Secretary or endeavour to dispose of tickets for the Art Union.

The following amounts have already been promised:

	£	s.	d.	
Sir Ralph and Lady Blois	50	0	0	1st Donation
C.F. Egerton Esq., and Mrs. Egerton	50	0	0	
Norman Graham, Esq.	50	0	0	
Rev. R.P. Wing	20	0	0	
Dowager Lady Blois	10	0	0	1st Donation
F.S. Stevenson, Esq., M.P.	2	10	0	
Miss Tatlock	2	10	0	
Seymour Lucas, Esq., R.A.	2	2	2	

II. NEWSPAPER CUTTINGS AND RELATED LISTS

[*From 1882 to 1884 advertisements were placed in Suffolk and Norfolk newspapers, appealing for donations and listing the contributions so far. The first list was published in the* Ipswich Journal *on 5 August 1882. Lists were then published weekly in that paper and the* Norfolk Chronicle *until 6 November 1883 when the frequency was reduced to monthly. The earliest surviving list is for 19 August 1882. The Restoration Committee decided at its meeting on 5 November 1883 to use only the* East Anglian Daily Times *but reverted to using the Norfolk and Ipswich papers from 7 January 1884. The text included with the list of 19 August 1882 was repeated in subsequent*

---

artist and the chance to win a painting in a lottery. See Joy Sperling, ' "Art, Cheap and Good." The Art Union in England and the United States, 1840–60', *Nineteenth-Century Art Worldwide* I, no. 1 (2002).

announcements. It has not been repeated below unless it changed. Unless otherwise referenced, the item is in both RCMB and SROI 2, 2. The newspaper cannot always be identified but generally the Norfolk Chronicle *cuttings are in SROI 2,2 and those from the* Ipswich Journal *in RCMB. There are sometimes small textual differences and spellings of proper names can vary.*]

1. *The Norfolk Chronicle*, **19 August 1882**[17]

BLYTHBURGH CHURCH RESTORATION

/: 'The first list of subscriptions etc. inserted Aug. 5 1882, Aug. 12 1882, Aug. 19 1882. Additional lists inserted Aug. 26 1882, Sept. 2, 9, 16, 23, Oct. 7, 14, 21, 28, Dec. 9, Jan. 13 1883, Feb. 10./

[*The newspaper reprinted the text from the appeal leaflet doc. 1.1 with an almost identical subscription list, the sum being £596 13s. 4¾d. There were additional entries for J. Turner £1 1s. 0d. and small sums £0 7s. 10½d. Collected in church and church box is now £8 11s. 4¼d. There are also spelling differences. Barber becomes Barker and Rev. H. Bartram is now E. Bartram.*]

2. *The Norfolk Chronicle*, **26 August 1882**

	£	s.	d.
Amount previously announced	596	13	4¾
Proceeds of Bazaar	211	14	2
F. Cross, Esq.	5	0	0
Miss Cross	3	0	0
E.G.	5	0	0
Rev. E. Bartrum	1	1	0
A.H. Aldous, Esq.	0	10	6
Rev. R.H. King	0	10	0
Mrs. Godfrey	0	10	0
Mrs. Hernan, collected by	0	10	0
	£824	9	0¾

3. **2 September 1882**[18]

	£	s.	d.
Amount previously announced	824	9	0¾
Rev. A.S. Ormerod, church fund	4	0	0
Thos. Reed, Esq., London	0	10	0
	£828	19	0¾

---

[17] An unannotated cutting is in SROI 2, 2. The list is almost identical with one published in the *Ipswich Journal* 5 August 1882 (SPAB 1), which has fewer names and a lower total of £595 12s. 2d.

[18] RCMB.

4. 9 September 1882

	£	s.	d.
Amount previously announced	828	19	0 ¾
Mrs. Hatcher, collected by	1	0	6
Mr. C.A. Bickers	1	0	0
Miss Elizabeth Smith, collected by	0	17	0
Collected in Church Box	0	10	6
Small Sums	0	7	6
	£832	14	6 ¾

5. The *Ipswich Journal*, 16 and 23 September 1882

	£	s.	d.
Amount previously announced	832	14	6 ¾
James Harvey, Esq., London	10	10	0
Alfred J. Harvey, Esq., M.A., Hampstead	1	1	0
W. T. Bensly, Esq., LL.D.	2	2	0
Collected in Church Box	0	11	0
Small sums	0	5	0 ¼
	£847	3	7

6. The *Norfolk Chronicle*, 30 September 1882

	£	s.	d.
Amount previously announced	847	3	7
Mrs. John Crowfoot	2	2	0
Lady Constance Barne	1	0	0
Mrs. F. Farrer	1	0	0
	£851	5	7

7. The *Ipswich* Journal, 7 October 1882

	£	s.	d.
Amount previously announced	851	5	7
Rev. G.I. Davies, Rural Dean	10	0	0
Rev. A.G. Adamson's Card	0	13	0
	£861	18	7

8. 14 October 1882[19]

	£	s.	d.
Amount previously announced	861	18	7
B.A. Wilcox, Esq.	5	5	0
Rev. S.B. Turner	5	0	0
Rev. T.D. Turner	5	0	0
Mrs. Braithwaite's Card	2	11	9
Railway Boxes	0	10	0
Church Boxes	0	11	6
Anonymous	2	2	0
	£882	18	10

9. 21 October 1882

	£	s.	d.
Amount previously announced	882	18	10
Rev. Canon Hinds Howell	5	0	0
Rev. E.J. Moor	5	0	0
Rev. Geo. Hamilton	3	3	0
Rev. P.L. Cantley	2	2	0
Anonymous	0	5	0
	£898	8	10

10. 28 October 1882

	£	s.	d.
Amount previously announced	898	8	10
Rev. J.N.I. Ewen	5	0	0
Rev. J.B. Pelham	3	3	0
Rev. Richard Gathe	2	2	0
Rev. John Thorp	1	1	0
Rev. J.J. Raven	1	1	0
Mrs. A. Crawfield	1	1	0
	£911	16	10

11. 9 December 1882

THE Committee urgently appeal for Funds to raise this noble edifice from imminent

---

[19] RCMB contains handwritten lists for 14, 21 and 28 October, 1882, and 13 January 1883, headed 'The following list is the first shortened list sent to the papers. See next column.'

ruin. Contributions towards the £4,865 required may be given to the Chancel, Church, or General Fund.

The following sums have been received or promised:-

	£	s.	d.
Amount previously announced	911	16	10
T. Percy Borrett, Esq.	5	0	0
Rev. J. Lancaster	2	2	0
Rev. I.H. White	1	1	0
Rev. W.H. Sewell	1	1	0
Rev. T. Chambers	1	1	0
James Garrould, Esq.	1	1	0
Rev. W. Blyth	1	0	0
Rev. G. Watson	1	0	0
Rev. J.R. Turnock	0	10	6
Small sums	0	10	0
	£926	3	4

12. 13 January 1883[20]

	£	s.	d.
Amount previously announced	926	3	4
Rev. R.W. Kennion	2	2	0
Ven. R. Blakelock	1	0	0
	£929	5	4

13. 10 February 1883
[*The required sum stated in the preliminary text changed*]

BLYTHBURGH CHURCH RESTORATION
The Committee urgently appeal for funds to rescue this noble edifice from imminent ruin. About £5000 will be required, towards which the following sums have been received or promised:-

	£	s.	d.
Amount previously announced	929	5	4
Lord Rendlesham, M.P.	5	0	0
Miss Stone	2	0	0
Miss M.E. Thorp, collected by	1	1	0
Lieut.-Col. Barne, M.P.	1	0	0
Rev. Canon Hankinson	1	0	0
Rev. H.T. Deacle /Ch. Fund/	1	0	0
Rev. T. Hildyard	0	10	0
A Friend	0	3	0

---

[20] Handwritten note in RCMB.

	£	s.	d.
	940	19	4

14. 10 March 1883[21]

	£	s.	d.
Amount previously announced	940	19	4
F.C. Brooke. Esq.	5	0	0
Lady Blois, Collected by	2	10	0
'Another Friend'	1	1	0
Mrs. Barne	1	0	0
Rev. F. Hildyard	0	10	0
Rev. H. Dickinson	0	5	0
Collected in Church Box	0	5	1
Small Sums	0	12	4
	£952	2	9	/ shd 952 12 0/

15. The *Ipswich Journal*, 12 May 1883[22]

THE Committee urgently appeal for funds to rescue this noble edifice from imminent ruin.

Contributions may be given to the *Chancel* fund, or to the *Church* fund as distinct from the *Chancel*; but where neither is specified all sums received will be placed to the *General* fund, which will be divided in the proportion of two-thirds to the *Church* and one-third to the *Chancel* fund. About £5,000 is required, and towards this sum the following subscriptions have already been received or promised.

	£	s.	d.	
Amount previously announced	951	12	9	/shd be 952 12 0/
S.S. Safford, Esq.	3	3	0	
Mrs. Cooper, collected by	1	12	6	
Ventriloquist Entertainment	1	1	4	
Rev. L. Price	1	0	0	
Sale of Prints	0	3	0	
	£958	12	7	/shd be 959 12 7/

16. 9 June 1883

BLYTHBURGH CHURCH RESTORATION

---

21 The total in the SROI 2, 2 copy is corrected by hand. The Revd F. Hildyard's donation has been crossed out in RCMB.

22 Corrections to totals are on the SROI 2,2 copy. RCMB copy has annotation 'Miss Hernan 10/-'

THE Committee urgently appeal for FUNDS to carry on the restoration of this truly magnificent but dilapidated Edifice.

About £5000 is required to preserve the building and render it fit for Divine Service, and towards this amount the following sums have been received or promised.

	£	s.	d.
Amount previously announced	958	12	7
'A Friend', per H.S.	2	2	0
Rev. Edward D. Stead	0	10	0
Small Sums	0	11	2 ¼
	£961	15	9 ¼

17. July 1883[23]

	£	s.	d.
Amount previously announced	961	15	9 ¼
Mrs. Cape, work sold (Church Fund)	4	4	0
Mrs. Braithwaite (Church Fund)	1	1	0
Anonymous, per H.S.	1	1	0
Mrs. Burrup	1	0	0
Mrs. Jilworth	0	10	6
Small sums	0	11	0
	£970	3	3 ¼

18. 11 August 1883

	£	s.	d.
Amount previously announced	970	3	3 ¼
C.H. Pinckard, Esq. (chancel fund)	10	10	0
G. Rennie, Esq. (chancel fund)	5	5	0
Captain Acton	1	1	0
Southwold Railway Box	0	19	0
Small sums	0	14	10 ½
	£988	13	1 ¾

---

[23] RCMB.

19. 13 October 1883[24]

BLYTHBURGH CHURCH RESTORATION

The First Contract for the restoration of this Church will be completed before Christmas; and the Committee urgently appeal for £100, to enable them to re-open it free of debt.

	£	s.	d.
Amount previously announced	988	13	1 ¾
Mrs. Braithwaite (*Chancel* Fund) 4th don.	5	0	0
Miss Wollage (*Chancel* Fund) 2nd don.	5	0	0
Arthur C. Pain, Esq. (*Chancel* Fund)	1	1	0
Mrs. Remnant	1	0	0
Mrs. Pryce Morris	1	0	0
Mrs. Hatcher, collected by	0	12	6
Blythburgh Station Box	0	12	6
Rev. H.T. Morgan	0	10	0
Rev. C. Thornton	0	10	0
Rev. H. Cobbald	0	10	0
Geo. Roberts, Esq.	0	10	0
Anonymous, per H.S.	0	10	0
Small sums	0	16	7 ½
Collected in Church Box	1	13	10
Harvest Thanksgiving	2	1	6
Interests on Deposits	11	7	11
	£1021	9	0 ¼

Subscriptions will be gratefully received by Lady Blois, Cockfield Hall, Yoxford; the Rev. H. Sykes, Walberswick, Southwold, *Vicar*; R. Briggs, Esq., Bulcamp, Wangford, and Chas. Youngs, Esq., Hinton Hall, Saxmundham, *Churchwardens*; and by Messrs. Gurneys and Co., Halesworth, Beccles, Lowestoft, Yarmouth and Norwich.

Collecting cards may be had on application to the Vicar.

20. *The Ipswich Journal*, 12 January 1884[25]

Blythburgh Church Restoration

The Committee hopes that the Church will be re-opened at Easter, and they earnestly appeal for £70 to enable them to re-open *free of debt*.

	£	s.	d.
Amount previously announced	1021	9	0 ¼
J.E. Grubbe, Esq., M.A. (Church Fund)	5	0	0

---

[24] This is the SROI 2, 2 version. In the *Ipswich Journal* text in RCMB, the church is 'magnificent' and the Braithwaite, Wollage and Pain donations are for the church, not the chancel fund. 'Cobbald' is 'Cobbold' and 'Anonymous' has been changed by hand to 'H.S.'

[25] Also Brooke.

Mrs. John Read, per Mrs. Cooper	5	0	0
Hy. Thompson, Esq., per Mrs. Cape (Church Fund)	5	0	0
A Friend, per H.S. (Church Fund) 2nd donation	2	2	0
Geo. H. Christie, Esq.	2	0	0
F.S. Waddington, Esq.	1	16	0
Edwd. P. Youell, Esq.,	1	1	0
Arthur C. Pain, Esq. (Church Fund), 2nd donation	1	1	0
Mrs. Baker	1	0	0
Rowland T. Cobbold, Esq.	1	0	0
Fishermen's Thanksgiving		13	7
Chas. Mann, Esq.		10	6
Lord Francis Hervey, M.A.		10	0
Rev. R.D. Pierpoint		10	0
Rev. R.R. Young		10	0
Mrs. Braithwaite, (Church Fund)		10	0
F. Ling, Esq.		10	0
'A Distant Friend'		3	0
Small sums	1	0	6
	£1051	6	7 ¼

Subscriptions will be gratefully received by Lady Blois, Cockfield Hall, Yoxford; the Rev. H. Sykes, Walberswick, Southwold, vicar; R. Briggs, Esq., Bulchamp, Wangford, and Cha[rle]s Youngs, Esq., Hinton Hall, Saxmundham, churchwardens; also by Messrs. Gurneys and Co., Halesworth, Beccles, Lowestoft, Yarmouth, and Norwich.

Collecting Cards may be had on application to the Vicar.

21. *The Ipswich Journal*, 29 March 1884[26]

BLYTHBURGH CHURCH RESTORATION
The First Contract is near completion, and the Committee appeal for Funds to carry forward this urgently needed Restoration.

The Church will be Re-opened for Divine Service at Easter. Particulars of Services, etc., next week.

	£	s.	d.
Amount previously announced	1051	6	7 ¼
Rev. W.N. Ripley	5	0	0
Lady Blois's children, collected by (Chancel Fund)	2	4	6
Rev. V.J. Stanton	2	0	0
Thos. Harrison, Esq.	1	1	0
Mrs. Godfrey's work (Chancel Fund)	1	0	6
C.H. Fison, Esq.	1	0	0
E.B. Fiske, Esq.	0	10	6
R.H. Gillett, Esq.	0	10	0

---

[26] RCMB has annotation 'Continued after minutes May 7. 1883'

Gooderham's Entertainment	0	11	0
	£1065	4	1 ¼

Contributions will be gratefully received by Lady Blois, Cockfield Hall, Yoxford; the Rev. H. Sykes, Walberswick, Southwold, *Vicar*; R. Briggs, Esq., Bulcamp, Wangford, and Chas. Youngs, Esq., Hinton Hall, Saxmundham, *Churchwardens*; and by Messrs. Gurney and Co., Halesworth, Beccles, Lowestoft, Yarmouth and Norwich.

Collecting cards may be had on application to the Vicar.

22. May 4 1884. Handwritten Note[27]

May 4 1884
'Explanation of Churchwarden's contribution to 'Restoration Fund'

Already advertized	42	0	0
Credited	21	0	0
	£63	0	0
Ap. 1884	13	0	5
Ap. 1883	36	6	7
Architect	10	10	0
Mr. Chilver's	3	3	0
	£63	0	0

23. 10 May 1884[28]

BLYTHBURGH CHURCH RESTORATION

This Church was Re-opened for Divine Service at Easter, but funds are still needed to carry forward this urgently needed Restoration.

	£	s.	d.
Amount previously announced	1065	4	1 ¼
Re-opening Services	30	17	0 [29]
'Diocesan Church Building Society'	25	0	0
Churchwardens (church fund), 2nd donation	21	0	0
Rev. Canon H. Howell, 2nd donation	5	0	0
Rowland T. Cobbold, Esq., 2nd donation	4	12	0
Rev. Canon Patteson	3	0	0
Chas. Lenny, Esq.	2	2	0
Miss H. Ward, collected by	1	1	0
Rev. P.L. Cautley (church fund), 2nd donation	1	1	0

---

[27] RCMB.
[28] The totals are handwritten in RCMB with the annotation for 29 June 1884.
[29] In SROI 2, 2 annotated by hand: '34 10 0'.

H.J. Debney, Esq., 3rd donation	1	1	0
Mrs. Barne	1	0	0
Mrs. Wm. Sykes	1	0	0
B. Sykes, Esq.	1	0	0
Miss Chapman	0	10	0
Small Sums	1	16	0
	£1165	4	1 ¼

Contributions will be gratefully received by Lady Blois, by the Vicar, and Churchwardens, and by Messrs, Gurney and Co. at their Banks.

/June 29/84 1201. 17. 7¼/

24. 29 November 1884[30]

This Church was re-opened for Divine Service at Easter, but funds are still needed to carry forward the work so well begun.

	£	s.	d.
Amount previously announced	1165	4	1 ¼
Dowager Lady Huntingfield, for Chancel (second donation)			
	20	0	0
Collected in Church	5	13	4
For N. Aisle and Nave Roofs –			
Ven. Archdeacon Groome, second donation	5	0	0
F.E. Babbington, Esq., second donation	2	2	0
H.J. Debney, Esq., fourth donation	2	2	0
Churchwardens (Ch. Fund)	1	2	0
Small sums	0	14	2
	£1201	17	7 ¼

III. MISCELLANEOUS

1. Example of collecting card, no date[31]

No. 202

BLYTHBURGH CHURCH RESTORATION.
COLLECTING CARD.
T.H.R. Oakes *Vicar.*

Churchwardens

---

[30] Also Brooke.
[31] SROI 1, 1. The date must be 1888 or later, but complete lists for this period have not survived.

Mrs. Jas. B. Cooper Collector

Date.	Name.	£.	s.	d.
May 16	Miss Wills		10	0
"	Mrs. Sargent		2	6
June 12	J.L. Barber		2	6
"	Octavia B.		1	0
"	Mrs. E H B		1	0
June 21	Mrs. J. Read		1	0
4th donation	A.F.H.C.		2	0
	C. Cooper		2	6
	Mrs. Jas. B. Cooper	2	2	0
		£3	4	6

carried over.

233

APPENDIX C

PRINTED NOTICES, REPORTS AND ARTICLES[1]

1. Diocesan regulations respecting faculties, May 1861[2]

REGULATIONS RESPECTING FACULTIES,
Which the Bishop of Norwich requests may be observed throughout the Diocese.

1.   In cases involving the sale of church property of value, such as lead, bells, etc., or where any questions relating to faculty and prescriptive pews are likely to arise, application should be made for a Faculty, as a protection to the Churchwardens, who might otherwise be proceeded against for illegally disposing of the property of the parish, or for interfering with private rights.

2.   So also, in cases, where there are *individual dissentients* to plans, to which the Parish in Vestry has agreed; or where the nature and extent of the works contemplated render it expedient, to secure their completion, and the protection of the Churchwardens from all after-questioning the authority of their proceedings, a Faculty should be applied for.

3.   In all other cases, where the proposed repairs and alterations have received the consent of the Vestry, duly convened for that purpose, a Notice of the same, according to a form to be procured of the Archdeacon's Registrar, should be affixed to the church-door for two consecutive Sundays. If no objection be raised, the Notice, with the plans and specifications of the proposed works, should be sent to the Archdeacon, who will forward them to the Bishop; and if the plans be approved, and it be satisfactorily shewn that a sufficient sum has been secured to ensure their completion, a Faculty will *not* be required.

Norwich, May, 1861.

2. Blythburgh glass. Articles by Hamlet Watling in the *Suffolk Chronicle*, 13 and 20 November 1875[3]

'The Fine Arts Long Ago.'
PAINTINGS ON GLASS IN SUFFOLK CHURCH WINDOWS. –
BLYTHBOROUGH: No. 3.

To enter upon the history of this fabric would be entirely out of place here; but the antiquity of it is unquestionably very great. How far it may extend anterior to the interment of King Anna and his son Firminus, who fell at the battle of Blythborough or Bullcamp, in 654, has never been handed down to us. The present beautiful

---

[1]   Persons have been referenced selectively, and details are in Appendix D.

[2]   RCMB.

[3]   Brooke.

Perpendicular pile in its palmy days must have almost defied description. The multi-plicity of its enrichments, bestowed upon it by its numerous donors, is a fact almost without a parallel in the records of ecclesiastical benevolence, exhibiting itself in the multiplicity of shields with arms scattered throughout the roof and windows. Amongst the most perfect I noticed were those of Hopton, Swillington, Crane, Rosse, Spencer, Tiptoft, Groswell, Wingfield, Barrington, Bacon, Kerdiston, Ufford, Meckilfield, Argentine, Cailey, Barett, and Scroop. A great many others made their disappear-ance during the visitation of that furious iconoclast Francis Jessop, the faithful agent of Dowsing, who visited the fabric on the 9th April, 1644. The windows and roof appear to have suffered most from his despoiling hands. How the 18 beautiful fig-ures, carved in chestnut wood, escaped his notice, is a matter of wonder. The bench ends, also, in the north aisle, representing the seven deadly sins, of which Sloth and Gluttony are as little injured as their antitypes in the world. The arca domini, lectern, and jack o' th' clock also still remain, and are fine specimens of church furniture of the days that are gone. At the present day, which has witnessed the restoration of so many fine churches throughout the kingdom, the condition of Blythborough is a wretched scandal. One of the finest fabrics in Suffolk, and connected with a place of so much historic note, and surrounded by fair and beautiful estates, stripped of its architectural ornaments, and reduced to a wretched state of squalor. The interior filled with rickety pews of the meanest wood. The windows blocked up with bricks and mortar, and besmeared with lime wash. The floor loose and unsafe to tread upon, and the whole throughout well besmeared with whitewash. Such was the condition of the place when I visited it some years since. I shall now proceed with the description of the glass that is still extant in the upper tracery of the windows.

The large subjects which filled the days [*bays?*] have long since disappeared. These were surmounted by the three arms of donors on shields, supported by three angels of exquisite work. In a window in the Hopton chantry, the gift of Sir Roger Swillington, are three bishops, the only ones left, that presided over the see at Dunwich; the others are gone. The most perfect are those of St. Felix, the first bishop of Dunwich; Boniface and Alsin. They are demi-figures. The former has a superbly decorated mitre upon his head with foliage and jewels. In his left hand he holds a crosier, and a book in the right. The collar of the chasuble is richly orna-mented, and beneath is written in old English St. Felix. His countenance is very youthful, and his snow white chasuble, studded with ornamental flowering, gives him a saintly appearance. I need add that St. Felix was the first Christian missionary in East Anglia; invited over by the good King Sigebert, he landed at Felixstowe in 630. The episcopal office, however, was not conferred upon him till some years afterwards when the truths and blessings he promulgated were extending themselves by his zeal and activity throughout the land. It is evident through the co-operation of the good King Sigebert and himself that Christianity was about to be permanently established, and that churches and monasteries were endowed, and there is much appearance of probability that this infant establishment fixed at Dunwich formed the germ whence the University of Cambridge afterwards sprouted. Felix died on the 8th of March, 647, and was interred in his own church at Dunwich. We have good authority, however, to suppose that his remains were removed, through the encroachments of the ocean, to Soham and interred in his own abbey. But in King Canute's reign they were again removed to the abbey at Ramsey, and there enshrined with splendour and his name canonised as the first saint of East Anglia. The second one on the list of survivors is Boniface, or Bosa, third bishop in succession. This prelate holds in his left hand a crozier, and a book open is held in his right. The mitre upon his head is beautifully ornamented. His consecration took place in 669. Bede informs us that when oppressed by old age and infirmities he divided his diocese into two parts, retaining that of Dunwich, which was to embrace Suffolk; the other see being at North Elmham in Norfolk, which was to extend over that county. The other that is imperfectly left is that of Alsin or Ælfun, buried at Dunwich, and the eighth in succession, the others have all disappeared – Acca or Etta, Astwolph, Edferth, Cuthwin, Alberth, Eglaf, Heardred, Tidferth, Weremund and Loybred. These, if left perfect, would have formed a truly interesting and valuable series, connected as they are with the renowned 'splendid city' of Dunwich. In the next window is glowing in rich tints the remnant of a subject, the gift of Robert Pinne, in 1457, who ordered his executors to 'glaze a window on the north side of the church next the window of St. John Baptist, and paint the same with the history of St. Anthony.' This is also in the Hopton chantry. I have been enabled to make but two copies from the filth and dirt that encrust them. The first represents the saint with a rugged staff in his right hand, with the head of one of the poor saint's cruel persecutors upon it. The beard is pointed and a turban covers the head, and a defiant scowl rests upon the countenance, whilst the saint's wears a smile. A long robe of purple covers him, and the hood is drawn tight over the head so that no hair is visible. Under his left arm he holds a closed book. The back ground is floriated. The other represents the saint holding up with his left hand the cross Tau, his usual emblem. He is also represented amongst the carved figures in the Hopton Chantry which has been mistaken for a square.[4] As St. Anthony and his emblems are truly interesting, I will give the reader a laconic sketch of the saint's life. The cross Tau crux ansata, key of the Nile, or emblem of life, as it is indifferently denominated, is frequently borne in the hands of Egyptian divinities, both male and female, by a ring attached to the transverse member. This sacred symbol was also wrought in various substances and worn as a necklace pendant, by the living subject of the Pharaohs, and also as an amulet on the breasts of their mummied corpses. The ladies in the Melford secular glass have the same ornament round their necks, which will be noticed hereafter. The Tau was aslo adopted by the Egyptians, Assyrians, Jews, Druids, Gnostics, and Knight Templars; the origin is not precisely known, but it is a curious fact the early Christians of Egypt adopted it in lieu of the cross, which was afterwards substituted for it. It is very probable that the saintly emblem and sacred crux are one and the same, and that its association with the saint was to point out that he was a native of the land of the Nile, he having been born at Coma, near Heraclea, A.D. 251. The relics of the saint were brought to Europe by the pious Joceline, and were efficacious as a cure against St. Anthony's fire and erysipelas.

I am sorry to say that the rest of the window below has been entirely destroyed. The saint there probably was represented with his other emblem – the 'pig,' with a bell hung about its neck, and a staff in his hand, etc. As I shall intrude too much upon space, in my next I will conclude this interesting series.

Guildhall, Stonham.   H. WATLING.

---

[4]   The carved stalls, later removed to the choir, were therefore still in the Hopton chapel when Watling made his observation for this 1875 article. See Correspondence 35.

'The Fine Arts Long Ago.'
ANCIENT PAINTINGS ON GLASS IN SUFFOLK CHURCH WINDOWS. No. 4.
– BLYTHBOROUGH (*continued*).

The next window which claims attention is that of St. John Baptist, as narrated in the will of Robert Pinne in 1457. Of this window only one perfect figure was left to remind us that it once existed. The remainder of the window is filled up with bricks and mortar as a substitute for the remainder of the saint's history. The copy which is now before me exhibits the saint holding with both his hands a closed book, on the cover of which is the Agnes Dei. The vest is purple, and his head surrounded with an ornamental nimbus of gold; the undergarment of camel's hair (as mentioned by St. Matthew) fastened by a leathern girdle about his loins. He stands with his feet upon a pavement of rich work. The background and canopy under which he stands are very rich in design. In a window south of the Hopton Chantry is a perfect representation of St. Andrew: in his right hand he holds his usual emblem, the cross soltire [*sic*], and in his left a closed book. His head is surrounded with a nimbus, and over his shoulders is a vest of purple, whilst the under garment is pure white studded with cinquefoil flowers of gold. The next figure to the last mentioned is that of St. Abercius, B.C., who destroyed the statue of Apollo. He is holding in his left hand the crosier brought to him by an angel from heaven; it is exquisitely wrought in foliated work and covered with pearls and gems. On his head is a superbly worked mitre of the same character. He is standing beneath a canopy of chaste work. Over the white alb is a vest of green. This beautiful figure undoubtedly escaped the hands of the dispoiler as well as the purloiner by being thickly encrusted with dirt and whitewash, which had to be removed before a copy could be made. Next in succession is the effigy of St. Bartholomew. The canopy of this figure is entirely destroyed, but the figure is in a perfect state. He is represented with a large flaying knife in his right hand, and under his left arm a book of the gospels. He is clad in a purple vest, with white under garment. In the tracery above this figure is St. Pancras or Pancratius, a youth with a stone held on his right arm and a palm branch in the left, the emblem of martyrdom. He was a Roman boy of noble family, who was martyred under Diocletian at the age of 14, and was thus regarded as the patron saint of children. St. Augustin dedicated his first church to this infant martyr after his arrival in England. The next figure which I shall notice is that of St. Blase, bishop martyr of the fourth century. This exquisite figure is holding in his left hand a wool comb, and in the other a crosier of exquisite design. Over the white tunicle and alb is a chasuble of crimson. On his head is a mitre richly set with pearls and gems, and surrounded with a nimbus of gold.

In the centre widow of the south aisle is a very perfect representation of St. Etheldreda, daughter of King Anna, who was slain at the battle of Baldcamp [*sic*] or Blythborough, as before narrated. This saint claims particular attention, seeing she was the foundress of Ely Cathedral. A few remarks, therefore, will be interesting to the reader. Her father was the son of Eni, who had a brother named Redwold, the Bretwalda. Her pious parent erected a stately monastery at Burgh Castle, near Great Yarmouth, then called Cnobhersburg (i.e. Cnober's town). Anna had four daughters, whose pure and holy lives gained for them an undying renown, viz., St. Sexburga, wife of Earcombert, King of Kent; St. Ethelberga, abbess of Brie in France; St. Withburga, the foundress of the nunnery of East Dereham, in Norfolk; and St. Etheldreda, the subject of our inquiry, the wife of Egrid, King of Northumbria. These ladies had a uterine sister, Sethird, also a saint, and abbess of Brie. Etheldreda was born at Exning, on the western boarders [*sic*] of Suffolk, circa 630. In the year 660 she espoused Egfrid of Northumbria, and twelve years, i.e. in 672, she severed herself from her royal partner, and entered on a pure religious life in the Abbey of Coluai or Coldingham, in Berkshire. Egfrid regretted the loss of so beloved a wife and sought her, without effect, as she fled to Ely, and there founded a religious house over which she presided as abbess. A curious legend is attached to her whilst on the road from the north. She lay down to sleep, planted her staff in the earth, and when she awoke she found it had grown into a vigorous tree. This incidence may be seen on the columns of Ely Cathedral. She is also represented sometimes holding a budding staff. This virgin Queen died of a swelling on the neck June 23, A.D. 679. It is reported by her historians that this disorder greatly delighted her, as she said that when a child she bore there the needless weight of jewels, and which she attributed to the divine goodness. She was interred in a wooden coffin, but her sister Sexberga sixteen years after had her exhumed, and the linen cloth which enveloped the body was found perfect and clean, and by the touch of which the devils were expelled and divers diseases cured. In the process of time her name got corrupted to Audery and Audry, and from this sprang the word 'Tawdry' as applied to showy articles of small value. Ely Cathedral, with St. Peter, is dedicated to her, and six churches in England. Much more might be mentioned of her, but space will not allow it. In the same window is the representation of St. Helen, Empress, A.D. 328, holding on her left arm a large cross and crowned. Next to her is St. Mary Magdalene, penitent, standing covered, with her hair flowing to the ground. The next perfect figure is St. Gabriel, archangel, clad in armour with sceptre and shield, and diapered back ground of purple. In another window is St. Jude, or Thaddeus, apostle. On his left arm he supports a ship without sails. The vest is pure white, over a garment of rose pink, and the head surrounded with a nimbus. The next figure delineated is that of St. Pantœnus, father of the church, A.D. 215, in the act of delivering an address or lecture. On his head is a tight cap of crimson, his vest white, over a dress of rose tint.

In the west window, north aisle, was painted in glowing colours most of the kings of East Anglia, but now entirely stripped of its glass and filled up with bricks and cement. The only fragment that has been saved to remind us of this assertion is a copy taken many years since by an antiquary in the neighbourhood. It is no other than the Mercian King Offa, who is said to have been the immediate predecessor of King Edmund. The story goes that Offa, having no issue, resolved to make a pilgrimage to Jerusalem to supplicate the blessing of an heir, and on his way thither paid a visit to his kinsman Alkmund, King of Saxony, whose Queen, Siware, had in the year 841 given birth to a boy, who in after time became renowned as St. Edmund. Offa on his road homeward was seized with a mortal illness, but before his death he nominated young Edmund as his successor to the throne of East Anglia. He is here represented crowned with a Saxon crown and a sceptre in his right hand. A tippet of ermine covers his shoulders; from this descends a vest of crimson, the under garment being of purple, bordered at the base with fur. He stands upon a pavement of a diapered and trellised pattern, and beneath is inscribed Offa, rex. The canopy is also rich in floriated work on a purple background.

Having thus described as far as I am able a few only of the sainted figures in glass in this once truly sublime fabric, I cannot quit it, without a sad feeling of regret that no care whatever has been bestowed to save them from utter ruin, and that from time to time they have disappeared without that laudable care in preserving them from destruction which our benevolent forefathers consecrated with great pains to the honour of God and His church.

The Gipping glass will form the subject of No.5.
Guildhall, Stonham.   H. WATLING.

3. Meeting of parishioners, 7 October 1881[5]

BLYTHBURGH CHURCH RESTORATION
A MEETING OF PARISHIONERS will be held in the National School-room, on
FRIDAY, OCTOBER 7TH, at 7 P.M.
As the Church belongs to the whole parish, it is hoped all will feel a deep interest
in preserving 'Our holy and our beautiful house in which our fathers praised' from
further decay, and in handing down to future generations this noble monument of the
piety of former times. Let no one say 'I am too poor.' Read 2 COR. VIII. 1 to 12v.
Remember what the Saviour said of the Widow's mite, and of another, 'She hath
done what she could.' Read also PROV. III. 9 and 10v.

Come to the meeting and encourage your Vicar and Churchwardens in this great
undertaking.
Walberswick Vicarage,
  October 4*th*, 1881.

4. Closure of Blythburgh church, *Morning Post*, 8 December 1881[6]

The parish church of Blythburgh, Norfolk, has been closed by order of the Bishop of
Norwich on account of the dangerous condition of its fine hammer-beam roof. The
church is one of the best examples of semi-Flemish 13th century architecture, but is
altogether in a very dilapidated condition.
/With Mr Kershaw's Compliments/

5. Death of G.E. Street, *Norfolk Chronicle*, 24 December 1881[7]

Mr. G. Edmund Street, R.A., the distinguished architect of the New Courts of Law,
was suddenly seized with paralysis on Thursday week, and expired on Sunday night
at his house, 14, Cavendish-place. Mr. Street was born at Woodford, Essex, in 1824,
and educated at the Collegiate School, Camberwell. His architectural studies were
begun under Mr. Owen Carter at Winchester, and completed under the late Sir George
Gilbert Scott, with whom he remained five years. He was only 57 years of age.

6. Newspaper cutting. Funeral of G.E. Street, no date[8]

FUNERAL OF THE LATE MR. G.E. STREET, R.A.
The remains of the late Mr. George Edmund Street were interred on Thursday in
Westminster Abbey. The funeral cortege included the family, assistants, and pupils of

---

5   RCMB.
6   SPAB I. The report is correct in placing Blythburgh in the diocese of Norwich and in describing the
    condition of the church as dilapidated. It is otherwise full of errors. Blythburgh is in Suffolk, not
    Norfolk; the church does not have a hammer-beam roof; and it is of the fifteenth century, with an
    earlier tower. 'Semi-Flemish' is a term used in the nineteenth and early twentieth centuries to attribute
    artistic and architectural styles in part to influences from the Netherlands.
7   RCMB.
8   RCMB. Source not identified.

the deceased; the president and council of the Royal Academy and Institute of British Architects. The pall bearers were Mr. Beresford Hope, Sir F. Leighton, Mr. Shaw-Lefevre, Mr. W.H. Gladstone, Mr. E. Freshfield, Professor Hayter Lewis, and the Bishop of Winchester. The Dean of Westminster officiated, assisted by Canons Farrar, Duckworth, Rowsell, and Barry, Rev. S. Flood Jones, precentor, &c. Among those present were Sir Phillip Cunliffe Owen; Mr. Symons, president of the Meteorological Society; the Right Hon. W.H. Smith, etc.

7. Newspaper cutting. Erection of memorial to the late G.E. Street. No date[9]

The Prince of Wales was present on Tuesday at a meeting of the committee to consider the erection of a memorial to the late Mr. G.E. Street, R.A., which was held in the new Law Courts – Mr. A. Beresford-Hope in the chair. His Royal Highness moved the first resolution, which was to the effect that the memorial should be a full-length figure of the late architect, and should be placed in the central hall of the new Law Courts; it was seconded by Sir F. Leighton, and unanimously agreed to, and Mr. Armstead, R.A., was appointed to carry out the work.

8. Formation of London committee, *Daily Telegraph*, 19 May 1882[10]

A committee has been formed in London for the preservation of the church of Blythburgh, in the eastern part of the county of Suffolk, a magnificent ecclesiastical monument now on the verge of ruin.

9. Formation of London committee, *Huddersfield Chronicle,* 19 May 1882[11]

/Cut from the 'Huddersfield Chronicle' May 19. 1882/
BLYTHBURGH CHURCH, SUFFOLK. – We are requested to state that a committee has been formed in London for the preservation of Blythburgh Church, Suffolk, which is now on the verge of ruin. The church is situate in the eastern part of the county, and is one of the finest specimens of semi-Flemish 13th century architecture in this country. The Bishop of Norwich has ordered the church to be closed, for it is no longer safe in its present state.
/The Church was closed for the Sunday services by the Bishop's permission./

10. Formation of London committee, *Morning Post,* no date[12]

BLYTHBURGH CHURCH, SUFFOLK. – A committee has been formed in London for the preservation of this church, now on the verge of ruin. The church is stated to be one of the finest specimens of semi-Flemish 13th century architecture in this country.

---

[9]   RCMB. Source not identified.
[10] Brooke.
[11] RCMB.
[12] RCMB. See Correspondence 3 and 12.

11. Report of fundraising concert, the *Ipswich Journal*, 8 July 1882[13]

BLYTHBURGH

THE CHURCH RESTORATION. – The movement set on foot to raise the necessary funds for the restoration of Blythburgh Church was materially assisted on Tuesday, when a most successful and interesting amateur concert was given at 38, Queen's Gate, London, by the kind permission of Mrs. Smith-Bosanquet, in aid of the restoration fund. The arrangements for the concert were undertaken by the Viscountess Midleton, Lady Blois, Lady Colthurst, and Mrs. Frederick Gaussen, and by special permission of Mr. D'Oyly Carte a selection of solos and choruses from 'Patience' was sung, under the able conductorship of Mr. Deacon.[14] The following programme was exquisitely rendered, and the characters from 'Patience' have seldom, if ever, been better sustained. Lady Jane, Bunthorne, and Grosvenor were simply perfect. Programme:-

PART I

| Duet (pianoforte) | 'Polonaise' | (*Rubenstein*) |

Miss Emma Cartwright and Hon. Albinia Brodrick.

| Song | 'I am the King' | (*Paul Henrion*) |

Mr Wyllys Betts.

| Song | 'Boléro Seguidille' | (*Emile Bourgeois*) |

Mdlle. D'Arbour.

| Song | 'Goodbye' (*Tosti*) | Mr. Harry Brooke. |
| Duet | 'Liebeslieder' (by desire) | |

(*Brahm*[*s*]) Misses Layton.

a 'Sarabande, A minor'   (*Hiller*)

b 'Gavotte'   (*H. C. Deacon*)

Mr. H.C. Deacon.

Lieder   (*Lassen*)   Mrs. Underdown.

PART II

Selections from 'PATIENCE'

Lady Jane	Mrs. Penrose Fitzgerald.
Patience	Miss Alice Colthurst.
Lady Saphir	Hon. Helen Brodrick.
Lady Ella	Miss Alice Gaussen.

---

[13] SPAB I. The cutting is annotated '4 August 1882', but the concert was held on Tuesday, 4 July 1882. Also in RCMB. The concert raised £54 for the restoration fund. See RCMB 21.

[14] 'Patience' was the fifth opera by Gilbert and Sullivan to be premiered by the D'Oyly Carte Opera Company. It ran at the Opera Comique from April to October 1881 and then opened the newly built Savoy Theatre in The Strand, London on 10 October 1881, where it played until 22 November 1882. The work was therefore a fashionable and popular choice for the concert.

Lady Angela	Miss Emily Hanbury.
Bunthorne	Mr. Wyllys Betts.
Grosvenor	Mr. Gumbleton.

Chorus

Hon. Misses Brodrick	Miss Evelyn Chapman.
Misses Smith-Bosanquet.	Miss Deedes.
Misses Chapman.	Miss Fleming.
Misses Cartwright.	Miss Eva Macnaughton.

At the piano:

Miss Emma Cartwright.

Miss Beatrice Cartwright.

Conductor	Mr. H.C. Deacon.

The spacious rooms were well filled by a fashionable audience. The rendering of the choruses by the well-trained choir under Mr. Deacon testified to the care with which the aesthetic opera had been prepared, and the overture of the Misses Cartwright elicited much applause. The hospitable addition of an afternoon tea was an agreeable conclusion to a most enjoyable entertainment. We understand that arrangements are in progress for providing a musical entertainment as an addition to the bazaar, which is to be held at Blythburgh in August.

12. Report of London concert, the *East Anglian Daily Times*, 10 July 1882[15]

BLYTHBURGH.

BLYTHBURGH CHURCH. – The movement set on foot to raise the necessary funds for the restoration of Blythburgh church was materially assisted on Tuesday last, when a most successful and interesting amateur concert was given at 38, Queen's Gate, London, by the kind permission of Mrs. Smith-Bosanquet, in aid of the Restoration Fund. The arrangements for the concert were undertaken by the Viscountess Midleton, Lady Blois, Lady Colthurst, and Mrs. Frederick Gaussen; and by special permission of Mr D'Oyly Carte, a selection of solos and choruses from 'Patience' was sung, under the able conductorship of Mr. Deacon. The spacious rooms were well filled by a fashionable audience. The rendering of the choruses by the well-trained choir testified to the care with which the aesthetic opera had been prepared, and the overture of the Misses Cartwright elicited much applause. The hospitable addition of afternoon tea was an agreeable conclusion to a most enjoyable entertainment.

13. Blythburgh church. Manuscript by J.M. Strickland, no date[16]

Blythburgh Church

---

[15] Brooke. This report is an edited version of the one that appeared in the *Ipswich Journal*. See document 11 above.
[16] SROI 2, 2. Quoted in the appeal leaflet dated 15 August 1882.

One of the oldest monuments of early Christianity meets the eye of the traveller on the London road on his way to the eastern coast of Suffolk. This striking object is the stately church of Blythburgh and its ruined monastic remains.

This noble temple, now alas fast hastening into decay, was founded on an earlier Saxon church – a church of the Heptarchy. Even then Christianity was not unknown to the natives of East Anglia, for it was tolerated and even outwardly professed by its sovereign Redwald, but as he retained in his temple the images of the Saxon idols and reverenced them, his baptism at the court of King Ethelbert of Kent had not made a Christian of him.

His successor Sigibert was a prince of pure faith and nobler character. He brought with him from France a pious Burgundian priest <who> who was at his request consecrated as the first bishop of East Anglia. The efforts of the missionary bishop whose seat was at Dunwich were so eminently successful that in a few years the whole people received the gospel. It was probably at this period that the Saxon church, upon which afterwards a nobler structure was founded, was erected.

The retirement of Sigibert to a Monastery was an inauspicious event for the people he governed, for Penda the heathen sovereign of Mercia, the most powerful kingdom in the Heptarchy, was determined to annex East Anglia to his dominions. He had defeated the successor of Sigibert and advanced as far as Bulcamp heath, where he was met by King Anna and his son-in-law St. Firminus.

We may imagine the anxiety of the worshippers within the church of Blythburgh during the engagement, and their grief and consternation when their beloved monarch and his saintly son-in-law were brought in to receive Christian burial. The victor, too, was near them who wasted the towns he conquered with fire and sword. To avert this calamity Ethelric, the mother of their late sovereign, entered into treaty with Penda, who consented to give the East Anglians peace upon payment of a large sum of money and receiving the new king's assistance in his wars.

We know little of Blythburgh church till the Black Canons received Henry first's grant to found a monastery and church, probably upon the previous edifice, but whether the former Saxon one had fallen into ruin or had been destroyed by the Danes we know not, as the grant from Henry 1st is the only mention of Blythburgh or its church from the time of the lost battle of Bulcamp – 'Tradition is the memory of the people' is the able remark of a celebrated French writer and tradition – oral tradition still links the ancient Saxon church with the present magnificent one by pointing to the tombs from which the remains of King Anna and St. Firminus were taken to be reinterred with suitable pomp in the abbey church of Bury.

The steeple was formerly crowned with a spire, which must have made a useful sea-mark to the home returning East Anglian fishermen. This was destroyed by lightning during an awful storm which shattered the steeple, threw down twenty people and struck dead two persons in its descent. This calamity occurred during divine service upon the fourth of August 1577. The fire that soon afterwards consumed the greater part of the town prevented the inhabitants from doing anything to keep up their church, which with its monastery had lost its endowments, its fisheries, and former importance.

The monks were not the indolent and useless persons they have too often been styled. They brought civilization, agriculture and learning to ignorant people. They built churches, founded schools, drained marshes and were the earliest missionaries. We will not speak of the errors of their creed, which mainly originated from the scarcity of the scriptures in a language understood by the people.

But the records of Blythburgh are not always of such a tragical nature as those we have narrated, for the antiquary who is curious respecting the costume of the medieval ages will find on the leads of the church the pattern of various shoes <such as> very unlike those of our own age. Shoes such as men of Suffolk wore during several centuries – of the possession of which the wearers appear to have been proud.

Another curious relic of the olden time, before the fine <old> oak screen was covered with churchwardenly whitewash, had escaped the prying eyes of Dowsing in the shape of a box with the words pro anima surmounted by a large, ostentatiously painted red tongue surrounded with flames. This appeal to the superstitious compassion of the ancient worshippers who frequented this church may possibly be still in existence concealed under the white veil so ignorantly bestowed upon the noble oak screen, unless it has been removed by some zealous protestant as inconsistent with the pure doctrine of the complete attonement made by our Lord. We of the Anglican church look upon this relic with far different feelings from those which induced the Suffolk man or maid while regarding this emblem of purgatorial torture with superstitious compassion to drop a small coin into the little box to procure the prayers of the church for the liberation of the souls of the dead from torment.

The church contained several chapels and was profusely ornamented with painting and imagery. The windows were very beautiful and had escaped the destructive hand of Dowsing, or else he had been bribed to overlook them, for the man could indeed be induced to do so if a better sum was offered him than 'the six and eightpence so sorely' he said 'begrudged him by the parish churls.' But what he did not do, a dreadful storm effected, by driving in the beautifully stained glass windows, of which the trifling remains prove what as a whole they had been.

We need not conclude that the present church is exactly the same as that founded by the black canons. It was doubtless embellished and improved both externally and internally during succeeding generations till it presents itself to our admiring eyes as a noble specimen of the Perpendicular style.

It is painful to Christian eyes to see this venerable and beautiful temple dedicated to the Holy Trinity so desecrated by the hand of ignorant men and so wasted by the encroachments of time and weather.

Efforts to save the beautiful but crumbling edifice are now being made and if these pious endeavours are seconded, as indeed they ought to be, it may be preserved, but without such help the fine old church must share the <gate> fate of the monastery and heap its ruins upon the nameless graves.

   'Of the hushed Choir
   Who lie with their hallelujahs
     Quenched like fire.'
BY – J. M. Strickland

14. Notice of bazaar, August 1882[17]

BLYTHBURGH CHURCH RESTORATION FUND
A BAZAAR
in aid of the above fund, will be held at Blythburgh, (D.V.) in August. Contributions of work, etc. will be gratefully received by

---

[17] RCMB.

Lady BLOIS, Cockfield Hall, Yoxford.
Mrs. F. GAUSSEN, 53, Eaton Square, London.
″ COOPER, Westwood Lodge, Blythburgh.
″ BRIGGS, Bulcamp, Wangford
″ YOUNGS, Hinton Hall, Saxmundham.
    AND
″ SYKES, the Vicarage, Walberswick.

15. Arrangements for Blythburgh bazaar, the *East Anglian Daily Times*, 4 August 1882[18]

FANCY FAIR AT BLYTHBURGH.

The arrangements for the bazaar and fancy fair, to be held at Blythburgh on Wednesday and Thursday next, the 9th and 10th inst., are being made on a most extensive scale, and will doubtless attract a large number of visitors to the quaint old village. The object of the bazaar is to aid the fund for the preservation of the grand old church, and the locality chosen for holding it seems to be most fortunate, being so near the church and the railway station. It will be a first-rate opportunity for many to meet, and to see the old church and the varied objects for sale that have been so judiciously collected. There will, in addition, be all kinds of amusements provided – shows, boating, music, lawn tennis, performing hen, and the magic well, which recently created so much sensation at the Lilipution [*sic*] Fair in London. Special return tickets will be issued by the Great Eastern Railway Company at single fares, from Ipswich, Lowestoft, Yarmouth, and all stations in the neighbourhood on both days of the bazaar.

16. Report of Blythburgh bazaar, the *East Anglian Daily Times*, 11 August 1882[19]

BLYTHBURGH CHURCH RESTORATION

Wednesday was a red-letter day for the usually quiet village of Blythburgh, and from early morning its inhabitants were astir making preparations for the bazaar to be held for the benefit of the parish church, one of the largest and most beautiful specimens of ecclesiastical architecture in East Anglia. But although the antiquity of the church is such as to rouse the hearts of antiquarians into unbounded enthusiasm, its present appearance is woe-begone and sad in the extreme. The patches and brick with which it has been clumsily repaired from time to time by some Goth and Vandal hands, has most grievously marred its magnificent proportions, while the roof is in so dilapidated a condition as to render it unfit for Divine service, and the villagers who ought to worship in this – we might almost say world-famed fane [*sic*] – have been obliged to adjourn to the adjacent school-room for the Sunday and week-day services. This at last became almost a scandal, and the necessity for restoration irresistibly forced itself upon those interested in the work. Accordingly subscriptions were solicited, and it was determined also to hold a bazaar. The bazaar, which was under the distinguished patronage of the Countess of Stradbroke, Lady Constance Barne, Lady Huntingfield, Hon. Mrs. Morton North, Hon. Mrs. H. Brodrick, Hon. Misses Thellusson, Lady Blois, Lady Knightley, Mrs. Blois, Mrs. Frederic Gaussen,

---

18 Brooke.
19 Brooke.

Mrs. Sykes, and Mrs. Cooper, was held in a large tent in the meadow adjoining the White Hart Inn, kindly lent free of charge by Mr. Mills. The customary useful and fancy articles were displayed for sale at prices which might be called fairly reasonable. Immediately on entering the tent was a stall of fancy articles presided over by Lady Huntingfield, Mrs. Sykes, wife of the Vicar, being in charge of the adjoining stall. A very pretty flower stall came next, where a brisk business was done by Master Bagot-Chester and Miss Adeline Blois. A very tasteful exhibition of lingerie, etc., was made by Mrs. Cooper, who has been untiring in her efforts to make the bazaar a success; and, assisted by the Misses Stanford, she was kept busy all day in distributing the articles she had taken such pains to gather. Mrs. Gaussen and Miss Clara Blois presided over a display as varied as it was attractive, while at Lady Blois' stalls could be purchased anything, from a pincushion to an original painting. Mrs. Blois dispensed refreshments, and little Miss Gertrude Blois sold dolls that were not much smaller than herself. In addition to the main tent there were three others, to enter which a small additional fee was charged. In one of these were to be seen the mechanical toys for which Messrs. Cremer and Co., of 210, Regent Street, London, are so justly famous. At another, pigeons, canaries, pet rabbits, and birds of all kinds were to be purchased of Masters Eardley and Ralph Blois, who were also extremely proud of a three-legged duckling, which it was said had been hatched in the parish, on the premises of the worthy landlord of the White Hart Inn, and was now on view in a glass case. An extraordinary novelty was the magic well – an illustration of which was given in a recent number of the *Graphic*, when it was under the charge of the young Princesses, daughters of the Prince of Wales, at the Liliputian Bazaar, at the Duke of Wellington's, and had been bought especially for this occasion by Lady Blois. The bazaar was largely patronised by the elite of the neighbourhood. Amongst those present we noticed Lady Huntingfield, Hon. Mrs. Morton North, Hon. Mrs. Henry Brodrick, Hon. Misses Thellusson, Sir John and Lady Blois, Lady Knightley, Mrs. Blois, Mrs. Frederic Gaussen, Lady Probyn, Lady Crossley, Miss Blois, Miss Clara Blois, Rev. C.H. Lacon, Mr. R.W. Burleigh, and Mrs. Charles Brown, Yarmouth, Miss Hickling, Miss Burleigh, Dr. Warwick, Rev. W. Bromley, Rev. R.S. Beloe, Rev. W. Hollond, Rev. T.S. Bartram, Rev. R. Gathorne, Mrs. D.P. Crooke and the Misses Crooke, and Mr. C. White. Two concerts were given under the superintendence of the Hon. Mrs. Brodrick in one of the rooms at the White Hart. At three o'clock the following programme was presented to an appreciative audience:- 'Polonaise' (*Chopin*), Hon. Mrs. Henry Brodrick; 'The Lost Chord' (*Sullivan*), Miss Pelly; 'To the Woods' (*F. Warner*), Rev. C. Lacon; 'Where the bee sucks' (*Dr. Arne*), Miss Gaussen; Recitation, 'The Pied Piper of Hamelin' (*Browning*), Mr. B. Pelly; 'Ruby' (*V. Gabriel*), Miss Pelly; Valse (*J. Schulhoff*), Miss Norton.

At four o'clock a still larger audience was present, when the programme annexed was admirably executed amid frequent applause:- 'Elsa's Wedding March,' 'Lohengrin' (*Wagner, Liszt*), Hon. Mrs. Henry Brodrick; 'The storm fiend' (*Pinsuti*), Mr. B. Pelly; 'Love is a plaintive song' (*Sullivan*), Miss Gaussen; song, Master Beloe; recitation, 'Wolsey and Cromwell' (*Shakespeare*), Mr. B. Pelly; 'Concert dans les bois' (*O. Schmidt*), Miss Norton; 'Thou art gone from my gaze' (*Linley*), Rev. C. Lacon; 'Good bye' (*Tosti*), Miss Pelly. The immense size of the church makes the undertaking an exceedingly onerous one, but we are pleased to record that up to Saturday evening last the Committee had been promised subscriptions amounting to £595, which included £100 given by Sir John Blois, the patron of the living; and the proceeds of the bazaar it is hoped will make a large addition to the restoration fund. The bazaar is continued to-day, when further attractions are promised, amongst others being an exhibition by Professor du Cane, of Norwich, and as the admittance fee will be reduced to half-price it is expected an even larger audience than that of yesterday will be the result. The band of the F Company (Halesworth) Rifle Volunteers, under Bandmaster Cowles, was in attendance, and played a choice selection of music during the day.

17. Report of Blythburgh bazaar, the *Ipswich Journal*, 12 August 1882[20]

RESTORATION OF BLYTHBURGH CHURCH
BAZAAR AND FANCY FAIR AT BLYTHBURGH

The village of Blythburgh and the district around are connected with associations of the most memorable and remarkable kind, and form a centre of considerable interest to historians, but perhaps infinitely more so to the archaeologist. Although at the present period it is but a small and humble village, there are unmistakable signs of its having been at some anterior date a large and probably thickly populated place, with a flourishing fishing trade, in which respect of the competition with the then neighbouring towns of Southwold and Dunwich was extremely severe. Dunwich, with its numerous churches, has now been nearly washed away, and Southwold has suffered to some extent by incursions of the ocean, whilst Blythburgh has also been the scene of disasters. Thus the trade in these former comparatively large commercial towns has been gradually exterminated, receiving an almost death-blow at the time of the Reformation, when for instance the inhabitants of Blythburgh were deprived of so many advantages in the suppression of their Priory. Through the ravages of the sea, and probably not having the means to adopt defensive measures, the river became almost choked up with silt, and the maritime trade was thus injured to an irreparable extent. Misfortunes of no mean or trifling character have at times befallen the inhabitants of this formerly flourishing port. On August 4th, 1577, when the parishioners were engaged in Divine service at the grand old church of Holy Trinity, a thunderstorm of unprecedented severity passed over the town, and with most disastrous results. No less than twenty persons, it is stated, were injured by the lightning, two killed, and several scorched. The sacred edifice, too, did not escape, but was damaged to a considerable extent, the spire and part of the steeple being thrown down. Then, again, in 1679, it is reported that a fire occurred in the place, by which several houses were burned to the ground, the sum of £18,020 being the estimated value of the damage caused by the conflagration. Other fires have occurred from time to time, and it appears from what even can now be seen that the inhabitants were fast becoming too poor as a body to replace the various buildings, and the decay thus commenced has continued down to the present day, when Blythburgh can lay claim no longer to be more than a little fishing village. Still it has surroundings of which the parishioners can well boast, and feel proud. The district in itself is exceedingly picturesque and offers an almost unlimited scope for the pen and pencil of the artists who visit the place during the season in fairly large numbers. Visiting at the time when the heather flower is in full development, one cannot but be struck with the glorious view extending far over the heath, so well known to travellers in that district, accompanied as it is by the beautifully fresh and invigorating breeze which at

---

[20]   RCMB.

times blow from across the neighbouring German Ocean. As to the antiquity of Blythburgh, there can be but little doubt. Discoveries have been made in the shape of Roman coins, Roman urns, and so forth, and it is stated that Anna, king of the East Angles, and Firminus, his son, slain in Bulcamp Forest while fighting against Renda [*sic*], King of Mercia, in 654, were buried in this place. The grand old parish church, of enormous dimensions when compared with the present number of inhabitants, is in itself sufficient proof that Blythburgh has seen more flourishing and successful times, because it is apparent that none but a fairly wealthy town could build such a significantly large structure as the Church of Holy Trinity. It is upon a slight eminence, some 100 yards from the ruins of the Priory for Augustine or Black Canons, a building founded in 1130, and thus probably of Norman architecture. The church is decidedly of the Perpendicular period, and the present structure was evidently in course of being built, or at any rate the workmen had not entirely withdrawn from it, during the years 1472 and 1473. In the former year John Grace left 20 marks for the re-building of the chancel. The sacred edifice naturally attracts the ordinary observer on account of the size of the structure, and it is especially noticeable in the journey to Southwold by the model little railway opened within the last two years. It bears evidence of the fact of its having been too great and expensive a burden for the people to keep in repair since the dissolution of the Monastery, as at intervals one can see ugly patches of brickwork inserted in the walls, and thus this extremely beautiful edifice has been from time to time mutilated in its character by injudicious and insufficient repairs. The windows, which are very numerous, have in some instances been in the same way patched up with bricks and mortar, but many of them have apparently afterwards been removed, and windows richly decorated with painted glass and tracery substituted. The tower, though well built and in a good state of preservation, does not attract the same amount of notice that the building itself does. The flint-work at the East end of the church is extremely beautiful, and beneath the chancel window there is to be observed a row of crowned letters. Many there are whose curiosity as to the meaning of these letters has, to their disappointment, been unsatisfied, their satisfactory deciphering being by no means easily accomplished.[21] The parapet on the South aisle is a remarkably beautiful work. It consists of a series of open wheel tracery, each wheel being quartrefoiled on its inner side, and with the exception of that portion which runs over the porch, is still entire. Some bands of flint and stone are worked together with a praiseworthy effect. The small squares, set in diamond form, have a considerable effect of relieving the monotonous appearance. The buttresses are of a very fine description, and in good order. On the South side, over each buttress, is the figure of an animal, whilst over the porch are grouped the figures of the four Apostles. The interior of the building is in a terrible condition, and presents a really pitiable appearance, but at the same time it is of such an interesting character that it more than repays the trouble incurred in paying it a visit. The roof is a depressed specimen of Perpendicular work, but still is very good. Its condition, however, is deplorable, the timber being perfectly rotten, and the decay set in has gone too far to ever be remedied. There are 54 brasses at the angles where the timbers intersect, and many of them contain the shields of old Suffolk families. The nave is 127 feet long, with two aisles, and the chancel is of a proportionate length. The arms

---

[21] See Timothy Beardsworth, 'The flint-work inscription under the east window of Blythburgh church', *PSIAH* 38 (1993), pp. 75–7, for the interpretation 'To the honour of Blessed Jesus, the Holy Trinity, Mary [and] St Anne, this chancel [has been] rebuilt'.

of two bishops of Dunwich, Felix and Boniface, are to be seen in the painted glass of the windows, and the corbels are conjectured to be portraits. The poppyheads of the benches in the North side of the nave are representations of the seven deadly sins of the Romish Church. They bear evidence, like the roof and other portions of the church, of the violence of Dowsing's work, and in many places they have been evidently wilfully cut away, whilst the roof contains innumerable shot holes, in some of which can be seen the leaden shots. The rood screen contains some remains of fine painting, and there are specimens of some wood carving scattered about throughout the sacred edifice. As referred to above, the body of King Anna is supposed to have been buried within the precincts of the church, but was afterwards removed to Bury. In the nave there are traces of where brasses have been removed, some of an interesting character. There is a very curious old donation box near the font, the construction of which is of an unique description. One of the old-fashioned wooden type Bibles is preserved in the church, with some documents of a valuable nature from a point of antiquity. In the course of the year there are large numbers who visit this somewhat renowned church, and all express their surprise that some means have not been taken to maintain and preserve so valuable an architectural structure. To rescue this grand old edifice from ultimate and complete ruin, has undoubtedly been a wish that has found an echo in the heart of almost every one of the inhabitants around, but it must be remembered that in an undertaking of such large dimensions, the responsibilities attached to its initiation are somewhat formidable. Thus it is that no action has been hitherto taken in the matter, and so the church has continued to decay, and in fact has become now so thoroughly dilapidated, that the congregation for the past six months or so have had to meet to worship in a building close by, rain and wind alike finding their way, with no great amount of obstruction, into the sacred edifice. This underirable [*sic*] condition of affairs, however, has had its effect, and at last there is the best prospect of some practical attention being paid to it, for with an amount of energy and zeal worthy of the warmest commendation, Lady Blois and a number of other ladies resident in the neighbourhood, with the ready assistance and co-operation of Sir John Blois, the patron of the living, have taken the subject up in a way that undoubtedly signifies a successful result. No sooner was it resolved to take steps for the restoration of the church than many came to the front, offering their help to forward the great and deserving object in view. It may be here mentioned that the late Mr. Street, R.A., who had taken such a very deep interest in the church, had expressed a wish 'to have a hand in rescuing so singularly interesting a church from further decay and ultimate ruin,' and up to the time of his illness and lamented death he engaged himself in preparing plans and specifications for the restoration, with an approximate estimate of the cost. From the carrying out of the work he was prevented, but after his death his son completed it. The amount required to put the sacred edifice in a satisfactory state is £4,856.[22] A committee was formed to consider the plans; these were adopted, and it is hoped before long to commence the work in the building. The restoration will be of such a general nature that it can scarcely be here detailed. The roof, which is in an actually dangerous condition, will, it is expected, have to be completely removed and a new one substituted, whilst the bricked up windows will be again opened and restored. The walls which are in a good, sound condition will be thoroughly cleaned and scraped, and everything needful done to

---

[22] This figure is incorrect. The correct estimate of £4,865 is given later in the article.

them. The tower as at present appears to have been unfinished in its construction, and by the plans this will be heightened to a certain extent. The now very irregular, not to say uncomfortable, method of finding accommodation for worshippers will be done away with and substituted by the more modern benches, for at present, while one part of the church has the old fashioned oak benches, in another portion there are existing the high back pews, more resembling sheep pens than anything else. That there is plenty of work to be done needs but one glance round the building to satisfy any curious mind, and that a great improvement can be effected there is still less doubt to be entertained. It is intended to begin with the South aisle, so that as early as possible the parishioners may worship within the four walls of their beautiful old parish church. As stated above, to thoroughly carry out the work of restoration it is anticipated that the sum of £4,865 is required, and it is very evident that in the district itself so large an amount cannot be raised. The Committee accordingly, considering that they have a claim upon all who take the least interest in the preservation of the churches of this country, and a still greater claim upon the county of Suffolk in maintaining one of its most interesting objects, have issued a circular appealing 'to all lovers of the grand and beautiful in architecture to help them in raising funds for the preservation of this noble edifice from the ruin which is imminent.' Three distinct funds were established, church, chancel, and general fund; in cases where subscriptions are received with no specification as to which fund it is to be applied, it will go towards the general fund to be divided in the proportion of two-thirds to the church, and one-third to the chancel restoration. The subscription list, which was immediately opened, was headed by the handsome donation of £100 by Sir John Blois. The Rev. E. Hollond put his name down for £50, the Hon. Mrs. H. Brodrick subscribed £25, Mrs. F. Gaussen £25, the Vicar (the Rev. H. Sykes) £25, the Lord Bishop of Norwich £20, and amongst the other influential contributors already subscribed to the list were Sir Wm. Rose, Lady Huntingfield, The Lord Bishop of Sodor and Man, Ven. Archdeacon Groome, the Dowager Lady Huntingfield, Lady Brassey, and many others too numerous to mention, the total sum as yet received from that source being about £600. This, so far as it goes, is very encouraging, but when that amount is compared with the estimated cost of the proposed restoration it is comparatively a small amount. Lady Blois, Lady Huntingfield, the Hon. Mrs. Brodrick, Mrs. Sykes, and Mrs. Cooper, in conjunction with a number of other ladies, determined by their personal efforts to assist in the general movement, and it was decided to hold a bazaar or fancy fair on behalf of the funds. Wednesday and Thursday last were the days fixed for the event, and fortunately for all concerned the weather was as much like what one expects in Summer as we have of late realised. It was at first suggested that the fair should be held on the ground in which the ruins of the old Abbey or Priory were enclosed, but then it was found to be impracticable. Mr. Mills, the landlord of the White Hart, came forward, and kindly offered the meadow at the back of the inn for the purpose. This site was eagerly taken as one having so many advantages, not the least of which were its close proximity both to Blythburgh station and to the church itself, which indeed is within a stone's throw of the meadow. Every publicity was given to the holding of the bazaar, announced to take place under the patronage of the Countess of Stradbroke, Lady Constance Barne, Lady Huntingfield, Lady Blois, Lady Knightley, the Hon. Mrs. Morton North, the Hon. Mrs. Henry Brodrick, the Hon. Misses Thellusson, Mrs. Blois, Mrs. Frederick Gaussen, Mrs. Sykes, and Mrs. Cooper. While Lady Blois had, so to speak, the superintendence of the fancy fair generally, the onerous duties connected with which it may be mentioned were so admirably and proficiently carried out, the arrangement and planning out of the ground was entrusted to Mrs. Cooper, who, assisted by the members of her family, proved herself quite equal to the occasion. One of Messrs. Rands and Jeckell's very large marquees was placed in the centre of the ground, whilst other tents were pitched about the ground for the various requirements. These were with flags and banners gaily decorated, whilst the entrance near the White Lion [*sic*] was made conspicuous by an artistic arrangement of flags and decorative materials. Immediately upon entering the large marquee, one could see arranged upon the various stalls in every conceivable form and fashion the numerous and varied articles common to bazaars and fancy fairs, and which have always such a magnetic influence upon the purses of the visitors. Turning directly to the right, the noticeable feature was the head stall of fancy work and articles presided over by Lady Blois. Here, arranged in the style most attractive to one and all, were everything that a visitor could desire. They included some very good oil colourings by Lady Blois, some water paintings by the hon. Mrs Morton North, and a very nicely-arranged screen by the children of Lady Blois, but perhaps the pièce de résistance was the screen presented by her Ladyship, and upon which were painted, in oil colours on a pretty background, various specimens of birds by Lady Blois. What can be done by a lady of advanced age, was shewn in a first-class specimen of modern worsted working by the Dowager Lady Huntingfield, and the pretty device was exceedingly attractive. An antimacassar of similar character, but different conception, had been specially worked by Lady Blois. At one end of the stall there was a very ingenious little construction in the shape of a pug dog, into which by a neat little mechanical contrivance the current coin of the realm could be passed by placing it upon the dog's face. In addition to these specialities, there was some porcelain pottery, hand-painted flower stand, wool work, cotton work, fans, covers, cushions, and fancy articles of various characters and fashions. The whole in their entirety made the stall present a very attractive appearance, reflecting infinite credit upon the taste of the stallkeeper. Right and left from this end stall were arranged the remaining stalls, presided over by Lady Huntingfield, Lady Probyn, Mrs. Frederick Gaussen, Mrs. Sykes, and Mrs. Cooper, at all of which were dispensed a miscellaneous collection of articles, and at prices which for a fancy fair were to say the least surprisingly reasonable. As can well be imagined a brisk trade was the result, but in addition to these particular stalls, there was a department especially assigned for refreshments, under the direction of Mrs. Blois, whilst Miss Clara Blois, Miss Gertrude Blois, Miss Adeline Blois, the Misses Stanford, and Master Bagot-Chester, were each busily engaged in their several self-imposed tasks as vendors of dolls dressed à la mode, fancy articles, and flowers. All worked unitedly in their efforts on behalf of the common cause, and a pretty sight indeed the busy scene within the model market presented. A novelty, especially to this locality, was to be met with in the shape of the now somewhat renowned Magic Well, such as was recently presided over by the daughters of the Prince of Wales, at the Lilidution [*sic*] bazaar. This was purchased by Lady Blois, and an exceptionally favourable source of income it became. It is not, perhaps, adviseable to disclose the secret of its structure and working, but suffice it to remark that the pail before descending to the magic well could be filled to any extent with coins, and after the chain had been lowered and the pail disappear from sight it would return having been emptied of its valuable contents, and refilled in a secret manner with articles which though perhaps of a more bulky nature were scarcely of such intrinsic worth, causing indeed a great deal of merriment amongst the lookers-on. Master Eardley and Master

Ralfe Blois were in charge of the tent containing the live stock, the chief characteristic of which was, as the young keepers took great care to point out, a three-legged duckling, but the collection also included some domestic animals and birds, a view of which was obtained by the payment of a nominal fee. During Wednesday there was an exhibition of some mechanical toys by a representative from the firm of Messrs. Cremer and Co., of London, and the hen that laid eggs at the will of its master, or of the visitors, was one which caused a great deal of fun. On the second day Professor De Cone, of Norwich, with his clever tricks of legerdemain, performed in a very neat and stylish manner, was the centre of an admiring gathering. During Wednesday three concerts were given by ladies and gentlemen volunteering their services, in a room attached to the White Hart, the following being included in the programmes:- 'Polonaise' (*Chopin*), Hon. Mrs. Hy. Brodrick; 'The Lost Chord' (*Sullivan*), Miss Pelly; 'To the Woods' (*F. Warner*), Rev. C. Lacon; 'Where the bee sucks' (*Dr. Arne*), Miss Gaussen; recitation, 'The Pied Piper of Hamelin' (*Browning*), Mr. B. Pelly; 'Ruby' (*V. Gabriel*), Miss Pelly; valse (*J. Schulhoff*), Miss Norton; 'Elsa's Wedding March,' 'Lohengrin' (*Wagner Liszt*), Hon. Mrs. Henry Brodrick; 'The Storm Fiend' (*Pinsuti*), Mr. B. Pelly; 'Love is a plaintive Song' (*Sullivan*), Miss Gaussen; song, Master Beloe; recitation, 'Wolsey and Cromwell' (*Shakespeare*), Mr. B. Pelly; 'Concert dans les bois' (*O. Schmidt*), Miss Norton; 'Thou art gone from my gaze' (*Linley*), Rev. C. Lacon; 'Good bye' (*Tosti*), Miss Pelly. It is almost needless to say that the various performers were well received, and the concerts proved to be an excellent break in what might otherwise have been a somewhat monotonous time. With fine weather the bazaar has proved a success, and the result has been extremely satisfactory. The convenient little railway on Wednesday was crowded with the visitors to the place, and perhaps it is some time since the village of Blythburgh presented so lively a spectacle. Carriages drove up in regular processions, and in the afternoon the brilliant costumes of the ladies made everything look cheerful and gay. Amongst those present can be mentioned – Lady Knightley, Lady Huntingfield, Sir John and Lady Blois, Lady Crossley, Lady Probyn, Hon. Misses Thellusson, Hon. Mr. H. Brodrick, Hon. Mrs. Morton North, Mrs. Blois, Miss Blois, and Miss Clara Blois, Mrs. Frederick Gaussen, Rev. C.H. Lacon, Rev. W. Bromley, Rev. R.S. Beloe, Rev. W. Holland [*sic*], Rev. T.S. Bartram, Rev. R. Gathorne, Rev. D.P. Crooke and the Misses Crooke, Mr. R.W. Burleigh and Miss Burleigh, Lady Hilda Rous, Lady Adela Rous, Mrs. Bagot-Chester, Col. St. John Barne, M.P., etc. That the fair proved successful may be gathered from the fact that on the first day alone £170 was taken, including the proceeds of the sale and the entrance money, a nominal charge having been made at the gate for admittance. It is to be hoped that the promoters of the restoration scheme will meet with every possible encouragement, and that they will be thoroughly rewarded for the responsible task they have undertaken. Too much cannot be said on behalf of the cause they have thus espoused, and in that they need the practical help and sympathy from all who are in a position to afford it. A generous response to the appeal of the Committee has already been received, but that will not suffice, and all are earnestly requested to do their utmost to promote the object in view, of realising the necessarily large sum required for the restoration of so interesting and grand a structure of architectural beauty as the Church of Holy Trinity, Blythburgh. For this purpose subscriptions will be gratefully received by Lady Blois, Cockfield Hall, Yoxford; the Rev. H. Sykes, vicar, Walberswick, Southwold; R. Briggs, Esq., Bulcamp, Wangford, and Charles Youngs, Esq., Hinton Hall,

Saxmundham, churchwardens; also by Messrs. Gurney and Co., Norwich, Yarmouth, and Lowestoft.

[*The Revd Henry Sykes appended this note*]: /In reply to the above report the following two letters appeared in the 'Ipswich Journal' Aug. 19. 1882./[23]

18. Report of bazaar, the *Norfolk Chronicle*, 12 August 1882[24]

BLYTHBURGH

The Church Restoration. – A bazaar in aid of the Church Restoration Fund was held on Wednesday in a large tent on the meadow adjoining the White Hart Inn. It was under the distinguished patronage of the Countess of Stradbroke, Lady Constance Barne, Lady Huntingfield, Hon. Mrs. Morton North, Hon. Mrs. H. Brodrick, the Hon. Misses Thellusson, Lady Blois, Lady Knightley, Mrs. Blois, Mrs. Frederic Gaussen, Mrs. Sykes, and Mrs. Cooper. Immediately on entering the tent was a stall of fancy articles presided over by Lady Huntingfield, Mrs. Sykes, wife of the vicar, being in charge of the adjoining stall. A very pretty flower stall came next, where a brisk business was done by Master Bagot-Chester and Miss Adeline Blois. A very tasteful exhibition of lingerie, etc., was made by Mrs. Cooper, who has been untiring in her efforts to make the bazaar a success; and, assisted by the Misses Stanford, she was kept busy all day in distributing the articles she had taken such pains to gather. Mrs. Gaussen and Miss Clara Blois presided over a display as varied as it was attractive, while at Lady Blois' stalls could be purchased anything, from a pincushion to an original painting. Mrs. Blois dispensed refreshments, and little Miss Gertrude Blois sold dolls that were not much smaller than herself. In addition to the main tent there were three others, to enter which a small additional fee was charged. In one of these were to be seen the various mechanical toys for which Messrs. Cremer and Co., of 210, Regent-street, London, are so justly famous. At another, pigeons, canaries, pet rabbits, and birds of all kinds were to be purchased of Masters Eardley and Ralph Blois, who were also extremely proud of a three-legged duckling, which it was said had been hatched in the parish, on the premises of the worthy landlord of the White Hart Inn, and was now on view in a glass case. An extraordinary novelty was the magic well – an illustration of which was given in a recent number of the *Graphic*, when it was under the charge of the young Princesses, daughters of the Prince of Wales, at the Liliputian Bazaar, at the Duke of Wellington's, and had been bought especially for this occasion by Lady Blois. The bazaar was largely patronized by the elite of the neighbourhood. Amongst those present we noticed Lady Huntingfield, Hon. Mrs. Morton North, Hon. Mrs. Henry Brodrick, Hon. Misses Thellusson, Sir John and Lady Blois, Lady Knightley, Mrs. Blois, Mrs. Frederic Gaussen, Lady Probyn, Lady Crossley, Miss Blois, Miss Clara Blois, Rev. C.H. Lacon, Mr. R.W. Burleigh, and Mrs. Charles Brown, Yarmouth, Miss Hickling, Miss Burleigh, Dr. Warwick, Rev. W. Bromley, Rev. R.S. Beloe, Rev. W. Hollond, Rev. T.S. Bartram, Rev. R. Gathorne, Mrs. D.P. Crooke and the Misses Crooke, and Mr. C. White. Two concerts were given under the superintendence of the Hon. Mrs. H. Brodrick in one of the rooms of the White Hart. At three o'clock the following programme was presented to an appreciative audience:- 'Polonaise' (Chopin), Hon. Mrs. Henry. Brodrick; 'The Lost

---

23 See Correspondence 32.
24 RCMB. This report is a shortened but essentially little different version from that in the *East Anglian Daily Times*, document C16 above.

Chord' (Sullivan), Miss Pelly; 'To the Woods' (F. Warner), Rev. C. Lacon; 'Where the bee sucks' (Dr. Arne), Miss Gaussen; recitation, 'The Pied Piper of Hamelin' (Browning), Mr. B. Pelly; 'Ruby' (V. Gabriel), Miss Pelly; valse (J. Schuloff), Miss Norton. At four o'clock a still larger audience was present, when the programme annexed was admirably executed amid frequent applause:- 'Elsa's Wedding March,' 'Lohengrin' (Wagner, Liszt), Hon. Mrs. Henry Brodrick; 'The storm fiend' (Pinsuti), Mr. B. Pelly; 'Love is a plaintive song' (Sullivan), Miss Gaussen; song, Master Beloe; recitation, 'Wolsey and Cromwell' (Shakespeare), Mr. B. Pelly; 'Concert dans les bois' (O. Schmidt), Miss Norton; 'Thou art gone from my gaze' (Linley), Rev. C. Lacon; 'Good bye' (Tosti), Miss Pelly. The immense size of the church makes the undertaking an exceedingly onerous one, but we are pleased to record that up to Saturday evening last the committee have been promised subscriptions amounting to £595, which included £100 given by Sir John Blois, the patron of the living; and the proceeds of the bazaar it is hoped will make a large addition to the restoration fund. The band of the F Company (Halesworth) Rifle Volunteers, under Bandmaster Cowles, was in attendance, and played a choice selection of music during the day.

19. History of Blythburgh church, *Halesworth Times*, 15 August 1882[25]

For the benefit of our many distant readers, we append a short account of the history of Blythburgh, as found in *Gardener's* [*sic*] and other works of a similar character:-

The now humble village of Blythburgh was formerly a flourishing little town and port, and had a considerable fishery and a goal for the Division of Beccles, for which Quarter Sessions were held here. The decline of Blythburgh is attributed to its river becoming so choked up as to be navigable to the town only for small barges, and to the suppression of its priory. In 1679 many of its houses, with their goods and furniture, were burnt by an accidental fire, and the damage was estimated at £18,030. A dreadful thunderstorm happened here on Sunday, August 4th, 1577, during divine service, when the lightning did great damage to the church, and struck down 20 people, of whom two were killed and others scorched. The spire and part of the steeple was blown down, and other parts of the church were 'rent and torn by the tempest, which took its course to Bungay, where it did much mischief.' Several Roman coins and urns have been discovered here; and it is said that Anna, King of Mercia [*sic*], in Bulcamp Forest, was buried here in 654. The revenues of the church of Blythburgh being given by Henry the First to the Abbey and Convent of St. Osyth, in Essex, they soon afterwards founded this Priory, which was endowed by Richard Bauveys, Bishop of London, and other benefactors. It was suppressed in the 26th of Henry VIII, when it contained only five canons, and its revenues were valued at £48 8s. 10d. per annum. The Church (Holy Trinity) is a large structure, which has been extremely beautiful, but has been much mutilated by time and injudicious repairs. The windows are numerous, and have been richly decorated with painted glass and tracery, most of which have given place to unsightly masses of brick. Internally the fine carved work has been covered with many coats of whitewash; and the carvings on the roof, consisting of angels bearing shields, have so long been in a decayed and mouldering condition, that many of them have fallen down. The porch is still decorated with grotesque heads, and at each corner stands an angel with expanded

---

25 RCMB.

wings. The tower, which formerly had a spire, is of inferior workmanship to the nave and chancel. There are two chapels at the east end, dedicated to the Blessed Virgin and her mother, St Anne; and in the church were several altars, and a great number of images of saints. At the east end of the north aisle is shown a tomb, said to be that of Anna, King of the East Angles; and in the chancel another to his son Firminus; but their remains are said to have been removed to the Abbey Church of Bury St. Edmund's.

/Halesworth Times Aug 15./

20. Manuscript note about Blythburgh priory, 2 March 1884[26]

<Blythb> Bliburgh, or Blythburrow Priory, Suffolk

This priory stands near the eastern extremity of the County, in the hundred of Blything, and the village of Bliburgh, from which it takes its name. This, tho' now but a mean place, is said to be of great antiquity, which appears probable, both from the termination of its name and a number of Roman urns dug up here about the year 1678.

This house was founded about the time of King Henry the First; it seems doubtful whether by that King, or an abbot of St. Osith in Essex, to which it was made a cell. Richard Beauveys Bishop of London, anno. 1108, was so great a benefactor, as to be esteemed almost a founder. It was a college of Black Canons, called Praemonstratenses, and dedicated to the Blessed Virgin. King Richard the 1st, by his charter, printed in the Monasticon, recites and confirms all the grants made to those Canons by the benefactors therein named.

From a framed picture of the old Priory etc. at Halesworth station. 2 March 1884.

21. Report on restoration, the *Ipswich Journal*, 11 March 1884[27]

BLYTHBURGH

THE RESTORATION OF THE CHURCH. – We are pleased to find that the work of restoration of this fine structure is making satisfactory progress, and it is hoped that it will be sufficiently advanced by Easter to admit of the holding of Divine service in the building. It is now two years since it was found imperatively necessary to disuse the church, and in the interim, service has been held in the schoolroom. The South side of the church is fully restored with the exception of the porch, and the appearance of the building on this side is very fine. All the clerestory windows on each side have been restored, and the aisle windows on the South have either been repaired or unblocked, and tracery inserted filled with tinted glass. The beautiful and unique quatrefoil parapet has been restored where necessary, and extended in new work at

---

26 RCMB. The reference to the canons of the order of Premonstatenses is in *Monasticon Anglicanum: or the History of the Ancient Abbies ... in England and Wales* (1718), p. 187 'Bliburg'. Founded in 1120 by St Norbert, the order followed more strictly the rules of St Augustine and came to England in 1143. They held the abbey of Leiston. This order of white canons seems to have been confused with the Augustinians already at Blythburgh.

27 RCMB.

the East end of the aisle. The appearance of the East end is now very imposing. The end windows of the North and South aisle, as well as the magnificent East window, have been unblocked, and the tracery restored in pure Perpendicular style, and filled with tinted glass. The windows on the North side are gradually being opened and tracery inserted. It is marvellous that so much of the tracery remains, considering the dilapidated state which it was in before the work of restoration was begun. Several of the windows, as yet untouched, bulge out; the mullions are perfectly loose, and apparently a stiff breeze would blow the windows out. The West window – the only one in the Decorated style – has two /*Sykes underlined 'two' and wrote in 'three'*/ lights, and although very beautiful, it appears small in comparison with the noble proportions of the building. This window has been thoroughly restored. A new roof has been placed upon the South aisle, the old work where possible being used, whilst everywhere a faithful restoration on the old lines has been carried out. Nothing was wanting in this finely proportioned building in the way of effect, and the architects have wisely not attempted to alter in any degree either the ornaments or the details of the original design. The box pews, which disfigured the nave, have been removed, and the original benches (or what was left of them) have been collected and arranged in the centre of the building. This change alone vastly improves the appearance of the church. Some of the poppy heads are remarkably good, whilst the carving of the choirstalls is in capital preservation, considering the vicissitudes through which the stalls have passed. The representations in the panels of the front benches are apparently of the twelve apostles; the figures are quaint, but evidently have not been interfered with either by the rude hand of the destroyer, or the meddlesome fingers of the curious, though their appearance has been enhanced by the rich deep brown of age. The roofs of the nave and North aisle have not been touched on account of want of funds, but they sadly need restoration; water comes in in a number of places, and many of the beams, especially in the roof of the North aisle, have quite rotted away, and barely reach the walls. The work, so far, has been carried out in a thorough manner; the workmanship appears to be of a sound character, and reflects high credit upon the skill of Mr. Allen, builder, of Southwold, who took the contract for this first portion of the restoration. The late Mr. Geo. Street, the eminent architect of the Royal Courts of Justice, interested himself greatly in the preservation of this noble ecclesi-astical building, and before his death prepared the plans, which are being faithfully carried out by his son. Much more needs to be done to make a complete restoration of this splendid specimen of ecclesiastical architecture of the 14th [*sic*] century, but the Vicar (the Rev. W.H. Sykes) is to be congratulated upon the near accomplishment of the first portion of the work, and it is to be hoped that his indomitable efforts will meet with such success as will enable him to entirely restore his grand old parish church.

22. Reopening of church, the *East Anglian Daily Times*, 14 April 1884[28]

RE-OPENING OF BLYTHBURGH CHURCH.

On Sunday (Easter Day) this beautiful, ancient, and historic church was re-opened for divine service, having been closed since November, 1881, when it had become so dilapidated as to render it almost dangerous to longer occupy it; and although for more

---

[28] RCMB. Also published in the *East Anglian Daily Times* on 16 April 1884. Brooke.

than a generation it had almost been deemed a scandal that so noble an ecclesiastical structure should have been so long neglected, yet up to that time nothing definite had been attempted further than receiving the report and estimates furnished by the late Mr. Street, which entailed an outlay of between £4,000 and £5,000. It was then decided something must be done, and despite the difficulties which it seemed almost impossible to overcome, the vicar, the Rev. H. Sykes, persevered and succeeded in forming a committee, composed of Lady Blois (wife of the lord of the manor), Sir J. R. Blois, the churchwardens – Mr. R. Briggs and Mr. C. Youngs, Mrs. Cooper, etc.; and to show how difficult and seemingly impossible was the task with which those who determined on its restoration were confronted, we may state that at the first meeting held, only a single shilling was promised, and the first real promise of any possibility of success came through the bazaar, held on the 9th and 10th of August, 1882, which netted the handsome sum of £211 14s. 2d. A concert given in London, under the auspices of Lady Blois, added another £50 to the funds, and a concert at Yoxford £18 10s. more. Sir J.R. Blois also gave a donation of £100, other munificent subscribers to the fund being Hon. Mrs. Brodrick, Mr. F. Gaussen, and the Vicar, £25 each; the late Rev. E. Hollond, with characteristic generosity, subscribed £50, and the Lord Bishop of Norwich £20 towards the repair of the nave roof. The funds were further augmented by subscriptions from Sir W. Rose, Mrs. Cooper, R. Briggs, Esq., Rev. G. Irving Davies, Lady Huntingfield, the Lord Bishop of Sodor and Man, Mrs. Cope, Ven. Archdeacon Groome, Miss Tatlock, Mrs. Savill Onley, etc.

The task of raising £5,000 all at once was even too herculean a task for the Vicar, and when the fund amounted to about £1,000 it was felt a commencement might be made, and accordingly on the 27th January, 1882, a contract for £1,049 was entered into with Mr. R.J. Allen. of Southwold, for the restoration of the south aisle and all the windows of the church which were not at that time blocked up with bricks and stone. The original terms of the contract placed September last as the time by which the work was to be completed, but the contractor found so much difficulty in getting the glazing finished that it has been delayed until now. We may say that Mr. Allen has conscientiously fulfilled the larger portion of his contract, and the church now presents a totally different aspect to that which saddened the spectator two years ago. The south aisle has been thoroughly restored according to the designs of Mr. Street, who has taken up his father's work, and has been especially careful to make the restored portion an exact reproduction of the original. We may instance the west window, which formed a part of a more ancient structure than the present one, has not been made to correspond with the other windows, but is a true copy of its predecessor, and the painstaking care and fidelity is manifest everywhere; wherever older tracery or carved work in wood or stone was not too far gone in decay it has been again used. The late Mr. Street put an almost priceless value upon the illuminations of the windows, and every scrap has been as carefully cleaned and re-glazed as if it were worth its weight in gold. As we have before stated, all the glazed windows have been wholly or partially restored, but the contract has been confined to the south aisle, the roof of which has been thoroughly restored with English oak. The old spandrels have, as far as possible, been again used, and those portions which were either gone or decayed, have been replaced. The old bosses, which were all gone, are now succeeded by others similar in design to those they replace. Three of the windows in the south aisle are adorned with shields emblematic of the Holy Trinity, and copied from shields in one of the north windows. They have been kindly given by Mr. Rowland Cobbold, who has taken great interest in the work. The shields are inscribed with symbols of the Holy Trinity. One of the arches and two of the columns of the south aisle have been scraped and restored, and the rest will be treated in a similar manner when sufficient funds are in hand to justify the Committee proceeding. The old unsightly high pews have been removed, and they were found to cover ancient benches with poppyheads, which are magnificent specimens of Early English carving. These occupy for the present the position in which they were originally placed, and harmonize well with their antique surroundings. The chancel end has been relieved with the best parts of the old deal pews. The beautiful [*stalls of the*] Hopton Chantry, with its matchless figures of the Apostles and Evangelists, has been somewhat altered in position, in order to give a better view of its rich carving, and the lectern, reading-desk, and pulpit have been placed in more appropriate positions. The north roof is in almost as dilapidated a state now as was the south previous to its restoration, and the Vicar is as determined as ever that the work of restoration shall not stop until all the plans of the late Mr. Street are executed, and if we may judge of the future from the past, we may confidently say that ambitious as is the project, it is not too ambitious for the boundless energy of Mr. Sykes, and before another decade shall have passed away Blythburgh Church will be worthy of its historic fame and of that religious enthusiasm of which it is so splendid an example. A portion of the open quatrefoil parapet running along the extensive roof of the south aisle has been restored, and when completed will render the church as pleasing to the eye as it is dear to the antiquarian.

At the services in connection with the re-opening, in the morning the prayers were read by the vicar, the Rev. H. Sykes, and the lessons by Mr. A. Cooper, after which the Vicar preached a suitable and earnest sermon from 1st Samuel, vii., 12 – 'Then Samuel took a stone and set it between Mizpeh and Shen, and called the name of it Ebenezer, saying, Hitherto hath the Lord helped us.' The rev. gentleman, during the course of his discourse, remarked that it had been suggested that no effort should be made for the restoration of their noble church, but it would be better to build a new chancel within the present one. To have done this would have been little better than a crime, and their hearts were filled with gratitude that day because God had heard their prayer and inclined the hearts of men to help them. Some from whom they had expected great things had failed them, but some who had never seen their church had come to their aid, and the language of their hearts was 'Hitherto the Lord has helped us.' There were those that even now said that in restoring the south aisle sufficient had been done, but he would never rest until the whole church was restored. He asked, could they be content to restore one little part and allow the rest to go to decay? No, the silver and the gold were the Lord's, and He had all hearts at His disposal; they acknowledged with gratitude His help in the past, and He would still bless them in this their work of faith and labour of love. He believed there were hundreds yet in the country who would come to their assistance, and those who had helped them in the past would not now desert them. In this work their only object had been God's glory, and they might still rely upon his Almighty arm. He would bless His own work. Their motto in the future should be 'Onward,' for they would yet bring in the top stone with shouting.

In the afternoon the prayers were read by the Vicar, and the lessons by the Rev. P.L. Cautley, vicar of Southwold, who subsequently preached an eloquent sermon based on Genesis, 28th chapter, 16 and 7 verses, 'And Jacob awaked out of his sleep, and he said, Surely the Lord is in the place and I knew it not. And he was afraid, and said, How dreadful is this place! this is none other but the house of God, and this is the gate of heaven,'

In the evening the prayers were read by the vicar, assisted by the Rev. R. Gathorne, vicar of Wenhaston, the sermon being preached by Rev. J. Thorpe, vicar of Darsham, who took for his text St. John, 20 chap., 11 verse, 'But Mary stood without at the Sepulchre weeping.' Before considering the text, the preacher said he desired to say a few words as to the occasion which called those present together. He thought the reopening day had been happily chosen, for no day could be more appropriate to celebrate the restoration of their beautiful house of God than Easter day. When they had such interesting churches as this handed down from their pious ancestors, it was their duty and ought to be their pleasure to hand it down in a proper manner to future generations. He hoped God's blessing would be abundantly shown in the work done for the church.

Good offertories were taken up after each of the services, which were well attended.

23. Reopening of church, the *Ipswich Journal*, 15 April 1884[29]

THE RE-OPENING OF BLYTHBURGH CHURCH.
In the Blythburgh Hundred, and in other parishes in 'high Suffolk,' there are magnificent specimens of church architecture. The church at Blythburgh is one of them, but time and neglect have operated to reduce it to something very far from what it was in its pristine beauty. Still, at every turn – though the building has suffered much from injudicious additions – there is much to catch the eye and excite the interest of the lover of the beautiful in church architecture. To restore it as it should be restored, taking good care to preserve its uniformity of style, and to make the new work harmonise with the old, would be an undertaking in view of which even the stoutest heart might well feel some fear. The vicar (the Rev. H. Sykes) has not attempted this all at once, but he has adopted the wiser course of doing the work by stages, and with indomitable courage and perseverance he has got over stage No. 1. Enthusiasm in a good cause is catching, and it is much to be hoped that the public will show their appreciation of his efforts thus far, and of the admirable way in which the first stage of the work of restoration has been carried out, by generously assisting him to continue the noble and difficult work to which he has set his hand. If, in course of time, Blythburgh Church should be so restored as to hold again the high place it once occupied amongst the most beautiful churches of the country, he will have earned the gratitude of Churchmen throughout Suffolk, while the beautiful building will be a monument to his energy and perseverance. If, by any unforeseen circumstance, he should not have the gratification of carrying the undertaking through, still the credit will be due to him, for he is the one who had the courage to begin the work, and the determination to carry it to a certain length.

The sum really required in order to complete the restoration, according to the designs of the late Mr. Street would be about £5,000. This is a large sum, and, as has been hinted, these are hardly the times, when agriculture is so much depressed, to raise so heavy an amount all at once. Many influential ladies and gentlemen in the county often at different times expressed a desire to see the church restored, while

---

[29] Brooke. Also RCMB.

as to the necessity of something being done there could not be two opinions, but in an undertaking of such large dimensions the responsibilities attached to its initiation are somewhat formidable. Thus it is that prior to 1882 no action was taken in the matter, and so the church continued to decay, until at last it became so thoroughly dilapidated that early in that year the congregation were obliged to meet to worship in a building close by, rain and wind alike finding their way, with no great amount of obstruction, into the sacred edifice. In August, 1882, the first considerable sum towards the restoration fund was raised by means of a bazaar, which was a very brilliant affair, and attended by the principal families in the neighbourhood. The report which appeared in the *Ipswich Journal* at the time of the interesting 'doings' on that occasion included also a minute description of the then condition of the church. The proceeds of the bazaar totalled up to rather more than £200. Subsequently there were munificent subscriptions by Sir John Blois, the late Rev. E. Hollond, the Dowager Lady Huntingfield, the Lord Bishop of Norwich, Sir Wm. Rose, K.C.B., Lady Huntingfield, the Ven. Archdeacon Groome, Hon. Mrs Brodrick, Mr. F. Gaussen, Miss Tatlock, Mrs. Cooper, the Rev. G. Irving Davies, Mrs. Savill Onley, and many other influential ladies and gentlemen whose names have appeared in the lists as they have been published from time to time. When the sum of £1,000 had been contributed, the Vicar, and the ladies and gentlemen acting with him as a committee, including Sir J.R. and Lady Blois, Mrs. Cooper, and the churchwardens, Mr. R. Briggs and Mr. C. Youngs, considered that they would be justified in commencing the work, and accordingly a contract was entered into with Mr. R.J. Allen, of Southwold, for £1,049, chiefly for the restoration of the South aisle, though the interior was in such a condition that it was necessary that the work should be of a rather more general character than that. The designs were prepared by Mr. A.E. Street, the son of the gentleman who took such a deep interest in the church that he expressed a wish 'to have a hand in rescuing so singularly interesting a church from further decay and ultimate ruin,' and up to the time of his illness and lamented death he engaged himself in preparing plans and specifications for the restoration. The effect of what has already been done is very striking, the utmost care having been taken to preserve the style of the building, which is Perpendicular, and to make the new work fit in with the old. This is strikingly apparent in the case of the West window. The greatest care has been exercised in the treatment of the windows, some of them containing illuminations of great age and value. Mr. Rowland Cobbold has very kindly adorned three of the windows in the South aisle with shields, copied from shields in one of the North windows. The roof of the South aisle has been thoroughly restored with English oak, the new bosses being similar to the old ones. The old high-back pews, which much resembled sheep pens, have been removed. As in the case of so many other churches in the county, so here, the old pews were found to cover ancient benches, with handsome poppyheads, and these were far too precious – considering the style of restoration being adopted – not to be utilized, and they occupy at present the place where they originally stood. The positions of the lectern, reading-desk, and pulpit have been changed, and various other changes made, not the least important amongst them being the altered position of the [*stalls from the*] Hopton chantry [*actually moved some years before*], which is very richly carved, containing some splendid figures of the Apostles and Evangelists. In the position it now occupies, a much better view is obtained of the whole of the carved work.

The re-opening of this ancient and magnificent church took place on Easter Sunday. Services were held in the morning, afternoon, and evening, which were

261

fairly attended, in the afternoon especially the provision made for seating being fully occupied. The Vicar read prayers and preached in the morning, taking for his subject, I Samuel vii, 12 [*Then Samuel took a stone and set it up between Mizpah and Jeshanah, and called its name Ebenezer, for he said, 'Hitherto the LORD has helped us. '*]. In his opening remarks, having alluded to the joyful season of Easter and its relation to Christianity, and the Christian's faith and hope, he briefly reviewed the objects aimed at in the restoration. While admitting that the state of the building was getting worse year by year, and everyone felt that something must be done, various plans had to be considered, but every proposition short of a complete restoration of the entire fabric was resisted and laid aside. The magnitude of the undertaking had to be considered, and the task to most minds seemed hopeless, but, as the Vicar remarked, the congregation were well aware that his faith in God, and the ultimate success of energetic and painstaking efforts had never wavered. The result had equalled, if not surpassed, their expectation. They had abundant cause for thankfulness that God had prospered the efforts made, and past mercies laid upon all the obligation to redouble their efforts to complete the work so well begun.

In the afternoon the Rev. P.L. Cautley, vicar of Southwold, preached the sermon, and took for his text, Gen. xxviii., 16, 17 [*Then Jacob awoke from his sleep and said, 'Surely the Lord is in this place; and I did not know it.' And he was afraid and said, 'How awesome is this place! This is none other than the house of God, and this is the gate of heaven,'*]. In his opening remarks he expressed his pleasure at seeing the great improvement effected in the church, and believed that from the Vicar to the poorest person in the parish all had contributed to the utmost extent of their abilities to the restoration of this house of God. He quite remembered the impression made upon his mind when he first looked upon its neglected condition. The piety and munificence of their ancestors had handed down from generation to generation one of the most beautiful temples in the land, and he could not help saying with the Psalmist, 'O God, the heathen have come into Thine inheritance; Thy holy temple have they defiled; they have laid Jerusalem on heaps.'

In the evening the prayers were read by the Vicar, assisted by the Rev. R. Gathorne, vicar of Wenhaston, the sermon being preached by Rev. J. Thorpe, vicar of Darsham, who took for his text St. John xx., 11, 'But Mary stood without at the sepulchre weeping.'

24. Historical notes by Hamlet Watling, the *East Anglian Daily Times*, 16 April 1884[30]

BLYTHBURGH CHURCH.

Mr. H. Watling, Stonham, has forwarded us the following notes upon this church, which was re-opened on Sunday last:-

To enter upon the history of this fabric would be entirely out of place here; but the antiquity of it is unquestionably very great. How far it may extend anterior to the interment of King Anna and his son Firminus, who fell at the battle of Bulcamp in 654, has never been handed down to us. The present beautiful Perpendicular pile

---

30 Brooke. 'A comparison with the first article from document C2 goes some way in revealing the development of Watling's thoughts about Blythburgh church between November 1875 and April 1884. He appears to have had the earlier article by his side while writing the second. Certainly, his opening in both is identical.

in its palmy days must have almost defied description. The multiplicity of enrichments bestowed upon it by its numerous donors, is a fact almost without a parallel in the records of ecclesiastical benevolence, of which the vast amount of shields with coats of arms scattered over its roof and windows, is a sufficient proof. The Hopton family and their connections contributed largely towards its erection, etc. Robert Hopton, Esq., married a daughter of John Skargill, and their son, Sir John, married Ann, the daughter and heiress of Sir Roger Swillington, Knight, of York, and their son and heir, Sir John Hopton, married three times – first, a daughter of John Heveningham, secondly, Margaret, daughter and heiress of Sir John Savell, and thirdly, Thomazine, daughter of John Barrington, county of Essex. This Sir John Hopton founded a chantry in the Church of Blythburgh in 1489, and left a sum of money for the church at Walberswick. Their arms were emblazoned throughout the church, as well as those of Swillington, Rous, Verdon, Scrope, Heveningham, Savell, Barrington, Wentworth, Jermy, Snowhill, Booth, Clere Owen, Echingham, Cocket, Pert, Crane, Bacon, and a considerable number of others. The windows, roof, and stalls, appear to have suffered most from the despoiling hands. How the beautiful figures, carved in chestnut wood, escaped his notice is a matter of surprise. The bench ends in the nave, representing Gluttony, Sloth, and the four seasons, are but little injured. The arca-domini, lectern, and Jack-o'-th'-clock are still preserved.[31] The last is sadly mutilated, as well as the ancient money-box, which has been repainted and decorated out of all character. The large subjects which filled the lower parts of the windows have long since disappeared. These were surmounted with the arms of the donors on shields, supported by three angels of exquisite workmanship. Fifty-seven windows were thus decorated with the saints and holy personages. The finest that still remain are three of the Bishops of Dunwich, St. Anthony of Egypt, St. Bartholomew, St. Jude, St. Helen, St. Etheldreda, St. Andrew, St. Abercius, B.C., St. Michael, and a few others in a mutilated condition. The figures of St. John Baptist, with those of St. Blaise, St. Pancras, and St. Anthony of Padua, and many others, have disappeared during the last forty years, and the west window of the north aisle bricked up, but which once had its tracery and painted glass representing the kings of East Anglia, Offa, King of Mercia, being the only one left. The stalls in the Hopton chantry, mentioned above, were removed to the choir a few years since, but are now removed to their original place.[32] These stalls, in front, under beautiful canopies, contain the effigies of the apostles and saints, 18 in number. Amongst them is St. Etheldreda, Henry VI, St. Stephen, etc. The roof perhaps is the most beautiful part of the fabric, having angels springing from decorated bosses, with expanded wings of great length. These angels hold in their hands shields emblazoned with the arms of the donors; the roof also is highly decorated with the letters I.H.S., etc. The south parapet is extremely beautiful and is perforated with quatrefoils, and upon the apex of the buttresses are grotesque figures representing St. Onuphrius Hermit, a hairy man, St. Vedast, St. Anthony, St. Matthew, etc. The fabric is dedicated to the Holy Trinity, and on the apex of the chancel roof is the figure representing it. It had two subordinate chapels in the north and south aisles dedicated to St. Ann and St. Mary, and had images raised in idolatrous pomp representing them. In the original fabric,

---

[31] The Arca Domini was the fifteenth-century 'Peter's Pence' box used to collect tax due to Rome: one penny per household, due to the Pope on the feast of St Peter in vinculis or Lammas Day (1 August). The box is illustrated in Suckling 1847, p. 152.

[32] The stalls were moved to the choir and remained there.

King Anna and his son were interred as before mentioned, but no traces of their tombs or inscriptions remain. No church, perhaps, has been so robbed of its beautiful historical relics, and the documents which were once preserved in the old chests as this. The ancient rood screen, fragments of which still remain, presents to us a specimen of its original beauty, and before the restoration was entirely besmeared with whitewash. The church is designed on a uniform plan, comprising a nave, chancel, two aisles, and a south porch, the roof of which was groined, and on the centre boss was carved the Holy Trinity. The tower at the west end is of inferior workmanship, and probably much older than the fabric itself. The chancel had a great benefactor in the person of John Greyse, in 1442. The font, which stands at the west end of the nave, is much mutilated, and was the gift of John Mason, and Katherine, his wife, as shewn by an inscription round it. The monuments in the church are probably those of the Hoptons and Swillingtons; those in the chancel probably to Sir John Hopton, who founded the chantry, and finished the chancel in the reign of Edward IV; and that in the north aisle to the last of the Swillingtons. The brasses which once graced the slabs upon the floor are now gone.

Blythburgh contains, including the hamlet of Hinton and Bulcamp, about 3,500 acres. There are no glebe lands, and the present annual value of this perpetual curacy is the miserable sum of £41. But the late Sir Chas. Blois consented to augment it with a sum of £200 from Queen Anne's Bounty.

25. Reopening of church, the *East Anglian Daily Times*, 18 April 1884[33]

RE-OPENING OF BLYTHBURGH CHURCH.

The re-opening services of this church were continued on Wednesday. In the morning, Rev. J.J. Raven, D.D., Rector of St. Georges's, Great Yarmouth, preached an eloquent discourse from Isaiah lxi. chap., 4 verse, 'And they shall build up the old wastes, they shall raise up the former desolation, and they shall repair the waste cities, the desolation of many generations.' In the afternoon the announcement that the Lord Bishop of Norwich would preach, brought together a large congregation, amongst whom were many of the elite of the neighbourhood. The Vicar, Rev. H. Sykes, read the prayers to the second collect, the Rev. J.A. Clowes (Westleton) continuing them to the end. The first lesson was read by Dr. Raven (Yarmouth), and the second lesson by Rev. V.J. Stanton (Rector of Halesworth and Rural Dean). Before the sermon the Bishop's favourite hymn was sung, commencing 'The Church's one Foundation.' The Lord Bishop took for his text, Haggai, 1st chapter, 8th verse, 'Go up to the mountain and bring wood and build the house, and I will take pleasure in it, and I will be glorified, saith the Lord.' His Lordship congratulated those who had earnestly laboured to bring about the restoration now partially completed. In the evening the Ven. Archdeacon Groome was announced to preach, but unfortunately was unable to fulfil his engagement through indisposition, and the Rev. J.A. Clowes, Westleton, officiated in his stead. The reverend gentleman took for his text the 84th Psalm, 1st and 2nd verses, 'How amiable are Thy tabernacles, O Lord of Hosts,' etc. All the services were well attended, especially that of the afternoon, and good offertories were taken up.

---

[33] Brooke.

26. Reopening of church, the *Ipswich Journal*, 19 April 1884[34]

THE RE-OPENING OF BLYTHBURGH CHURCH

The services in connection with the re-opening of Blythburgh Church, after partial restoration, were continued on Wednesday. In Tuesday's edition of the *Journal* we gave a brief report of the alterations which have been made in this magnificent church and of the services held on Easter Sunday. The sum, amounting to about £1,000, which has been already raised and expended, has certainly served to whet the appetite to continue the good work. The utmost care has evidently been exercised not to spend a penny where it was not absolutely needed; there is little or nothing in the way of ornamentation pure and simple, the repairs being substantial and good. A considerable part of the money has been expended in undoing the injudicious 'restorations' of former periods, such as removing bricks from many of the beautiful windows which served to make the original building so exceptionally attractive. The taking down of the high-backed pews was another matter that had to be attended to, though the trouble, if not the expense, of this was in a large degree compensated for by the uncovering of several old benches with carved poppyheads that had thus been hidden for many generations. Very much more in the same direction will have to be done before the second stage in the work of renovation has been reached, especially the scraping of the ragged walls and of the handsome pillars of the grand old nave, the length of which, by the way, with the chancel, is 127 feet, having timbers artistically embellished with ecclesiastical emblems. There is no difficulty in pointing out what needs to be done. The real difficulty that has to be faced is how the money is to be raised to do it. The judicious laying out of the money could very well be left in the hands of the architect, Mr. A.E. Street. The rector [*sic*], the Rev. Henry Sykes, will now probably take a little breathing, and then perhaps begin de novo. We have no authority for saying so much, but nothing, it is said, succeeds like success, and success has pre-eminently marked his efforts and the efforts of the influential ladies and gentlemen who have been associated with him as a Committee in the noble undertaking. The real discouragement that had to be encountered was the deplorably neglected condition of the sacred edifice before anything was attempted. Now that such a marked improvement has been effected by the expenditure of £1,200, there is some encouragement for renewed effort to raise an additional thousand, which would serve the purposes another stage in the restoration, though he would be a bold man who would say off-hand how many such stages would have to be covered before the building was brought into a state it should be brought into, from its fine proportions, and the many architectural and antiquarian features that have been preserved notwithstanding the determined efforts of the most vicious iconoclast. There are, for instance, intact, sixteen carved figures on the panel work in front of the chancel pews. There is also some very beautiful old glazing, which has been carefully re-used. There are many other most interesting features which serve to increase the desire to extend the work of renovation. There is a good deal that must be done before long, and still more which might be done. In the former category may be placed the careful restoration of the chancel and nave roofs with new lead throughout, the thorough restoration of the North aisle roof, and the opening and restoration of the clerestory and two larger windows in the chancel. It would also be satisfactory to do something

---

[34] RCMB.

to beautify the chancel, but that might be left for a time. The other works which are not absolutely necessary are the restoration of the screen, stalls, parvis, etc., but on the other hand there is a certain amount of external work which might well be done. The idea is, however, when a new start is made to attempt nothing beyond what is necessary for the preservation of the building. At the morning service on Wednesday, prayers were read by the vicar, the Rev. H. Sykes. The first lesson (2 Chronicles vii. to verse 17) was read by the Rev. J.N.F. Ewen., M.A., rector of Frostenden, and the second lesson (Ephesians ii) by the Rev. T.S. Curteis, rector of Brampton. These two clergymen also took the ante-Communion service. The Rev. J.J. Raven, D.D., head master of the Grammar School, Yarmouth, preached from Isaiah lviii., 12, 'And they that shall be of thee, shall build the old waste places: thou shalt raise up the foundations of many generation; and thou shalt be called the repairer of the breach, the restorer of paths to dwell in.' The rev. gentleman spoke of the deep interest he had taken in Blythburgh Church for many years. About 14 years ago he was deputed by the Suffolk Archaeological Society to visit the church and write an article upon its history and character.[35] From that time he had been a great admirer of this noble structure, and could not but deplore its dilapidated condition. Dr. Raven expressed the great satisfaction the work accomplished gave him, and felt confident that what had been so well begun would be eventually carried though, to the credit of those engaged in it, and to the gratification of all admirers of church architecture. In the afternoon the prayers were read by the vicar, assisted by the Rev. J.A. Clowes, vicar of Westleton. The first lesson (Haggai i, ii. to verse 10) was read by Dr. Raven, and the second lesson (Hebrew x. 19 to 26) by the Rev. V.J. Stanton, M.A., rector of Halesworth. The Lord Bishop of the Diocese[36] preached, and took as his text (Haggai i, 8), 'Go up to the mountain and bring wood, and build the house: and I will take pleasure in it, and I will be glorified, said the Lord.' The right rev. Prelate said the Jews had, 15 years before the time that Haggai wrote, returned to Jerusalem from their captivity in Babylon, and they had been specially charged by the Lord to rebuild the Temple. When they came to Jerusalem and looked upon the Temple in ruins, and realized the circumstances in which they were placed, they were greatly discouraged. They were discouraged at the greatness of the undertaking, and at their inability to re-erect the house of God in its former magnificence. They also felt the insecurity of the city in which they were dwelling and the harassing position of their enemies, but more than that, they were hindered from undertaking and prosecuting the work by a selfish regard to their domestic comfort and earthly prosperity. Under these circumstances God spoke to them as he had ever spoken to men, and as He spoke in the present day by His providential dealings. All classes, all the authorities both in the State and in the Church listened to the Word of God, and went to work with a will and a purpose. What a blessed thing it was when in a nation, or in a church, or in a parish, or in a home the command of the Lord was thus obeyed, and the promise of the Lord graciously fulfilled as it was in this case. The command of God to the Jews was in some respects distinct and peculiar to the Temple, in reference to which it was addressed. As with the Tabernacle, so with the Temple – the whole fabric, its internal arrangement, and its furniture, were all in accordance with a divinely revealed pattern. This could not be said of our churches, but they were alike in this, that they were set apart for the celebration of God's appointed ordinances, for the assembly of

---

35 Raven, 'Blythburgh'.
36 John Thomas Pelham, Bishop of Norwich, 1857–93.

congregations, for the service of prayer and praise, and the hearing of the Word; and though we had no divinely revealed pattern, yet as the House was for Him and His worship, it ought to [be] built and furnished, and, if needed, restored in a way that should evidently show our regard and reverence for Him and for His Word, and in a manner well adapted for all its several uses. His Lordship spoke of the promise contained in the text, and remarked that it was very suggestive to mark how God's glory was to be manifest in the rebuilt and restored Temple in Jerusalem. The aged ones in Jerusalem regarded with tears the contrast between the building that was then being restored with the magnificence of the former one, yet God declared that the glory of the latter house should be greater than the former, 'I will fill this house with glory.' The material splendour was evidently far inferior. No visible cloud of manifested glory ever filled its courts. Wherein, then, was to consist the excelling glory of the restored house over and beyond that which had distinguished the first temple? This was it – 'God manifest in the flesh,' the Messiah, called in the 7th verse of the 2nd chapter the 'Desire of all nations.' The manifestation of the Christ, and in Him the opening of the doors of God's house to all nations, was to be the distinguishing feature of the excelling glory of the latter house. As the bodily presence of God incarnate, our Lord Jesus Christ was that by which God was glorified in this second restored temple; so was the spiritual presence of the same Lord Jesus, by which God doth glorify Himself in the churches and assemblies of His saints now, whether in the magnificent cathedral, or in the village church, or 'where two or three are assembled together' in His name, that which gave efficacy to our ordinances, and it was through this alone that our services of prayer and praise found acceptance, and were well-pleasing to God. My dear brethren, continued the right rev. prelate, I am thankful to have met you this afternoon in this House of God, and together with you to express our thankfulness that one good step has been taken towards this restoration, and that what has been attempted has been well done; but we cannot look around and not feel, especially as we look upon the work that has been done, how very much yet remains to be done, how much requires to be done. Who can look upon that which remains to be performed by the light of that which has been done, and not long and desire that the whole work was accomplished? This is a great work, and so was that which the Jews had to do, but I hope that we shall none of us answer as they did, that 'The time is not come.' I hope there will be a different spirit amongst us than that. I hope we shall consider our ways and know that if we would indeed honour the Lord with our substance, and with the first fruits of our increase, we should find it true, not only that the house of God would be restored, and His services blest, but our earthly prosperity would be increased.

In the evening the prayers were again read by the Vicar, and also the first lesson (Ezra iii). The Rev. J.A. Clowes read the second lesson, and preached the sermon from Psalm lxxxiv, 1,2. After reading his text, 'How amiable are Thy tabernacles, O Lord of hosts! my soul longeth, yea, even fainteth for the courts of the Lord; my heart and my flesh crieth out for the living God,' the rev. gentleman explained that his appearance in the pulpit was occasioned by the sudden indisposition of Archdeacon Groome, who had been taken ill at Southwold after his arrival there the previous evening. The Vicar had heard services [*'services' crossed out by Sykes and replaced by 'several times'*] during the day from the Archdeacon, who hoped almost to the last to take his part in the deeply interesting services of the day. Mr. Clowes preached an excellent sermon, in which he dwelt upon the deep interest of the Psalmist in the services of God's house, urging upon his hearers the importance of attending regularly the public worship of God.

The Rev. H.L. James, of St. Clement's, Ipswich, who kindly came over for the purpose, ably presided at the organ.[37] The energy and ability with which the rev. gentleman conducted the musical portion of the services, in the double capacity of organist and choirmaster, left nothing to be desired. The musical portions of the services were as follows:- *Morning*: 'Venite,' *Jones* in D, special Psalms (as approved by the Bishop), 47 and 48, to *Hayes* and *Aldrich* in F (transposed); 'Te Deum' and 'Jubilate' to *Lord Mornington's* Chants in D. The hymns sung were the 'Old 100th' Psalm, and 'Jerusalem the Golden' to tune *Ewing*. Concluding voluntary, 'The Priests' March,' from the oratorio, 'Athalie.' *Afternoon*: The opening hymn was *Miss Elliott's* 'The Hour of Prayer,' sung with much feeling to *Stewart's* 'Palestrina.' Special Psalms, 84 and 85, to *Robinson* in E flat; 'Magnificat,' *Mornington* in D (transposed). The 'Deus Misereatur' being sung to the beautiful *Gregorian* 'Tonus Peregrinus.' Hymns 'The Church's one Foundation,' and 'O God of Bethel,' to tunes 'Aurelia' and 'Belmont' were sung with great vigour. The concluding voluntary was a march in G by the Rev. H.L. James. *Evening*: For the opening voluntary was played a symphony in G (*Glück*); special Psalms, 148, 149, and 150, were sung to *Hayes* in F, *Cooke* in G (transposed), and *Pelham Humphrey's* 'Grand Chant,' the latter being sung in unison. Cantate, *Cooke* in F, 'Nunc Dimittis,' to *Rev. H. L. James's* chant in F. The hymns were – 'Pleasant are Thy Courts above,' to tune 'Maidstone,' and the evening hymn, 'Abide with me.' The concluding voluntary was one of a series of six 'Bagatelles' in F and B flat.

27. Progress of restoration, *Morning Post*, 12 May 1884[38]

RESTORATION OF BLYTHBURGH CHURCH, SUFFOLK.

The restoration of this magnificent and venerable edifice is making rapid progress towards completion. The work includes the thorough restoration of the south aisle, with the exception of the porch, as also the restoration and extension of the beautiful and unique parapet in the east end of the aisle and around the porch. The windows on the south-east and west of the aisle have been unblocked and restored, and filled in with tinted glass. A roof of English oak, including many valuable portions of the old work, is completed, and the south side of the church presents a very fine appearance – a most pleasing contrast to its dilapidated condition two years ago. The east end, as it now appears, is truly imposing. The magnificent chancel window and the one east of the north aisle have been fully restored in accordance with the original design. The north aisle is almost completed so far as the windows are concerned, as also the west end, including a very handsome decorated one in the tower. The improvement internally is as striking as the outward appearance. The old box pews which disfig-ured the nave and south aisle have been removed, and the original oak benches, with their antique and interesting poppy heads, have been collected and arranged in the centre of the building. Other excellent improvements have been effected, and the work has been done to the complete satisfaction of the Building Committee. The work of restoration so far has cost only £1,1000 [*sic*]. The projected restoration of the north aisle and nave roofs will cost £1,035 in addition, and the Rev. H. Sykes, the

---

37 He was to be vicar of Blythburgh, 1885–8.
38 RCMB.

vicar, hopes to receive assistance in his effort to preserve this magnificent specimen of 14th [*sic*] century ecclesiastical architecture.

28. Debenham church. Thackeray Turner, SPAB, to the *Ipswich Chronicle*, 27 November 1884, published 29 November[39]

DEBENHAM CHURCH

Sir, – The attention of my Committee has just been called to the long letter from the Vicar of Debenham which appeared in your issue of the 22nd inst., and I am directed to say that the Committee is pleased to hear of the partial success of its efforts to save Debenham Church from what we consider, as will be seen from our report, to be nothing less than destruction.

It is, however, a matter of regret to the Committee that its advice was not followed more fully, and that the Restoration Committee, who it is true wrote to say that it had complete confidence in its architect, did not avail itself of the suggestion contained in the last clause of our report, and allow this Society to discuss the points upon which we differ. I am directed to say that I have acted throughout entirely in accordance with the instructions of my Committee, and that the restoration of Debenham Church has not been singled out by the Society, as may be proved by the large number of reports which are yearly sent out by this Society to incumbents and churchwardens or restoration committees. Our report was lithographed because, as the Debenham Church Restoration Committee was a large body, it was cheaper than making copies by hand, and it would not have been either courteous to that Committee, or business like, if a copy had only been sent to the Vicar.

My Committee hopes the Vicar's suggestion will be taken, and that many will visit the church, for although they will not, of course, be able to see the old work of the south aisle which has been destroyed, they will at least be able to see the beautiful flint and stonework and stained glass of the north aisle, and my Committee sincerely hopes that no one, after seeing it, will subscribe towards the work of repair unless there is a promise that it shall be dealt with in accordance with our report, and that the windows, with one exception, shall not be taken out and rebuilt as suggested by the Vicar.

The Committee believes the Vicar earnestly desires to do the best for the building, but from his letter it is clear he does not understand or appreciate the art of medieval workmen, and that to him a modern copy of their work is practically as good as the original.

It has been found by experience that when once old window tracery has been removed it cannot be replaced without cutting many of the original stones and replacing many by new. This alone is a sufficient reason, without naming the old glass, for not removing the north aisle windows of Debenham Church. – I am, Sir, yours obediently,
THACKERAY TURNER,

---

[39] RCMB. This is one of a series of letters in the *Ipswich Journal* concerning differences between the SPAB and the Debenham church restoration committee. Although not about Blythburgh, the retention of this cutting shows that Sykes was aware of the intervention of the SPAB in other church restoration debates. The south aisle of St Mary Magdalene church, Debenham, was restored by H.J. Green in 1883–6. Bettley and Pevsner, *East Suffolk*, p. 189.

The Society for the Protection of Ancient Buildings, 9, Buckingham-street, Adelphi, W.C. November 27th 1884.

29. Newspaper cutting. Report on bazaar, [?]1886[40]

Bazaar at Blythburgh.

The inhabitants of Blythburgh have made up their minds that the fine old historic fabric, bequeathed to them by their ancestors, shall be thoroughly restored to a condition worthy of its ancient fame. The church, which is one of the finest in the diocese, contains some 50 windows, all in the Perpendicular style. It also has a Perpendicular carved oak roof, painted in the original style of Henry VII. The roof of the north aisle is in a dilapidated and unsafe condition, and totally unfit for worshippers to sit under. It is proposed to restore this aisle, and tenders have been received for the work. A tender of £700, which will include the repair of the roof of the nave and north aisle, is under consideration, and subscriptions towards this amount have been received. In aid of this object a successful bazaar was opened in the rectory grounds on Wednesday; and if the necessary funds are forthcoming, the repairing of the north aisle will be commenced with as little delay as possible.[41] The stalls at the bazaar, which were laden with useful articles of every description, were arranged in a gaily-decorated and spacious tent. The stall-keepers were – Lady Blois (Cockfield Hall), assisted by Miss Maude Blois; Lady Huntingfield; Mrs. James, assisted by the Misses Cross; Mrs. F. Gaussen (Southwold) and Miss Gaussen; Mrs. Cooper, Miss Cooper and friends; Mrs. Tuthill and Miss E. J. Hardy and Mrs. Youngs. The flower stall, containing a profusion of choice blossoms, was presided over by Miss Blois, assisted by Miss Adeline Blois; whilst the refreshment stall was under the charge of Miss Blois (Southwold). In addition to these there was a live stock stall, managed by Mr. E. S. Blois, a fish-pond in which amateur and professional anglers exercised their skill with equal success, under the care of Mr. S.K. Blois; a 'magic well,' in which the 'dip' never failed to produce something new, under the presidency of Miss Violet Blois and Miss Cecil Blois. Special attractions were provided in the form of conjuring by Mr. Walter H. Purssord (Yarmouth), who introduced his sleight-of-hand tricks with great success. Two excellent concerts were also given at three o'clock in the afternoon and six in the evening, in which Lady Blois, Miss Blois, Mrs. Gaussen, Miss Gaussen and other ladies took part. Exhibition games of lawn tennis were played during the day. Among the articles worthy of special note upon the stall of Mrs. James were six water-colour drawings by Mrs. S. Spedding James and the Rev. H. J. James [sic] (the Vicar); some delicate and skillfully worked leather brackets by Miss Hanbury (Ipswich); a pair of hand-painted bellows by Miss Pemberton-Barnes, of the Hall, Havering; silk embroidery and crewel work by Mrs. Crowther, Bradford, Yorkshire; the new macrame work for brackets; crewel work in sofa cushions, by Mrs. James; and a five guinea silk counterpane, made by Mrs. Cape, containing some of the silk of King George III's sash. The stall presided over by Lady Blois also contained many interesting and valuable articles. During the day the bazaar was visited by Lord Stradbroke, Lady Constance Barne and family, Mr. and Mrs.

---

[40] SROI 2, 2. Newspaper not identified.
[41] The 1882 bazaar was in the field behind the White Hart, but this is the only reference in a document to the location of the 1886 bazaar. Walberswick and Blythburgh were one benefice and the 'rectory' was at Walberswick, so it is plausible that a bazaar to raise money for Blythburgh could be held there.

Brook (Sefton), Mr. and Mrs. Holland (Huntingfield), and the Rev. P.L. Cautley and Mrs. Cautley (Southwold). Among the subscriptions sent in by those unable to attend the bazaar were subscriptions from Lady Huntingfield, Lady Rose, Mrs. Lomax, and Mrs. Bromley. The proceedings were enlivened by the band of the Halesworth Company 1st Suffolk Rifles. The bazaar will be open again today (Thursday). The Rev. H.L. James (who is a most earnest and untiring worker), the Vicar of Blythburgh and Walberswick, is very anxious to obtain further subscriptions towards completing the tender for £700. The Great Eastern Railway have made special arrangements for the issue of return tickets at single fares.

30. Newspaper cutting. Proceeds of bazaar, [?]1886[42]

BLYTHBURGH
THE BAZAAR. – the gross receipts at the bazaar held on the 11th inst. are:- Stalls: Lady Blois, Lady Huntingfield, Mrs. F. Gaussen, Miss Blois (Southwold), and Miss Blois (Cockfield), £69; Mrs. James, £34 12s. 2d.; Mrs. Cooper, £20; Mrs. Tuthill, £6 7s. 6d.; Mrs. Youngs, £2; taken at gate and sundries, £10 14s. 4d.; cash donations to Vicar during the bazaar, £7 6s.; total £150. The expenses have not yet been ascertained, but will probably amount to about £20.

31. *The Blythburgh and Walberswick Parish Magazine*, September 1894[43]
[Not all transcribed, but relevant extract is:]

GOOD WORKS IN BLYTHBURGH
The month past has proved an eventful one in Blythburgh. One kind proposal for the improvement of the interior of the Church has followed another. Mr. and Mrs. Bellairs first asked permission to wash the whitewash off the beautiful oak screen, and when this was readily granted, a band of willing workers joined them, none working harder than our good leaders themselves, and after a whole week's perseverance, the great task was very happily accomplished. Meanwhile the removal of the whitewash from the stone columns and arches of the chancel was proposed; then the adornment of the sacrarium with tile flooring, and hangings for the walls; and eventually the Vicar announced in Church on the following Sunday that a subscription list for the necessary expenses was already handsomely headed, and called for further contributions. In thus kindly initiating the good work, and in actually labouring in it with their own hands, besides their gifts of money, our good friends have earned, and may feel assured of the lasting gratitude of the parishioners. About £20 is required, and subscriptions will be gladly received by the Vicar and Churchwardens.

---

[42] SROI 2, 2. Newspaper not identified.
[43] SROI 2, 1.

APPENDIX D

NOTES ON PEOPLE

Notes in lists 1 to 3 are on people named in correspondence, architects' reports and other main documents. Section 3 does not include people who appear only as contributors to appeals or those who attended or performed at the 1882 Blythburgh bazaar and London concert. Contributors to appeals are listed in Appendix B.

1. Vicars of Blythburgh

1879–1885	Sykes, the Revd Henry (b. *c*. 1830)
1885–1888	James, the Revd Henry Lionel (b. *c*. 1858)
1888–1896	Oakes, the Revd Thomas Henry Royal (*c*. 1854-1945)
1896–1902	Woodruff, the Revd Arthur William, BA, MA (b. *c*. 1858)
1902–1923	Wing, the Revd Richard Plowman, BA (1852-1936)
1924	Naylor, the Revd Arthur Herbert Douglas
1925	Shakespear, the Revd Samuel Henry
1928	Thompson, the Revd Arthur Donald

2. Churchwardens of Blythburgh

1879–1890	Robinson Briggs and Charles Youngs
1890–1891	Charles Youngs[1]
1891–1894	Charles Youngs and Arthur B. Cooper
1894–1895	Arthur B. Cooper and Henry A. Gray
1895–1896	H.A. Gray and George Goldsmith
1896–1901	H.A. Gray and William F. Parkington
1901–1902	H.A. Gray and Philip C. Rock
1902–1907	H.A. Gray and Claude F. Egerton
1907–1190	C.F. Egerton and James Nutt
1910–1911	J. Nutt and W.F. Parkington

---

[1] Robinson Briggs died in 1890. A vestry meeting held on 13 May 1890 to elect churchwardens for 1890–1 was found to be illegal and the chairman, the Revd Thomas Oakes, did not record the business. A meeting held on 14 August 1890, attended by the unusually high number of 36 people, was again deemed by Oakes to be illegal. The meeting ended in disorder at 12.40 a.m. A meeting held on 31 March 1891, attended by 10 people, successfully appointed two churchwardens for 1891–2. SROI FC198 A1 1 Vestry Minute Book.

3. People

Adamson, A. George (*c.* 1822–85). Bank agent. The Bank House, Framlingham. Wrote letter forwarded by the Revd Henry Sykes to the *Ipswich Journal*, 1881.

Allen, Robert J., builder, High Street, Southwold. Successful bidder for restoration work, 1882.

Aplin, Francis W. Hon. Treasurer, SPAB 1906.

Bagot-Chester, Master. Either John Massey (b. 1868) or Hugh Augustus (b. 1871), sons of Col. Heneage Charles (1836–1912) and Madeline Elizabeth Bagot-Chester. Bazaar 1882.

Baker, Oliver (1856–1939). Artist and antiquary. SPAB committee.

Bardell and Brothers, builders, London Road, King's Lynn, Norfolk. Unsuccessful bidders for restoration, 1882.

Barne, Lady Constance Adelaide Seymour (1852–1915), of Sotterley Hall. Daughter of Francis George Hugh Seymour, 5th Marquis of Hertford (1812–84). Married Lt-Col. Frederick St John Newdigate Barne (1842–98) in 1871. Patroness of 1882 and 1890 bazaars.

Barne, Mrs Violet Ella. Daughter of Archibald Ernest Orr Ewing, 3rd Bt, married Major Miles Barne (1874–1917) in 1904. Patroness of Yoxford exhibition, 1905.

Bartram, builders, Aylsham, Norfolk. Unsuccessful bidders for restoration, 1882.

Bellairs, (William) Charles (1861–98). White House Farm, Bulcamp, Blythburgh. Supporter of Blythburgh church.

Bence Lambert, Mrs Ida Millicent (1860–1951), of Thorington Hall. Patroness of 1890 bazaar. Patroness of Yoxford exhibition 1905.

Bickers, Charles Arthur (1848–1908). Coal merchant, Blythburgh. Sunday-school teacher. Restoration committee 1881.

Blois, Miss Adeline Louisa (d. 1941). Daughter of Sir John Blois, 8th Bt. Bazaar 1882.

Blois, Miss Alice Clara (b. *c.* 1848–1940). Daughter of Sir John Blois, 8th Bt. Killed by enemy action. Bazaar, 1890.

Blois, Eardley Steuart (1869–1955), second son of Sir John Blois, 8th Bt. 'Master Eardley' at bazaar 1882. Inherited the estate of F.C. Brooke (d. 1886)

Blois, Lady Eliza Ellen (d. 1924). Daughter of Capt. Alfred Chapman, R.N. Sister of Mrs Brodrick and Mrs Gaussen. Married Sir John Blois in 1865. Restoration committee from 1882. Patroness of 1882 bazaar.

Blois, Miss Gertrude. Not identified. Bazaar, 1882.

Blois, Sir John Ralph, 8th Bt of Cockfield Hall, Yoxford (1830–88). Second son, his older br. d. unmarried 1849. Succeeded his uncle, 1855. Blythburgh church patron. Restoration committee from 1882.

Blois, Sir Ralph Barrett Macnaghten, 9th Bt (1866–1950) of Cockfield Hall, Yoxford. 'Master Ralph' at bazaar, 1882. Succeeded his father, Sir John Blois, in 1888. Married, 1898, Winifred Grace Hegan (d. 1963). Blythburgh church patron. Secretary restoration committee appeal, 1905.

Blois, Lady Winifred Grace (d. 1963). Daughter of Col. Edmund Hegan Kennard. Married Sir Ralph Blois, 9th Bt, in 1898. Patroness of 1890 bazaar. Restoration committee, 1905.

Blois, Dowager Lady. Patroness of Yoxford exhibition, 1905. See Lady Eliza Ellen Blois.

Blois, Mrs. Patroness, 1882 bazaar. Not further defined. The wives of two brothers of Sir John Blois, 8th Bt, were alive at this date: Claudine Francis (d. 1928), who married, 1870, George Vanneck Blois (d. 1872), and Fanny Elizabeth (d. 1912), who married, 1874, William Thornhill Blois (d. 1889).

Blomfield, Sir Arthur William (1829–99). Architect. Knighted 1889. Consulted by London committee, 1882.

Bodley, George Frederick (1827–1907). Architect. Designer of churches, with a talent for decorative detail and an approach that was the antithesis of the beliefs of the Arts and Crafts Movement. Consultant architect to Peterborough, Exeter and Manchester cathedrals towards the end of his career.

Bosanquet, Mrs Cecilia J. Smith- (b. *c.* 1834). Wife of Horace J. Smith-Bosanquet (b. *c.* 1829) of 38 Queen's Gate, London. Provided venue for London concert, 1882.

Brewer, Henry (1836–1903). Architectural draughtsman. SPAB restoration committee.

Briggs, Mrs Ellen J. (b. *c.* 1826). Wife of Robinson Briggs. Church restoration committee, 1881.

Briggs, Robinson (*c.* 1822–90). Farmer, Bulcamp, Blythburgh. Churchwarden 1879–90. Restoration committee, 1881.

Bristol, Marchioness Geraldine Georgiana Mary of, of Ickworth (d. 1927). Married Frederick William John Hervey (1834–1907), 3rd Marquis of Bristol, 1862. Patroness of Yoxford exhibition, 1905.

Brodrick, the Hon. Mrs Henry. Alice, daughter of Capt. Alfred Chapman, married 1869, second wife of Henry Brodrick (1838–77), son of 6th viscount Midleton. Sister of Lady Eliza Ellen Blois and Mrs Gaussen. Patroness of 1882 bazaar.

Brooke, Francis Capper (1810–86), of Ufford Place. Related to patrons of Blythburgh church by descent through mother from Sir Charles Blois, 1st Bt. Brooke's complex will led to estate passing, on the death of daughter Constance in 1930, to Eardley Steuart Blois, second son of 8th Bt. He changed his name to Brooke.

Brooke, Mrs. Probably Helen Beatrice (1855–97), first wife (1882) of John Kendall Brooke (1856-1939) of Sibton Park. Patroness of 1890 bazaar.

Brooke, Mrs Katherine Frances Kendal. Daughter of Arthur Heywood of Glevering. Second wife (1901) of John Kendal Brooke of Sibton Park. Patroness of Yoxford exhibition, 1905.

Cautley, the Revd Proby Littler (1845–1934), BA Cantab. 1871, MA 1880. Vicar of Southwold, 1877–90, and rural dean, 1889–90.

Cautley, Mrs Anne Frances Ovendon (b. *c.* 1847). Wife of Proby Cautley. Patroness of 1890 bazaar.

Clarke, Sir Caspar Purdon, G.S.I., FSA (1846–1911). Museum director and architect. Director of South Kensington Museum (later renamed Victoria & Albert Museum), 1896–1905; director Metropolitan Museum, New York, 1905–11. Restoration committee, 1905.

Clarke, Mrs. Not identified. Patroness of Yoxford exhibition 1905.

Clowes, the Revd James Aaron (b. *c.* 1820). Vicar of Westleton, 1861. Reopening, 1884.

Cobbold, Lady Evelyn (1867–1963). Daughter of Charles Adolphus Murray, 7th Earl of Dunmore. Married, 1891, John Dupois Cobbold (d. 1929) of Holy Wells, Ipswich. Patroness of Yoxford exhibition, 1905.

Cobbold, Roland Townsend (1822–95), of Dedham Lodge, Essex. Paid for emblems in south windows.

Colthurst, Lady Edith Jane Thomasina (d. 1930). Married, 1881, Sir George St John Colthurst (1850–1925), 6th Bt of Ardrum, Co. Cork. London concert 1882.

Cooper, Arthur Barber (b. *c*. 1861). Farmer, Westwood Lodge, Blythburgh. Son of Catherine Cooper. Churchwarden, 1892–95. Restoration committee, 1881.

Cooper, Miss Clara L. (b. *c*. 1863). Daughter of Catherine Cooper. Restoration committee from 1882.

Cooper, Mrs Catherine (*c*. 1830–95). Farmer. Westwood Lodge, Blythburgh. Widow of James Benjamin Cooper (*c*. 1832–74). Restoration committee, 1881. Patroness of 1882 and 1890 bazaars.

Crofts, Ernest, RA (1847–1911). Artist. Created picturesque house, The Green, Priory Road, Blythburgh, from two old cottages in the early twentieth century. An immediate neighbour of the church. Restoration committee and donation of sketch for 'Art Union' 1905.

Crooke, Mrs Emily Ann Sayer Parry- (1836–1912). Married, 1860, Douglas Parry-Crooke (1834–1916), of Darsham House, Saxmundham. Patroness of 1890 bazaar.

Crossley, Dowager Lady Martha Elizabeth Brinton (d. 1891). Widow of Sir Francis Crossley (1817–72), 1st Bt, of Somerleyton Hall. Patroness of 1890 bazaar.

Crossley, Lady Phyllis (d. 1948). Daughter of Gen. Sir Henry de Bathe, Bt, married 1887 Sir Savile Brinton Crossley (1857–1935), 2nd Bt (and 1st Baron 1916) of Somerleyton Hall. Patroness of 1890 bazaar. Patroness of Yoxford exhibition 1905.

Curteis, the Revd Thomas Spencer (b. *c*. 1843). BA Cantab. 1865. Rector of Brampton, 1873. Reopening, 1884.

Dowsing and Sons, builders, Norwich. Unsuccessful bidders for restoration, 1882.

D'Oyly Carte, Richard (1844–1901). Impresario. Permission for use of music, London concert, 1882.

Duleep Singh, Prince Frederick (1868–1926). Landowner and antiquarian. Son of Duleep Singh (1838–93), former Maharaja of Lahore, deposed by the British and established at Elveden Hall. Supporter of SPAB and member Blythburgh church restoration committee, 1905–6.

Egerton, Claude Francis Arthur, MICE (1864–1957). Engineer. Churchwarden and hon. treasurer restoration committee appeal 1905. Rented White House farmhouse, Bulcamp, from the earl of Stradbroke. Member of the Leveson-Gower family, related to the earls of Sutherland. Married, 1900, Alexandra Elizabeth Ritchie, widow of Charles Bellairs (d. 1898).

Egerton, Mrs Alexandra Elizabeth (d. 1938). Wife of Claude Egerton. Restoration committee and patroness of Yoxford exhibition, 1905.

Ewen, the Revd John Norris Frederick (b. *c*. 1840). BA Cantab., 1861; MA, 1866. Rector of Frostenden, 1873–90. Reopening 1884.

Fildes, Sir Samuel Luke, RA, FSA (1843–1927). Illustrator, and genre and portrait painter. Knighted 1906. Restoration committee and donation of sketch for 'Art Union', 1905.

Gathorne, the Revd Richard (b. *c*. 1847). BA Cantab., 1870; MA, 1873. Vicar of Wenhaston, 1879. Reopening, 1884.

Gaussen, Alfred William George (1855–1910). Matric. Christ Church, Oxford, 1874. Son of Mrs Frederick Gaussen. Member of London committee, 1882–3.

Gaussen, Mrs Frederick (*c*. 1826–1915). 53 Eaton Square, London. Letitia Maria Chapman, daughter of Capt. Alfred Chapman, married Frederick Charles Gaussen

(1817–67), barrister, 1852. Sister of Lady Eliza Ellen Blois and Mrs Brodrick. Patroness of 1882 and 1890 bazaars.

Gibson, Mrs Susannah Arethusa Milner (1814–85). Society hostess and political activist. Daughter of the Revd Sir Thomas Gery Cullum, 8th Bt, of Hardwick House, Bury St Edmunds, and wife of Thomas Milner Gibson (1806–1884), radical politician, of Theberton House. Patroness of Yoxford exhibition, 1905.

Goldsmith, George (b. *c.* 1849). Churchwarden, 1895–6. Stationmaster.

Gooch, Lady Florence Meta (d. 1932). Married, 1902, Sir Thomas Vere Sherlock Gooch (1881–1946), 10th Bt of Benacre Hall. Patroness of Yoxford exhibition, 1905.

Goodram, Miss. Not identified. Restoration committee from 1882.

Goscombe, Sir John William RA (1860–1952). Sculptor. Donation of sketch for 'Art Union', 1905.

Graham, Norman. Not identified. Restoration committee 1905.

Gray, Henry A. (b. *c.* 1843). Schoolmaster, Dunwich Road, Blythburgh. Churchwarden, 1894–1907.

Grimwood and Sons, builders, Sudbury. Unsuccessful bidders for restoration, 1882.

Groome, the Ven. Robert Hindes (b. *c.* 1810). BA Cantab., 1832; MA, 1835. Archdeacon of Suffolk, 1869. Reopening, 1884.

Hamilton, Mrs. Not identified. Restoration committee, 1905.

Helder, Sir Augustus (1827–1906). Solicitor. MP for Whitehaven, 1895–1906. Restoration committee, 1905.

Hill, Arthur George (1857–1923), BA Cantab., 1880; MA, 1883. Docteur des Lettres Lille 1913. Ran family organ-building company from 1893. Fellow of the Society of Antiquaries of London, 1882.

Hollond, Mrs. Probably the wife of Francis Egbert Hollond of Satis House, Yoxford, neighbours of the Blois family at Cockfield Hall. However, another Suffolk possibility is the wife of Edward William Hollond of Benhall Lodge. Patroness of 1890 bazaar. Patroness of Yoxford exhibition, 1905.

Huntingfield, Louisa Lady (d. 1898). Wife of Charles Andrew Vanneck (1818–97), 3rd Baron Huntingfield of Heveningham Hall. His mother, Lucy Anne, was the third daughter of Sir Charles Blois, 6th Bt. Patroness of 1882 and 1890 bazaars.

Irving-Davies, the Revd George. BA Oxon., 1856; MA, 1861. Rector Kelsale-cum-Carlton, 1868. Rural dean Dunwich, 1881. Restoration committee from 1882.

James, the Revd Henry Lionel (b. *c.* 1858). Vicar Walberswick with Blythburgh, 1885–8. Perpetual curate of St Clement's, Ipswich, 1880–4, and incumbent of Laxey, Isle of Man, 1884–5. He left for St. Cuthbert's, Everton. Participated in reopening service, 1884.

Johnston, Philip Mainwaring, FSA, FRI, BA (1865–1936). Architect. Blythburgh church restoration, 1905–6. Restored numerous churches and houses and designed war memorials.

Kent, John (d. 1911). Assistant secretary SPAB.

Kershaw, Samuel Wayland (1836–1914). Antiquary and librarian, Lambeth Palace library from 1870. SPAB committee member who provided historical background on certain cases.

Knightley, Lady Louisa Mary (1842–1913). Daughter of General Sir Edward Bowater. A Suffolk connection through grandmother Emilia Mary, daughter of Col. Michael Barne, of Sotterley. Married Sir Rainald Knightley (1819–95), 3rd Bt and 1st Baron, 1892, politician, of Fawsley, Northants. Patroness of 1882 bazaar.

Lawrence, the Ven. Charles D'Aguilar BA Oxon., 1872; MA,1874 (b. *c.* 1848). Archdeacon of Suffolk, 1901–1916; rector, St Margaret's Lowestoft, 1889–1901; rural dean of Lothingland from 1892; restoration committee, 1905.

Lenny, Charles (b. *c.* 1818). Halesworth land agent. Auditor of restoration fund accounts.

Lethaby, William R. (1857–1931). Architect, designer and teacher. SPAB committee.

Lomax, Mrs. Probably Ann (b. *c.* 1827), wife of Thomas Lomax (b. *c.* 1826), barrister, of Grove Park, Yoxford, neighbours of the Blois family at Cockfield Hall. Patroness of 1890 bazaar.

Long, Mrs. Probably Muriel née Wentworth. Married 1898 William Evelyn Long (1871–1944) of Hurt's Hall, Saxmundham. Patroness of Yoxford exhibition, 1905.

Louise, HRH. The Princess, Duchess of Argyll (1848–1939). Daughter of Queen Victoria, married Marquess of Lorne 1871. Artist, sculptor and active president of infant National Trust. Restoration committee and patroness of Yoxford exhibition and donation of sketch for 'Art Union', 1905.

Lowther, the Hon. C. Alice (1828–1908). Daughter of James Parke, Lord Wensleydale, and wife of the Hon. William Lowther (1821–1912), of Campsea Ashe. Patroness of Yoxford exhibition, 1905.

Lucas, John Seymour RA, FSA (1849–1923). Artist. Created picturesque house The Priory, Priory Road, Blythburgh, from old cottages in early twentieth century. Restoration committee and donation of sketch for 'Art Union', 1905.

Lucas, Mrs Marie Cornelissen Seymour (1850–1921). Married, 1877, John Seymour Lucas. Restoration committee, 1905.

Lushington, Vernon, QC (1832–1912). SPAB committee. Called to the Bar 1857 and took silk eleven years later. In 1864 appointed Judge-Advocate-General and became Secretary to the Admiralty in 1869. Judge of the County Courts for Surrey and Berkshire, 1877–1900.

MacColl, Norman (1843–1904). Journal editor and Spanish scholar. Edited literary weekly *The Athenaeum*, 1871–1900.

Micklethwaite, John Thomas (1843–1906). Architect and ecclesiologist. Not a member of SPAB but frequently consulted by them. In Suffolk worked on Orford church and restored screen at Ranworth, Norfolk.

Middleton, Professor John Henry (1846–96). Architect and archaeologist. Director Fitzwilliam Museum, Cambridge, 1889, and of art collections at South Kensington Museum, 1892. SPAB committee and honorary secretary, 1882–95.

Midleton, Visountess Augusta Mary (d. 1903). Daughter of 1st Baron Cottesloe married 1853 William Brodrick (1830–1907), 8th Viscount Midleton of Midleton. London concert 1882.

Mills, George (*c.* 1825–1921). Landlord, White Hart, Blythburgh, *c.* 1875 – *c.* 1895. Restoration committee, 1881.

Moore, W. Secretary, Norwich Diocesan Building Society 1885.

Morris, William (1834–96). Socialist, campaigner, writer and designer. Founded SPAB, 1877. Visited Blythburgh church, 1895.

Murray, Sir David, RA (1849–1933). Artist. Knighted, 1918. Donation of sketch for 'Art Union', 1905.

Norman, Philip, FSA (1842–1931). Artist, author and antiquary. Treasurer of Society of Antiquaries of London, 1897–1913, and vice-president, 1913–17. Member of SPAB committee.

North, the Hon. Mrs Henry Morton. Not identified. Possibly related to the North family, earls of Guilford, Glemham Hall. Patroness of 1882 bazaar.

Nutt, James (b. *c.* 1858). Schoolmaster, London Road, Blythburgh. Churchwarden, 1908–11.

Oakes, Mrs Ada (b. *c.* 1865). Wife of Thomas Oakes.

Oakes, the Revd Thomas Henry Royal Oakes (*c.* 1854–1945). Vicar of Blythburgh with Walberswick, 1888–96. Born in India, educated at theological colleges in the USA and London. Curate St Philip's, Girlington, Bradford, Yorkshire, W.R., before Suffolk. Vicar of Netley St Matthew, Hampshire, 1896–1921 (exchanging with the Revd Arthur Woodruff) then rector of Thurgarton, Norfolk, until retirement in 1932.

Pain, Arthur C. M. Inst. C.E. (1844–1937). Engineer. Supervised the construction of the Southwold Railway, which opened in 1879 and ran through Blythburgh.

Parkington, William Fisk (b. *c.* 1862). Blacksmith, Priory Road, Blythburgh. Churchwarden, 1896–1901 and 1910–11.

Patterson, H. S. Correspondent from Arthur Street, architect's office 1890.

Pelham, the Hon. and Rt Revd John Thomas (1811–94). BA Oxon., 1832; MA and DD, 1857. Bishop of Norwich, 1857–93.

Pelham, the Revd Sydney (1849–1926). BA Oxon., 1873; MA, 1875. Vicar St. Peter Mancroft, Norwich, 1879–81.

Phipson, Evacustes (Edward) Arthur (1854–1931). Artist.

Powell, Alfred Hoare (1865–1960). 'Arts and Crafts' artist, designer and decorator of pottery. Supporter of SPAB. Reported on Blythburgh church, 1903–5.

Pretyman, Lady Beatrice Adine (1870–1952). Daughter of George Cecil Orlando Bridgeman 4th Earl of Bradford. Married, 1894, George Ernest Pretyman (1860–1931) of Orwell Park. Patroness of Yoxford exhibition, 1905.

Price, Mrs Gertrude, of Carlton Hall, Saxmundham. Married, 1873, Captain George Edward Price RN (1842–1926). Patroness of 1890 bazaar and Yoxford exhibition, 1905.

Prior, Edward Shroeder (1857–1932). 'Arts and Crafts' architect and scholar.

Probert, Capt. (later Col.) William Geoffrey Carwardine (1864–1938) of Bevills, Bures. Soldier, scholar and antiquarian. From 1903 equerry and subsequently comptroller to HRH Princess Louise, Duchess of Argyll.

Probyn, Lady. Possibly Letitia Maria Thellusson, who married, 1872, Gen. Sir Dighton MacNaughton Probyn, VC. Bazaar, 1882.

Quilter, Lady Mary Anne Bevington, (d. 1927). Wife of Sir William Cuthbert Quilter, 1st Bt (1841–1911). Art collector and politician, of Bawdsey Manor. Patroness of Yoxford exhibition, 1905.

Randall, the Revd Henry Lawrence (1855–1926). BA Cantab., 1878; MA, 1908. Vicar St Michael's, Halesworth, 1883–8.

Raven, the Revd John James (1833–1906), BA Cantab., 1857; MA, 1860; DD, 1872. Antiquary and campanologist. Headmaster Great Yarmouth Grammar School, 1866–85, and vicar of St George's, Great Yarmouth, 1881–5. Lifelong antiquarian studies in East Anglia. Restoration committee, 1905.

Rawlinson, Thomas (b. *c.* 1831). Sexton. Restoration committee, 1881.

Rayner, John. Building contractor of East Hanningfield, Essex. Visited church with Philip Johnston, 1905.

Rix, Samuel Wilton (1806–94). Beccles nonconformist, attorney and solicitor who retired 1879. Restoration committee from 1882.

Roberts, Mrs. Not identified. Patroness of 1890 bazaar.

Rock, Philip C. (b. *c.* 1864). Farmer, Hinton Lodge, Blythburgh. Churchwarden, 1901–2. Chairman parish council, 1896.

Rose, Lady the Hon. Sophia Andalusia Mary (d. 1900), of Leiston Old Abbey. Daughter of 2nd Baron Thellusson of Rendlesham Hall. Married, 1856, Sir William Rose (d. 1888). Patroness of 1890 bazaar.

Rous, Augusta, Countess of Stradbroke (d. 1901). Wife of John Edward Cornwallis Rous (1794–1886), 2nd Earl. Patroness of 1882 and 1890 bazaars.

Rous, Helena Violet Alice, Countess of Stradbroke (d. 1949). Wife of George Edward John Mowbray Rous (1862–1947), 3rd Earl. Patroness of Yoxford exhibition, 1905.

Rous, John Edward Cornwallis (1794–1886), 2nd Earl of Stradbroke, of Henham Hall. He owned land in Blythburgh, and Henham adjoined the parish to the north.

Safford, Samuel Sutherland (b. 1853) of Parkshot, Richmond, Surrey. Founder and secretary of short-lived London committee (1882–3) to support Blythburgh church. A Suffolk connection from his father John Burham Safford, of a Mettingham Castle line, and mother Maryanne, daughter of John Sutherland, surgeon and mayor of Southwold, after whom Sutherland House in the High Street is named. Secretary of charitable organisations including the Cabdrivers' Benevolent Association, the Universal Beneficient Society and the Home of Rest for Horses.

Sainty, Miss Mary A. (b. *c.* 1859). Blythburgh schoolmistress. Restoration committee, 1881.

Scott, George Gilbert (1839–97). Architect and scholar. Early in career used William Morris and firm for decoration and stained glass. In East Anglia designed Roman Catholic cathedral, Norwich, and his only country house, Garboldisham Manor, Norfolk (*c.* 1868–73, demolished).

Scrivener, Mrs Mary Millicent Levett- (1864–1948), of Sibton Abbey. Cousin and second wife of Egerton Bagot Byrd Levett-Scrivener (1857–1954), who inherited Sibton in 1889. His first wife died in an accident in 1890. Patroness of Yoxford exhibition, 1905.

Sheepshanks, the Right Revd John (1834–1909). BA Cantab., 1856; MA, 1859. Bishop of Norwich 1893–1909. Restoration committee, 1905.

Southall, Joseph Edward (1861–1944). Artist and pacifist, from Quaker background. Trained as an architect. Active in Arts and Crafts movement; often visited Southwold and reported on Blythburgh church for SPAB, 1903.

Stallybrass, Basil Thorold (1879–1922). 'Arts and Crafts' architect. Suggested as possible architect for Blythburgh, 1903.

Stanford, Misses. Not identified. Bazaar, 1882.

Stanton, the Revd Vincent John (b. *c.* 1818). BA Cantab., 1842; MA, 1850. Rector of Halesworth, 1863. Rural dean N. Dunwich, 1877. Reopening, 1884.

Street, Arthur Edmund (d. 1938). Architect. Son of George Edmund Street. Oversaw completion of many of his father's works. Architect for Blythburgh and Walberswick churches, 1881–90.

Street, George Edmund (1824–81). Architect and architectural theorist. Published numerous articles in *The Ecclesiologist* and was principal shaper of 'High Victorian' style. Prepared proposals and cost estimate for restoration of Blythburgh church, shortly before his death in 1881.

Strickland, Jane Margaret (1800–88). Author. One of a number of sisters who all became writers. Family lived in Reydon Hall, 1808–64. With proceeds from

1854 school history *Rome, Regal and Republican* she bought Park Lane Cottage, Southwold.

Sykes, Miss Sarah Ann (b. *c.* 1858). Daughter of the Revd Henry Sykes. Restoration committee from 1882.

Sykes, Mrs Anne (b. *c.* 1832). Wife of Henry Sykes. Patroness of 1882 bazaar.

Sykes, the Revd Henry (b. *c.* 1830). Vicar of Walberswick with Blythburgh, 1879–85. Ordained, 1877. Came from Freethorpe, Norfolk, and returned to Norfolk as vicar of Potter Heigham. Chairman restoration committee, 1881.

Thellusson, the Hon. Misses. Daughters of Frederick William Brook Thellusson (1840–1911), 5th Baron Rendlesham of Rendlesham Hall. Married Lady Egidia Montgomerie, 1861. They had five daughters. Patronesses of 1882 bazaar.

Thomas, Carmichael (1856–1942). Editor, *The Graphic*. Restoration committee, 1905.

Thompson, the Revd Arthur Donald (1893–1978). Univ. of London, 1919. Vicar of Walberswick with Blythburgh, 1928–1964.

Thorp, the Revd John (b. *c.* 1834). BA Oxon., 1859; MA, 1860. Vicar of Darsham, 1866–89. Reopening, 1884.

Turner, Hugh Thackeray (1853–1937). Architect. Pupil of George Gilbert Scott but became revolted by 'Gothic Revival' design. Paid secretary SPAB, 1883–1912. Ardent traveller and promoter of society. His insistence that additions to old buildings should be 'frankly modern' influences current restoration practice.

Tuthill, Mrs Maria (b. *c.* 1859). Wife of Thomas Tuthill. Restoration committee, 1881.

Tuthill, Thomas (b. *c.* 1840). Farmer, of Hawthorn Farm, Dunwich Road, Blythburgh. Restoration committee, 1881.

Vanneck, the Hon. Anne Jane (1843–1933). Daughter of Charles Andrew Vanneck (1818–97), 3rd Baron Huntingfield of Heveningham Hall, and Louisa Arcedekne (d. 1898), and sister of 4th baron. Unmarried. Patroness of Yoxford exhibition, 1905.

Vanneck, the Hon. Mrs Walter. Catherine Medora (d. 1932), married 1877 Walter Vanneck (1848–1931), younger brother of Joshua Charles Vanneck (1842–1915), 4th Baron Huntingfield of Heveningham Hall. Patroness of Yoxford exhibition, 1905.

Vanneck, the Hon. Mrs William. Mary Armstrong (*c.* 1864–1919), married the Hon. William Arcedeckne Vanneck (1845–1912), son of 3rd Baron Huntingfield. Patroness of Yoxford exhibition, 1905.

Vanneck, Baroness Lucy Anne (d. 1889 aged 90). Daughter of Sir Charles Blois, 6th Bt, second wife of Joshua Vanneck (1778–1844), 2nd Baron Huntingfield. Dowager Lady Huntingfield at bazaar, 1882.

Wardle, George (d. 1910). Bookkeeper and draughtsman to Messrs Morris, Marshall, Faulkner & Co. (Morris & Co., 1874) and business manager, 1870–90. Founder member of SPAB. Provided colour studies of many churches he visited.

Wardle, Thomas E. (1863–1931). Son of George Wardle, born in Southwold.

Waterlow, Sir Ernest Albert, RA (1850–1919). Landscape and animal painter. RA 1903 and knighted 1902. Donation of sketch for 'Art Union', 1905.

Watling, Hamlet (1818–1908). Schoolmaster and antiquarian. Wrote about visits to Blythburgh church, 1837–94. Watercolours in SROI of Blythburgh window glass.

Webb, Philip Speakman (1831–1915). Architect. In 1856 while an assistant with George Edmund Street, then Oxford diocesan architect, met William Morris, a new pupil. Designed Red House for Morris (1859–70) and with him was founder of SPAB in 1877. Reported on Blythburgh church, 1882.

Weir, William (1865–1950). Principal architect for the SPAB and committee member from 1902. Had early positions with Philip Webb and J.T. Micklethwaite. Reported on Blythburgh church, 1905–6, 1926–33 and 1947.

Wells, (Albert) Randall (1877–1942). Architect. Joined SPAB in 1901 and became active campaigner against over-restoration of ancient buildings. As a 'wandering architect' worked with Edward Shroeder Prior on Voewood, Holt, Norfolk 1905. Suggested as possible architect for Blythburgh, 1903. Visited church with Alfred Powell.

Wentworth, Mrs. Possibly Mrs Mary Emily Vernon-Wentworth (d. 1948), daughter of Lt. Gen. John Christopher Guise, CB, VC. Married, 1899, Frederick Charles Ulick Vernon-Wentworth (1866–1947) of Black Heath, Friston. Patroness of Yoxford exhibition, 1905.

Wing, the Revd Richard Plowman (1852–1936). BA Cantab., 1876. Vicar of Walberswick with Blythburgh, 1902–23. Came from Huntingfield with Cookley and retired to Walberswick.

Wise, Thomas. Chartered accountant and SPAB secretary 1881.

Woodruff, the Revd Arthur William (b. *c.* 1858–1919). BA Oxon., 1880; MA, 1884. Ordained, 1881. Vicar of Walberswick with Blythburgh, 1896–1902. Came from Netley St. Matthew, Hampshire, and left Blythburgh to become licensed priest in Winchester diocese before appointment as rector of Ardley, Oxfordshire, 1904.

Youngs, Charles (*c.* 1828–94). Farmer, Hinton Hall, Blythburgh. Churchwarden, 1879–94. Restoration committee, 1881.

Youngs, Mrs Victoria Louisa (b. *c.* 1839–1908). Wife of Charles Youngs. Restoration committee, 1881.

Lists 4 to 7 are of correspondents and addresses compiled by or for Blythburgh vicars and a selective list of Blythburgh residents.

4. List of addresses, no date[2]

The Revd Edmund Hickling, The Grove, Frostenden, Wangford
Geo. Adamson, Esq., The Bank House, Framlingham
S. Wilton Rix, Esq., Beccles
F.E. Babington, Esq., Halesworth Bank
Revd H.L. James, <1 St. Clement's Terrace> 44 Christ's Church St, Ipswich
Revd R. Brown, St Clement's, Ipswich
Jas. Garrould, Esq., Cookley
S.W. Woods, Esq., Bank House, Newnham, Gloucestershire
Revd M.B. Moorhouse, vicar St Mary's Bredin Dane John Cant
Lady Sutton, Benham Park, Newbury, Berkshire
Mrs R.G. Bosanquet, 15 Prince of Wales Terrace, Kensington, London
Mrs H. Smith Bosanquet, Broxbourn-Bury, Hoddesdon, Hertfordshire
Mrs Wingfield, Burrington Park, Burford, Oxfordshire
Revd Peter Wood, Neasdens Rectory, Gloucester

---

[2] RCMB, therefore before 1885.

5. List of correspondents, no date[3]

F.S. Waddington, Esq., 16 Clapton Square, Lower Clapton, London
George Wardle, Esq., 9 Charlotte Street, Bedford Square, London
Mr Bradbeer, Fish Salesman, Lowestoft
J. Henry Middleton, 4 Storey's Gate, Westminster
Revd Edward Hickling, The Grove, Frostenden, Wangford
Church Bells, 8 May 1880, per 'Blythburgh Church'.
Arthur C. Pain, engineer etc., 6 Claremont Road, Surbiton, London
S. Sutherland Safford, Esq., Parkshot, Richmond, Surrey
Mr F.U. Glass, 182 Leighton Road, Brecknock Road, London, N.W.
Harry Corran, <The Globe, 367.> 7 Beaufort Buildings, Strand, London, W.C.
107 Pall Mall (Athenaeum Office)
Mr Woolnough, Hall Farm, Henham, Wangford
Dickson's Almanack, Beccles
Chas. Lenny, Esq., Halesworth
The Incorporated Society for Promoting the Enlargement, Building, and Repairing of
    Churches and Chapels, 7 Whitehall
Mercer's Company
Messrs Wells Gardner, Darton and Co., 2 Paternoster Buildings, E.C.
H. Watling Esq., Pembroke Villa, Earl Stonham, Stonham
Miss Wollage, c/o Mrs Tucker, 15 Selbourne Road, Hove, Brighton
c/o Mrs Entwistle, 24 Mile St, off Trafalgar Road, <u>Burnley</u>
William Smith, Esq., 33 Ludgate Hill, London
Miss Wollage, c/o Mrs Tucker Selbourne Road, Hove, Brighton [*repeated entry*]
H. Thompson, Esq.   )
George Wooston Esq., 38 Mincing Lane, E.C.)
Church Patronage Society, Secretary of
Revd W.H. Barlow, Oakfield, King's Road, Clapham Park, S.W.
Alex. Strahan and Co. ('Good Words'), Edinburgh
G. Millican, Chestnut Lodge, Mendham, Harleston
Fred. Ling, Esq., Blaxhall Hall, Wickham Market
Revd A. Griffith<s>, St. Andrew's Vicarage, Hastings
N.W. Lavers, Endell Street, Bloomsbury, W.C.
        do   The Woodlands, Long Ditton, Surrey.

6. List of names and addresses, no date[4]

/√/ <Wm. Morris   (a) 55 Beaufort St, Chelsea, S.W.>
                     (b) 31 Bedford Row, W.C.
                     (c) 28 Caxton St, Bow, E.

---

3   RCMB, therefore before 1885. The book also contains printed 'Directions for Commencing and
     Addressing Letters to Persons of Rank'.
4   SROI 2, 3. Handwritten on notepaper from the Swan Hotel, Southwold. The deletions are lightly done.
     The meaning of the numbered ticks is not known. The names follow almost exactly the list of SPAB
     committee members printed on the form dated 1892, stating the principles of the society, which had to
     be signed by prospective members before nomination. W.C. Alexander and the last six of the names on
     the printed list are missing and Major E.C. Griffith has been added. The addresses are also additions.
     SPAB file 'Membership 1893–1904'.

(d) 13 Campden House Rd, W.

The Rt Hon. A.J. Mundella, M.P., F.R.S., 16 Elvaston Pl., S.W.

Revd T.W. Norwood

Coventry Patmore (Mrs) 9 Doughty St, W.C.

              (Mr) 53 Lawford Rd, N.W.

              (Wm) 10 Wellington Rd, St John's Wood, N.W.

<C. Kegan Paul, 38 Ashburn Pl., S.W.>

Revd Preb. Philpott

<Ernest Radford, Fountain Court, Temple, E.C.>

/1√/ Essex E. Reade, 2 Pont St, S.W.

<W.B. Richmond, A.RA, 20 York St, Portman Sq. W.>

T.J. Cobden-Sanderson

<Temple \H. H./ Soanes, 7 Palace Gate, Kensington, W.>

/√/ <Leslie Stephen, 22 Hyde Park Gate, S.W.>

J.J. Stevenson, FSA, 4 Porchester Gardens, S.W.

L. Alma Tadema, RA

Revd Precentor Venables

Emery Walker

George Y. Wardle

<Philip Webb, 1 Raymond Bldgs, Grays Inn, W.C.>

<Thomas Wells   (a) 14 Manchester Sq., W.>

                (b) 25 Upper Grange Road, S.E.

                (c) 6 Pembroke Sq., W.

<Griffith, Major E.C., F.S.S., Carlton Chambers, 4 Regent St, S.W.>

Society for the Protection of Ancient Buildings

Thos. Armstrong, 14 Sheffield Gardens, W.

<Eustace James A. Balfour, 32 Addison Rd, W.>

<J.W. Barnes, F.R.C.S., 3 Bolt Court, E.C.>

<Rt Hon. the Earl of Bective, M.P., F.R.G.S., Carlton Club, S.W.>

J. Edmund Bentley, 7 Camden Sq., N.W.

/2√/ <Detmar J. Blow, 96 Cheyne Walk, Chelsea, S.W.>

/4√/ <Geo. Price Boyce, West House, 35 Glebe Place,> Chelsea, S.W.

H.W. Brewer, 83 St. Quintin Avenue, W.

/7√/ <Revd Stopford A. Brooke, MA, 1 Manchester Sq., W.>

/8√/ <Professor James Bryce, M.P., D.C.L., 54 Portland Pl., W.>

Sir Fred. Wm. Burton, FSA, L.L.D., 43 Argyle Rd, W.

<Ingram Bywater, 93 Onslow Sq., S.W.>

<Rt Hon. Lord Carlingford, K.P., P.C., 24 Mount St, Berkley Sq., W.>

Rt Hon. the Earl of Carlisle, Kensington Palace Green, W.

J. Comyns Carr, 19 Blandford Sq., N.W.

C.G. Clement, 58 Victoria St, S.W.

(Sam. Pepys?) <S.C. Cockerell, 35 Phillimore Gardens, S.W.>

<Sidney Colvin, British Museum, W.C.>

/3 √/ <Rt Hon. Leonard \H./ Courtney, M.P., 15 Cheyne Walk, Chelsea, S.W.>

Rt Hon. the Earl Cowper, K.G., P.C., 4 St James's Sq., S.W.

Sir George Webb Dasent, [*Belgrave Mansions, S.W.*]

/5√/ <W. De Morgan, The Vale, Kings' Road, S.W.>

<Frank Dillon, 12 Buckingham St, Strand, W.C.>
F. <S.> Ellis. F.S.I., 16 Leamington Road Villas, W.
<Revd Whitwell Elwin.> <Canon Elwin>
G. Rutter Fletcher, 7 Milner St, Islington, N.
/6√/ <Wickham Flower, Old Swan House, Chelsea Embankment, S.W.>
Ernest W. Gimson
Revd Canon Greenwell
<Hon. R.C. Grosvenor, 35 Park St, Grosvenor Square, W.>
<Major Alfred Heales, FSA, 45 Carter Lane, E.C.>
John Hebb
J.P. Heseltine, 196 Queen's Gate, S.W.
J. <R.> Holliday, 203 Harrow Rd, W.
A.W. Hunt, 1 Tor Villas, Campden Hill, W.
W. Holman Hunt
E. Burne Jones, A.RA
H.C. Kay, 11 Durham Villas, Kensington, W.
Alderman William Kenrick, M.P., 71 St Ermine's Mansions, Caxton St, W.
S. Wayland Kershaw, MA, Lambeth Palace Library, S.E.
Chas. G. Leland
Revd W.J. Loftie, BA, 3A. Sheffield Terrace, Kensington, W.
Rt Hon. the Marquis of Lothian, K.T., P.C., F.R.G.S., 39 Grosvenor Sq., W. and
    Blickling Hall, Aylsham, Norfolk
Hon. J. Russell Lowell
Rt Hon. Sir John Lubbock, Bt, M.P., D.C.L., F.R.S., L.L.D., 117 Piccadilly, W.
Vernon Lushington
Norman Maccoll, 4 Notting Hill Sq., W.
F. Macmillan, 7 Northwick Ter., Maida Hill, N.W.
Revd Newton Mant
Alfred Marks, 155 Adelaide Rd, N.W.
Professor J. Hy Middleton

7. List of Blythburgh residents, 1886[5]

Chilvers George	)
Ballard Robt	)
Tuthill Sarah	) Lodge
Harvey D	)
Westgate W	)

Stannard Jas	)
Bailey Thos	) Walberswick
Phillips Jac	)

---

[5]   SROI 2, 2. The composition and purpose of this list is not clear. The churchwardens Robinson Briggs
and Charles Youngs, and the churchgoing Coopers of Westwood Lodge, for example, are not included.
The list contains 103 names. The 1881 census lists 136 households in Blythburgh including the hamlets of Bulcamp and Hinton. The population was 612, not including the Bulcamp workhouse. Location
names at the beginning of the twenty-first century are given in square brackets.

Westgate Robt)
Borrett James) Street Walk [*Stone Cottage, Dunwich Road*]
Wilson Jno)

Miles Lewis
Godbolt J

Gray H)
Walker) Mill Corner [*Dunwich Road*]
Hurren)
Piper Geo)

Tuthill Thos   Farm [*Hawthorn Farm, Dunwich Road*]

Shade)
Goldsmith) opposite Tuthills
Knights Jno)
Gilbert Jno)
Smith Willm)

Girling J
Keable Mrs   Corner House
Piper W   – Shop
Crawford – Mrs
Hunt Robt   Lodging House

Woods Tom)
Cole Mrs)
Eade Sam)

Fairhead   Shop
Etheridge Publican   [*The Street*]

Mrs D Hatcher)
Mrs W Fiske)

Ben Elmy)
Alfred Aldis)
Crawford W)

Kett John)
Gooding W)
Fiske Jno)
Goodwin Maria) opposite church [*Church Road*]
Fiske Mrs)
Broom J - Senr) opposite church
Broom J – Junr)

Meadows Mrs)
Hunt Willm)
S. Etheridge Farm) Lane called
Paske Mrs) Gorleston [*Church Lane*]
Elmy Harry)

Pinkney Jno
Attoe Robt   [*Church Lane*]

Fiske Cornelius)
Kett Edgar) Gorleston [*Church Lane*]
Meadows Horace)

Borrett Jno
Aldis Wheelwright   [*Priory Road*]

Crawford Jno)
Baxter Robt)
Rawlingson Tom)
Haycock Herbt)
Eade John) Lane from
Aldis Simeon) church past
Mr and Mrs Cobb) Blacksmiths [*Priory Road*]
Eade Harry)
Hatcher Chas)
Maria Adams)

Mr & Mrs Woodyard   House up step

Smith Peter)
Bird James) opposite White Hart [*London Road*]

Mr Mills   White Hart

Boulton   Old Toll Bar House
Chandler   Cottage by White Hart

Knights W)
Bird Harry) Barracks
Adams Charlotte)

Garrod Police Officer [*Station/London Road*]
Mr & Mrs Fuller   Corner House [*Corner London Road and Angel Lane*]

Keable Jas) near Hart Inn
Elmy Wm)

Burton Jas Snr
Burton - Junr   – Shop [*The Street*]

Stannard Sam

Farrington G   ) over Bridge
Mills J   )

Napthine by Mrs Briggs

Woodgate Mrs   ) Toby's Cottage
Lovatt J   )

Mrs Rose   House on Walks [*Toby's Walks*]

Reave W   )
Clarke Jsc   ) Fen [*Blythburgh Fen*]
Muttitt Mrs   )
King D   )

King G

Ben Chapman   ) Hinton
Clarke Saml   )

Walkers   Bulcamp

Garwood   )
Cracknell   ) Hinton
Moore   )

[*Signed*] May 1886 C. Cooper[6]

---

6   Mrs Catherine or Miss Clara Cooper, of Westwood Lodge.

BIBLIOGRAPHY

UNPUBLISHED SOURCES

Suffolk Record Office, Ipswich

Documents transcribed in this volume

Blythburgh Church Restoration Committee Minute Book, 1881–84. SROI FC198 E2 1

Blythburgh Churchwardens' Accounts, Easter 1879 to Easter 1911. SROI FC185 E1 1 (summarised)

A collection of papers from F.C. Brooke of Ufford Place, 1882–84. SROI HD 80 4 2

Blythburgh church, miscellaneous papers. SROI FC 185 E3 2 Parts 1–3

Documents not transcribed

Blythburgh Vestry Minute Book, 1884–1902. SROI FC198 A1 1

Blythburgh church miscellaneous papers. Deposited in Suffolk Record Office, Ipswich, May 2016. Provisional list dated March 2016.

Society for the Protection of Ancient Buildings, 37 Spital Square, London, E1 6DY

Documents transcribed in this volume

Blythburgh Box I, 1881–95, and II, 1901–6, and 'Additional Documents'

Documents not transcribed

'Restoration' in East Anglia. No. 1. A report to the Society for the Protection of Ancient Buildings upon the condition and prospects of the cathedrals of Ely and Norwich, and certain churches and other buildings in East Anglia (1879)

ONLINE SOURCES

Oxford Dictionary of National Biography www.oxforddnb.com

The British Newspaper Archive www.britishnewspaperarchive.co.uk

The Times Digital Archive www.gale.cengage.co.uk

Who's Who and *Who Was Who* www.ukwhoswho.com

UK Census Records and Birth, Marriage and Death Registers, and Crockford's Clerical Directory www.ancestry.co.uk

PRINTED WORKS

Except where otherwise stated, the place of publication is London.

Anon., Heraldry of Suffolk churches, *Suffolk Heraldry Society* 10 (1980)

Bailey, Mark, *Medieval Suffolk: an economic and social history, 1200–1500* (Woodbridge, 2007)

Beardsworth, Timothy, 'The flint-work inscription under the east window of Blythburgh church', *PSIAH* 38 (1993)

Becker, M. Janet, *Blythburgh* (Halesworth, 1935)

Bettley, James, 'A month in the country: Revd Ernest Geldart at Kelsale, 1881', *PSIAH* 42 Part 4 (2012)

Bettley, James, 'The Wool Hall, Lavenham: an episode in the history of preservation', *Transactions of the Ancient Monuments Society* 57 (2013)

Bettley, James and Pevsner, Nikolaus, *The buildings of England: Suffolk: East* (2015)

Blair, John, *The church in Anglo-Saxon society* (Oxford, 2005)

Blatchly, John, *Isaac Johnson of Woodbridge: Georgian surveyor and artist* (Dorchester, 2014)

Blatchly, John and Peter Northeast, *Decoding flushwork on Suffolk and Norfolk churches* (Ipswich, 2005)

Bloore, Peter and Edward Martin (eds), *Wingfield College and its patrons: piety and prestige in medieval Suffolk* (Woodbridge, 2015)

Boulting, Nikolaus, 'The law's delays: conservationist legislation in the British Isles' in Jane Fawcett (ed.), *The future of the past: attitudes to conservation, 1147–1974* (1976)

Brown, Cynthia, Birkin Haward and Robert Kindred, *Dictionary of architects of Suffolk buildings, 1800–1914* (Ipswich, 1991)

Brown, Sarah, *Stained glass: an illustrated history* (1995)

Bujak, Edward, *England's rural realms: landholding and the agricultural revolution* (2007)

Cautley, H. Munro, *Suffolk churches and their treasures* (5th edn, Woodbridge, 1982)

Church, Dani and Ann Gander, *The story of the Southwold–Walberswick ferry* (Holton, 2009)

Cooper, Trevor (ed.), *The journal of William Dowsing: iconoclasm in East Anglia during the English Civil War* (Woodbridge, 2001)

Crockford, *Clerical directory* (various editions, 1876–1906)

Crook, J. Mordaunt, *The dilemma of style* (1987)

Curl, James Stevens, *Encyclopaedia of architectural terms* (1992)

Delafons, John, *Politics and preservation: a policy history of the built heritage, 1882–1996* (1997)

Dellheim, Charles, *The face of the past: the preservation of the medieval inheritance in Victorian England* (Cambridge, 1982)

Drury, Michael, *Wandering architects* (Stamford, 2000)

Duffy, Eamon, *The stripping of the altars* (New Haven and London, 1992)

Dutt, William Alfred, *Highways and byways in East Anglia* (1901)

Dymond, David and Edward Martin (eds), *An historical atlas of Suffolk* (3rd edn, Ipswich, 1999)

Dymond, David and Peter Northeast, *A history of Suffolk* (2nd edn, Chichester, 1995)

Dymond, David and Clive Paine, *Five centuries of an English parish church: 'The state of Melford church', Suffolk* (Cambridge, 2012)

Dymond, David and Roger Virgoe, 'The reduced population and wealth of early fifteenth-century Suffolk', *PSIAH* 36 (1986)

Fairweather, Janet (trans.), *Liber Eliensis: A history of the Isle of Ely* (Woodbridge, 2005)

Fawcett, Jane (ed.), *The future of the past: attitudes to conservation, 1147–1974* (1976)

Fleming, Abraham, *A strange and terrible wonder* (1577)

Foster, Joseph, *Alumni Oxonienses, 1715–1886*, 2 vols (Oxford, 1888)

Gardner, Thomas, *An historical account of Dunwich, Blithburgh and Southwold* (1754)

Glyde, John Jun., *Suffolk in the nineteenth century* (1856)

Gomme, George Laurence (ed.), *Topographical history of Staffordshire and Suffolk* (1899)

Gowers, Sir W.R., 'The flint-work inscription on Blythburgh church', *PSIAH* 11 (1901)

Grace, Frank, 'A historical survey of Suffolk Towns', *Suffolk Review* 5 (1982)

Harper-Bill, Christopher (ed.), *Blythburgh priory cartulary*, I (Suffolk Charters 2, Woodbridge, 1980)

Haward, Birkin, *Suffolk medieval church arcades* (Ipswich, 1993)

Hawksley, Lucinda, *The mystery of Princess Louise, Queen Victoria's daughter* (2013)

Hervey, S.H.A. (ed.), *Suffolk in 1674: being the hearth tax returns, 1674* (Woodbridge, 1905)

Kelly, *Directory of Suffolk* (various editions, 1879–1908)

Kelvin, Norman (ed.), *The collected letters of William Morris* (4 vols, Princeton, 1984–2014)

Lawrence, Rachel, *Southwold River: Georgian life in the Blyth Valley* (Exeter, 1990)

Love, Rosalind C. (ed.), *Goscelin of Saint-Bertin: the hagiography of the female saints of Ely* (Oxford, 2004)

MacCarthy, Fiona, *William Morris* (1994)

MacCulloch, Diarmaid, *Suffolk and the Tudors: politics and religion in an English county, 1500–1600* (Oxford, 1987)

Mackley, Alan, 'Clerks of the works', *The Georgian Group Journal*, VIII (1998)

Middleton-Stewart, Judith, *Inward purity and outward splendour: death and remembrance in the deanery of Dunwich, Suffolk, 1370–1547* (Woodbridge, 2001)

Miele, Chris (ed.), *From William Morris: building conservation and the arts and crafts cult of authenticity, 1877–1939* (2005)

Miele, Chris (ed.), *William Morris on architecture* (Sheffield, 1996)

Miele, Chris, 'Morris and Conservation', in Chris Miele (ed.), *From William Morris: building conservation and the arts and crafts cult of authenticity, 1877–1939* (2005)

Morrice, Richard, 'Ecclesiastical exemption in England', www.buildingconservation.com, accessed 24 March 2015

Mosley, Charles (ed.), *Burke's peerage and baronetage* (106th edn, 1999, Crans)

Muttitt, Mick, 'Witness to the first Kennedy tragedy' and 'Joe Kennedy Jnr's last mission' in Alan Mackley (ed.), *The poaching priors of Blythburgh* (Blythburgh, 2002)

Parker, J.H., *The ecclesiastical and architectural topography of England: Part VII, Suffolk* (Oxford and London, 1855)

Powell, Kerry (ed.), *The Cambridge companion to Victorian and Edwardian theatre* (Cambridge, 2004)

Plunkett, Stephen J., 'Hamlet Watling: artist and schoolmaster', *PSIAH* 39 Part 1 (1997)

Pugin, August Welby, *Contrasts: or a parallel between the noble edifices of the fourteenth and fifteenth centuries, and similar buildings of the present day; showing the present decay of taste; accompanied by appropriate text* (2nd edn, 1841), and *The true principles of pointed or Christian architecture; set forth in two lectures delivered at St Marie's Oscott* (1841)

Radcliffe, Enid and Nikolaus Pevsner, *The buildings of England: Suffolk* (Harmondsworth, 1974)

Raven, J.J., 'Blythburgh', *PSIAH* 4 (1874)

Riches, Anne, 'Victorian church building in Suffolk', in H. Munro Cautley, *Suffolk churches and their treasures* (5th edn, Woodbridge, 1982)

Richmond, Colin, *John Hopton: a fifteenth-century Suffolk gentleman* (Cambridge, 1981)

Rimmer, Michael, *The angel roofs of East Anglia: unseen masterpieces of the Middle Ages* (Cambridge, 2015)

Scarfe, Norman, 'Blythburgh, Holy Trinity Church', *PSIAH* 34 Part 2 (1978)

Scarfe, Norman, *Suffolk in the Middle Ages* (Woodbridge, 1986)

Sperling, Joy, '"Art, cheap and good". The Art Union in England and the United States, 1840–60', *Nineteenth-Century Art Worldwide* I, no. 1 (2002)

Steinbach, Susie, *Women in England, 1760-1914: a social history* (2013)

Stell, C.F., *Nonconformist chapels and meeting-houses in eastern England* (Swindon, 2002)

Suckling, Alfred, *The history and antiquities of the hundreds of Blything and part of Lothingland, in the county of Suffolk* (1847)

Tate, W.E., *The parish chest* (3rd edn, Cambridge, 1969)

Thompson, Owen, 'Rev. Henry Sykes and the restoration of Blythburgh Church: late Victorian church restoration', *Suffolk Review* 31 (1998)

Thrush, Andrew and John P. Ferris (eds), *The history of parliament: the House of Commons, 1604–1629* (Cambridge, 2010)

Timmins, T.C.B. (ed.), *Suffolk returns from the census of religious worship, 1851* (Suffolk Records Society 39, 1997)

Urban, Sylvanus, *The gentleman's magazine and historical chronicle for the year 1808*, 78, Part 2 (1808)

Venn, J, and J.A. (eds), *Alumni Cantabridgienses Part II*, 6 vols (Cambridge, 1922–54)

Wake, R., *Southwold and its vicinity, ancient and modern* (Great Yarmouth, 1839)

Warner, Peter, *Bloody marsh: a seventeenth-century village in crisis* (Macclesfield, 2000)

Webster, Leslie and Backhouse, Janet (eds), *The making of England: Anglo-Saxon Art and Culture, AD 600–900* (1991)

Werner, Julia S., *The Primitive Methodist connexion* (University of Wisconsin, 1984)

Wessex Archaeology, *Blythburgh priory, Blythburgh, Suffolk: archaeological evaluation and assessment of results,* Ref. 68742 (2009)

White, James F., *The Cambridge movement: the ecclesiologists and the Gothic revival* (Cambridge, 1962)

Williams, Ann and G.H. Martin (eds), *Domesday Book: a complete translation* (1992)

Woodforde, Christopher, 'The fifteenth-century glass in Blythburgh Church', *PSIAH* 21 (1931–33)

Young, Arthur, *General view of the agriculture of the county of Suffolk* (1813)

UNPUBLISHED WORKS

Baty, Revd Edward, 'Victorian church building and restoration in the diocese of Norwich', PhD thesis, University of East Anglia, 2 vols (1987)

Gee, Eric, Notes on a visit to Blythburgh church in August 1964. Typescript in the National Monuments Record, Swindon

Parr, Robert T.L., *Yoxford Yesterday,* SROI, S. Yoxford 9

Watling, Hamlet, 'Blythburgh Church. Also the painted glass in the church windows and other antiquities' (no date). Bound manuscript in the possession of the editor

INDEX OF PEOPLE AND PLACES

All places are in Suffolk unless otherwise shown. Place names have been given in their modern form. Those not identified are in italics. Places appearing in Appendix D, Notes on People, are indexed only when they refer to people appearing elsewhere in the text. For people and places represented as images in Blythburgh church window glass see BLYTHBURGH, church, fabric, windows, images. Place names in letter addresses have not been indexed. Ranges of three or more consecutive pages for a given term are listed in the form pp.186–98 for both continuous and separate mentions of the term.

INDEX OF SUBJECTS

THE SUFFOLK RECORDS SOCIETY

For sixty years, the Suffolk Records Society has added to the knowledge of Suffolk's history by issuing an annual volume of previously unpublished manuscripts, each throwing light on some new aspect of the history of the county.

Covering 700 years and embracing letters, diaries, maps, accounts and other archives, many of them previously little known or neglected, these books have together made a major contribution to historical studies. At the heart of this achievement lie the Society's members, all of whom share a passion for Suffolk and its history, and whose support, subscriptions and donations make possible the opening up of the landscape of historical research in the area.

In exchange for this tangible support, members receive a new volume each year at a considerable saving on the retail price.

Members are also welcomed to the launch of the new volume, held each year in a different and appropriate setting within the county, giving them a chance to meet and listen to some of the leading historians in their fields talking about their latest work.

For anyone with a love of history, a desire to build a library on Suffolk themes at modest cost and a wish both to see historical research continue to thrive and to bring new sources to the public eye in decades to come, a subscription to the Suffolk Records Society is the ideal way to make a contribution and join the company of those who give Suffolk history a future.

THE CHARTERS SERIES

To supplement the annual volumes and serve the need of medieval historians, the Charters Series was launched in 1979 with the challenge of publishing the transcribed texts of all the surviving monastic charters for the county. Since that date, nineteen volumes have been published as an occasional series, the latest in 2011.

The Charters Series is financed by a separate annual subscription leading to receipt of each volume on publication.

CURRENT PROJECTS

Volumes approved by the Council of the Society for future publication include *The Diary of John Clopton, 1648–50*, edited by John Pelling, *Crown Pleas of the Suffolk Eyre of 1240*, edited by Eric Gallagher, *Household Inventories of Helmingham Hall: 1597, 1626 and 1707/8*, edited by Moira Coleman, *The Woodbridge Troop of the Suffolk Yeomanry, 1794–1818*, edited by Margaret Thomas, *Loes and Wilford Old Poor Law Records*, edited by John Shaw, and *Monks Eleigh Manorial Documents*, edited by Vivienne Aldous; and in the Charters Series, *The Charters of the Priory of St Peter and St Paul, Ipswich*, edited by David Allen, *Bury St Edmunds Town Charters*, edited by Vivien Brown, and *Rumburgh Priory Charters*, edited by Nicholas Karn. The order in which these and other volumes appear in print will depend on the dates of completion of editorial work.

MEMBERSHIP

Membership enquiries should be addressed to Mrs Tanya Christian, 8 Orchid Way, Needham Market, IP6 8JQ; e-mail: membership@suffolkrecordssociety.com

The Suffolk Records Society is a registered charity, No. 1084279.